INDIAN FIGHTERS TURNED
AMERICAN POLITICIANS

INDIAN FIGHTERS TURNED AMERICAN POLITICIANS

FROM MILITARY SERVICE TO PUBLIC OFFICE

THOMAS G. MITCHELL

Westport, Connecticut
London

Library of Congress Cataloging-in-Publication Data

Mitchell, Thomas G., 1957–
  Indian fighters turned American politicians: from military service to public office/Thomas G. Mitchell.
    p. cm.
  Includes bibliographical references and index.
  ISBN 0-275-98130-4 (alk. paper)
  1. Political culture—United States—History. 2. Indians of North America—Wars. 3. United States—Politics and government. 4. Soldiers—United States—History. 5. Generals—United States—History. 6. Politicians—United States—History. I. Title.
  E183.M698 2003
  355'.0092'273—dc21   2003053028

British Library Cataloguing in Publication Data is available.

Copyright © 2003 by Thomas G. Mitchell

All rights reserved. No portion of this book may be reproduced, by any process or technique, without the express written consent of the publisher.

Library of Congress Catalog Card Number: 2003053028
ISBN: 0-275-98130-4

First published in 2003

Praeger Publishers, 88 Post Road West, Westport, CT 06881
An imprint of Greenwood Publishing Group, Inc.
www.praeger.com

Printed in the United States of America

The paper used in this book complies with the Permanent Paper Standard issued by the National Information Standards Organization (Z39.48-1984).

10 9 8 7 6 5 4 3 2 1

Contents

Preface		vii
1	The Militia and Indian Wars	1
2	The Revolutionary War	25
3	The War of 1812	45
4	The Second-Party System: Democrats and Whigs	69
5	The Mexican Fighters and the Collapse of the Whig Party	87
6	Indian and Mexican Fighters as Presidents	127
7	Indian Fighters on the Frontier: Kentucky, Ohio, Tennessee, and Texas	151
8	The End of the Indian-Fighter Era	197
Appendix: The Indian Fighter and the Arab Fighter		215
Bibliography		231
Index		235

Photo essay follows Chapter 5.

Preface

Everyone who has grown up in the United States and has watched Westerns on television or at the movies knows who Indian fighters are. Indian fighters in the awkward lexicon of the time were those whites who fought Indians—not fighters who were Indians, as one would assume from the term. From the first white settlement in Jamestown, Virginia, in 1607 to the last significant Indian fight at Wounded Knee, South Dakota, in 1890, there were about 380 years of Indian warfare in North America in the area that became the continental United States. (This is excluding early Spanish settlement in Florida.) When most Americans think of Indian warfare and Indian fighters, they think about a twenty- to twenty-five-year period following the Civil War because this has been the experience portrayed in the media: in the Western novels, the television serials, the movies, and even the documentaries. These media deal with Indian warfare in the West, among the Plains Indians, and in the Southwest with the Apache and Navajo Indians.

From this period, the one real—as opposed to fictional—Indian fighter that is best known to Americans is George Armstrong Custer. Custer was the "boy general" of the Civil War and was the youngest major general in American history. Custer managed to develop fame as an Indian fighter largely because he cultivated the media and wrote about his career while he was still on active duty rather than waiting to retire as did his competitors. This was a wise decision considering his fate. He was also killed in a manner that was presented in the contemporary media as heroic. That portrayal, begun in the press and continued through several films and even a television series, is what most Americans remember. Few Americans know the names of Custer's contemporary Indian fighters of superior ability—names like George Crook, Nelson Miles, and Ranald Mackenzie. These three were superior in large part because they lived long enough to accumulate a much bigger base of experience than Custer did, and they worked hard at analyzing and learning from it.

But there was an earlier experience of Indian warfare in the East by Americans, those old enough to spend much of their adult lives in an independent United States; that experience lasted about a century. Most Americans older than forty can think of at least two famous Indian fighters from that period: Daniel Boone and Davy Crockett. This is again due to the influence of the media and a single actor—Fess Parker—who played the two in two television series that aired in the 1950s and 1960s. This book deals with both of these figures—as well as others—because they belonged to a class of Indian fighters who became famous during this period: the *Indian-fighter politicians*.

These are politicians who used their early experience of Indian fighting to win an election and build a political career or who used Indian fighting as a means of accelerating an existing political career. Boone and Crockett were actually rather minor members of this class. Boone served in the Virginia state legislature in the 1780s at the end of the American Revolution. Crockett served in the Tennessee state legislature and then served three terms in Congress in the 1820s and 1830s. Crockett became briefly a national figure, first as an object of ridicule and scorn and then, very briefly, as a serious figure. But these two were not by far even the most important Indian-fighter politicians in their states. Isaac Shelby became the first governor of Kentucky. At least three governors of Tennessee were Indian fighters while Crockett was active in politics, as well as several members of Congress and even a president from Tennessee—Andrew Jackson. Jackson was one of four Indian fighters who became president, the other three being George Washington, William Henry Harrison, and Zachary Taylor. Most American historians normally rank George Washington and Andrew Jackson as among the great presidents. The Confederacy's only president was also an Indian fighter. Even Abraham Lincoln nearly became an Indian-fighter president—he participated in the war but was demobilized like most of his companions from the militia without seeing any action. In addition to Kentucky and Tennessee, at least three other states—Illinois, New Hampshire, and Texas—had Indian-fighter governors. Thus, this is a fairly important phenomenon that warrants investigation.

Wesleyan University English professor Richard Slotkin has written a trio of books dealing with the theme of the Myth of the Frontier.[1] He deals with the interaction between the myth and American politics, but not in a systematic fashion. Slotkin deals with real persons more as mythological characters than as actual individuals. His first two works focus on a number of famous

Indian fighters, starting with Benjamin Church of Massachusetts and ending with George A. Custer. But Slotkin examines the Indian fighters—in particular, Daniel Boone and David Crockett—more as sources for legend and mythology than as actual politicians.

Many biographers have dealt with the individuals mentioned in this book, but always in an individual rather than an environmental fashion as part of a political class or typology. Why does this theme warrant such a treatment? For two reasons: First, they were the first class of war hero in American politics. The phenomenon of electing war heroes on a regular and widespread basis, while not unique to America, is still rare among Western democracies. Second, at least two other Western societies have had a similar phenomenon. The first is South Africa in the second half of the nineteenth century. When Custer and others were conquering the West, the Afrikaner Kaffir fighters were conquering the North. The second is Israel, where the influence of their Indian fighters, the Arab fighters, has lasted for over forty-five years and shows no signs of stopping. Many scholars have noted the tendency of Americans to elect victorious generals as presidents after major wars, but none have really tied this to the story of the conquest of continent. It is this feature that separates the phenomenon of the *native fighter* from the phenomenon of "the man on horseback" as, for example, in France or Poland or Latin America.

Originally this book grew out of a comparative study of *native fighters* in these three societies (the United States, South Africa, and Israel) and an attempt to find a few European native-fighter politicians. The needs of my publisher, however, were different; and the book was transformed into one concentrating exclusively on American Indian fighters. This change actually allowed me to expand some of the themes that I had originally developed and take the book from the 1850s to the post–Civil War period. And it allowed me to start the book well before the Revolution as a means of developing the stage. I found that I was also able to articulate all of the important themes regarding Israel into a final "chapter"—the Appendix.

The purpose behind this book and its original idea was to examine the role of military figures in Israeli politics and see what lessons could be learned by the experience of Indian-fighter politicians in nineteenth-century America. Israeli Arab fighters have been involved in every major peace negotiation with the Arabs and have played a major role in Israeli politics for over thirty years. I looked to history to possibly suggest when that role might come to an end. The reader will have to decide if the research was worth the effort.

In order to make these comparisons, it is necessary to understand how the Indian fighters fit into both the party political system and the political culture of the United States. For this reason I have devoted a good portion of the book to a discussion of the second-party system of the United States and its two component parties, the Democrats and the Whigs. I also discuss the multiparty phase that existed from 1848 to 1860 as the United States was in transition from the second- to the third-party system that we have at present. This is a unique period in American history as several major parties existed simultaneously in the mid-1850s as the Whig Party was dying and several parties—including the Republicans and the Know-Nothings—were struggling to inherit the remains. There are some parallels between the 1850s and the 1990s. I have also taken the discussion of war heroes beyond the Civil War into the 1880s to demonstrate how the basic underlying principle remained the same, even as the details changed.

I could have written just a series of biographical chapters dealing with the various Indian-fighter politicians, but this would have been less effective in demonstrating how they fit into the political system as a whole. This is an approach that is more suited to a military discussion of Indian fighters and has been used in the past in discussing those of the post–Civil War West. I have attempted to keep discussion of the actual military exploits of the Indian fighters to a minimum in order to keep the focus on what the average voter would know and how the military career impacted the political career.

Much of the historiography dealing with the antebellum period of 1820–60 attempts to explain the outbreak of the Civil War. It is written "backward" from 1861 rather than forward from 1834 or some other turning point, with treatment being much less detailed and analytical the farther one goes back in time. It is also vested with the quality of a Greek tragedy in which the end is unavoidable. Because Andrew Jackson is a hero of the modern Democratic Party, at least in terms of paying lip service, his presidency has been very well covered. There had been a gap in American historiography between the period of Jackson and that of Lincoln covering a roughly twenty-year period from 1837 to 1856. In the last two or three decades this has started to change as Jackson scholars like Robert Remini have written biographies of some of the other important political figures of the Age of Jackson extending coverage forward into the early 1850s. This, combined with recent interest in the Mexican War and even the Whig Party itself, has narrowed the "gap" to about a three-year period or less, from roughly 1852 to 1855—from the death of Henry Clay and Daniel Webster to the outbreak of conflict in Kansas.

There is still the "gap" between the Age of Jackson (1815–45) and the Age of Lincoln (1856–65). But if one thinks in terms of the Age of the Indian Fighter, it all seamlessly flows together. Abraham Lincoln and Jefferson Davis served together in the Black Hawk War of 1832, during the presidency of Andrew Jackson. Lincoln gained first state and then national attention campaigning on behalf of two Whig Indian-fighter presidents—Harrison and Taylor. Davis was briefly the son-in-law of Zachary Taylor, who first gained his military fame fighting Indians. The cement that holds the two periods together is the Whig Party, which became dependent on Indian fighters to win the presidency. And it goes even farther back. Jackson served briefly in the American Revolution against the British; this is the war that made Washington our first Indian-fighter president. And Jackson's first great political enemy was John Sevier, the most important Indian-fighter politician from the American Revolution.

Thanks to the work of scholars like Remini, Norma Peterson, Merrill Peterson, Michael Holt, Jack Bauer, John Eisenhower, and others, I was able to tie the Indian-fighter era of the Age of Jackson to the Mexican-fighter era of antebellum and Civil War period.[2] Holt wrote an almost encyclopedic study of the Whig Party, but this tends to focus on the rise and fall of the party and on the national conventions for choosing presidential candidates. Although it was very good source material, it did not deal with the phenomenon of the Whig Party's dependency on war heroes to win the presidency. Previously, Merrill Petersen and Remini had concentrated on the two most prominent individuals within the Whig Party, Henry Clay and Daniel Webster. Kinley Brauer in his work on the Conscience Whigs dealt with the nexus between the Mexican War and slavery and how this contributed to the rise of the multiparty system. Fine biographies of Taylor and now Scott have been written. But no one has completed the picture by tying all the information together and explaining why the Indian-fighter politician emerged and why he disappeared in such a relatively short space of time.

Thanks to the W. W. Norton series of bicentennial state histories and a few state histories by scholars specializing in frontier history, I was able to explore a few regional Indian-fighter politicians who did not make a splash on the national level. Existing histories of frontier Tennessee and Texas were the closest that one comes to finding a discussion of the Indian-fighter phenomenon. This has enabled me to expand the picture of the depth of the phenomenon of the Indian-fighter politician and also has allowed me to make more intelligent comparisons, with the African-fighter politicians in South Africa. But it has been limited by my inability—for financial reasons—to conduct primary research at the local level delving into local archives. Had I been able to do so, the longest chapter, which deals with state politics, would have been much longer and more detailed. My own research "gap" concerns the possible existence of Indian-fighter politicians in the trans-Mississippi West. I had to guess that none of any importance existed, but I was not able to prove this by exhaustive research. If I have been wrong in my surmise and conclusions regarding this period, I hope that professional historians will be forgiving of an amateur historian without their professional training and funding.

The expansion of interest in American Indian history by professional historians in the United States and Britain has also aided this project. I was able to find background material on the major Indian wars and Indian tribes in the East. This enabled me to more intelligently write about the American Revolution as a complex racial conflict and not just a national liberation struggle between settlers and their metropole. Because this is a work dealing with American politics and not Indian tribal politics, Indians are not the focus of this book; but some figures like Tecumseh and Black Hawk are necessary to mention in order to make the story intelligible.

I have chosen to use the singular collective form of the noun when referring to Indian tribes. Any reader who finds this disconcerting can merely mentally add the word "Indians" behind the name of the tribe. There is an old tradition in English of referring to African and Indian tribes by the singular form of the noun, and I have continued this rather than making all the tribal names plural. This is not exclusive to Third World peoples—the English, Spanish, and French are examples of European peoples with collective adjectival names.

Chapter 1 tells the story of the militia tradition in colonial America and in the early United States through the Mexican War. It also explains the development of colonial politics and Indian warfare leading up to the American Revolution. Chapter 2 is the story of the first wave of Indian-fighter politicians—those who went into politics after the French and Indian Wars and the American Revolution. The main figures considered are George Washington, John Sevier, and John Sullivan. Chapter 3 tells the story of Indian warfare in the War of 1812 and focuses on three individuals: Tecumseh, William Henry Harrison, and Andrew Jackson.

Chapter 4 deals with the politics of the period: the development of the second-party system of Democrats and Whigs following the end of the Era of Good Feelings. It opens with the quest of Andrew Jackson for the presidency and then takes the Whig Party through the first decade of its existence to about 1845. The parallel development of the Democratic Party is also narrated. Chapter 5 tells the story of the Mexican War and the careers of veterans of that war. These include the top two generals who both became Whig candidates for president, and figures of the 1850s like Governor Quitman of Mississippi, Governor Joseph Lane of Oregon, Lieutenant Governor Jim Lane of Indiana, and Senator Jefferson Davis of Mississippi. This chapter also narrates the collapse of the Whig Party in the 1850s and its replacement by the Republican Party, initially led by Mexican War veteran John Fremont. Chapter 6 is the story of the presidencies of the Indian-fighter presidents: George Washington, Andrew Jackson, Zachary Taylor, and Jefferson Davis, the last two also being Mexican War veterans.

Chapter 7 is the story of the Indian fighters from the Revolution and the War of 1812, and Texas Indian fighters who only made it at the state level. Chapter 8 explains why there was no prominent Indian-fighter politician from the Indian wars of the West and looks at the military careers of the top Indian fighters. The Appendix examines the development of a similar native-fighter tradition in Israel.

NOTES

1. Richard Slotkin, *Regeneration Through Violence, Fatal Environment,* and *Gunfighter Nation* (New York: Harper Perennial, 1996, 1994, and 1995). Only the first two were relevant to this work. The third book deals mostly with the Myth of the Frontier as portrayed in novels and films in the late nineteenth and twentieth centuries.

2. See the Bibliography for complete citations of works.

1

The Militia and Indian Wars

INTRODUCTION

One of the first institutions founded in the New World by the English colonists—whether in religious colonies as in Massachusetts or Pennsylvania or in royal colonies like Virginia—was the militia. The militia has a long history in Europe in general and England in particular. As relations with the native population deteriorated, the militia grew in importance. Later the interjection of European imperial rivalries into North America increased the need even more as the French began actively aiding the Indians against the British settlers.

During the eighteenth century, as the colonists became more established, they began to exert their independence; and the legislatures of the colonies became training schools for American politicians and statesmen. As the century went on there arose a power struggle in nearly every colony between the royal executive in the form of the governor and the "democratic" legislatures. The colonists saw themselves as Englishmen, with all the rights of Englishmen won in the English Civil War and the Glorious Revolution. As taxes were levied after the French and Indian War in an attempt to make the Americans pay a greater share of their own defense, the cry of "no taxation without representation" was taken up.

Eventually the militia and the legislature came together as the Second Continental Congress began to organize the militias for revolution. Throughout the American Revolution, the militias played a crucial part in providing both a basic manpower pool from which to recruit for the

Continental army and an emergency backing for the army in local battles. They also provided the Patriot generals of the Revolution, men like blacksmith Nathaniel Greene, bookseller Henry Knox, tavern keeper Israel Putnam, Benedict Arnold, Benjamin Lincoln, and Daniel Morgan.

The war ended with independence for the thirteen independent states, and a weak confederacy was established. This soon gave way to the federal government, and the plural United States became singular. An ideological aversion to large standing armies led to the United States relying on the militia to protect against local Indian attacks and to defend the country in the event of a foreign war. A small professional army, which was reorganized during the Washington administration as the Legion of the United States, was retained for Indian fighting in the Northwest. The militia supplied many of the leading generals of the War of 1812: William H. Harrison, Jacob Brown, Peter Buel Porter, Samuel Smith, and, of course, Andrew Jackson.

During the War of 1812 volunteer units made up of citizen soldiers, many members of local militia, played a major role. This role would only increase in importance during the Mexican War and the Civil War. Two of the final Indian wars in the East, the Black Hawk War of 1832 and the Third Seminole War of 1855–58, were fought with large contingents of militia troops. This chapter considers the various forms of citizen soldiers during the seventeenth to nineteenth centuries and the Indian wars before the American Revolution. Subsequent chapters look at Indian warfare during the American Revolution and the War of 1812.

THE NEW WORLD MILITIA

An old European and English tradition dating from the Middle Ages made all white males eligible for military service in defense of their local communities. This system had gone out of use in England as the threat of foreign invasion receded, but it was revived in the New World. The New Model Army of the English Civil War left a residue of fear in the minds of middle-class men of standing armies and military dictators. The limits of armies from the Glorious Revolution became embodied in the Constitution.

The Pilgrim militia system was a "pickup team"—temporary, not permanent. All citizens were required to own arms. The colony would loan any citizens the funds to buy them if they lacked their own. The militia wore no uniforms, except for some of the officers who provided their own. They usually lacked a professional commander, instead choosing their own officers through election.[1]

Pennsylvania, because of its Quaker tradition of pacifism, was the last English colony to enact a militia act obligating mandatory service in 1755, during the French and Indian War. Most of the original thirteen colonies had passed militia acts in the seventeenth century when they began establishing regiments: Massachusetts in 1643, Virginia in 1651, Connecticut in 1653, Maryland in 1658, and South Carolina in 1685. The basic unit of the militia was the company, which had a geographic rather than a numeric basis and was based on a town, county, or part of a city. In New England militia members could elect their own officers. But the governor and legislature had a hand in selecting regimental officers. Citizens could buy their way out of militia service, so the upper crust usually did not serve. The militia was solely defensive so that they could be used only within the borders of the colony, with a few notable exceptions. North Carolina allowed its militia to be used within South Carolina and Georgia—probably in recognition that the three colonies had a common enemy in the Cherokee. A governor could call for each militia unit to provide a quota of volunteers or draftees for an expedition. If the unit did not come up with a sufficient number of volunteers to fill the quota, constables were sent into the populace to "recruit" or draft the remainder, usually from the lowest socioeconomic strata as in Europe; but, unlike Europe, few of these draftee professional soldiers remained in the army for the rest of their working careers.[2]

New England colonies cooperated militarily during King Philip's War (1675–77), which was the first major Indian threat to the New England colonies. Militia units were used during King William's War (1689–97) for protection against French raids, with volunteer units doing the offensive work. A joint volunteer New England force serving under a single commander marched against Montreal and Quebec during Queen Anne's War (1702–13), and a South Carolina volunteer force with auxiliary Indian allies invaded Florida. Militia successfully defended Deerfield, Massachusetts, against a surprise Indian attack on February 28, 1704. The survivors of the attack gathered in the town blockhouse and were defended by the militia soldiers.[3]

Americans had a very different attitude toward war from Europeans: for Europeans war was a matter of high politics that was relevant only to the monarch and the court; in America it was a defense of "home and hearth." In Europe rulers distrusted an armed citizenry, but in America it was necessary. Because of the great distances and poor communications, decentralized command was essential. Bloody Indian wars in Virginia in 1622 and 1644 remained a part of folk memory. Nathaniel Bacon's Rebellion in Virginia in 1676 was over the demand of settlers for more help from the authorities in fighting Indians. This demand would be echoed a century later in the Declaration of Independence as one of America's complaints against King George III—and 185 years later in Texas' secession from the United States. The New Englanders never got over the initial successes of the Indians in King Philip's War. The garrison house in each small settlement remained the visible sign of this fear that remained in existence through the end of the French and Indian War. The American scene created a new form of adventure literature—stories of Indian captivity. And after 1700 there was a fear in the South of a slave revolt, something that only occurred once—Nat Turner's revolt in Virginia in 1830. There was also the intermittent threat of invasion by the European powers: the French and Dutch in the North and the Spanish in the South.[4]

On the frontier all settlers were soldiers; even women were expected to defend themselves against Indians, and, if not good shots themselves, they were at least proficient in loading weapons for their men. Settler youths became proficient with both gun and tomahawk. The Pennsylvania—later Kentucky—rifle was common on the frontier at a time when it was practically unknown in England. The American rifle had many advantages over the European version with which the British were equipped. During the American Revolution many British regulars expected every American to be a sharpshooter and this had an effect on their morale. Everyone was partly a soldier, but no one was completely one as there was no military class in America.[5]

On the night of September 23, 1675, an alarm at a town thirty miles from Boston brought twelve hundred militiamen under arms within an hour. The militia disbanded just as quickly once the emergency was over. The militia system tended to disintegrate after each Indian war was over. The militia system was inadequate, lacking both a central commissariat and a central command. The settlers were willing to build local defenses for defense against Indian attacks or European invasion but not strategic defenses such as coastal forts. Forts fell into disrepair in Boston Harbor and in Virginia because the colonists were unwilling to be taxed to pay for their upkeep. Each colony wanted to control its own army and not cooperate with other colonies for the general defense, except in very limited circumstances. Questions of imperial strategy were of no interest to ordinary Americans. Twentieth-century isolationism and antiwar sentiment during the Vietnam War were simply reflections of traditional, very deep attitudes. The colonies were willing to revolt and unwilling to unite for the same reason—an intense localism.[6]

AMERICAN SOCIETY IN THE EIGHTEENTH CENTURY

Many people think of the white population of colonial America as being predominantly English, but it is more accurate to think of it as northern European and predominantly Protestant. Although English colonists dominated during the seventeenth century, only eighty thousand English immigrants came to America between 1700 and 1775 compared with 350,000 in the previous century. There were also some fifty thousand convicts who were deported to America between 1718 and 1775 and sold at about one-third the price of male African slaves. They were often bought by wealthy planters, including George Washington, for use as field hands and were treated like slaves. The largest group of white immigrants in the eighteenth century was the Scots who numbered some 145,000 immigrants between 1707 and 1775.

The Scots were further divided into three groups: the Lowland Scots, who settled in New England; the Highland Scots, who settled in the frontier valleys of New York, North Carolina, and Georgia; and the Ulster Scots, known in America as the Scotch-Irish, who settled along the frontier from Pennsylvania to Georgia. The next largest group of immigrants was the Germans, who numbered some one hundred thousand during the eighteenth century and settled on farms in Pennsylvania, Virginia, and Maryland.

By far the largest group of immigrants was made up of African slaves who came involuntarily but still came at a rate greater than triple that of white European immigrants. Some 1.5 million black slaves were imported to British colonies in the New World with the bulk going to the West Indies and the Chesapeake Bay colonies of Virginia, Delaware, and Maryland. Before 1775 very few Britons, either in America or Britain, objected to slavery. Births outnumbered deaths among slaves so there was a natural population increase, even if blacks had a higher mortality rate than whites.[7]

Despite a shortage of professional ministers, some two-thirds of colonial whites were churched—that is, they belonged to an organized denomination and belonged to a church of that denomination. Originally, in the seventeenth century, most settlers came to America not seeking religious freedom so much as seeking religious domination by their particular denomination. This led to most colonies being dominated by a particular denomination. By the end of the seventeenth century most colonies had less religious freedom than was found in England or Scotland. Anglicans were the most important denomination, followed by Congregationalists, with the latter very strong in New England with the exception of Rhode Island. Most Scots were Presbyterians and most Germans were Protestants of a wide range of denominations from Lutherans to Moravians to Baptists. There were a few Catholic churches, mostly in Maryland, and even a handful of Jewish synagogues distributed throughout the largest cities. Most Africans at this time were not Christians as most slave-owners did not want them evangelized. Only 1 percent of blacks in America in 1775 were free men, so most had little opportunity to become converted from Islam or animist beliefs.

Many of the colonial elite, including even a majority of the Anglican clergy as well as a minority of other clergies, were Christian rationalists. That is, they believed in the God of the Bible but did not accept the Bible as the inerrant word of God. In some cases, like that of George Washington and Thomas Jefferson, this had moved from Christianity into Deism—the generalized belief in an abstract God. Quakers were the only denomination that actively opposed either slavery or wars against the Indian population. Other denominations accepted both practices. The most interesting religion that arose in the colonies was a syncretistic religion among the Delaware Indians consisting of some Christian religious practices adapted to the existing native religion starting in the 1750s. This was the beginning of a trend that would continue for at least the next century.[8]

THE COLONIAL INDIAN WARS

Richard Slotkin, an American studies professor specializing in analysis of literature, contends that the Indian wars were the distinct national event of American history.[9] They lasted for over 250 years—150 years during the colonial period and a century after independence. Initially, relations between the Puritans in Massachusetts and the local Indians were good and the Indians taught the settlers many of the skills that were necessary for their survival. This period of peace is recalled in the American holiday of Thanksgiving celebrated on the third Thursday of each November. But the Pequot Indians were nearly exterminated by the Puritans in 1636.[10]

The first generation of leaders died by 1660, depriving the two sides of the interpersonal ties that were necessary to preserving the peace. Settler hunger for land, different concepts of land ownership and usage, and heavy-handed treatment of the natives by the colonial government led to the outbreak of war in 1675. In 1662 settlers took Wampanoag leader Wamsutta to Plymouth for questioning at gunpoint. Shortly afterward he sickened and died. Wamsutta's brother Metacom, known to the whites as Philip, became the Wampanoag leader. Plymouth's tendency to treat native leaders as inferiors and the murder of the liaison between the two peoples led to war. The war spread as far north as New Hampshire and as far southwest as Connecticut.[11]

Most Christian Indians either remained neutral or sided with the English, while those who remained traditional sided with Philip and the Wampanoag. The Nipmuck sided with the Wampanoag. The Nipmuck ambushed a force of militia led by Captains Hutchinson and Wheeler. Eight soldiers were killed, and the rest fled in terror back to their garrison at Brookfield. The town of Brookfield was burned to the ground by the pursuing Indians, and the settlers and soldiers huddled in the garrison house in the center of town, which the Indians soon set on fire with a burning cart. The settlers used their last drinking water to slow down the flames and were waiting to perish when a downpour from the sky put out the flames. Soldiers from eastern settlements soon arrived, and the town's surviving members were rescued.

The two tribes then turned to attacking settlements in the Connecticut River Valley. Scattered farms were attacked. In the autumn of 1675 several tribes that lived along the Connecticut River joined the first two tribes. The Indians attacked the Pioneer Valley and drove the settlers out of the town of Deerfield. They also ambushed a militia force under the command of Captain Lothrop sent to gather any remaining grain in Deerfield. Seventy-one of the militia were killed within minutes at a roadblock along "Bloody Brook." A relief force arrived too late to save most of the men. The Puritans resorted to imprisoning and hanging neutral and Christian Indians and persecuting the Quakers. In October there were raids on the towns of Hatfield, Northampton, and Springfield. The latter town was burned.

In December 1675 General Winslow and Captain Benjamin Church led a thousand-man force from three separate New England colonies against the neutral Narragansett tribe in southern Rhode Island in a preemptive strike. A local Narragansett told the force where the Indian town was located. The Indians' winter camp was located deep in a swamp and was surrounded by both a moat and a log wall. The settlers attacked in a blizzard, crossing the moat on a single log and losing many men in the assault. They avenged themselves by killing over five hundred of the enemy, many women and children, in the Great Swamp Massacre. The surviving Narragansett Indians then entered the war on the Indian side. They burned at least seven settler towns including Plymouth and Providence.

In February 1676 the Indians attacked Lancaster, Massachusetts, and stormed the garrison where the settlers had taken refuge. One of the survivors, a woman named Mary Rowlandson, was taken prisoner and spent six weeks in captivity. She was eventually ransomed. The Indians were running low on food, muskets, and shot and powder.

In May 1676 Captains Turner and Holyoke raided the main Wampanoag and Nipmuck camp on the northern end of the Connecticut River. They entered the camp at dawn and cut down scores of the inhabitants as they tried to flee. Warriors from surrounding areas launched a counterattack killing one of the leaders. The settlers were chased back to Hadley. But the alliance soon collapsed and Philip was left with few warriors as most of the Indians fled north.[12]

Philip with his remaining force returned to his tribal capital at Mount Hope, near Swansea where the war had started. Benjamin Church spent the summer tracking him using friendly Indians as scouts. In a final battle King Philip was killed by a musket shot through the heart from a Wampanoag fighting with Captain Benjamin Church, who became the first celebrated Indian fighter in American literature. This effectively ended the war and Indian resistance in New England. One out of every ten soldiers and warriors on both sides was a casualty, and the settlers took years to recover from the effects of the war. Brookfield remained abandoned for eleven years. The war was proportionately the most costly in American history in terms of casualties. Not until the Fort Mims massacre of 1813 and the Sioux rebellion of 1862 in Minnesota were there Indian attacks to compare with those of Philip's War.[13]

The war, the last fought in New England without the aid or intervention of outside powers, led to a great outpour of Indian war narratives with religious themes. Captive literature, the story of settlers—usually women—held captive by Indians during the Indian wars, was the most popular literature published in America between 1680 and 1716. Four works gained the status of best sellers between 1680 and 1720—three of these were captivity narratives, and the fourth was the novel *Pilgrim's Progress*, a classic work of American literature. This period spans the period from just after

King Philip's War to just after Queen Anne's War. Between 1716 and 1784 the Puritan version of the New World underwent a great revision under the impact of rationalism and the enlightenment. The captive narrative with its religious themes and biblical exegesis was replaced as a leading form of literature by more practical works aimed at showing how to get along with and, if necessary, fight the Indians.[14]

There were four wars between Britain and its Indian allies and the French with their Indian allies between 1689 and 1763, which are known collectively as the French and Indian War by historians. The wars can be divided into two cycles with a long peace in between them. The first cycle lasted from 1689 to 1713 and was followed by a twenty-six-year peace until 1739 when Britain went to war with Spain. From 1744 to 1763 there was a second cycle of wars. The Indians held the balance of power in North America by controlling the forested buffer zone between the British and French empires. They could make the difference between victory and defeat by weakening or even destroying an invading army through guerrilla attacks on the army itself or its line of supply.[15]

King William's War began in Europe in May 1689 when King William III joined the League of Augsburg and the Netherlands to resist Louis XIV's invasion of the Rhenish Palatinate. In Ireland this became known as the War of the Three Kings. In North America hostilities broke out between the English and French along Hudson Bay and between the Iroquois and the French in the area between the Mohawk River and the St. Lawrence River. The war was fought more in Canada than in the American colonies but did involve French raids against Schenectady, New York, in February and against New England in the spring and summer of 1690. Abenaki Indians periodically raided New England in 1692, 1694, and 1697. Massachusetts troops seized the fort at Port Royal, Quebec, in 1690; but a year later the French recaptured it. The war ended in 1697 with a treaty that restored the status quo ante. This was the first of the French and Indian wars that were fought between the two European powers for control of North America.[16]

The next major French and Indian war was Queen Anne's War, also known as the War of the Spanish Succession. The war began in Europe with the Grand Alliance, concluded in 1701, declaring war on France in order to prevent the union of France and Spain under a single sovereign. The Abenaki Indians raided Maine settlements in August 1703 and destroyed Deerfield, Massachusetts on the night of February 28–29, 1704. The attackers killed fifty and took another one hundred captive before burning the town. They again attacked Maine in September 1707. Colonel Benjamin Church led a force of five hundred New Englanders in an attack on French villages on July 28, 1704, in order to eliminate the source of Abenaki supplies. This added to Church's military reputation. Three expeditions were sent against Port Royal, only the last being successful. In September 1702 the South Carolina assembly authorized an expedition to seize Fort Augustine, Florida.

In December a force of five hundred colonists and Indians seized, looted, and burned the town but failed to capture the garrison. In 1704 a force under former Governor James Moore destroyed thirteen of fourteen missions in the Apalachee country in West Florida, opening up the road to Louisiana. But the colonists were never able to penetrate the Choctaw screen that protected the French Gulf Coast settlements. In the Treaty of Utrecht in 1713 the French lost some of their Canadian possessions.[17]

King George's War, also known as the War of Jenkins' Ear and the War of the Austrian Succession, began in Europe in 1739 and in North America in 1744. In 1744 the French entered the war on Spain's side putting New England in danger. In June 1745 a three-thousand-man force of volunteers from three New England colonies forced the Canadian French fortress of Louisbourg to surrender after a six-week siege. The fort had been dubbed "the Gibraltar of North America" and was considered impregnable. The French retaliated by raiding settlements in New England and New York. The New England colonies prepared to invade Canada in 1746; but promised troops and the fleet never arrived, having been diverted to attack the French coast. Skirmishing continued along the New England frontier, but colonial expeditions against Canada were at an end. The Treaty of Aix-la-Chapelle in 1748 returned Louisbourg to France in exchange for French concessions elsewhere. This made American colonists cynical as they saw that their interests would always be subordinated to British imperial interests. Henceforth, the British and colonial adventurers would carry out military expeditions on behalf of Britain in North America.[18] A decade later Britain fought its largest war with France for North America.

The French were at a serious numerical disadvantage during the French and Indian wars. In 1689 when the wars began, New France had only twelve thousand inhabitants while the English colonists numbered over two hundred thousand or about a 1:17 disadvantage. By 1760 the population of New France had approximately quintupled to about sixty thousand, but the population of the British colonies had increased by a factor of eight to 1.6 million so that the odds were then 1:27. During the wars the English colonists engaged in two main military activities: privateering against French shipping and fighting Indians who were backed by the French.[19]

The first Indian war that large numbers of future citizens of the United States took part in was the French and Indian War. They began with an expedition of Virginia militia led by Lieutenant Colonel George Washington to the Ohio Valley in 1754. The force consisted of one hundred Indian traders who wanted to keep French competition out of their market and two hundred lower-class volunteers. The force was too small, and logistical support was virtually nonexistent. Washington was forced to surrender their position and withdraw. Washington complained of the poor quality of men he received—paid substitutes for the men chosen—in 1756–57, and many other commanders made similar complaints.[20]

General Braddock was unable to raise more than a few recruits or obtain substantial assistance from the colonial assemblies. Local suppliers charged exorbitant prices and saw the war primarily as a profit-making opportunity. Lord Loudoun arrived in America to recruit a colonial army in 1756, following Braddock's death in combat, and managed to recruit about seventy-five hundred troops; and the British Isles supplied another forty-five hundred troops. The following year he managed to recruit in America only twelve hundred men but received eleven thousand troops from Britain. When the Americans operated with their British counterparts, friction always seemed to arise. Colonial militiamen were much better paid than British regulars, and British army officers refused to recognize the ranks of militia officers or treat them as equals.[21]

When William Pitt the elder came to power as prime minister in England, he promised to reimburse the colonies for any expenses incurred in prosecuting the war on Britain's behalf. Pitt asked for twenty thousand American militiamen, and the system began to work in 1758–59. Colonel John Bradstreet, with colonials from New York, New Jersey, Rhode Island, and Massachusetts, captured Fort Frontenac at the head of the Saint Lawrence River. This was like a repeat of the capture of Louisbourg or Port Royal in previous wars. But General Wolfe, who defeated the French at the Plains of Abraham and captured Montreal in 1759, had nothing but contempt for his six companies of American irregulars. These troops were probably draftees and paid substitutes. In the final victorious phase of the war from 1759 to 1763, fought mainly in Canada and in Europe, it was British regulars who fought the war.[22]

The French lost five major fortresses in North America in the course of the war, before finally losing their entire empire on the continent as a result of the peace. The North American war was closely tied to what happened in Europe, where the war was known as the Seven Years War, and in India. For example, British naval superiority in European waters allowed it to destroy the French navy and merchant marine. This in turn impacted on France's ability to fight the war in North America. But the war began as an attempt to protect two British colonies—Virginia and Nova Scotia—from French expansionism. So some historians have decided that "the Great War for the Empire" is the best of a number of poor names for the war.[23]

Colonial militias varied greatly in quality from colony to colony. The New England militias tended to be the best as the Puritan church was very supportive of them. Boston had the best units in New England, and Rhode Island had the worst. In the mid-eighteenth century the militias of New York and Pennsylvania were weak, Virginia and Maryland had fair militias, and South Carolina—especially Charleston—had a very good militia. One British observer rated the French-Canadian militia units as being much better than their British colonial counterparts in that they were more self-sufficient and hardy and were better Indian fighters.[24]

In the eighteenth and nineteenth centuries there were four basic types of citizen soldiers:

1. standing militia—each man had a legal obligation to provide his own firearm and to train periodically;
2. volunteer militia—self-financing, it consisted of elite units (artillery, cavalry, and elite infantry such as riflemen) who provided their own arms and uniforms;
3. war volunteers—volunteered for specific expeditions and could serve longer than three months and could serve outside the colony; and
4. involuntary servers—drafted either from the militia or the lower classes to fill a quota.[25]

THE BATTLE FOR POWER AND THE ROAD TO REVOLUTION

Politics during the American colonial period, from the establishment of Jamestown to the American Revolution, can be roughly divided into three periods. First was the period of executive supremacy from 1606 to 1689; then second came the period of executive-legislative parity from 1690 to 1763. The final period was one of legislative supremacy from 1763 to 1776. The lower houses of the legislatures in America developed in a similar fashion during the eighteenth century. During the early eighteenth century the assemblies could battle the governors on equal terms. By 1763—if not earlier—the assemblies were the dominant political element in America. The assemblies were most powerful in Rhode Island and Connecticut where they had nearly complete power. The next most powerful lower houses were in Pennsylvania and Massachusetts. The Pennsylvania house gained prominence in the 1730s and 1740s. The Massachusetts house had the unique privilege of a hand in selecting the council that advised the governor. The South Carolina Commons and the New York House of Assembly were only slightly less powerful. The assemblies in New Jersey, North Carolina, and Virginia developed more slowly and did not really take the upper hand until during the French and Indian War. Only the Maryland House of Delegates and the New Hampshire House of Assembly failed to reach this final stage before 1763.[26]

The houses all faced similar problems and drew upon common traditions and imperial precedents. Many families had members in more than one colony, and newspapers from one colony were often available from another; so news of developments in one colony soon reached the other colonies. Similar executive policies by the royal governors stemmed from a common royal policy dictated from London. This presented the colonists in the thirteen colonies with a similar, if not uniformly common, challenge. So, as in any profession, several members might attempt a similar approach independently of each other purely by chance, and word of successes and failures spread and influenced the other colonies.[27]

The lower houses were in a continuous struggle to enlarge their spheres of operation and influence. The houses responded forcefully and sometimes violently when the governors threatened to deprive them of their new rights. This was a struggle for political influence by a new economically powerful class of merchants, planters, and professionals. The process had previously occurred in Britain and would subsequently repeat itself in numerous countries around the world until it became a pattern if not an iron law. Executives insisted that the houses existed as a privilege to the colonies—the houses saw themselves as existing by right as the right of ordinary Englishmen. The Americans—like their English counterparts—saw men as deeply flawed creatures incapable of ruling over other men without abusing their positions of authority. They were suspicious of the executive because of the record of the monarchy in seventeenth-century England. The houses emerged from the French and Indian War with a self-confident assertion of their rights.[28]

Britain emerged from the Great War for the Empire with a huge war debt of 137 million pounds sterling, which was unprecedented for the time long before an annual income tax for ordinary citizens, nearly twice the prewar debt. Annual per capita tax in Britain was several times that of the most heavily taxed colonies in America—those that had contributed most to the war effort, Connecticut and Massachusetts—let alone compared to lightly taxed colonies like Maryland and Georgia. As a result of the war, Britain began to impose a number of sales taxes on common goods and services. They started with the Sugar Act in 1764 that prohibited the importation of rum from non-British areas and imposed a tax on a number of luxury goods including sugar, wines, silk, and coffee. The British began operating aggressively against smugglers. This had a very harmful effect on merchants in New England who had come to rely on smuggled goods in producing rum and other liquors. Next was the Currency Act that prohibited using promissory notes as currency. As the colonies typically ran a trade deficit, hard currency was always in short supply and prohibiting alternatives really pinched upon commerce. Then there was the Stamp Act in 1765, which required a stamp on official papers such as licenses or contracts, as well as on newspapers. This act affected nearly all the members of the rising new economic classes from merchants to professionals to even planters who needed to pay the tax to read the newspaper. Riots broke out in several colonies, mobs of angry citizens forced customs agents and tax collectors to resign, and the mobs destroyed the hated stamps. The Virginia House of Burgesses, spurred on by Patrick Henry, passed a series of resolutions denouncing taxation without representation. Ironically, Britain actually preferred taxation without representation to taxation with representation—which would have meant heavier taxation. A Stamp Act Congress met in Massachusetts in October 1765 with delegates representing nine of the thirteen colonies to draw up a set of petitions to London asking for repeal of the act. With the support of the British merchant classes, which were also opposed to the new taxes, the inexperienced Rockingham government in Britain repealed the Stamp Act in 1766. This only served to encourage the colonists to believe that if they were vigorous enough in their complaints and protests, with sympathetic supporters in Britain they could overturn the legislation.[29]

Meanwhile, ordinary poor colonists were disturbed by the Royal Proclamation of 1763, which prohibited settlement west of a line running down the crest of the Appalachian Mountains in order to appease Indians living in the West and prevent the outbreak of further violence similar to Pontiac's Rebellion. These colonists, many of them Scotch-Irish (Ulster Scots) from Ulster, Ireland, were settled on poor unproductive land in the Carolinas, Virginia, or Pennsylvania and wanted the opportunity to acquire more productive lands in the West. Many simply ignored the proclamation and went on to settle in the prohibited areas regardless of the consequences—and then resented the lack of protection from the Crown—or like Daniel Boone and the "long hunters," went on "long hunts" in Kentucky and Tennessee. Others remained in the colonies and formed the backbone of the forces striving for independence and played an important role in the Revolution.[30]

In 1765 an underground revolutionary society was formed—the Sons of Liberty—in order to oppose the new taxes. The group existed in several colonies, particularly in New England, where it led protests and riots against the Stamp Act. Later it agitated against the stationing of British soldiers in American homes and opposed a tax on tea with the famous Boston Tea Party in 1773, when Sons of Liberty thinly disguised as Indians tossed crates of tea into Boston Harbor in protest. From this point onward the colonies were in a downward slide to revolution and open warfare. Ironically, the war that had been meant to secure the colonies for Britain helped to lose them through its costs and the means taken to recover them.[31]

In the state houses of America in the two decades before independence, there emerged a class of great legislators: John Adams, Samuel Adams, and James Otis in Massachusetts; William Livingstone in New York; Ben Franklin and John Dickinson in Pennsylvania; Richard H. Lee, Thomas Jefferson, and Patrick Henry in Virginia; and others. These politicians played major roles in the Continental Congresses, the confederation, the Constitutional Convention, and after 1789 in the federal government.[32]

THE MILITIA IN THE AMERICAN REVOLUTION

The First Continental Congress, only in existence for seven weeks in September and October 1774, urged the thirteen colonies to improve the state of their militias. At this point there were some 2.5 million Americans, very few of whom were contemplating national independence from Britain.

The Second Continental Congress constructed a uniform table of organization for the militias and recommended that companies elect their officers and that they group the companies into regiments whose officers would be designated by the colonial legislatures. Massachusetts, the most radical of the colonies and the likely starting point for any revolution, ordered the first Minuteman units, so-called because the men would be ready on a minute's notice by keeping their firearms at the ready at their place of business or residence. These Minutemen did not do well at Lexington and failed to stop the British force sent to collect munitions and return with them to Boston, but the Minutemen performed very well at Concord—the British force failed to accomplish its mission and had to be rescued by another force from Boston. The relief commander, Lord Percy, was very impressed by the martial spirit and skill of the Americans, "I never believed . . . that they would have attacked the King's troops, or have the perseverance I found in them."[33]

A twenty-thousand-man militia army from New England soon converged on Boston but dissolved as soon as the situation evolved into a stalemate. This demonstrated both the strength and weakness of the militias: they could react relatively quickly in an emergency but had little capacity for sustained warfare.

Congress constituted twenty-six regiments to serve during 1776—this was the beginning of the Continental Army and of the U.S. Army. During the Revolution there were the Continental Army of Washington and thirteen state armies, as well as local militias, all competing for men, for officers, for rank, and for glory. The troops had a contractual spirit—not surprising in a cause based on a notion of contractual individual rights and in a nation imbued with the Scottish notion of contractual loyalty to the sovereign—and did not feel obliged to reenlist after their contracts had expired. As a result, Massachusetts felt compelled in 1776 to draft men to its army.[34]

The colonial armies tended to be seasonal, fighting in the late spring and summer and early fall between the time of planting and the time of harvest. Like the Indians, the colonists would suffer if the farmers did not have a chance to plant and harvest their crops during the year. The men would return to their communities in the fall for the harvest and spend the winter at home. The truth is that the majority of militiamen did not spend the winter at Valley Forge, Pennsylvania, in the winter of 1778 learning how to operate as a cohesive unit. After the spring planting they would reenlist for duty. This served to provide the farmers with employment during the summer. Desertion was commonplace. The colonial armies and the Continental Army were dependent on townsmen and city dwellers or teenagers who had not yet married and could be spared from the farms. Some defeats came about because Patriot commanders felt obliged to rush into battle under the pressure of short-term enlistments and the imminent departure of their men. Militiamen often fled the battlefield in terror, spreading defeatism, and even the best of commanders were let down by their troops. In all states the militia commanders refused to subordinate themselves to Continental officers, and as a result there was endless bickering over relative rank. The militia was also unpredictable: calls for action could produce more men than needed, fewer men, or even no men at all.[35]

In the nineteenth century the Prussian military theorist Von Clausewitz developed the concept of "center of gravity," meaning the one thing that was crucial to the enemy's (or one's own) war effort. This was usually the enemy capital or its army. During the Revolution there was no conventional American center of gravity. During the first four years of the Revolution, all four main cities (Boston, New York, Philadelphia, and Charleston) were occupied by the British to little effect. Washington's Continental Army was possibly the center of gravity in the early days, but once the Revolution got going and independence was declared, the individual state armies could have survived and carried on even if Washington had been forced to surrender. Militia was crucial to the conflict in all areas during the Revolution. Major General Charles Lee defended Charleston in 1776 with a force of two thousand state troops, twenty-seven hundred local militia, and nine hundred Continentals. General Burgoyne was forced to surrender to a group of American militia units in October 1777.[36]

After France entered the war on the American side in February 1778 following the Battle of Saratoga, the British shifted their strategic focus to the South. The militia played a key role in the fighting in the Carolinas, particularly in the Battles of King's Mountain (discussed in the next chapter) and Cowpens. In the latter battle in January 1781, General Daniel Morgan beat the British with a militia army backed by "regulars." Britain suffered 110 killed and 702 taken prisoner at the cost of 12 killed and 60 wounded for the Americans. Morgan rose through the ranks to the rank of brigadier general. He had started his military "career" in the French and Indian War and deserted following Braddock's defeat. He started as a captain in 1775, was captured in Quebec in 1775, and was exchanged the following year. Morgan was nearly illiterate, but his imposing size, common sense, willingness to listen to others, and courage endeared him to his men. After this loss Lord Cornwallis retreated to Virginia where he was defeated at Yorktown in October 1781 by a force of seventy-eight hundred French soldiers, fifty-seven hundred Continentals, and thirty-two hundred militiamen. The militia was crucial to completing the siege that forced Cornwallis to surrender.

Morgan was typical of Continental officers in that he came out of the militia. John Sullivan, a leading general in the North, began as a major in the New Hampshire militia. Benedict Arnold, the most skilled American commander in battlefield tactics before his treason, began as a captain in Connecticut. And Benjamin Lincoln was colonel of a Massachusetts regiment—which his father had commanded before him. Even the two American officers with widespread experience in the British army before the Revolution—Charles Lee and Horatio Gates—had confidence in the militia, and Lee even authored a pamphlet to demonstrate that they were superior to British regulars.[37]

The Patriots gained a number of co-belligerents—"allies" would be too generous a term for them—in the late 1770s. Spain joined France as a co-belligerent in 1779, which was a disastrous year for the latter. And the Netherlands eventually joined in the war. France's entry into the war actually prolonged the North government in London and prevented its replacement until after the Battle of Yorktown.

As early as April 1779 Spain proposed peace on the basis of *uti possidetis,* or each side retaining what it actually possessed. France, who had been bankrupted by the war, had already broken the spirit if not the letter of her two treaties with the United States by 1779 in terms of discussing peace terms with Spain and others without American knowledge. By February 1781 France was ready to accept a proposal by Austrian and Russian mediators for a peace on the basis of territory held—except for New York, which would go to the United States despite British occupation. This would have effectively meant a partition of the United States, with New York and New England winning their independence and the Southern colonies and Western territories remaining under British rule. After all, the conquests of George Rogers Clark had disappeared by the end of the war. The French foreign minister seriously considered this. But it was unacceptable to both the United States and Britain—who each wanted to retain New York. The siege of Yorktown then changed the entire calculus of victory in late 1781.[38]

There were major weaknesses with the militias besides those already mentioned. Mutinies broke out in Pennsylvania in January 1781 and in June 1783 over nonpayment of wages. The Pennsylvania militia also massacred ninety defenseless Christian Indians encamped at Gnadenhutten in 1782. Pennsylvania had probably the worst of the state militias.[39]

Historian John Shy has identified three crucial roles the militia played during the Revolution. First, it held communities for the Patriot cause: by encouragement if possible, by intimidation if necessary. Second, the militia provided large numbers of men that could quickly report for combat in an emergency as at King's Mountain, Cowpens, or the defense of Charleston. Third, the militia served as a recruiting pool for volunteers for the Continental Army and a training ground for both soldiers and officers.[40]

The American military ideal and model was not Caesar but Cincinnatus, the soldier who returned to his farm after the emergency. American military officers even created a fraternal organization at the end of the Revolution—the Society of Cincinnati, headed by a reluctant Washington. Even in Britain where there was little fear of coups during the eighteenth and nineteenth centuries, military men rarely became prime ministers—the Duke of Wellington being the prime exception. Turning military success into a political career was almost a uniquely American phenomenon until the late nineteenth century when the Afrikaners in South Africa began to copy the American model. Israel has since copied it. The reasons for this heritage are the subject of the remainder of this book. But historian Daniel Boorstin gives one reason, "Precisely because there was no military caste, the citizen soldier easily found a place in American political life."[41]

THE MILITIA IN THE EARLY REPUBLIC

The United States was initially formed as a confederacy with a weak central government under the Articles of Confederation in 1783. There was no federal army, no central currency, and no method of forcing the payment of debts between states. In 1786 a group of men living in western Massachusetts led by former Captain Daniel Shays, a successful militia officer in the Revolution, revolted against foreclosure by creditors living in the eastern part of the state. The rebellion was ultimately put down because sectionalism within the state allowed militia recruited in the east to proceed to the west and crush the rebellion. This was one of the key reasons for the calling of the Constitutional Convention in Philadelphia in 1787.[42]

When Lieutenant Colonel Josiah Harmer led 1,775 men to the Ohio frontier in the summer of 1790, three-quarters of them were militiamen. Harmer blamed his poor performance on the poor quality of his manpower. General Arthur St. Clair, the military governor of Ohio, was sent to attack the Indians in 1791 and was ambushed near Fort Washington. He suffered over seven hundred men killed—in absolute terms the largest loss of any American force in Indian warfare and the largest proportional loss of a major force until the Little Bighorn in 1876. Congress conducted an investigation of the defeat and ordered President Washington to turn over all papers related to the expedition. Washington readily complied, setting a major precedent in legislative-executive relations for the Republic.

A law establishing a uniform militia was passed on May 8, 1792. But there were no provisions in the law for either individuals or states that refused to comply. The law was observed more in the breach than in the observance. Washington and Congress organized a new federal army—the Legion of the United States—under the command of Major General Anthony Wayne, who was after Washington and Lee the leading general in the Revolution. This rescued Wayne from a scandal that had ruined his budding political career after only a single term in the House from Georgia. In 1794 he defeated the Indians of the Northwest at the Battle of Fallen Timbers with no help from the militia. This established a pattern for the United States: the Indian wars would be fought mainly by the professional army, and the militia would provide local defense and volunteers for wars with foreign powers. That same year George Washington took to the field to personally lead a 12,950-man militia force made up of contingents from Pennsylvania, New Jersey, Virginia, and Maryland. The governors of the first three states personally led their contingents. The occasion was the crushing of the Whiskey Rebellion in western Pennsylvania by farmers who objected to paying a tax on whiskey production. The rebellion was put down with only two accidental civilian deaths. Four years later there was a mutiny by the militia of Bucks County, Pennsylvania, who rebelled against property tax assessors and began arresting them. President Adams called out a small contingent of regular troops to subdue the rebellion. Most of the Federalist leaders had been officers in the Continental Army and were more inclined to rely on the army than on militia. The Republicans believed in militia to the extent that they supported a military at all.[43]

In 1800 there were 28,000 militia officers. The militiamen seldom had uniforms, but the officers did. In 1804 there were 525,000 militiamen, but of these only 10 percent owned firearms. By then state units were no longer interchangeable, with great divergences in size of regiments among the various states. By the time of the War of 1812, the requirement of six annual training days had been cut back to four due to complaints by local militiamen.[44]

THE MILITIA IN THE WAR OF 1812

When the United States declared war on Britain in June 1812—ironically just as the ostensible causes of it were being addressed and corrected by Britain—the U.S. Army was in a poor condition. A 36,000-man army, 50,000 volunteers, and 100,000 alerted militia were authorized by Congress for the war, but it never reached that strength. Over a hundred thousand men came and went for short tours.

Every militia had two commanders: the president and the state governor; and if the two disagreed, then the force was paralyzed. The performance of the militia had a very negative impact during the opening stages of the war. Brigadier General William Hull was ordered to invade Canada with a mixed regular and militia force. But the militia refused to cross into Canada. As a result Hull lost all confidence in the militia and surrendered Detroit to an inferior force of British and Indians on August 17, 1812. A force of some fifty-five regulars at Ft. Dearborn was ordered by Hull to evacuate the fort and head for Fort Wayne in Indiana. But the garrison, a number of civilians and a force of some thirty Miami scouts sent to deliver the evacuation order, were all ambushed and massacred by a force of some five hundred Potawatomi a short distance from the fort. By surrender or abandonment, the United States lost most of its forts in the Northwest in the opening months of the war, Fort Harrison held by Captain Zachary Taylor being a notable exception.[45]

Winfield Scott was forced to surrender to an inferior force at Queenstown, Canada, on August 17, 1812, because militia refused to cross into Canada to back him up. Incidentally, a small force of Mohawk was fighting with the British at Queenstown and one nearly killed Scott as he came bearing a white flag to surrender as they had killed two other officers, but he was saved by British officers. This and his near escape from capture by Indians while breakfasting at the home of a Canadian woman who had both invited and betrayed him before the Battle of Chippewa on July 5, 1814, were the extent of Scott's close experience with Indians.[46]

According to militia historian John K. Mahon, William Henry Harrison "knew how to get the most out of militia troops." He would dress up in buckskins, like his men, and harangue them with patriotic exhortations. According to Mahon, "his campaign displayed almost the perfect use of citizen soldiers." Morale among the Kentucky militia was especially high because they were led by their governor, Revolutionary hero Isaac Shelby. But unfortunately, Harrison's army was good for one campaign only of just over a year.[47]

New York militia left the Canadian border undefended during the war, and as a result Black Rock and Buffalo were looted and burned by a British invasion force. Major General Jacob Brown used an ingenious strategy to convert defeat into victory at Sackett's Harbor, New York. After the militia had fought for some time against British regulars, it broke and fled the battlefield. Brown sent runners throughout the town and the surrounding area to announce that a victory had been won. Not wishing to miss out on the spoils and glory of victory, the militiamen trickled back and Brown reformed them and drove the British from the town and area. It had achieved the victory that he had announced prematurely. This marked Brown as one of the more successful officers of the war, and he went on to achieve fame in the border fighting in 1814. In September 1814 fifteen hundred militiamen were persuaded to cross into Canada, and they achieved a victory at Fort Erie.[48]

In Maryland the militia fled in terror from the amphibious force of General Robert Ross at the village of Bladensburg, some six miles northeast of Washington, and the battle became known as the "Bladensburg races." The British burned the White House (not yet called that) and other public buildings in Washington. But the local Chesapeake militia recovered Maryland's honor by performing as they were designed to do in theory and successfully defending Baltimore. General Ross was even shot dead by an American sniper from the militia.[49]

In July 1814 when a twenty-thousand-man army of Napoleonic veterans threatened to invade the United States, it was not the militia that prevented it. Rather, it was a small fleet of one schooner, three sloops, and ten gunboats under Lieutenant Thomas Macdonough that defeated an even smaller British fleet of four ships on Lake Champlain and left the British invasion force vulnerable to having its supply route interdicted. Even though the naval battle was really a draw, the British failed to establish "command of the lake." The cautious British commander declined to press his luck and refused to invade. The British had learned to respect the Americans and did not regard them as mortal enemies like the French.

This was just as well for the Americans, as a convention of delegates from five New England states meeting in Hartford, Connecticut, had met to deal with the war. The convention claimed it was unconstitutional to put regular officers over militia troops and to try and classify a state's militia. As the British and Americans were negotiating the Treaty of Ghent to end the war in Belgium, the Hartford Convention denounced the war and claimed that it was ruining the economy. In reality, the merchants had actually prospered in many areas by charging steep prices for trade with both armies. Some of the delegates advocated secession if the war was not brought to a swift conclusion, but they were a minority. The convention was basically a Federalist enterprise, and it had the effect of branding the party as disloyal and leading to its collapse as a national party. But Daniel Webster of Massachusetts had spoken in Congress denouncing Secretary of War James Monroe's plan for a one-hundred-thousand-man force of reserves, which would require conscription. The bill was never enacted.[50]

The militia was very successful at producing leaders of citizen soldiers, including William Henry Harrison, who had actually been trained in the regular army; Jacob Brown; Peter Buel Porter; Richard M. Johnson; and Samuel Smith. The most conspicuous militia graduate was Andrew Jackson, who was the commander in the Creek War and the defense of New Orleans. Jackson put down a rebellion by militia who were ending their service, and he even criticized Governor Willie Blount, the leader of his own faction, for not being energetic enough in keeping an army in the field. Blount forgave Jackson's remarks, which were addressed to him in a private letter, as Jackson was a valuable political asset. At New Orleans with a militia force, Jackson was able to inflict casualties on the British in the ratio of 7:1.[51]

Throughout the thirty-month war some 398,000 men served less than six months, 60,000 served slightly more than six months, and only 10,000 volunteers served with no restrictions on their service. Some $65 million dollars were paid out in pensions for War of 1812 service between 1872 when the pensions began and 1946 when the last pension was paid out. The pensions were paid not only to veterans but also to their wives and widows and to some family members, and many veterans married quite young women late in their lives.[52]

THE MILITIA AFTER 1815

The next war in which the militia played a role was the Black Hawk War of 1831–32. The United States took ten thousand citizen soldiers on its payroll for the war—7,787 of them from Illinois and the remainder from Michigan and Wisconsin (the latter still being part of Michigan). Governor John Reynolds, who rode in the field with his militia in the summer of 1832, often ignored General Henry Atkinson, who was the senior army commander, and issued orders directly to his troops. A group of Illinois militiamen came upon a group of Black Hawk's men who were trying to arrange a surrender. The Indians did not speak English, and the settlers attacked the Indians. They were in turn ambushed by a small group of Indians and raced away in terror and did not stop for some twenty-five miles. The incident, which took place near Stillman's Ferry, became known as Stillman's Run; and Zachary Taylor described it as "unutterably shameful." The Illinois militia also committed a number of atrocities during the war. Brigadier General James Henry was the only effective militia commander, and he played a significant role at the beginning of the Battle of Bad Axe on August 4, 1832, that ended the war.[53]

The next war in which citizen soldiers played a role was the Second Seminole War from 1835 to 1842. Two commanders from the regular army emerged from this war with a national reputation: Colonel Zachary Taylor, who commanded in the only major conventional battle of the war at Lake Okeechobe on Christmas Day 1837; and Brigadier General Thomas Jesup. Taylor was promoted to brigadier general as a result of the battle. Senator Thomas Hart Benton accused Taylor of sacrificing the Missouri volunteers in order to protect his regulars. Taylor pleaded that he was only making sure that seasoned troops were in position to back up the volunteers if they showed signs of faltering. Jesup controlled nine thousand men in 1837, forty-one hundred of them volunteers. Volunteer battalions came from Florida, Louisiana, Georgia, Tennessee, and Missouri; two companies came from Pennsylvania; and one company each came from New York and the District of Columbia. Jesup, like Taylor, disliked the volunteers and preferred to do without their service. Horses made the volunteers more expensive than regulars, but the volunteers refused to walk like the regulars. When Brigadier General Walker Armistead assumed control of Florida in 1840, the volunteers were relegated to a purely defensive role.[54]

The Mexican War of 1846–47 was the first American war in which long-term volunteers played a major role. The militia was the common source of procuring volunteers. Some 12,500 militiamen were mustered into service during the war. Initially the men were given the choice between enlisting for one year or enlisting for the duration of the war. In May 1846, after the war began, the one-year enlistment option was deleted. Some 27,000 men enlisted for one year and another 33,500 for the duration. Only about 3 percent of the military-age population served in the Mexican War compared to about 40 percent in the War of 1812 and an even greater percentage in the Revolution. Nineteen out of twenty-nine states—mostly Southern and border states—sent volunteers, as did a few cities such as Saint Louis and Louisville. The composition of the force in Mexico was: 58 percent volunteers, 30 percent regulars, and 12 percent militia.[55]

The volunteer troops tended to riot when idle, and there were instances in which officers, both volunteer and regular, were shot while attempting to quell riots. The volunteers with their racist attitudes also mistreated the Mexican population by robbing, raping, and even murdering the natives. This created guerrilla resistance to the American armies operating in Mexico—particularly Taylor's army. Both Taylor and Winfield Scott had low opinions of the volunteers, both formed from their previous service in the War of 1812 and in the Black Hawk War, with Scott having an even worse opinion than Taylor did but being more effective at controlling his volunteers.[56]

The national consensus after the war was that the volunteers "had vindicated the national honor." Congress cut the army from 29,512 authorized in 1847 to 11,685 in 1855. This was at the beginning of the Third Seminole War in Florida. This war was fought mainly by the Florida militia, which committed many atrocities; and only about a hundred Indians remained in Florida at the end of the war.[57]

NOTES

1. John K. Mahon, *History of the Militia and the National Guard* (New York: Macmillan, 1983), pp. 6–11, 13; Daniel J. Boorstin, *The Americans: The Colonial Experience* (New York: Random House, 1958), pp. 354–55.
2. Mahon, pp. 14–15, 18, 19, 21.
3. Ibid., pp. 23, 25–26.
4. Boorstin, op. cit., pp. 348, 352–53.
5. Ibid., pp. 349–51.
6. Ibid., pp. 356–58, 360, 361, 362.
7. Alan Taylor, *American Colonies* (New York: Viking, 2001), pp. 314–17, 323–24, 337.
8. Ibid., pp. 339–40, 342, 344, 358, 360.
9. Richard Slotkin, *Regeneration Through Violence* (New York: HarperCollins, 1996), p. 78.
10. Mahon, op. cit., p. 31.
11. "King Philip's War," *Pilgrim Hall Museum* on the Internet at www.pilgrimhall.org/philipwar, accessed in September 2002.
12. Michael Tougias, "King Philip's War in New England," *The History Place*, at www.historyplace.com/specials/kingphilip, accessed in September 2002.
13. Ibid., and *Pilgrim Hall*, op. cit.
14. Slotkin, op. cit., pp. 95–96, 180–81.
15. Taylor, op. cit., pp. 421, 424.
16. Jeffrey and Richard Morris, "WARS—King William's War," *Encyclopedia of American History: 7th ed.* (New York: HarperCollins, 1996) reprinted on the Internet at *USA History* at www.usahistory.com/wars/william, accessed in September 2002.
17. Jeffrey and Richard Morris, "WARS—Queen Anne's War: War of the Spanish Succession," *Encyclopedia of American History: 7th ed.,* op. cit., and "Gorton Carruth," *The Encyclopedia of American Facts and Dates: 10th ed.* (New York: HarperCollins, 1997) at *USA History* at www.usahistory.com/wars/spansucc, accessed in September 2002.

18. "King George's War," *Small Planet Communications* at www.smplanet.com/colonial/french/george, accessed in September 2002.

19. "French and Indian Colonial Wars," *Small Planet Communications* at www.smplanet.com/colonial/french/overview, accessed in September 2002.

20. Mahon, op. cit., pp. 28, 29; see next chapter for details on Washington's Indian-fighting career.

21. Boorstin, op. cit., pp. 364, 365.

22. Mahon, op. cit., pp. 29, 30.

23. Lawrence H. Gibson, "The American Revolution as an Aftermath of the Great War for the Empire, 1754–65," in Abraham S. Eisenstadt, ed., *American History Recent Interpretations Book I: to 1877* (New York: Thomas Crowell, 1969), pp. 149–65, see p. 151.

24. Ibid., pp. 31, 33.

25. Ibid.

26. Jack Greene, "The Role of Lower Houses of Assembly in Eighteenth Century Politics," in Eisenstadt, op. cit., pp. 80–99, 81–84.

27. Ibid., pp. 84, 86.

28. Ibid., pp. 88, 91, 95.

29. "American History: Road to Independence," and "Stamp Act, 1765" in *Webster's World Encyclopedia 2000* (New York: Webster's Publishing, 1999); Gibson, op. cit., pp. 158, 159, 161; Taylor, op. cit., p. 439.

30. Gibson, p. 157.

31. "Sons of Liberty," in *Webster's*, op. cit.; Gibson, p. 165; Taylor, op. cit., p. 440.

32. Greene, op. cit., p. 95.

33. Taylor, op. cit., pp. 442, 443; Mahon, op. cit., p. 36.

34. Mahon, p. 37; Boorstin, op. cit., p. 367.

35. Mahon, op. cit., pp. 37, 40, 42–43; Boorstin, pp. 368, 369.

36. Boorstin, p. 369; Mahon, pp. 38, 39.

37. Mahon, pp. 40, 41, 43–44.

38. Richard Morris, "The Diplomats and the Mythmakers," in Eisenstadt, op. cit., pp. 178–201, see pp. 187–89, 194, 196, 200.

39. Boorstin, op. cit., p. 370; Mahon, p. 42.

40. John Shy, "Mobilizing Armed Forces in the American Revolution," in John Parker and Carol Urness, eds., *The American Revolution a Heritage of Change* (Minneapolis: University of Minnesota, 1973), pp. 96–106, quoted in Mahon, p. 44.

41. Boorstin, op. cit., pp. 371–72.

42. Mahon, op. cit., p. 47.

43. Mahon, pp. 51, 52, 54, 55.

44. Ibid., pp. 57, 63, 66.

45. Ibid., pp. 67, 68; John R. Elting, *Amateurs, To Arms!: A Military History of the War of 1812* (New York: Da Capo Press, 1995), p. 35.

46. Mahon, op. cit., p. 68; Elting, p. 48; John Eisenhower, *Agent of Destiny* (New York: Free Press, 1997), p. 82.

47. Mahon, pp. 69–70.

48. Ibid., pp. 71–72; Elting, op. cit., pp. 130–31.

49. Mahon, p. 73.

50. Ibid., pp. 74–75, "Hartford Convention," *Webster's*, op. cit.

51. Mahon, op. cit., pp. 75–77.
52. Ibid., p. 77.
53. Ibid., p. 87.
54. Ibid., pp. 89–90.
55. Ibid., p. 91.
56. Ibid., pp. 92, 94.
57. Ibid., pp. 94, 96.

2

The Revolutionary War

INTRODUCTION: THE AMERICAN REVOLUTION
IN INDIAN COUNTRY

The American Revolution was another in a long series of wars in North America involving European powers allying themselves to local Indians in order to accomplish their goals. This process began in 1689 and would not end until the War of 1812. The difference between the Revolution and previous wars was that instead of the French siding with the Indians against the settlers and the British protecting them, the British and Americans were each siding with various Indian tribes—some of these tribes being split down the middle. Often the tribal leaders only dimly understood the balance of power among the whites. The American Revolution was more complicated in its interaction with the native population than was the later War of 1812, because it was less a matter of most of the natives lining up clearly on one side.

At the end of the colonial period there were approximately 150,000 woodland Indians surviving in the eastern area. There was much contact between these Indians and local whites with many Indians having assimilated European culture to various degrees, some of them having even studied at American or English universities. There were also many whites who lived among the Indians and acted as "cultural brokers" between the European and native cultures. There were twenty odd whites living in the Shawnee capital of Chillicothe in the winter of 1772–73 and as many as three hundred English and Scots living among the Creek by the beginning of the Revolution. Indian and colonial economies became interdependent, with many whites using herbal medicines procured from Indians and Indians dependent on whites for alcohol, tobacco, and many trade goods.[1]

The Indian population had just suffered a major reduction in numbers due to the introduction of a host of European diseases to which they had no immunity: smallpox, plague, measles, influenza, pneumonia, tuberculosis, diphtheria, and yellow fever. It was one of history's greatest biological catastrophes and one that was mostly not planned. There was one incident of Indians being deliberately infected with smallpox during the Pontiac War of 1763 when they were given blankets from smallpox sufferers. But around the Great Lakes region and in the lower Mississippi Valley, the Indian populations were actually on the rise, partly due to the absorption of refugees from areas farther east.[2]

Interaction between whites and Indians had alternated between periods of conflict and peace—with the latter occurring when settlers were territorially satiated or prevented by the authorities from expanding. In fact, many whites learned how to hunt from Indians. Conflict between European and Indian civilizations was increasing by the time of the Revolution. This was primarily because British victory in the French and Indian War had opened Indian country up to a flood of new settlement at the expense of the Indians. The Treaty of Stanwix in 1768 infuriated the Shawnee who felt that the Iroquois had sold out *their* lands to the whites. British authorities recognized the justice of Indian complaints about fraudulent land purchase from Indians by settlers. On the eve of the Revolution, bloodshed typified Indian–white relations on the frontier.[3]

The best that Indians could hope for at the beginning of the war was damage control rather than victory. In Indian country the American Revolution amounted to a civil war with no neutrals: Indians fought Indians, Indians fought whites, and whites fought whites. Many Indians did not know which side to take in the Revolution. Many Indians, particularly educated Indians intrigued by the idea of liberty, voluntarily enlisted in the colonial cause. Many militant Indians saw this as an opportunity to ally with the British and win back territory lost in recent years. This was the same motive that Irish republicans had in 1798 and in 1916. But participation in fighting tended to be episodic and brief.[4]

The Iroquois Confederation had managed to obtain a pivotal position in North American affairs due to their neutrality in earlier conflicts. In 1775 the Oneida and other Iroquois tribes took a neutral stance, but by 1777 they were actively involved in the war. The Iroquois Confederation split during the war: the Tuscarora, the newest member of the confederation, fought for the Americans; the Mohawk, Seneca, and Onondaga sided with the British; the Oneida split, with most going with the Americans and some with the British. The Pequot of Connecticut, who sided with the Patriots, suffered 50 percent casualties among those who volunteered. The Seven Nations of Canada stayed neutral.[5]

Shawnee leader Chief Cornstalk tried to remain neutral despite pressure from young warriors to join the British side. But frontiersmen proved to be their own worst enemies, murdering Cornstalk under a flag of truce in 1777 causing his followers to side with the British. This unleashed a wave of attacks on Kentucky. The Catawba in South Carolina supported the Americans simply because they were surrounded by them and to do otherwise would have been suicidal. In the western Great Lakes region, the late revolutionary period saw a struggle for Indian sympathies between George Rogers Clark and British agent Charles Langlade.[6]

A thousand British and Indians attacked Spanish Saint Louis in May 1780 and failed to take the city—a major blow to British prestige. This caused many Sauk and Fox to switch allegiance from the British to the Spanish. In February 1781 a Spanish and Indian force captured St. Joseph, Missouri, and held it for a day before retreating back to St. Louis in triumph. The Choctaw supported the British except for in the Six Towns district near New Orleans where they sided with the Spanish. The Creek supported the British against the Spanish and Americans—an alliance that would continue into the next war. The Revolution was a Cherokee civil war with the Chickamauga under Dragging Canoe splitting off from the main tribe to form a new pro-British tribe.[7]

Many backwoodsmen, infused with a racial hatred of Indians and often unable to distinguish one tribe from another, murdered peaceful Indians, thus undoing the hard work of professional Indian agents to keep the Indians neutral or pro-American. American strategy was to take the war to the Indians and to burn the corn crop late in the season, leaving them without food. Corn for the woodland Indians was the equivalent of the buffalo for the Plains Indians. Colonial militias were used more for revenge than for protection against Indians. South Carolina paid seventy-five pounds for male scalps, whereas Pennsylvania offered one thousand dollars for every Indian scalp—Indians by then being rarer in Pennsylvania than in the Carolinas. The Americans, the British, and the Spanish all interfered in the internal tribal politics of the various tribes. These circumstances in turn often allowed war chiefs to prevail over peace chiefs during the Revolution. Prime examples of this are Mohawk Chief Joseph Brant and Chief Dragging Canoe of the Cherokee. Many Indians ended the war with bitter scores to settle not only against whites but against other Indians as well. And if the fighting was not bad enough by itself, several epidemics occurred during the Revolution. Smallpox hit the Onandaga in the winter of 1776–77, killed Cherokee and Creek in 1779 and 1780, and hit the Cherokee again in 1783. The hardships caused by the fighting and the epidemics marked the end of the old ways for the Cherokee and the beginning of a new period during the mid-1780s.[8]

There were three main areas of conflict in the East between Indians and American settlers, each producing its own Indian-fighter politicians: New York and Pennsylvania, where the settlers faced the Iroquois; Kentucky, where the settlers suffered from Shawnee raids and in turn raided into Ohio; and in the Carolinas, eastern Tennessee, and Georgia, where the settlers battled the Cherokee.

GEORGE WASHINGTON

Those who would eventually call themselves Americans gained their first experience of Indian warfare in the French and Indian War, the North American extension of the European Seven Years War, where many served with General Braddock in the Pennsylvania–New York state area.

One of those who served Braddock was a young Virginia planter named George Washington, who had been appointed an adjutant in the militia of southern Virginia in December 1752 with the rank of major. A few months later he switched his office to northern Virginia, which was closer to his home. In November 1753 Governor Dinwiddie sent Washington on a diplomatic mission to demand that the French withdraw their forts in the Ohio Valley south of Lake Erie, as he claimed this territory as part of Virginia for King George. Washington met with the French, who declined the request, and returned to Virginia after a difficult journey of two months. Washington had friendly contacts with Indians on the mission as well as one hostile incident by an Indian that tried to lead Washington's party into an ambush and fired at them. Washington was appointed a lieutenant colonel in the Virginia militia in the spring of 1754 and became the executive officer of a three-hundred-man regiment. The unit was formed in order to drive the French out of the Ohio Valley. The commander of the expedition was killed en route, leaving Washington in command. He began building a base on the Monongahela River about forty miles from the French fort. Washington, acting under prior authorization from Dinwiddie, attacked a French party on May 27, 1754, and killed ten of the enemy and forced the others to surrender. Both sides had Indians fighting alongside them. This was the beginning of the French and Indian War—the North American portion of the Seven Years War in Europe, which began in 1756. Washington had another fight with the French and Indians on July 3, 1754, when he was attacked in his base—poorly situated from a tactical perspective—by the French and allowed to withdraw after signing a surrender document.[9]

The following year Washington volunteered to serve on General Braddock's staff as a volunteer after he learned that Braddock could appoint no one to a rank higher than captain. In the major battle of the campaign, Washington served as a rider during the battle and had two horses shot out from under him and had four bullets pierce his coat—but he remained untouched. Braddock's force was ambushed by some six hundred Indians while passing through an open area surrounded by woods. Braddock was mortally wounded in the battle on July 9, 1754. Some one thousand men of Braddock's force were killed while the French and Indians only lost about forty. Washington was weak with fever before and after the battle. He returned home in late July as a local hero and was appointed the commander of the regiment with the rank of full colonel upon his return. Washington made friends in the Virginia House of Burgesses, but his ambition for rank caused him to fall out of favor with the governor. Dinwiddie, however, did recommend him for a commission in the British army. Washington garrisoned the Shenandoah Valley to protect it from Indian attacks. Washington went to Boston in the late winter of 1756 to seek a commission in the British army but was turned down by General Shirley who had no authority to grant commissions. The British brought over British and foreign mercenary officers to lead four colonial regiments known as the Royal Americans. Hence they felt they had little need for American officers.[10]

There were Indian attacks in the spring of 1756; but by the time Washington could raise a militia force to respond, the Indians were gone from the colony. Washington respected the skill of Indians in frontier warfare and considered them superior to most white troops in battle.

Washington served under General John Forbes in the fall of 1758 in recapturing Fort Dequesne from the French. The French burned the fort and retreated when the expedition approached. During this campaign Washington suffered from repeated bouts of dysentery, which caused him to resign from military service at the end of the campaign. He had been in service for four years and had been involved in one major battle and several smaller skirmishes.[11]

Washington was elected to the House of Burgesses from Frederick County in 1758. He had been defeated for the same seat three years earlier. Washington got married, settled down to the life of a wealthy Virginia planter, and served as a delegate to the legislature until September 1774 when he was elected as one of seven delegates from Virginia to the First Continental Congress in Philadelphia. Washington began raising a volunteer company of militia in early 1775 and drilling them.

When the delegates returned to Philadelphia in May 1775 as agreed for the Second Continental Congress, the colonies—or at least Massachusetts—were in a state of war with Britain. Local militia had battled British regulars at Lexington and Concord the month before. The first order of business was to choose a commander in chief for a united American army. The delegates wanted someone who was not from New England so as to ensure that the battle was not perceived as a purely regional fight. In any case, neither New England nor the Middle Colonies had suitable candidates for the post. In fact, Washington had only two real rivals for the position: Horatio Gates and Charles Lee, both Englishmen rather than Americans, who had decided to throw their lot in with the colonies. Gates had no field experience but was a qualified administrator. Lee was the strongest candidate on paper. He had served in his father's regiment to help crush the Jacobite rebellion in Scotland at a young age. Like Washington, he went on to fight in Braddock's campaign. But afterward he served in the campaign in Canada that decided the war in North America and then went on to fight in Portugal in 1762. After the Seven Years War, Lee won an appointment as a major general in the Polish army and observed the Russo-Turkish war. But like Gates, Lee was suspect because he was not a colonial. Washington was appointed commander in chief, a job he felt that he was not qualified for by experience, after being nominated for the position by his future vice president, John Adams.[12]

After 1758 Washington never fought Indians again, but it was those earlier experiences that gave him the experience and authority to win high military command and glory. This was then translated into high office. Washington was chosen to preside over the Constitutional Convention that met in Philadelphia in 1789. He was then chosen to be the first president and was reelected without opposition. Some wanted to choose Washington to be a pseudo-dictator or even a king, but Washington would have none of it. This is the difference between Washington and the Latin Indian-fighters in Latin America in the following century. Washington's path was later copied by, first, Arthur Wellesley—the Duke of Wellington—and then by Sam Houston and Andrew Jackson. Washington was not only first in war, first in peace, and first in the hearts of his countrymen but also the first Indian-fighter president. His period as president is considered along with the other Indian-fighter presidents in a later chapter.

Lee provided valuable service in the early years of the American Revolution but grew increasingly contemptuous of Washington's military abilities and, as a result, increasingly insubordinate. Lee and Washington exchanged harsh words on the battlefield during the Battle of Monmouth in the summer of 1778. Afterward Lee was tried by a court martial for cowardice as a scapegoat for the American failure to win a decisive victory. He was found not guilty of cowardice or treachery but guilty of insubordination and was ordered to give up his command for one year. He resigned from the army and never served again because the army refused to wipe the stain of dishonor from his record. He died a bitter man in Philadelphia in 1782.[13]

JOHN SULLIVAN

The Iroquois Confederation, also known as the Six Nations, consisted of six separate tribes that made decisions jointly. Collectively they remained neutral until 1777, at which point, under heavy British pressure with offers of gifts and so on, four of the tribes (Mohawk, Cayuga, Onandaga, and Seneca) joined the British; the Oneida split, with some siding with the Americans and others with the British; and the Tuscarora remained neutral.

In June 1778 the Seneca went to war with a major raid on the Wyoming Valley in northern Pennsylvania followed by further raids into the Cherry Valley in New York in November. The following July the Iroquois struck in New Jersey. Washington vowed "to carry the war into the Heart of the Country of the six nations [sic]; to cut off their settlements, destroy their next Year's [sic] crops, and do them every other mischief of which time and circumstances will permit," after he was unable to defend against Iroquois raids along the frontier in 1779.[14] Washington looked for volunteers among his generals to deal with the Indian threat. General Gates, the senior American general after Washington, declined on grounds of health. So Washington gave the job to John Sullivan who had provided valuable service at the early battles including Trenton and Princeton. In August 1779 the Americans invaded the Iroquois homeland from two directions. Colonel John Brodhead, leading a small force, invaded from the southwest from Pittsburgh, Pennsylvania. The main force under Sullivan, numbering some thirty-seven hundred men, invaded from the south. Sullivan met the Iroquois under Chief Joseph Brant, numbering some five hundred braves, along with several hundred loyalists and a few British regulars at Newtown. The combined British-Indian force was compelled to flee, and Sullivan proceeded with the invasion. He destroyed some forty Indian towns, burning both dwellings and crops. The troops destroyed an estimated 160,000 bushels of corn and great quantities of vegetables; soldiers spent days burning crops and cutting down fruit trees. By the end of 1779 the Mohawk, Cayuga, and Onandaga towns had been destroyed and all but two of the larger Seneca towns as well. Women and children in the towns were killed, and young women were raped. The winter of 1779–80 was by chance one of the coldest winters on record in North America. This greatly reduced Iroquois participation in the remainder of the American Revolution and made them a supply drag on the British army that was required to supply their food needs for the remainder of the war.[15]

Poor health forced Sullivan to leave the army in November 1779. Sullivan returned home to New Hampshire and resumed his career as a lawyer. Before the war Sullivan had not been well liked because he had a habit of engaging in nuisance suits in order to intimidate neighbors. But his military service rehabilitated him. He served as state attorney general before being elected for three one-year terms as president (governor) of New Hampshire in 1785, 1786, and 1789. Washington had him appointed a federal judge for the New Hampshire district, and Sullivan kept this position until his death in 1795 at age fifty-five.[16]

DANIEL BOONE AND GEORGE ROGERS CLARK

Among those who served with General Braddock in the French and Indian War was Daniel Boone, born in southeastern Pennsylvania to a Quaker family that relocated to North Carolina. Boone participated not only in

Braddock's campaign but also in campaigns against the Cherokee in 1759 and 1761. In 1769 Boone went on a hunting trip to Kentucky and was captured by Shawnee in December of that year. He so impressed his captors that he was adopted by one of the chiefs and lived with the Indians for some eighteen months. In 1771 Boone returned to North Carolina after nearly two years in Kentucky. Two years later he led a party of family and friends to Kentucky, but an Indian attack at the Cumberland Gap turned them back and Boone lost one of his sons to the Indian attack. The following year he was sent by Virginia authorities to warn Kentucky surveyors of a pending war with the Shawnee; he also lead the defense of the Clinch River settlements during the conflict known as Dunmore's War.

The following year an entrepreneur hired Boone to cut the Wilderness Road into Kentucky from North Carolina. He founded a settlement that he christened Boonesboro, one of the first in Kentucky. That September he brought his family to settle in Boonesboro. The following year his daughter Jemima and two neighbor girls were kidnapped by Indians. Boone led a rescue that succeeded in recovering all the girls and immortalized him in frontier legend. In December 1776 Kentucky was given the status of a separate county within the state of Virginia. In the spring of 1777 the revolution came to Kentucky in the form of repeated Shawnee attacks against the settlements. In March 1777 the Kentucky militia had its first muster—it consisted of 121 men to defend 280 settlers in three major settlements. Major George Rogers Clark was the commander of the Kentucky militia. Boone was one of only four captains and the commander in Boonesboro. The American Revolution began in Kentucky two days after the muster. Boone was wounded in the initial attack and saved by a neighboring youth who dragged him to safety. The fighting continued on and off over the next five years. Boone's brother Squire suffered eight wounds in seventeen separate engagements.

In February 1778 Boone and his men were captured by Shawnee while making salt at a lick. Boone was taken in captivity to Detroit, which served as the British headquarters in what eventually became the Northwest Territory after the war. While a captive, Boone learned that the British and Indians were planning an attack on Boonesboro. He was then taken to the Shawnee town of Piqua where he spent three months. He managed to escape and traveled some five hundred miles in only four days running nonstop overland to make it back to Boonesboro. Boone led the defense of Boonesboro during an eleven-day siege in September. Boone negotiated with Shawnee Chief Blackfish at the beginning of the siege. The following month Boone was tried in a court martial on charges of collaborating with the British and was acquitted.[17]

In May and June 1779 Colonel John Bowman of Kentucky led an attack on the Shawnee capital of Chillicothe. The Shawnee suffered only light losses except for the death of Chief Blackfish, Boone's adopted father, who stayed behind to make a stand while the women and children escaped.[18]

In September 1779 Boone led a large party of emigrants to Kentucky and founded a second settlement, Boone's Station. In October of the following year, Boone lost a brother to the Shawnee. In the 1780s Boone attempted to make the transition to respectable businessman from frontiersman and scout. In November 1780 Kentucky was divided from a single county into three separate counties. Boone became the head of the militia in Fayette County with the rank of lieutenant colonel and was elected to the Virginia state assembly. In 1781 he was elected county sheriff. During the next decade he served at least three times in the state assembly. While attending the state assembly in Richmond in June 1781, he was captured during the British invasion of the state and was paroled on the condition that he not take up arms against the British and their allies for the remainder of the war. Despite the American Revolution coming to a virtual end after the surrender of Lord Cornwallis to General Washington in October 1781, the war between the Indians and the settlers continued on the frontier.[19]

On August 17, 1782, Boone urged caution about attacking an Indian position at the Blue Licks. A hothead militia officer accused Boone of cowardice and thereby goaded him into participating in the attack. Just as Boone had warned, the situation was a trap that resulted in a large Indian force ambushing the militia. Boone had a son and a nephew killed in the attack. It was the low point of the war for the Kentuckians, and many of them returned to Virginia. It was also the last major battle of the American Revolution.[20]

For Americans and Europeans, the real Indian fighter who had a significant impact on the American Revolution was General George Rogers Clark. Clark was born in 1752 in Virginia. Although Boone would later become a frontier legend known to generations of Americans, Albemarle County, Virginia, which was then on the American frontier, he was too young to participate in the French and Indian War; but at age twenty-two he fought in Lord Dunmore's War: an invasion of the Ohio River Valley. The war bought two years of peace on the frontier for the settlers.

In 1775 Clark went to Kentucky and offered his assistance to the settlers. Clark was chosen one of two delegates to Richmond to win county status for Kentucky. Clark went to see Governor Patrick Henry to beg gunpowder for the defense of the settlements in Kentucky. Because Indians had likely killed a messenger, Clark had to go to Pittsburgh to retrieve the powder for himself. Getting the powder to Kentucky involved a four-hundred-mile dash down the Ohio River while being chased by Indians. Clark was forced to bury the powder, flee, and return to retrieve the powder at a later date. It took the better part of a year but resulted in Kentucky being armed when the Indian attacks began in the spring of 1777. Clark was in charge of the defense of Harrodsburg, the largest settlement in Kentucky, with the rank of major.[21]

During the summer of 1777, Clark sent a pair of scouts to slip through the Indian encirclement of the camps and report on the condition of the French settlements in Illinois that were located along the Mississippi River.

The scouts reported back to Clark that the French were not interested in helping the Americans but that the settlements were thinly garrisoned. Clark decided to mount an expedition to capture the towns. On June 26, 1778, Clark started down the Ohio River from Pittsburgh with 178 men intent on capturing Kaskaskia and Cahokia. The expedition left its boats at the former French outpost of Fort Massac at the mouth of the Tennessee River and continued on foot cross-country so as to escape detection. They made the 125 miles to Kaskaskia in only six days and arrived on the second anniversary of American independence. When the French inhabitants were informed of the new alliance with France, they agreed to take a loyalty oath without question and several French militia units volunteered to serve with the Americans. Cahokia and Vincennes in Indiana surrendered as easily, eliminating the entire British presence south of Detroit.

In Detroit the lieutenant governor of Canada, Henry Hamilton, had been planning to mount an expedition against Pittsburgh. When informed of Clark's exploits, he determined to recapture the settlements. With about 250 men he made his way into Vincennes in mid-December 1778 and the inhabitants switched their allegiance back to the British. Clark received news of the fall of the town six weeks later from a trader who had been released by Hamilton. He determined to recapture the town. He set off a week later with 170 men, about half American and half French. Clark once again traveled overland so as to escape detection. Three weeks later he wandered into the town of Vincennes and liberated it. The Americans, posing as British, greeted an Indian war party returning from a raid into Kentucky. Five were killed and seven captured. Five of the captured Indians were then brained in front of the British fort on Clark's order. The British were allowed to march out of the fort under arms, and Hamilton was sent in captivity to Virginia. This was the highpoint of Clark's career, just as the recapture of Vincennes had been the highpoint of Hamilton's career.

Clark had disrupted plans by the British for a major Indian offensive against the settlements of Kentucky and the Ohio Valley. Hamilton had artillery, which could have easily broken through the wooden stockade defenses of the Kentucky settlements. In gratitude for his exploits, Clark was promoted by Washington to brigadier general and put in charge of the defense of Kentucky. In early August 1780 he invaded the Ohio Valley with a force of about a thousand men, including Boone and every major Kentuckian male. Boone served as a scout for the expedition. The expedition captured the Shawnee capital of Chillicothe, burned by the Shawnee themselves before they retreated, and the village of Piqua, where a young Indian boy named Tecumseh lived. The Shawnee made their stand in Piqua. Clark used a small cannon against the village council house, where many of the Indians had taken refuge. His men spent two days burning cornfields and robbing graves so that they could collect bounties on Shawnee dead that had died previous to the battle. Out of the ashes of that village grew two new Indian wars and another generation of Indian fighters.

Clark returned to the Ohio Valley in the summer of 1782 following the Battle of Blue Licks, accompanied by a Boone thirsting for revenge. The Kentuckians burned five villages, but the Shawnee suffered minimal losses by refusing to give battle. There were eight invasions of Shawnee settlements in the Ohio Valley between 1774 and 1794. Chillicothe was attacked four times between 1779 and 1790. Each time the Shawnee simply rebuilt the village in a different location.[22]

In December 1780 Clark was in Richmond arguing for an expedition against Detroit. But the war suddenly changed with the invasion of Virginia by Cornwallis in the spring of 1781, rendering any offensive action in the West by the Americans impossible. Cornwallis burned a number of government papers at Richmond including the financial records for Clark's expeditions. Clark's commanders had kept their own records, which they sent back to Virginia without his signature, forcing a reconciliation of accounts. Clark was awaiting this reconciliation, which would enable him to recover considerable out-of-pocket expenses that he had made to reimburse his subordinates, when the British burned the records. The records were all either burnt or lost. This ended up reducing Clark to a life of poverty.[23]

Before the war officially ended in 1783, Clark invaded the Ohio Valley with a force of eleven hundred men and in three weeks of campaigning burned six towns and a British trading store but killed only twenty warriors. In the first four years after the end of the American Revolution in 1783, three hundred Americans were killed and twenty thousand horses stolen along the Ohio River. This situation resulted in Clark's final expedition in 1786 against the Shawnee. The invasion was a disaster: just past Vincennes, about half the force mutinied because they feared a shortage of supplies. Clark was forced to call off the expedition.[24]

In October 1786 Boone commanded a company of militia in another invasion of the Ohio Valley led by Colonel Benjamin Logan. Hugh McGary, the militia officer who had accused Boone of cowardice before the battle of Blue Licks, killed a captive Indian chief because he thought that he had been at Blue Licks four years before. McGary was tried by a court martial and lost his rank but was not otherwise punished. This was Boone's last major battle against Indians—he had been fighting them off and on for thirty years. About this time, Boone befriended a young American turned Indian, who went by the name of Blue Jacket. He had been kidnapped by Indians as a teenager during the Revolution and preferred the company of Shawnee to whites. Boone used to hunt with him and helped liberate him by a ruse after settlers captured him. Blue Jacket would go on to fight in the Ohio Valley wars of the early 1790s and become a major Shawnee ally of Tecumseh.[25]

Clark retired after the American Revolution to live as a surveyor in the Louisville area of Kentucky. In 1812 the state of Virginia voted to award him an engraved sword in gratitude for his services in the American Revolution. His younger brother William became a career soldier in the American army and served as co-leader of the famous 1804–1806 Lewis and Clark expedition that explored the West from the Mississippi to the Pacific Ocean. During the War of 1812 he served as territorial governor of the Louisiana territory and as commander of the Louisiana militia. In that capacity he liberated Prairie du Chien, the western-most British post in the interior of America, from the Canadian garrison that had been holding it in 1814.[26]

During much of the post-revolutionary period of the 1780s, Boone was a tavern owner in Maysville, a small settlement in eastern Kentucky. Boone used his profits to engage in land speculation in the 1780s to buy up land cheaply to sell to new settlers. In 1787 voters in Bourbon County elected him to represent them in the state assembly in Richmond. Boone attended the assembly from October to January 1788. In 1789 Boone moved his family to Kanawha in eastern Kentucky and once again became a lieutenant colonel in the local militia, making him the third ranking official in the county. In 1791 Boone was elected to the assembly from Kanawha County, and that year Kentucky became a state. During this time Boone won a contract from Richmond to supply the militia units in Kentucky with ammunition and provisions but was eventually replaced for nonfulfillment of the contract after he encountered a few problems with credit. During the early 1790s Boone lost title to most of his landholdings in court in Virginia and he was forced to give up his idea of becoming an entrepreneur. He returned to the wilderness life of earning his living from hunting and trapping. In 1798 Kentucky honored him by naming a county along the Ohio River after him.

In 1800 he followed one of his sons westward and settled in the Spanish province of Missouri. He was made a minor official in the local Spanish government. He once again suffered at the hands of the legal system when his land titles in Missouri were not recognized by the American government following the Louisiana Purchase. He was finally granted a plot of land to live on by the government in return for his services during the Revolution, and he died in Missouri in 1820.[27]

Boone came to represent one type of Indian fighter—the frontiersman and scout—a type that included the later mountain men such as Jim Bridger and Kit Carson, as well as David Crockett. Crockett was the only one of this group that made a successful career in politics, partly by piggybacking on the legend and myth of Daniel Boone. In 1784 a newly arrived settler from Pennsylvania named John Filson wrote a pamphlet on the history of the settlement with a special section devoted to *The Adventures of Col. Daniel Boon* [sic]. The pamphlet was reprinted repeatedly—often without attribution to Filson—over the next several decades. Boone became a mythic figure in both America and Europe. He was portrayed as both a mythic civilizer and philosophic individual, a white version of the "noble savage" myth that was popular in Europe, and later as a white savage in the derogatory image that Americans had of the native population. The height of the Boone myth was reached during the 1820s and 1830s, the period when the Indian-fighter politician was at his peak.

In 1822 Lord Byron devoted seven stanzas to Boone in his epic canta *Don Juan*. Byron's Boone was pure fantasy. It was also rather vague. From 1823 to 1841 James Fennimore Cooper, America's first popular novelist, published his five "Leatherstocking Tales" novels. The lead character, Nathaniel "Natty" Bumppo, was based on Boone. The first novel, *The Pioneers*, sold thirty-five hundred copies on its first day of publication, allowing Cooper to become one of the first Americans to support himself as a novelist. The second novel, *The Last of the Mohicans*, was published in 1826. The captive sequence of this novel was based on Boone's rescue of his daughter Jemima and the Callaway girls in July 1776. This was followed the next year by *The Prairie*. Cooper then waited thirteen years before taking his character back to an earlier time in *The Pathfinder*. The last of the novels, *The Deerslayer*, was published in 1841. Although the novels were set in the Lake George country of upstate New York, Bumppo was based on episodes out of Boone's life. The *Cambridge History of American Literature* called Bumppo "the most memorable character American fiction has given to the world."[28]

While it is probably unlikely that the Cooper Leatherstocking novels had much effect on the elections of 1824 and 1828—considering Jackson's hero status on the frontier, they were part of the genre of frontier tales—both fiction and nonfiction—popular in the 1830s that helped to create a cult around the Indian fighter in the popular imagination. They may have helped to boost the political fortunes of lesser figures such as Richard Johnson and William Henry Harrison.

JOHN SEVIER AND ISAAC SHELBY

Two Indian fighters from the American Revolution emerged as fairly major politicians. These were Isaac Shelby and John Sevier, co-commanders at the Battle of King's Mountain in 1780. Shelby's military and Indian-fighting career began as a lieutenant in his father's Fincastle Company in the battle of Point Pleasant in Lord Dunmore's War on October 10, 1774. He served in the militia during the first several years of the Revolution, rising to the rank of major. In the spring of 1779 he was elected to the Virginia legislature for Washington County. In the second half of 1778, following Washington's victory at Monmouth Courthouse in June 1778, the war moved from the northern and central colonies to the southern colonies. It was in the Carolinas that the war was fought most fiercely. Shelby went into the army on a regular basis in 1780. Shelby and Sevier led a combined force of about three hundred frontiersmen, which combined with William Campbell's Virginia militia and climbed King's Mountain and assaulted a much larger British force of eleven hundred under the command of British Major Robert Ferguson. Shelby was thanked for his service by the legislature of North Carolina and received an engraved sword in gratitude.

He served briefly as a member of the legislature before moving to Kentucky. He was a member of the convention that framed the first constitution of Kentucky, and he became the first governor of the state. He declined reelection and retired to farm and raise cattle. He also raised horses and mules, which he sold throughout the South to cotton planters. He was once again elected governor of Kentucky in 1812 and served for four years. He commanded a force of three thousand Kentucky militia under General William Henry Harrison and played an important role in the victory at the Battle of the Thames. A grateful President Monroe offered him the position of secretary of war, which he declined, and Congress awarded him a gold medal. He later served with Jackson as a commissioner to negotiate a treaty with the Chickasaw after the war in 1818. He died in 1826 at age 76. There are nine different counties named after Shelby, in as many different states.[29]

Sevier was born in Virginia on the frontier in September 1745 and helped to found the town of New Market as a young man. His father was a storekeeper and land speculator. In 1770 Sevier moved to Millerstown in Frederick County in the present Shenandoah County. Tennessee historians assert that he was a captain in the Virginia militia before moving to the Watauga Valley. In 1773 his father Valentine moved the entire Sevier clan, consisting of himself and his wife and all of his sons and their families, to the Watauga Valley in then western North Carolina, where he soon became active in politics. The Watauga Association was founded in 1771, and John Sevier was said to be one of the commissioners—indicating that he was committed to moving there two years before he actually did. On March 19, 1775, Charles Robertson leased a large tract of land from the Cherokee in the Holston, Watauga, and New rivers area. Robertson and Sevier were elected delegates along with two others (one did not go) to the Provincial Congress of North Carolina at Halifax in November 1776.[30]

Sevier's career as an Indian fighter began in 1776 with his appointment as lieutenant colonel of militia in Washington County. The settlers were convinced that British agents were stirring up the Indians against them. Two British agents in the South, John Stuart and Mr. Cameron, were suspected of attempting to drive all the settlers from the Indian territory in Virginia, the Carolinas, and Georgia. There was a fear that a British army would land on the coast of West Florida and pass through Creek and Chickasaw country to strike at the settlers with the help of the Indians. In reality, the British had actually tried to prevent the Indians from attacking the settlers. They were at this point probably confident of winning the war and did not want to alienate their future subjects. The settlers, however, were fed stories from eastern Patriots.[31]

Nancy Ward, an Indian woman sympathetic to the whites, warned the whites of attacks by the Cherokee. Colonel Christian of Virginia, Colonel Williamson of South Carolina, and General Rutherford of North Carolina led militia armies against the Cherokee. These militia armies laid waste to Indian towns and villages and destroyed the offensive strength of the Cherokee. They burned the settlements and destroyed the grain stores. The treaties of Dewitt's Corner and Long Island brought the war to an end in July 1777.

At this point Dragging Canoe, war chief of the Cherokee, entered into communications with Governor Hamilton in Detroit. Hamilton supplied free trade goods to the Chickamauga to encourage them to attack the whites. Colonel Evan Shelby (Isaac's father) went to war against the Chickamauga of Dragging Canoe and destroyed eleven towns and burned twenty thousand bushels of corn. Sevier did not take part in Shelby's campaign but first campaigned against the Indians in 1780 when he commanded a small group of ten to twenty scouts along the Holston and Tennessee Rivers.

In 1780 Sevier moved again, coming to his final residence in 1783. After King's Mountain Sevier commanded the Washington County militia—about 170 men, or a modern company sized unit—against the Cherokee. He skirmished with Indians at Long Creek, and he forced the Indians to retreat. Sevier continued on into Indian country and had a small group, of which he was part, decoy the Indians into his force at Boyd's Creek. He attempted a complete envelopment of the Cherokee force, but one of his subordinate commanders was slow in closing the trap allowing the Cherokee to escape. The Cherokee had between twenty-eight and thirty killed as compared to only one wounded for the militia. Sevier experienced a close escape when a bullet passed through the hair on the back of his head during the decoy chase. The force burned Cherokee towns along the Tennessee River.[32]

Sevier led a second expedition against the Cherokee in the spring of 1781 targeting the Middle Towns. The militia killed fifty warriors and captured many Cherokee women and children. He burned fifteen to twenty towns. The settlers had only one killed and one wounded. In the summer of 1781 Sevier led another expedition against the settlements of the Indian Creek and routed Indians at Indian Ford.

Immediately after this Sevier raised two hundred mounted militiamen to operate against General Lord Cornwallis in South Carolina in support of Francis Marion (the famous "Swamp Fox" who was played by Mel Gibson in a very thinly disguised character in the movie *Patriot*) in "mopping up" operations in South Carolina. They took part in the capture of Monk's Corner. Sevier's men were part of a larger force of six hundred, made up also of Isaac Shelby's troops. In 1782 Sevier led two hundred men against the Cherokee in Georgia. Peace then followed for four years.[33]

Like Boone, Sevier continued his Indian fighting after the Revolution. In 1786 he led 160 men against the Valley Towns of the Hiwasse Valley and fought against John Watts, Dragging Canoe's successor as war chief of the Chickamauga, who had about a thousand warriors. Sevier avoided a trap and prudently retreated in the face of this uneven contest. This was while he was governor of the failed State of Franklin. He again led the Franklinites against the Cherokee two years later—as Franklin was collapsing.

The Cherokee accused him of stirring up the settlers against them. The settlers usually did not need much stirring up after settlers were murdered or driven from their homesteads on Indian land. Some thirty Cherokee were killed in this campaign, and the rest fled to the Lower Towns. The settlers moved against the Indians in an attempt to pressure them into selling their lands. This last campaign was an attempt by Sevier to restore his authority with the settlers after the collapse of the Franklin project. During this last campaign a survivor of an Indian massacre murdered several Indian prisoners. Sevier never punished the man and for this was held by his opponents to have been culpable in the murders. Indian Agent Richard Winn wrote to the governor of North Carolina complaining about Sevier following this incident.[34]

In 1789 Washington County (one of the three Franklin counties) elected Sevier to represent them in the North Carolina senate. Upon entering the senate, Sevier was appointed to the Indian Affairs Committee. In December 1789 the Assembly determined that his commission as brigadier general of militia dating from 1784 was still valid.

Sevier's last major Indian or military campaign was in 1793. The Cherokee had begun attacking settlers the previous year for settling on their lands. A Captain Beard and his militiamen murdered a group of twelve to fifteen Cherokee, some of whom were chiefs invited to a conference with a representative of President Washington. Sevier mobilized between six hundred and seven hundred men to fight the Indians when they invaded Ish's Station. He destroyed the village of Etowah near present-day Rome, Georgia.[35]

Sevier's technique as an Indian fighter was to invade Indian territory and destroy Cherokee towns and food supplies, after the warriors had first either retreated or been defeated in battle. His men destroyed more than thirty-one Cherokee towns in three campaigns from 1780 to 1782. Sevier was more responsible for conquering and pacifying the Cherokee than any other person—including his rival Andrew Jackson—through his military efforts over thirteen years and policy as governor for another dozen. Sevier and his friends held no treaty with the Indians to be sacred. Sevier's tomb bears the legend: "fought 35 battles, won 35 victories."[36] This probably turns very minor skirmishes into battles, if not inventing the number out of whole cloth. He conducted some seven campaigns against the Cherokee from 1780 to 1793—each of which featured only one or two battles; plus, he participated in two major battles in the Revolution against the British.

After the war, North Carolina ceded its western lands to the United States and as a result local settlers formed a new state that they dubbed Franklin. Sevier served as the first—and only—governor of Franklin. Congress failed to recognize the new state, and North Carolina repealed its cession of the lands and attempted to reestablish title to the three counties (Washington, Sullivan, and Greene) in 1784. Sevier was arrested for treason in 1788 and brought to trial, but he escaped from the courthouse at the beginning of the trial and the trial was never held. The following year he was elected to the state senate and pardoned by the governor. Sevier was made a brigadier general in the "territory south of the river Ohio" in 1791. He was also appointed to the ten-man legislative council for the western area. In 1796 the new state of Tennessee was formed partially out of the territory of the failed state of Franklin, and Sevier was elected its first governor. Sevier served as governor in two separate periods, from 1796 to 1802 and again from 1803 to 1809. Thus, along with Sam Houston, he is the only individual to have been governor of two different states—and for a much longer total period than Houston: fifteen years compared to three years for Houston.

During the period between Sevier's two periods as governor, a young Andrew Jackson challenged Sevier in an 1802 election for the position of major general of militia. Jackson had been seriously preparing for the election after having been previously defeated in 1796, partly because of Sevier's opposition. Sevier considered Jackson to be a mere "petty-fogging lawyer" and not his military equal. The major general was elected by all of the field-grade officers in the three separate districts plus the three brigadier generals. The election resulted in a tie, which was then decided in Jackson's favor by the governor, an ally of Jackson. The election resulted in the two becoming serious political enemies. Eventually they "fought" a duel that turned into a farce and Jackson publicly accused Sevier of fraud and gave evidence to this effect to the governor. Sevier had his revenge by having his allies in the legislature divide Tennessee into two militia districts, leaving Jackson in command only over the western district. Sevier ended his public career by serving in the state senate from 1809 to 1811 and in Congress from 1811 to 1815, where he was a leading war hawk. His career is covered in more detail in the Tennessee section of the chapter on Frontier Fighters.[37]

In addition to his public career and his career as an Indian fighter, Sevier had at least two other careers. He was a leading land speculator. In 1782 North Carolina rewarded her Continental soldiers and militia officers with land grants varying in size from 640 acres for a private to twelve thousand acres for a brigadier general. Sevier had extensive holdings in the Watauga Valley area before the land office opened there in 1777, to which he added his military service grants. This was followed by at least 70,215 acres in 1795 in the Cumberland Valley area. He helped to establish new settlers and did not charge exorbitant fees for the land that he sold. He continued to enjoy a good reputation in spite of some questionable land schemes. And he was the leader of one of the two main political factions within the Republican Party—the only established party in Tennessee during this period—until his death. He was immensely popular in East Tennessee but not nearly so popular in Middle or West Tennessee.[38]

NOTES

1. Colin G. Calloway, *The American Revolution in Indian Country* (New York: Cambridge University Press, 1995), pp. 3, 15–16.
2. Ibid., p. 5.

3. Ibid., pp. 18–23.
4. Ibid., pp. 26, 28, 33.
5. Ibid., pp. 33–34.
6. Ibid., pp. 39, 41, 43.
7. Ibid., pp. 42, 44, 45.
8. Ibid., pp. 47–48, 58–59, 60, 62, 64.
9. John R. Adler, *George Washington: A Biography* (Baton Rouge: Louisiana State University Press, 1984), pp. 9, 17, 25–26, 29.
10. Ibid., pp. 28, 34, 41, 43, 45, 48–49, 51; Alan Taylor, *American Colonies* (New York: Viking, 2001), p. 429.
11. Adler, pp. 53–54, 65, 69.
12. Ibid., pp. 71, 102, 106, 110–12.
13. Ibid., pp. 178–79.
14. Calloway, op. cit., p. 51.
15. Ibid., pp. 51–53; John R. Adler, *George Washington: A Biography* (Baton Rouge: Louisiana State University Press, 1984), pp. 183–85.
16. "Sullivan, John," *Webster's World Encyclopedia 2000* and the website on the 1779 campaign at www.generalsullivan.com, accessed in February 2001.
17. John Mack Farragher, *Daniel Boone* (New York: Henry Holt, 1992), pp. xi–xiii chronology and pp. 145–50, 188; Norman K. Risjord, "Tecumseh: Indian Statesman," in Risjord, *Representative Americans: The Revolutionary Generation* (Lexington, MA: DC Heath, 1980), p. 214.
18. Calloway, op. cit., p. 53.
19. Ibid., pp. 213–14.
20. Ibid., pp. 217–22.
21. Norman K. Risjord, "Conqueror of the Northwest: George Rogers Clark," in Risjord, *Representative Americans: The Revolutionary Generation,* op. cit., pp. 176–80.
22. Calloway, op. cit., pp. 53, 55.
23. Ibid., pp. 182–89; Farragher, op. cit., p. 210.
24. Farragher, p. 250; Risjord, op. cit., p. 190.
25. Farragher, pp. 252–55, 260.
26. "George Rogers Clark and the Illinois Campaign (1778–79)," www.locustgrove.org; and John R. Elting, *Amateurs, To Arms!* (New York: Da Capo Press, 1995), pp. 36–37, 276.
27. Farragher, pp. xiii–xiv, 237, 245, 266–69, 274.
28. On Cooper and Bumppo see Farragher, op. cit., pp. 331–33; and Richard Slotkin, *Regeneration Through Violence* (New York: Harper Perennial, 1996), pp. 466–516. See Slotkin's earlier chapter, pp. 394–465 for a complete history of the publishing of Boone's various biographies. Slotkin gives a psychological and cultural treatment of Boone and Cooper that is very speculative and argumentative.
29. This is based on biographies on three separate websites: *The Columbia Encyclopedia, Sixth Ed. 2001* at www.bartleby.com; and www2.dgsys.com; and www.expage.com; and a description of the Battle of King's Mountain in Mark Derr, *The Frontiersman* (New York: William Morrow, 1993), p. 39.
30. Carl Driver, *John Sevier: Pioneer of the Old South West* (Chapel Hill, NC: University of North Carolina Press, 1932), pp. 6–7, 10, 12, 14, 16.
31. Ibid., pp. 16–17.

32. Ibid., pp. 21–22, 25–26.

33. Stanley Folmsbee et al., *Tennessee: A Short History* (Knoxville: University of Tennessee Press, 1969), pp. 69–70; Driver, op. cit., pp. 27–28. The producers used a fictional name for Marion because Marion was a slave-owner, something that they did not want to deal with in the film.

34. Driver, pp. 28, 29, 31.

35. Ibid., pp. 32–36.

36. Ibid., pp. 37, 38, 41, and quote on p. 217; Mark Derr, *The Frontiersman* (New York: William Morrow, 1993), p. 39.

37. "John Sevier," and "Franklin, State of," in *The Columbia Encyclopedia* at www.bartleby.com; "John Sevier," *Webster's World Encyclopedia 2000;* Robert V. Remini, *Andrew Jackson and His Indian Wars* (New York: Viking, 2001), pp. 16, 36–37, 46; and Robert Remini, *The Life of Andrew Jackson* (New York: Harper & Row, 1988), pp. 45–46.

38. On his career as land speculator see Driver, op. cit., pp. 62–64, 69, 149–50.

3

The War of 1812

INTRODUCTION AND CAUSES

The War of 1812 is a forgotten war in both American and British history; it is remembered mainly by the Canadians. But it is the war that made the Indian fighter a force in American politics, producing two presidents, one vice president, and two unsuccessful presidential candidates. Before examining the course of the war, I lay out the prewar biographies of the two main Indian-fighter generals of the war, Andrew Jackson and William Henry Harrison. After narrating the battles of the war, I then discuss the biographies of lesser Indian fighters.

Three main reasons are given by historians for the War of 1812. First was the impressment of Americans into British service on the high seas on the ruling of a British officer that they sounded British (or Irish) when they spoke. Britain felt free to stop American ships at will and search them for suspected deserters. This was complicated by the American doctrine that allegiance to the crown was conditional and could be traded in for a different allegiance and the British position that once a subject, always a subject. This was the official cause of the war, but it was a justification rather than the real underlying cause. Second was the supply of British arms and ammunition to Indians, particularly in the Northwest Territory, in New York, and along the Gulf of Mexico. This ran parallel to the increasing tension over forced impressment. It is caught up in Tecumseh's struggle to maintain an Indian confederacy—a pan-Indian alliance uniting as many of the tribes in the East as possible. Between the battle of Tippecanoe and the outbreak of war, Indians in Indiana scalped twenty whites.¹ Third was the desire by a group of young congressmen—the War Hawks—who had entered the House in 1811 and wished war so that they could annex Canada and/or Spanish Florida and populate them with Americans. These War Hawks included both existing Indian-fighter politicians such as John Sevier and future Indian fighters such as Richard M. Johnson, as well as completely civilian politicians such as Henry Clay of Kentucky, John C. Calhoun of South Carolina, and congressmen from other Southern states. Ironically, President James Madison finally caved to political pressure and declared war in June 1812 about two weeks before Britain removed the hated Orders in Council that allowed for the searching of American vessels. But by then it was too late.²

The war, which lasted from June 1812 to January 1815, was fought in four separate theaters within the United States and Canada: first, along the western Great Lakes and Mississippi River of the Northwest Territory; second, along the international border between New York and Canada, particularly along the Niagara frontier; third, along the Chesapeake Bay at Washington and Baltimore; and last, along the Gulf of Mexico. Initially the war took place in the first two theaters in 1812–13. The war then spread south to the Mississippi Territory with the massacre at Fort Mims in present-day Alabama in August 1813. The Creek War lasted for six months from September 1813 to March 1814. In July there was major fighting along the Niagara frontier with two large battles: Chippewa and Lundy's Lane. August and September saw the fighting around the Chesapeake Bay. In November 1814 Jackson captured Pensacola in West Florida. In late December 1814 the Treaty of Ghent was signed, officially ending the war. And in January 1815 the Battle of New Orleans resulted in the largest victory of the war for the Americans. The period of the Indian fighters was June 1812–October 1813 in the West and September 1813–January 1815 in the South.³

TECUMSEH AND HARRISON

This is a good point to introduce another main character that would be involved with the careers of several Indian fighters. Tecumseh was born in the Shawnee village of Piqua—burned by Clark in 1780—in about 1768; his father was a Shawnee and his mother was a Creek—so he could speak both languages, a fact that was of immense consequence in 1812. When General Clark and Colonel Benjamin Logan, with Major Daniel Boone serving as a guide in his last major Indian campaign, invaded Ohio in October 1786 and destroyed six villages and brought back thirty women and children as prisoners, Tecumseh fled to a Miami village and offered his services to Chief Little Turtle. This raid touched off nine years of border warfare in the Ohio Valley.

In late 1789 or early 1790 Tecumseh went with his older brother to live with the Chickamauga. There he acquired a Cherokee girlfriend, and some Cherokee to this day claim to be descended from him. There he participated in a number of ambushes of whites—both settlers and soldiers—in Georgia and began to acquire a reputation as a warrior. Tecumseh returned to Ohio in the fall of 1790 as a minor war chief. Tecumseh was credited with helping to spring the trap that led to the ambush of St. Clair's force in 1791, but a recent biographer claims that he was not at the battle. The multitribal force was led by Miami Chief Little Turtle, Shawnee Chief Blue Jacket, and Delaware Chief Buckongahelas.[4] By 1792 Tecumseh was a chief among the Shawnee and was beginning to travel widely. He visited the Creek and along with his older brother lived among the Chickamauga. In October 1792 the brother was killed while leading an attack on Buchanan's Station near Nashville. John Watt, who followed Dragging Canoe as war chief of the Chickamauga, was shot through both hips in the same attack. Tecumseh returned to Ohio at the end of 1792. He also traveled widely throughout the northeastern United States from New York to Illinois and from Virginia to Indiana.[5]

In October 1792 the Shawnee hosted a Congress of tribes from the Great Lakes region and Canada to organize a confederacy against the United States. This was not a new idea. In 1763–64 in what is known as Pontiac's War, Chief Pontiac of the Ottowa of northern Ohio organized a "conspiracy" of several Indian tribes to simultaneously attack British forts along the Great Lakes. The initial attacks led to the capture of eight forts, but the alliance collapsed when the British counterattacked in force. Pontiac spent his remaining years attempting to rebuild the conspiracy but died in 1769 without having reaped any further success. Tecumseh, who must have heard stories of the war when he was growing up, decided to take up Pontiac's dream. After the Revolution, Mohawk Chief Joseph Brant, who had led the pro-British Iroquois during the Revolution, attempted to emulate Pontiac and succeeded in creating a viable coalition. The idea was that this coalition would not only exist in wartime but also operate in negotiations during peacetime and that only land sales that were approved by the confederacy as a whole would be permitted. The high-tide period of this confederacy was the period of 1791–95.[6]

William Henry Harrison was born in February 1773 into one of the most aristocratic and celebrated families in Virginia. One ancestor was a founder of William and Mary College. His father, Benjamin Harrison, was not only a signer of the declaration of independence—but one of the committee members that approved the language along with John Adams, Benjamin Franklin, and Thomas Jefferson. He was also governor of Virginia when William was a child. Harrison briefly studied medicine in Richmond and Philadelphia in 1790 and 1791 before deciding upon a military career. He received his commission as an ensign in the new United States Legion directly from President Washington in August 1791 in the First Regiment of Infantry. Harrison recruited his own company of eighty men and marched them over the mountains to Fort Pitt, from where they took flatboats down the river to Fort Washington (Cincinnatti). They arrived in time to witness the aftermath of General St. Clair's defeat at the hands of the Indian confederacy. It was here that Harrison befriended William Clark, the younger brother of George Rogers Clark who later became famous as a Western explorer.[7]

Chief Little Turtle had defeated a force of Kentucky militia in about 1793, killing about 150 Americans. Major General Anthony Wayne constructed a string of forts as he moved north. At that time, the United States and Britain were on the verge of another war as a result of British seizures of American ships on the Atlantic. The British had told their Indian allies that they would determine the borders through warfare. Harrison parleyed with Little Turtle while he was in the process of building a fort, but no agreement was reached. Both sides suspended hostilities for the remainder of the year. That year Little Turtle decided to give up leadership of the Indian forces to a younger man. He chose the Shawnee Chief Blue Jacket, Boone's hunting companion of almost a decade previous. This had the effect of raising the stature and profile of Tecumseh. Blue Jacket made the strategic mistake of laying siege to Fort Recovery in the summer of 1794. Without cannon, they were unable to prevail against the fort. The Americans recovered some of the shot from the logs in the walls and discovered that it was British. Messengers were sent south to Kentucky with the word, and hundreds of angry Kentucky volunteers streamed north to join Wayne.[8]

With a fortified army, Wayne resumed the march northward. Wayne left Greenville, Ohio Territory, with a force of thirty-five hundred men including fifteen hundred mounted Kentucky volunteers. Blue Jacket decided to make his stand at a spot along the Maumee River where the wind had leveled the forest—hence, the name of the battle, Fallen Timbers. There were at least five tribes fighting at the battle: Delaware, Miami, Ottowa, Shawnee, and Wyandotte. Wayne delayed his attack for two days once he was on the battlefield, because he knew that Indians usually fasted before a big battle. He wanted to weaken them. Many of the Indians were absent on the day of the battle, visiting relatives or hunting, leaving only about five hundred to six hundred warriors, so that the Indians were outnumbered about six to one. Wayne's infantry advanced on the Indian lines, and a tight volley followed by a bayonet charge served to break the Indian ranks. The Indians lost about five hundred men compared to thirty-one Americans killed and 102 wounded. The Indians retreated to a nearby British fort, Fort Miami, but the British refused to open their gates and admit them. The retreating Indians were slaughtered, and Tecumseh learned not to completely trust the British, whom he considered henceforth to be just another brand of whites. The Americans burned Indian cornfields for miles around the battlesite, so that the Indians would be too occupied merely surviving to organize a counterattack. During the battle, Harrison served as a courier delivering messages from Wayne to his commanders. Harrison had a number of close calls. He was mentioned by Wayne to Washington in dispatches sent after the battle.[9]

The following summer the twelve main tribes of the eastern portion of the Northwest Territory sent ninety-two chiefs and subchiefs to meet with Wayne at Greenville, Ohio Territory, and negotiate a peace agreement. After being well fed and well lubricated with liquor, the chiefs signed the Treaty of Greenville on August 10, 1795. The Indians conceded the lower half and eastern quarter of the present state of Ohio, so that they ended up with about a third of the present state. This had the effect of moving them much farther away from Kentucky, making it harder to raid the white settlements there—although they could still take the Miami River south to the Ohio and then take the Kentucky River south into the heart of Kentucky. This was the last treaty signed by the Indian confederacy; shortly thereafter it collapsed as individual tribes began to once again sign land deals with the Americans.[10]

Wayne promoted Harrison to captain in 1795, but the promotion did not become official until May 1797. Harrison started sending long, detailed reports to Washington on everything he did. In June 1798 President Adams offered Harrison the position of secretary of the Northwest Territory under General St. Clair, who was the governor. Harrison accepted the post and resigned from the army. Harrison served as the delegate of the territory in the House from March 1799 to May 1800. While there he passed the Harrison Land Act, which was supported by Vice President Jefferson. The act allowed settlers with very few means to buy land in the territory. Harrison was at this time a Republican sympathizer rather than a Federalist. In 1800 the Northwest Territory was divided into the Ohio and Indiana Territories along the present state borders and Harrison was made governor of Indiana starting in January 1801. He remained governor for the next 11.5 years until the outbreak of the War of 1812. It was common practice in the early nineteenth century to make men with a military background governors of territories on the frontier so that they could lead militia forces in war against the Indians if necessary. In addition to General St. Clair and Harrison, Lewis Cass was made a governor of the Michigan Territory after his service in the War of 1812.[11]

Tecumseh was the only major Indian leader to refuse to accept the Treaty of Greenville. The year after the peace he married a half-breed woman and then rejected her after she bore him a child. Tecumseh was involved romantically with a white woman, Rebecca Galloway—the daughter of a trader; she taught him to read and taught him the history of the Americans as well as some literature. But she wanted him to convert to Christianity, which he refused to do, and so the romance died. Tecumseh began to develop a reputation and a following both because of his prowess as a warrior and his stand of defiance. Tecumseh had attained the status of both a war chief and a civil chief and had his own village of followers with about 250 inhabitants of whom forty-five to fifty were warriors. He moved to Greenville and built a house on top of the treaty line. After a couple of years, when Greenville became too crowded, he moved to central Indiana. After Harrison was appointed governor, a showdown was inevitable.[12]

Harrison signed a total of thirteen separate treaties with the Indians while he was governor at Vincennes. Harrison was an aggressive land buyer. In 1803 he negotiated the purchase of a major tract around Vincennes. The following year he acquired 15 million acres in Illinois and Wisconsin from the Sauk (also known as the Sac) and Fox. In 1805 he purchased a very large portion of southern Indiana from the Ohio River north to the White River. Between 1802 and 1805 Harrison negotiated seven treaties that added to American territory southern Indiana, most of Illinois, and parts of Missouri and Wisconsin, all at about the rate of just over two cents an acre. In 1809 he acquired 3 million acres from four different tribes in Indiana. By 1809 he had purchased about 40 percent of the present state of Indiana. Harrison in fact exceeded his authority for the land purchase by President Madison, by going ahead with purchases knowing that they would create "apprehension" among the Indians—something that he was instructed not to do.

Harrison's technique before a purchase was to wine and dine the Indian leaders while demonstrating American power with subtlety, without making any overt threats. He also used the poverty-stricken Pottawatami from Michigan, not to be confused with their more militant cousins in Illinois, to pressure the Kickapoo and Wea to surrender their land in the Treaty of Fort Wayne in February 1809. The Indians, who owned land collectively in their culture, did not understand the concept of private ownership of land. They would sell land expecting to be able to traverse it and hunt on it freely after the sale. Harrison probably did not make great efforts to enlighten the Indians on the legal specifics of the documents they were signing. If he could not get the senior chief from the tribe to sell, he would find other chiefs who would.[13]

Tecumseh denounced these deals as crooked. But he was opposed not just to those land sales he considered crooked but to any sales at all. He saw the sales as merely feeding the expansion of American settlement into Indian lands, leading to a day in the not-too-distant future when all Indians would be dispossessed. He traveled throughout the eastern United States organizing an alliance of Indian tribes against the Americans, for the day when Britain and the United States would once again be at war.

In 1805 Tecumseh's younger brother, a notorious alcoholic known as Laulewasika or "loudmouth," began to have a series of visions. He founded a settlement near Greenville, Ohio, in November 1805. He took a new name, Tenskwautawa, which means "the open door" from the quote from Jesus in the New Testament—"knock and the door will be opened to you."[14]

He created his own new religion with three basic demands: first, no drinking of alcohol; second, no fighting with other Indians; third, no use of white customs, dress, or goods. This was the same sort of practice that later flourished among the Lakota and Cheyenne during the 1860s and 1870s. The Americans called Tecumseh's brother simply "the Prophet," in recognition of his status, and this is how he is known to history. The Prophet had little competition from white missionaries, who at this stage were not very successful in converting the Indians.[15]

Harrison perceived the Prophet as a threat to his treaty making with the Indians and so urged Indians to demand that he perform a miracle. The Prophet did just that in June 1806: he told Indians that he would make the moon eat the sun and then free it again. Scientific expeditions had come from the East to observe a solar eclipse, and the Prophet had been informed of the upcoming event. This feat only served to increase his reputation.

In the spring of 1808 the Prophet established his headquarters at the conflux of the Wabash and Tippecanoe Rivers in northern Indiana near the site of present-day Lafayette. Tecumseh ventured westward to Wisconsin and Illinois to talk with the Sauk and Fox in Illinois and the Winnebago and Menominee in Wisconsin.[16]

Tecumseh's biggest Indian opponent was the paramount chief of the Shawnee, Black Hoof, with his impressive war record dating back to the French and Indian War. But Black Hoof had decided that the time for fighting was past and that the Indians should make their peace with the whites, adapt to white civilization, and become farmers. But he fiercely resisted encroachments upon Shawnee territory and made repeated trips to Washington and pressed for a statement of the recognized limits of Shawnee territory. He used his influence to prevent the Shawnee from uniting behind Tecumseh. In many ways the relationship between Black Hoof and Tecumseh parallels the later relationship between Chief Red Cloud and Crazy Horse among the Oglala band of the Lakota Sioux. Crazy Horse's activities in the period between 1868 and 1876 parallel those of Tecumseh following the Greenville Treaty.[17]

On August 14, 1810, Tecumseh visited Harrison's house in Vincennes with an escort of 250 Indian warriors and the two made speeches to each other and exchanged threats. Tecumseh threatened to execute any Indian who made a treaty with the whites and to go to war if any whites attempted to occupy the land ceded in the treaties. War was only a matter of time. During 1810–11 word of a coming Indian war against the Americans began leaking out through French traders and Indian spies who worked for the Americans. In July 1810 Harrison had sent a warning with a French trader warning the Prophet against planning to go to war against the United States. By 1810 there were some 270,000 whites living in what is today the states of Ohio, Michigan, Indiana, and Illinois compared to only seventy thousand Indians; thus, the latter were outnumbered nearly four to one.[18]

Harrison sent Tecumseh a message in July 1811 offering to let him speak with President Madison about the Treaty of Fort Wayne in Washington. But, at the same time as a precaution, Harrison appealed to Washington for more troops and the secretary of war sent reinforcements to Vincennes. The two opponents met for a second time in Vincennes on July 30, 1811, nearly a year after their first meeting. Tecumseh was again defiant and boastful—he exaggerated his success in recruiting Indian allies, which only further alarmed Harrison. Tecumseh also openly revealed to Harrison his plans to go south on a recruiting trip.[19]

In the late summer of 1811 Tecumseh traveled south to recruit new allies for his conspiracy. He visited the Creek and passed out bundles of red sticks to those who supported him. He told them that they were to wait until they had heard that war had been declared and then throw away a stick per day until the bundle was gone and then attack. It was an ingenious method of coordinating a mass attack over a wide area. He also took a cue from his brother and told the Creek that when the earth shook violently they would know that he had arrived back home at Prophet's Town in Indiana. This was either a bit of bravado or a sign that the Prophet really was psychic as there was no way he could have predicted the famous New Madrid earthquake of December 1811 with its epicenter in Missouri.[20]

The word that Tecumseh was away on a recruiting mission reached Harrison in Vincennes, in confirmation of Tecumseh's early revelation that he was going, and he decided to take advantage of it. Harrison called out the militia and marched on Prophet's Town with an army of about one thousand armed men, including both soldiers and civilians. Harrison camped in an open field along the Wabash River, about two miles from Prophet's Town. That afternoon he met under a flag of truce with the Prophet and the two agreed to negotiate the next day. Possibly Harrison planned to cow him into submission and force him to sign a new treaty. Or possibly he planned to attack in the open if the negotiations broke down. The Indians captured a black cook named Ben who told them that the Americans planned to attack on the following day. But instead the Prophet whipped his followers into a frenzy and attacked the military camp at dawn.

The Indian warriors found Harrison's camp unprepared, and they penetrated nearly to the center. Most of the Americans slept fully clothed and with their weapons at the ready. Most of the Indians were armed with muskets, but they lacked enough powder for more than a single shot or two. So the attack would have to depend largely on Indians using hand weapons such as tomahawks and war clubs to fight their way to the center supported by covering fire from Indians hiding in the dark. Harrison was nearly killed at the start of the battle. He and his aide, Colonel Abraham Owen, rushed to the site of the main attack, the northeast corner of the camp, to take charge and rally the men. Owen was mortally wounded almost immediately. The battle last two and a quarter hours from about 4:30 to after dawn on November 6, 1811. But due to his superior numbers, Harrison was able to rally his men and prevail. Harrison suffered sixty-eight men dead or fatally wounded and 120 wounded. Indian casualties are uncertain: thirty-eight were found dead on the battlefield, but the Indians probably dragged off many more. A Kickapoo later claimed that the total number of Indians killed was fifty-one. The Prophet abandoned Prophet's Town, and his followers retreated to the surrounding wilderness. Harrison's men spent the entire day and waited until after dark on the following day before they ventured forth and burned Prophet's Town and the surrounding cornfields. They also killed many Indians in a nearby swamp. In the ashes of Prophet's Town, they found British muskets still in their cases along with cases of ammunition. A recent biographer estimated the Prophet's forces at Tippecanoe to be about five hundred to six hundred warriors but claimed that many of the warriors went off to steal horses during the attack, leaving as few as a hundred warriors to do the fighting.[21]

Even though Harrison's march into Indian territory violated Madison administration policy of preserving the peace with the Indians, he was not censured. Word of the British muskets had stirred up war sentiment throughout the West. Sentiment in favor of war with Britain had been growing since the *Leopold-Chesapeake* affair of 1807 when a British warship attacked an American merchantman that refused to be boarded to search for British deserters. As a result of this attack, in April 1808 Congress tripled the size of the army, turning it into a permanent institution. Both Zachary Taylor and Winfield Scott, future generals in the Mexican War, joined the army as lieutenants at about this time.[22]

THE WAR IN THE WEST

Thirteen garrisons in the western Great Lakes region surrendered or were evacuated in July and August 1812. The surrender of Detroit on August 16, 1812, by Brigadier General William Hull left the frontier defenseless. There were attacks on outposts along the upper Mississippi Valley in early September 1812. Captain Zachary Taylor had only sixteen healthy men to defend Fort Harrison in September 1812 against attacks by Indians and the British. Thirty-four men, including Taylor himself, were sick from an outbreak of fever. The fort was attacked by 450 warriors who proceeded to set the barracks on fire. Two men were killed, two were wounded, and two of the defenders deserted. Part of the stockade wall was burned up, and Taylor had to find some logs to patch the gap. Taylor was brevetted major for his defense of the fort.

After the fall of Detroit, Harrison started sending out columns to attack the Indian villages that served as enemy bases. Taylor served as an aide to militia Major General Samuel Hopkins from Kentucky, who was also a congressman. It was while serving with the Kentucky volunteers that Taylor developed his lifelong dislike of volunteers and militia. Hopkins led a twelve-hundred-man force of Kentucky volunteers and regulars to burn Prophetstown in Indiana and some Winnebago villages.

In July 1813 Colonel William Russell led a sweep through Indiana, but most of the villages were empty—the soldiers burned them—because the Indians had gone to Canada with Tecumseh. Taylor was put in charge of a 140-man garrison at Vincennes. It was safe enough for him to bring his family north. His only remaining fight was with Indians led by Chief Black Hawk at Credit Island on the Rock River on August 22, 1814, when he had fourteen men wounded, three of whom subsequently died.[23]

There were two main land battles fought in the West in 1813: the Battle of Frenchtown on the River Raisin in January 1813 and the Battle of the Thames in October 1813. There was also the British siege of Fort Meigs in May 1813. The first was a disaster for the Americans that resulted in four hundred dead and the capture of Brigadier General James Winchester, ending his career as an Indian-fighter politician. After rising to the rank of captain in the American Revolution, Winchester moved from Maryland to Tennessee in 1784. He served in a number of campaigns against the Cherokee, probably in Sevier's 1793 campaign. He served as speaker in the first senate in Tennessee. After six weeks in captivity, Winchester was exchanged and was later given command of the garrison in Mobile, Alabama, by General Jackson. He was saved from a second disaster only by the war's end. He died in July 1826.[24]

In August 1812 Harrison was made a major general of the Kentucky militia. Harrison had forced James Winchester, commissioned a brigadier general by Madison in March 1812, into allowing him to lead the relief expedition to Fort Wayne, Indiana. Harrison used his political influence in Kentucky to also get himself a federal commission as a brigadier general in September. Following Winchester's capture in January 1813, Harrison was promoted to major general in the army in March and made the commander of the entire Northwest division. During the spring he was ordered by the secretary of war to remain on the defensive within Fort Meigs until the United States could build a naval squadron and take command of Lake Erie. Harrison commanded a garrison of twelve hundred men—half regulars and volunteers and half militiamen from Kentucky and Ohio. Harrison was blessed with a brilliant engineer, Captain Eleazor Wood, who continually strengthened the fort's defenses. During May British forces led by Brigadier General Henry Procter, promoted from colonel for his victory at Frenchtown, were besieging the Americans at Fort Meigs. A fresh contingent of Kentucky militia led by Brigadier General Green Clay arrived during the siege and, in accordance with a plan worked out with Harrison, attacked the British artillery in the enemy camp before coming into the fort. They managed to spike only a few guns, and many of the men foolishly followed the Indians into the woods where they soon found themselves outnumbered and were forced to flee for their lives back to the fort, outside of which they met a determined British counterattack. Most of the American force was compelled to surrender. The siege had cost the British only 14 killed, 47 wounded, and 41 taken prisoner compared to 135 killed, 188 wounded, and 630 captured for Harrison—or nearly a thousand casualties.[25]

On September 10, 1813, Commodore Oliver H. Perry won "command of the sea" over Lake Erie, allowing him to ferry troops to the other side. Secretary of War John Armstrong had ordered Harrison to recruit an army of seven thousand and prepare to invade Canada. Harrison had only managed to recruit three thousand when Governor Isaac Shelby of Kentucky offered three thousand militiamen from Kentucky if Harrison would pay for them. On September 27 Perry ferried forty-five hundred infantrymen from the mouth of the Detroit River. Harrison started out in pursuit of Brigadier General Proctor, the victor of Frenchtown. Procter's army consisted of about four hundred British troops, a few Canadians, and about a thousand Indians commanded by Tecumseh.

The night before the battle, one of Tecumseh's chiefs, Walk-in-the-Water, deserted with sixty followers and surrendered to Harrison. Large quantities of English stores were continually falling into the possession of the Americans during the retreat that preceded the battle. Tecumseh went down river on a scouting mission and afterward proposed to Proctor an attack on the Americans, but Proctor preferred to defend against an American attack.

On October 5, 1813, Proctor halted west of Moraviantown, on the north bank of the Thames River. Harrison brought up his infantry and was expecting to send his infantry, under the command of General Lewis Cass, up the road at the British position when he noted the loose spacing of the British lines. Richard Johnson, commander of a thousand-strong mounted infantry regiment, armed with rifles rather than with sabers and pistols, offered to charge the British positions. Johnson sent one battalion of cavalry under the command of his brother James against the British Forty-first Foot Regiment, while the remainder rode into the swamp where the Indians were positioned. James Johnson managed to completely surprise the British by hitting their left flank and rolling up their entire line. The British suffered forty-three casualties, and many surrendered to the attacking Kentuckians. They fled in terror, ending that portion of the battle in ten minutes. Only about 180 men managed to reach the center division at Burlington Heights—and some of these had not been present at the battle. The others were either killed or captured by the Americans. As soon as this occurred, Procter grabbed his carriage and with an escort of dragoons and mounted Indians fled the battlefield and proceeded down the road to Moraviantown.

The Kentuckians dismounted in the swamp and fought Indian style, moving from tree to tree as they advanced. The Indians put up a much stiffer resistance than their British comrades had. As soon as Shelby heard the firing from the swamp, he led up his men and joined the action. The battle lasted at most thirty minutes and resulted in 477 British and Canadian troops being taken prisoner. The bodies of thirty-three Indians were found on the field. Only about fifteen Americans were killed and thirty wounded.

Richard Johnson was badly wounded—hit four times, he still remained in the saddle—but was wrestling his horse into cover after it was hit, and he collapsed. While he was preoccupied, an Indian approached, leveled a musket at him, and then fired. Johnson managed to kill the Indian, who was dressed in a gaudy shirt, with his pistol. Johnson remained convinced until he died that he had killed Tecumseh himself. Initially he only claimed to have killed an Indian—who had in turn shot him in the hand crippling it for life. But he let others claim that the Indian was Tecumseh during his campaigns in 1836 and 1840. And in 1843 he started making the claim for himself. In 1839 a Shawnee named Shabeni gave an interview at the United States Hotel in Chicago repeating the story that Johnson had killed Tecumseh. Shabeni had met Johnson in Washington in 1836 and was probably merely repeating the tale related to him by Johnson of his encounter with the Indian. Tecumseh's body was found on the battlefield after the battle with the scalp missing and portions of his skin gone where frontiersmen had taken pieces for razor strops. Henry Clay supposedly exhibited one in Washington in the winter of 1814. Harrison and Perry viewed the body on October 6, and Harrison was upset about the mutilation.[26]

Harrison captured the chief who took over command after Tecumseh's death. He complained bitterly of the cowardice of Procter. Harrison returned to Detroit with his army without sending Johnson in pursuit of Procter's remaining force. A determined general might have managed to capture Proctor.[27]

More political careers were made—or could have been made—out of the Battle of the Thames than any other battle in American history. The battle served to drive the British back into Canada where they stayed for the remainder of the war; it also destroyed the alliance between the British and the Indians by killing off the head of the Indian confederacy. Harrison became the ninth president of the United States, and Richard Johnson preceded him as vice president under President Martin Van Buren. In 1817 President Monroe offered Isaac Shelby, commander of the Kentucky militia at the battle, the post of secretary of war in his cabinet. Shelby declined.

John Crittenden, a Kentucky militia officer serving as Shelby's aide at the battle, later became a leading Whig politician and served as Harrison's and John Tyler's attorney general in 1841 and again as attorney general under President Fillmore, following the death of Zachary Taylor. President Adams nominated Crittenden to the U.S. Supreme Court, but his nomination was delayed until Jackson became president and then the nomination was killed. Crittenden also served as a longtime member of the Kentucky legislature and as governor of Kentucky from 1848 to 1850. Before that he served as

U.S. senator from 1842 to 1848. He initially replaced Henry Clay when the latter resigned but was elected in his own right. He became the king-maker in the Whig Party, helping to determine who the presidential nominee would be. Of interest is the fact that Crittenden had two sons who were generals in the Civil War—one Confederate and one Union. He also had a son who fought in the Texas revolution in 1836 and in the Mexican War. So his example seemed to have inspired his children.

Brigadier General Lewis Cass served as the military and civil governor of the Michigan Territory between 1813 and 1831. He served as President Jackson's secretary of war and was involved in executing the Indian removals of the 1830s. He served as ambassador to France from 1836 to 1842. Cass was elected a senator from Michigan in 1845 and again in 1851 and was the unsuccessful Democratic candidate for president against Zachary Taylor in 1848. Including those already mentioned, the Battle of the Thames helped create: "one president, one vice president, three governors, three lieutenant governors, four senators, and twenty congressmen."[28]

Research by historian John Sugden credits Tecumseh and his Indian allies with capturing or killing fifty-five hundred people in the Old Northwest Territory and in the South from 1810 to 1815 compared to 948 men lost by the U.S. Army between 1866 and 1890 in the various western Indian campaigns.[29]

JACKSON AND THE CREEK WAR

Andrew Jackson was already a successful politician and businessman/lawyer before he began his military career. He was born in 1767 in the Piedmont area of South Carolina shortly after the death from disease of his immigrant Scotch-Irish father. Jackson possibly had an older brother that was killed by Indians either before Jackson was born or when he was young. In any case, his mother was an Indian hater and passed her prejudices along to all of her sons. Jackson learned to fear and hate Indians from a young age—as did most settlers. He was able to detect the sound of Indians communicating with one another by the use of animal and bird calls. Jackson's attitude toward Indians was typical of the frontier: Indians were barbaric and not trustworthy, regularly violated agreements and treaties, and were incapable of living in harmony with whites.

In 1780 the British army led by the notorious Lieutenant Colonel Banastre Tarleton invaded South Carolina. Jackson and his brother joined an American force as messenger boys and served with the force until betrayed to the British by a Tory neighbor. In captivity Jackson refused to shine the boots of a British officer who swung his sword at the youth, severely cutting him in the hand and forehead. This was enough to give Jackson a lifelong hatred of the British. His mother contracted cholera while nursing American soldiers in Charleston. He was thus an orphan while still only a young teenager. In 1784 he moved to North Carolina to study law and clerked for a local lawyer for two years. Jackson lived a rather wild life gambling and playing pranks on everyone. In 1788 one of his fellow law students was elected to the legislature in North Carolina and appointed a superior court judge. He offered the position of public prosecutor to Jackson. Jackson crossed the mountains to Jonesborough. In September 1788 Jackson headed overland as part of a 183-person party to Nashville. Jackson saved the group by detecting the calls of gathering Indians and rousing the group to move on in silence during the night before the Indians could strike. During the next several years Jackson moved back and forth between Nashville and Jonesborough a total of twenty-two times. Once Indians chased him for several miles.[30]

When Jackson arrived in Nashville, the Cherokee were killing settlers within a five-mile radius of the city at the rate of one every ten days. Shortly after arriving, Jackson was pressed into a punitary expedition against the local Indians. He soon looked forward to opportunities to fight Indians and gained a reputation as an excellent Indian fighter. Indian warfare was constant on the frontier because whites ignored Indian treaty boundaries. Jackson, like most settlers, was opposed to the treaties in any case during this period. Later, as a judge and general he would have to defend the integrity of the treaties. Jackson was very active as an Indian fighter during the Chickamauga War of 1792–94. Jackson planned an attack on the Indian village of Nickajack in which a force of about 550 mounted infantry attacked the village (population three hundred). In total Jackson spent some thirty years, off and on, fighting Indians—a career total matched by very few men, Boone being one of them.[31]

In 1796 Jackson was one of five delegates from Davidson County to the Tennessee constitutional convention, where he played a fairly minor role. As soon as Tennessee became a state, Jackson became its sole representative in the House. That year he won compensation for all those who took part in General Sevier's 1793 expedition against the Cherokee. This would have guaranteed Jackson a second term in the House had he opted to run again. He was elected to the U.S. Senate in September 1797 to replace William Blount, who was forced to resign after being involved in a conspiracy with Britain to seize Spanish Florida. Jackson complained directly to President John Adams about the administration's Indian policy. As a result of this, Adams negotiated a new treaty with the Cherokee giving the disputed land to the whites. This merely whetted their appetite for new concessions. Jackson always sided with the settlers against the Indians. Jackson resigned from the Senate in April 1798 after only one session, realizing that he was out of his depth in the body. Vice President Thomas Jefferson, serving as presiding officer over the Senate, noticed Jackson's terrible passion and rages when he was too angry to speak. Jackson served as a judge in Nashville from December 1798 to 1804.[32]

Following the killings in the Duck River area, Jackson published an article in the *Democratic Clarion* on July 8, 1812, in which he called for vengeance for the victims. He instructed his men, "Hold yourselves in readiness: it may be but a short time before the question is put to you: Are you ready to follow your general to the heart of the Creek nation?"

Shortly afterward Jackson raised an army of militia and marched it to Natchez for transportation down the Mississippi for an attack on Spanish Florida. In Natchez he received a second command ordering him to dismiss his troops and for them to make their own way home. The Czar of Russia had offered to mediate in the war with Britain, and it was felt that an attack on neutral Spanish territory would be diplomatically damaging. Knowing that many of his men lacked the money to make it back home by themselves, he reinterpreted the order and marched the army back to Nashville without losing a single man. Jackson often walked so that sick or tired men could ride his horse. His men dubbed him "Old Hickory" for his toughness, and he became the most popular man in Tennessee when word of his care broke out.[33]

On August 30, 1813, the Red Stick Creek warriors managed to kill between 250 and 275 soldiers, white settlers, friendly Indians, and mixed-race persons at Fort Mims when they managed to enter through the open gates and attack. Jackson was still recovering from his wound from the altercation with the Hart-Bentons when the news of the massacre reached Tennessee. The Madison administration ordered a four-pronged invasion of Creek territory to end the rebellion, but only Jackson made a real invasion—the other commanders, in Georgia and the Mississippi territory, either only made very limited raids or did not bother to turn out at all.[34]

On September 24, 1813, Jackson mobilized the militia for action against the Creek. The first battle at Tallushatchee in November was largely a massacre of innocents. It was also the only battle that David Crockett participated in. Jackson wrote Governor Blount after the battle, "[W]e have retaliated for the destruction of Fort Mims." Jackson adopted an orphaned Indian boy, Lyncoya, who was found wandering around on the battlefield. The boy lived at Jackson's home at Hermitage until he died of a disease at age sixteen.[35]

Throughout the campaign Jackson was plagued by a manpower shortage due to the short three- or six-month enlistments of his militia troops. He faced this problem from late November to January. Jackson stopped one mass desertion by riding in front of his troops and personally threatening to shoot the first man who stepped forward to leave for Tennessee. The mutineers backed down. It was later found that the musket that Jackson held was defective and would likely have exploded had Jackson actually discharged it. By December 1813 Jackson was left with only a regiment of infantry.

After 850 new recruits arrived, Jackson marched toward the enemy encampment at Horseshoe Bend. On January 21, 1814, he was attacked at Emuckfaw Creek, three miles from Horseshoe Bend, and his army nearly cut to pieces. He ordered a retreat back to their base at Fort Strother. The army was again ambushed at Enotachopco Creek while crossing. Jackson rode into the thick of the action and organized a counterattack. He suffered twenty killed and seventy-five wounded compared to some two hundred dead Indians left on the battlefield.

On March 14, 1814, Jackson left Fort Strother with an army of about thirty-three hundred men—mostly from troops freshly raised for him by Governor Blount—to engage about one thousand Red Sticks at Horseshoe Bend. They arrived at the enemy fortress on March 27 and attacked. Many friendly Indians, both Cherokee and Creek, accompanied Jackson in his assault. The Creek War was really a civil war between the young radical followers of Tecumseh—the Red Sticks—and the older more conservative leadership that wished to remain at peace with the United States.[36]

The friendly Indians initiated the battle by finding high ground from which they could fire down upon the defenders. Under this covering fire, Jackson's troops assaulted the fortifications. The first man over the parapet was a Major Montgomery who was killed instantly. The next man over was Ensign Samuel Houston, who had enlisted in the army a year before when recruiters visited his town. Houston was hit by an arrow in the groin. Houston had a lieutenant pull the arrow out so that he could remain in the battle. Jackson ordered him out of the battle, but Houston managed to lead his platoon in an assault on a Red Stick Blockhouse during which he was shot twice in the shoulder and the arm. He was left for dead on the battlefield.[37]

The killing went on for about five hours. The Red Sticks were utterly defeated, and many women and children who were encamped with the warriors were massacred as well in the frenzy. There were 557 Indian bodies counted on the battlefield, and an estimated further three hundred drowned or bled to death in the creek surrounding the fortress. So there were probably about nine hundred Red Sticks dead with only about a hundred managing to flee. Jackson had 47 Americans killed and 159 wounded and 23 Indian allies killed and 47 wounded.[38]

A few days after the battle the Red Stick leader, Chief Red Eagle—also known as Bill Weatherford, as he was of mixed race—entered Jackson's camp and boldly made his way up to Jackson's tent. He surrendered himself to Jackson and threw himself on Sharp Knife's (as the Indians called Jackson) mercy, but Jackson's men called for him to be killed. Jackson was impressed by his great courage and released him in order to persuade remaining holdouts to surrender. Jackson also distributed rations to starving friendly Creeks after the battle to prevent mass starvation. The Red Sticks inflicted some seven hundred casualties during the war between November 1813 and March 1814 inclusive, but the British estimated that the Creek suffered some eighteen hundred men killed in the war in exchange—or about 2.5 men killed for every casualty they inflicted.[39]

Jackson managed to end the war just as the British were preparing to land troops and supplies on the Gulf in support of the Red Sticks. This would have made the war much more costly and harder to contain. Jackson perceived the Creek Nation as a threat to the national security of the United States and saw it as his personal mission to reduce it until it was no longer a threat.[40]

Throughout the Creek War, Jackson had only had general's rank in the militia and not in the regular army. Jackson was offered the rank of brigadier general in the army after the Creek War but held out for major general. Secretary of War Armstrong told him that no disrespect of his abilities was intended but that he had only three major general commissions to distribute and all were taken. At that point Harrison resigned in the midst of one of his spates with the Madison administration—but urged his Kentucky supporters to pressure Washington to reject the resignation, and his commission was offered to Jackson at the end of May. Jackson happily accepted in mid-June. Jackson was in charge of the Seventh Military District, which included Tennessee, Louisiana, the Mississippi Territory, and the Creek Nation. Jackson then called a peace convention for the Creek Nation to begin on August 1, 1814.[41]

In July two battles were fought inside Canada along the Niagara frontier, Chippewa and Lundy's Lane. The first was an American victory, and the second was a tactical draw and a strategic victory for the British as the American invasion force was compelled to withdraw. Chippewa was the first battle in which the Americans defeated a large force of British regulars. Brigadier General Winfield Scott, the man responsible for the victory at Chippewa, was seriously wounded in the shoulder at Lundy's Lane and evacuated from the battle and the war. He became the newest American war hero replacing Harrison.[42]

Jackson moved his army by river down to Mobile, Alabama, where it could easily be deployed to anywhere along the Gulf coast by sea. Jackson was faced with the threat of British landings on the Gulf coast, especially as Napoleon had abdicated and gone into exile at Elba, thus freeing up thousands of British troops for deployment in North America. Vice Admiral Sir Alexander Cochrane, the supreme British commander in North America, recommended an invasion of the Gulf coast where the British troops could link up with both the Indians and the Spanish. Spain had been liberated from French occupation by the British and was thus a British ally, and the Americans were perceived as a threat to Spain's North American possessions in Florida and Texas.

Many Red Sticks had fled to Florida after the Battle of Horseshoe Bend, and Jackson considered Spain to be in violation of its neutral obligations. Never one to defer to Washington when he perceived the national security to be threatened, Jackson decided to act. He invaded Pensacola, West Florida, and compelled the Spanish garrison to surrender on November 6, 1814.

Jackson suffered seven dead and eleven wounded compared to fourteen killed and six wounded for the Spanish. Jackson then turned control of Pensacola back over to the Spanish governor. He then ordered his friend General John Coffee to take two thousand men to Baton Rouge and link up with newly mustered militia said to be coming from Kentucky and Tennessee. Jackson then turned over command of Mobile to the disgraced Brigadier General James Winchester and departed for New Orleans with two thousand troops on November 22, 1814.[43]

Jackson reached New Orleans on December 1. He agreed to accept the aid of free blacks in the defense of the city, and he made a bargain with the Haitian mercenary pirate Jean Lafitte for his aid in exchange for a share of the booty. Jackson had a total force of between thirty-five hundred and four thousand men. Lieutenant General Sir Edward Michael Packenham, the Duke of Wellington's brother-in-law and a very experienced professional soldier, opposed him. The Treaty of Ghent, ending the War of 1812 on the basis of the *status quo ante bellum* or prewar situation, was signed on Christmas Eve 1814, but word of the signing did not reach New York until February 11, 1815.

The largest, most decisive battle of the war took place on January 8, 1815, after the war was officially over. Packenham made the mistake of sending infantry to assault a fortified American position of breastworks located behind a canal at a ninety-degree angle from the Mississippi River and supported by artillery. Packenham possibly thought that the raw American militia would break and run as soon as his men got within firing range. The American guns were manned by sailors and by Lafitte's pirates. They cut the advancing British ranks to pieces as they emerged out of the fog. Repeated volleys of musket fire from the breastworks shattered those that survived the artillery. The British suffered 291 killed, 1,262 wounded, and 484 prisoners or missing. Many of the prisoners had simply fallen down on the battlefield as dead and surrendered afterward. Jackson suffered thirteen killed, thirty-nine wounded, and nineteen missing, mostly from the West Bank of the Mississippi.[44]

American folklore later attributed the victory to the marksmanship of riflemen from Kentucky and Tennessee. But most of the riflemen were on the West Bank of the river and hence did not see much action. The militiamen from Kentucky, Louisiana, and Tennessee were all armed with muskets, which were indeed superior for this type of linear warfare because of their more rapid rate of fire. Jackson himself played into this myth during his presidential campaigns by adopting "the Hunters of Kentucky" as his unofficial campaign song.[45]

Jackson's determination, favorable terrain, and luck had turned him into the great war hero of 1815. New Orleans was "by far the greatest victory of the war." Jackson eclipsed Scott and became "the undisputed darling of the public," to quote Scott's most recent biographer. Jackson was feted at numerous public receptions when he went to Washington on business in November 1815.[46]

Once Jackson had made peace with the Creek, his next obsession was the threat from the Seminole of Florida. The Seminole were actually a confederacy of different tribes, some closely related to the Creek, who were considered by whites to be one tribe as a means of simplifying negotiations. Jackson perceived them as a threat because they harbored both Creek refugees from the Creek War and runaway slaves. Many of these slaves were raiding into Georgia in an attempt to free family members who were still enslaved. Thus, they were a threat to white property. Jackson ordered Brigadier General Edmund Gaines to destroy a fort occupied by runaway slaves on the Apalachicola River in West Florida. Jackson coerced the Spanish governor into granting permission for the intervention by means of a vague threat to act without it. Gaines bombarded the fort on July 27, 1816—resulting in a massive explosion when the armory was hit.

On December 26, 1817, Secretary of War John C. Calhoun ordered Jackson to form a force at Fort Scott in southern Georgia to act against the Seminole but not against the Spanish. Jackson wrote to Monroe directly, bypassing Calhoun, and asked for permission to seize Florida from Spain. Monroe instructed Calhoun to tell Jackson not to attack any Spanish troops. Calhoun never passed on the message to Jackson, and Monroe never checked back to see that the message had been passed. On March 10, 1818, Jackson invaded Florida with a force of three thousand Americans and two thousand friendly Indians. Jackson wrote a letter to the Spanish governor demanding the right of safe passage in pursuit of the Seminole. The war, known to history as the First Seminole War, was over by late April 1818. Jackson hanged two British nationals who had been trading with the Seminole, even though a court martial that tried the two had sentenced one to "only" fifty lashes and twelve months hard labor. The incident could have provoked a new war with Britain, but Britain was in no mood for a new war and was mollified by reading a copy of the court martial transcripts. Jackson then followed this up by invading Pensacola in May and forcing the Spanish governor to surrender the fort at Barrancas. Jackson then wrote to President Monroe offering to capture Saint Augustine as well and even Cuba.[47]

Jackson's moves in Florida were very popular with the public but did not go over so well with the political elite. Speaker of the House Henry Clay moved a censure motion against Jackson for acting with authority in Florida, but it was defeated by a vote of 107 to 100. This earned Clay the lifelong enmity of Jackson. In the cabinet, only Secretary of State John Quincy Adams spoke in favor of Jackson's actions. Adams used Jackson's action as leverage to negotiate the purchase of Florida from Spain for $5 million in February 1819. Jackson had at this time two important personal goals for the country. The first was the expulsion of any foreign presence from the South. The second was the removal of the Indians from the South. Jackson started working on the second as soon as he had accomplished the first.[48]

JACKSON AS INDIAN COMMISSIONER

Secretary of War John Armstrong appointed General Thomas Pinckney and Benjamin Hawkins as Indian commissioners to negotiate a peace treaty with the Creek on March 14, 1814, as Jackson was marching south from Fort Strother toward Horseshoe Bend. Hawkins was considered a friend of the Indians, and both of them were opposed by Tennesseans who wanted to take over Indian land. Jackson ignored the official commissioners and instead ordered Creek chiefs to report to Fort Jackson for a convention on August 1, 1814. "Destruction will attend a failure to comply with these orders," threatened Jackson in his "invitation." Jackson wrote to his friend General John Coffee, threatening to strike against any Indian bands failing to attend.

Only friendly chiefs attended the convention. Jackson demanded about 23 million acres or roughly half the land claimed by the Creek—about 60 percent of Alabama and 20 percent of Georgia. Jackson also wanted 4 million acres of Cherokee land worth about $40 million and a strip along the Florida border from the Perdido River to the Pearl River. Jackson justified his demands on the grounds that the Creek had failed to report the appearance of Tecumseh before them in the fall of 1811. Jackson told Shelocta, who had provided troops to fight alongside Jackson, that the Creek must be cut off from contact with the northern tribes for the security of the United States. "You know that the part you desire to retain is that through which the intruders and mischief-makers from the Lakes reached you and urged your nation to those acts of violence, that have involved your people in wretchedness and your nation in ruin . . . That path must be stopped."[49]

When the Creek—who thought that the subsequent civil war was sufficient payment for any dereliction of duty on their part—balked at his terms, Jackson got nasty. "Your rejecting the treaty will show you to be the enemies of the United States—enemies even to yourselves." The Creek, not desiring a second war with the United States, felt obliged to comply with Jackson's terms. They offered Jackson a three-square-mile tract of the portion they were forced to cede as a personal present. In reality it was probably a sign of contempt. Jackson said he would accept only if Washington allowed him. The Creek signed the peace treaty on August 9, 1814. The treaty was in violation of Article IX of the Treaty of Ghent, which required the Americans to return to the Indians any lands held by them in 1811. Jackson probably would have justified his ignoring the treaty on three grounds. First, he had not signed the treaty. Second, the treaty with the Creek was completed before the Treaty of Ghent and was between the Creek and the

United States. Third, it was a question of the national security of the United States and thus *raison d'etat* took precedence. The British never attempted to enforce Article IX of the Treaty of Ghent—it was merely a sop for their own consciences. The Treaty of Fort Jackson was stalled in the Senate by the two senators from Tennessee until after the Battle of New Orleans. It was then rushed to the floor and unanimously ratified on February 16, 1815.[50]

The Cherokee complained to the Monroe administration that part of the land that the Creek were forced to cede was actually Cherokee land. After examining past treaties, the Monroe administration awarded part of the land to the Cherokee and also awarded damages for property (livestock) taken by Jackson's army during the Creek War. Both parts of this ruling infuriated both Jackson and Tennessee in general, as well as other western governors who saw it as a bad precedent. General Coffee was told by several Creek chiefs that the land that the Cherokee were forced to give up was in reality Creek land and that it had only been loaned to them after they were defeated by General Sevier in 1794.[51]

As a result of political pressure brought on the Monroe administration, Secretary of War William Crawford ruled that final disposition of the land in question must be dealt with by peace commissions with the Cherokee, the Chickasaw, and the Choctaw to settle the conflicting claims. Armstrong appointed Coffee; Colonel John McKee, who was the Choctaw agent; and Congressman John Rhea of Tennessee to deal with the Choctaw. He appointed Jackson, General David Meriwether of Georgia, and Jesse Franklin to deal with the Cherokee and the Chickasaw. Jackson wrote Crawford daily on the subject and told him he would not use the militia to surrender land to the Cherokee. "The people of the West will never suffer any Indian to inhabit this country again," wrote Jackson.[52]

Jackson, who considered himself to be in charge of the Cherokee-Chickasaw delegation, wrote to Coffee, whom he considered to be his counterpart on the Choctaw delegation, and suggested a joint strategy for dealing with the Indians. Jackson urged Coffee to tell the Indians that white settlers would never agree to move off of the land. Coffee should tell them that the number of white settlers would constantly increase. Then he should offer them "a fair consideration for this doubtful claim of theirs in money." Jackson urged a combined strategy of three separate weapons: first, the use of intimidation by military presence and bearing—a covert tactic; second, the secret bribery of key chiefs; third, overt threats of violence if bribery did not work.[53]

Negotiations began on September 8, 1816. The Cherokee delegation was under instruction not to give away any lands. Jackson grew angry from Indian refusal to immediately surrender to his demands. The Chickasaw produced a charter from President Washington signed in 1794 guaranteeing their claims. An 1801 treaty recognized the charter. After the use of the Jackson strategy, the Chickasaw delegates accepted a bribe on September 20,

1816, and signed the treaty. Jackson disliked bribes as demeaning and unseemly and preferred to simply dictate terms and make threats, but the Monroe administration did not want any further Indian problems.[54]

Jackson was forced to bribe the Cherokee tribal council to ratify the agreement. Later eighteen chiefs complained that the treaty had been confirmed by the chiefs of only four towns and not by the entire nation. This claim was made nearly a year after the treaty was signed and simply ignored by the commission. The Choctaw gave up their lands for $16,000 annually for twenty years and $10,000 in merchandise.[55]

As a result of his dealing with Crawford in 1815–17, Jackson considered Crawford to be his political opponent and personal enemy. Jackson would hold on to this grudge until Crawford retired from politics following his unsuccessful presidential bid in 1824. Jackson wrote to President Monroe on inauguration day in March 1817 that he did not consider the Indian nations to be sovereign states and that Congress was entitled to legislate on Indian affairs. Indians were subjects living on U.S. land. He went on to write: "too true that avarice and fear are the predominant passions that govern the Indian—and money, is the weapon, in the hands of the commissioner, wielded to corrupt a few of their leaders, and induce them to adopt the plans embraced by the views of the Government." Monroe wrote back that Jackson's ideas were "new but very deserving of attention."[56]

In July 1817 Jackson told a convention of Cherokee chiefs, "Look around you and recollect what had happened to your brothers the Creek." Jackson then bribed the chiefs to sign a treaty giving up 2 million acres in Georgia, Alabama, and Tennessee in exchange for the land in Arkansas that had been given to the Cherokee who moved there in 1809. The annuities to be paid out to the Cherokee Nation would be divided proportionately between the Arkansas and eastern Cherokee. Those agreeing to go to Arkansas were each given a rifle and ammunition, one blanket, and either a brass kettle or a beaver trap. The treaty was signed on July 8, 1817, and ratified unanimously by the Senate on December 11, 1817. For Jackson the treaty established a "principle" or precedent that he intended to apply to all of the five tribes.[57]

Jackson bribed the Chickasaw chiefs to cede their land in Tennessee and Kentucky, north of the Tennessee River, to the government in October 1818. Jackson was afraid that threatening them would result in war. After this the Chickasaw only retained a relatively small territory in northeast Mississippi and northwest Alabama.

Jackson personally benefited from his treaty making, as he was able to buy land out of the ceded territory at $21 an acre, which was well below market price, because no one was willing to bid against him. Jackson speculated in land, like many other entrepreneurs in the West, in order to grow wealthy.[58]

NOTES

1. Rebecca Stetoff, *William Henry Harrison: 9th President of the United States* (Ada, OK: Garret Educational Corp.), p. 88.
2. See Elting, op. cit., pp. xiii–xv for a short review of the causes.
3. This summary is based on a review of the works by Remini, Eisenhower, and Elting cited earlier.
4. John Sugden, *Tecumseh: A Life* (New York: Henry Holt, 1998), pp. 55, 61, 63; Norman K. Risjord, *Representatative Americans: The Revolutionary Generation* (Lexington, MA: D.C. Heath, 1980), makes the claim that Tecumseh scouted for the force and sprang the ambush.
5. Stetoff, op. cit., pp. 49, 51; Risjord, op. cit., p. 215; Sudgen, pp. 73–75, 79.
6. Sugden, op. cit., pp. 80–82.
7. "William Henry Harrison" *Encyclopedia Americana* online version at www.grolier.com/presidents; accessed July 12, 2003.
8. Risjord, p. 216.
9. Ibid., Stetoff, op. cit., pp. 58–62; Sugden, op. cit., p. 89.
10. Stetoff, p. 67; Risjord, p. 218 for a map of the boundary lines; Sugden, p. 106. The twelve tribes were: the Shawnee, Wyandotte, Delaware, Ottowa, Chippewa, Potawatomi, Kickapoo, Kaskaskia, Wea, Piankeshaw, Eel River, and Miami.
11. Stetoff, op. cit., pp. 70, 72, 75.
12. Risjord, op. cit., p. 217.
13. Stetoff, op. cit., p. 79; Risjord, op. cit., pp. 218–19; Sugden, op. cit., pp. 106, 183–85; see Miriam Gurko, *Indian America: The Black Hawk War* (New York: Thomas Crowell, 1970), pp. 78–80, for details on Harrison's technique.
14. Matthew 7: 7.
15. Sugden, op. cit., p. 109.
16. Stetoff, op. cit., p. 79; Risjord, op. cit., pp. 218–19; Sugden, p. 131.
17. Sugden, pp. 128–31. But it was Sitting Bull who did the political work of forming a pan-Indian alliance among the various Lakota bands and the Northern Cheyenne. But this was much smaller than Tecumseh's federation in terms of participating tribes and numbers of warriors. Red Cloud was also a very successful chief—the only Indian to win a war against the United States in the post–Civil War period.
18. Sugden, op. cit., pp. 189–90, 197.
19. Ibid. pp. 222–23.
20. Risjord, p. 224; Remini, *Indian Wars*, op. cit., pp. 1–5 for a description of Tecumseh's mission to the Creek.
21. Risjord, pp. 224–25; Stetoff, op. cit., p. 84; Elting, op. cit., p. 23; Sudgen, pp. 231–36.
22. David R. Collins, *Zachary Taylor: 12th President of the United States* (Ada, OK: Garret Educational Corp., 1989), p. 10; John S. D. Eisenhower, *Agent of Destiny* (New York: Free Press, 1997), pp. 10, 14.
23. K. Jack Bauer, *Zachary Taylor: Soldier, Planter, Statesman of the Old Southwest* (Baton Rouge, LA: Louisiana State University Press, 1985), pp. 13–20, 24.
24. www.rootsweb.com/~tnsumner/winchest.htm for a short biography of Winchester, accessed in January 2002; see Elting, op. cit., pp. 55–63, 319–21 for his war record in 1812–15.
25. Sugden, op. cit., pp. 331–38.

26. Sugden, op. cit., pp. 376, 379 on Tecumseh's death; Risjord claimed that his corpse was removed from the battlefield and buried elsewhere, but this appears to be mistaken, see Risjord, op. cit., p. 228.

27. See Risjord, op. cit., pp. 227–28; Elting, op. cit., pp. 110–13. Stetoff, op. cit., p. 89 gives the British/Indian total as 1,600 compared to 2,400 Americans, giving the Americans a 3:2 advantage. A detailed account of the battle is found on the Internet at www.publicbookshelf.com/public_html/The_Great_Republic_By_the_Master_Historians; accessed in February 2002. It is a late nineteenth century account of the battle by the historian Henry Adams, himself a descendant of John Quincy Adams.

28. "Cass, Lewis, 1782–1866," at www.clements.umich.edu/Webguides/Arlenes/C/Cass.html; Risjord, op. cit., p. 228; "John Jordan Crittenden," at www.virtualology.com/johnjordancrittenden, both accessed in January 2002; Eisenhower, op. cit., pp. 211–12; the quote is from Donald R. Hickey, *The War of 1812: A Forgotten Conflict* (Chicago: University of Illinois Press, 1989), p. 307, and is based upon chapter eight of Bennet H. Young, *The Battle of the Thames* (Louisville, KY, 1903).

29. Sugden, op. cit., p. 398.

30. Robert V. Remini, *Andrew Jackson and His Indian Wars* (New York: Viking, 2001) (hereafter *Indian Wars*), pp. 12–24.

31. Ibid., pp. 26–30, 33–34.

32. Remini, *Indian Wars*, pp. 39, 43–45; Remini, *Life of . . .* , op. cit., p. 40.

33. Remini, *Indian Wars*, op. cit., pp. 58–60.

34. Ibid., pp. 6–7.

35. Ibid., p. 64.

36. Remini, *Life of*, op. cit., pp. 71, 73, 81.

37. Jean Fritz, *Make Way for Sam Houston* (New York: G. P. Putnam's Sons, 1986), pp. 12–13.

38. Remini, *Indian Wars*, p. 78; *Life of*, p. 82.

39. Sugden, op. cit., p. 385.

40. Remini, *Life of*, op. cit., pp. 87–89.

41. Ibid., p. 86; Elting, op. cit., p. 114.

42. Eisenhower, op. cit., pp. 84, 93–94, 97.

43. Remini, *Life of*, op. cit., pp. 87–89.

44. Casualty figures are from Elting, op. cit., p. 308.

45. Ibid.; Faragher, op. cit., p. 335.

46. Eisenhower, op. cit., pp. 104–05; Remini, *Indian Wars*, p. 101.

47. Remini, *Indian Wars*, pp. 137–38, 142, 147, 156, 160–61.

48. Ibid., pp. 164, 166–68.

49. Ibid., pp. 88, 90.

50. Ibid., pp. 90, 92, 95–96.

51. Ibid., pp. 102–103.

52. Ibid., pp. 103, 105.

53. Ibid., pp. 106–107.

54. Ibid., p. 112.

55. Ibid., pp. 114, 116.

56. Ibid., p. 118.

57. Ibid., pp. 120–29, quote is on p. 127.

58. Ibid., pp. 176–80.

4

The Second-Party System: Democrats and Whigs

Jackson was in poor health in 1819 and seriously considered retiring from public life. But he stayed on to work as an Indian commissioner, negotiating treaties with the Five Civilized Nations of the South. President Monroe appointed Jackson territorial governor of Florida in February 1821 as soon as the Senate had ratified the purchase treaty. Jackson took care of regularizing the administration of the new territory and then resigned as governor in November 1821. Jackson had been in charge of the military district in the South and had used his home in Hermitage, outside Nashville, as military headquarters while managing his business affairs from 1818 until June 1821, when he finally resigned from the army. The next several years were spent waiting to be president.[1]

During the "era of good feelings" between the first and second party systems, there was no regular method for nominating presidential candidates. Party conventions did not become a part of American politics until the early 1830s, and Monroe refused to name his successor, as earlier presidents had. The Tennessee legislature nominated Jackson for president in 1822. On October 1, 1823, the Tennessee legislature elected him to the U.S. Senate by a vote of 35 to 25.

By 1824 there were five candidates, all from the Republican Party, running for president. These were: Treasury Secretary William Crawford, Secretary of State John Quincy Adams, Secretary of War John C. Calhoun, Representative Henry Clay, and Jackson. This involved: two Southerners (Calhoun and Crawford), two Westerners (Jackson and Clay), but only one

Northerner (Adams). Calhoun soon realized that he did not have much chance after Pennsylvania came out in favor of Jackson and so switched to running for vice president, where he was unopposed. Crawford suffered a stroke (brought on by his doctor's treatment for a fever) and so was in no physical shape to serve as president, although this was concealed from the public. Adams desperately wanted to be president—if for no other reason than as a positive confirmation of his success as secretary of state—and tried at various times to have Monroe send Jackson, Clay, and Calhoun on diplomatic missions to either Europe or Latin America in order to keep them out of the country. Monroe saw through this transparent ploy and refused to go along with it. Adams refused to openly campaign for president, but he did send "anonymous" defenses of his career to several newspaper editors.

In February 1824 a Republican congressional caucus nominated Crawford for president. On March 16, 1824, Monroe presented Jackson with a medal for the Battle of New Orleans in a White House ceremony. His supporters emphasized the Battle of New Orleans during the campaign. The Federalist Party, which still existed in the North, did not even bother to nominate a presidential candidate in 1824.[2]

The 1824 election was the first for which the popular vote was important, as most states (eighteen out of twenty-four) had passed laws connecting the selection of members of the electoral college directly to the popular election. Jackson won both the popular vote with 152,901 votes and the electoral college with 99 votes compared with Adams's 114,023 popular votes and 84 electoral votes; Clay had 47,217 popular votes but only 37 electoral votes compared to Crawford's 46,979 popular votes and 41 electoral votes. Jackson took Tennessee, Pennsylvania, New Jersey, Indiana, most of Maryland, and most of the South. New England and most of New York voted for Adams. Clay carried Kentucky, Ohio, and Missouri; whereas Crawford captured only Virginia and Georgia. As no candidate had a majority in the electoral college, the election would go to the House (for the second and final time in American history—the 1800 election being the first), with only the top three candidates in terms of electoral votes eligible for selection as president. This eliminated Clay who had fewer electoral votes than Crawford. The House delegations would then cast their votes as a unit with each state having only one vote. All the managers of the top three candidates attempted to win Clay over to their side, as he could deliver Kentucky and would be instrumental in winning the votes of other states as well.

Clay did not like Adams personally but considered him the most qualified of the three. He considered Crawford medically unfit for office and Jackson to be a mere "military chieftain" lacking the necessary political and intellectual experience. But he wanted to secure his own future interests before he supported Adams. "That I should vote for Mr. Crawford? I cannot. For Gen. Jackson? I will not," wrote Clay in his diary. Clay met with

Adams at the latter's house on January 9, 1825, and "spent the evening with me [sic] in a long conversation" according to Adams's diary. Adams probably agreed to adopt Clay's American System as his economic system—with which he had no problems—but whether he made any other promises was a matter of speculation. Exactly a month later the House elected Adams president on the first ballot with thirteen states voting in favor, followed by seven for Jackson and four for Crawford. Adams promptly offered Clay the office of secretary of state. Clay took a week to think over the offer, and his desire to be able to promote Latin American independence overrode his fear of accusations of a "corrupt bargain." According to Jackson and Clay biographer Robert V. Remini, Clay's acceptance was the "worst mistake of his life."

Jackson immediately resigned from the Senate in disgust with Congress and returned home. His supporters cried foul. "I weep for the Liberty of my country. The rights of the people have been bartered for promises of office," Jackson wrote his friend and former subordinate John Coffee. "So you see, the Judas of the West (Clay was popularly known as Harry of the West) has closed the contract and will receive the thirty pieces of silver." The 1828 election campaign began in February 1825.[3]

At this point, Martin Van Buren, a professional politician and lawyer from New York City who had been Crawford's campaign manager, realizing how popular Jackson was with the public, switched sides. He and Calhoun joined forces in support of Jackson and founded the Democratic Republican Party, initially as a faction within the Republican Party but eventually as the dominant faction until the party became known simply as the Democratic Party. Van Buren had been courted as campaign manager by several prospective presidential candidates for the 1824 race and, by January 1823, had decided to support Crawford. He considered Adams to be too unpopular and Clay incapable of withstanding "the severe ordeal of public opinion for two long years." He also disliked Adams because he suspected him of being like Monroe in that he would distribute political patronage on a nonpartisan basis rather than using it as a partisan tool for the good of the party.[4]

Van Buren, who was a senator from New York, and Jackson sat quite near each other in the Senate and so got to know one another. From 1826 to 1828 Van Buren almost single-handedly forged the Democratic Party by uniting the followers of both Crawford and Calhoun behind Jackson. Van Buren wanted to substitute party loyalty for loyalty to a particular candidate. By 1827 Van Buren had managed to make a large number of friends within the Jackson camp. That same year Clay attempted to imitate Van Buren by forging an anti-Jacksonian party, the beginning of the National Republicans that would be known popularly by that name by 1830.[5]

The 1828 campaign was a rematch of the 1824 race, except that Jackson had a straight shot at Adams. Neither of the two candidates took much active personal part in the campaign. Jackson did no active campaigning except to go to New Orleans in January for a ceremony marking the anniversary of the battle. Jackson had a distinct advantage over Adams in terms of personality and image—he was a romantic war hero and Indian fighter, whereas Adams was a rather dour, curmudgeonly lawyer. The campaign was one of the most negative in American history with Jackson's wife Rachel accused of being a bigamist because she had inadvertently married Jackson before her divorce from her first marriage had come through. Jackson was accused of being a brutal murderer for having six men shot for desertion during the Creek War, and his mother was called a prostitute. In turn, Jackson's supporters accused Adams of being a pimp for the Russian czar during his period as ambassador to Russia. Jackson and Adams biographer Robert Remini has written that "[w]ithout question the election of 1828 was the filthiest in American history." Van Buren managed a tariff bill in the Senate that raised the duties on the principal products of western states in an attempt to win votes away from Clay's friends. Rallies were held throughout the country with hickory poles to remind the public of "Old Hickory," and parades were held. At the rallies all sorts of hickory merchandise were sold to raise funds.

Kentucky, Missouri, and Ohio, which had all voted for Clay in 1824, voted for Jackson in 1828. Jackson captured the South, the West, and the Northwest for a total of 178 electoral votes compared to 83 for Adams, mostly from New England. New York split its votes: 20 for Jackson and 16 for Adams. Jackson won the popular vote 647,276 to 508,064 for Adams. Jackson's election was described in one contemporary account as "notoriously the work of Martin Van Buren." Jackson's biographer describes Van Buren's management of the election as "brilliant." Van Buren had been promised the position of secretary of state if Jackson was elected. Longtime Jackson biographer Robert Remini attributes Jackson's election to three factors: first, his enormous popularity with all sectors of the population as a hero; second, the belief that Adams had been elected by deceit; third, the superior organization of the Democratic Party.[6]

During 1832 the National Republicans developed the tactic of attacking Jackson as "King Andrew," which later became the strategy of the Whig Party. The campaign was fought over the issue of the Bank of the United States with Jackson opposing it and Clay supporting it. Henry Clay, in the second of his five campaigns for the presidency, suffered a humiliating defeat. Jackson beat him in the electoral college 219 to 49 with Jackson winning 55 percent of the popular vote compared to only about 37 percent for Clay. Clay managed to carry only Kentucky, Delaware, and three New England states. The Anti-Masons, a populist party made up of conspiracy theorists, were a powerful political force starting in the late 1820s. Clay, who was himself a Mason, wanted to run as the joint candidate of both the National Republicans and the Anti-Masons without making any concessions to the latter. Whig Party historian Michael Holt concluded, "The election of 1832 clearly stamped the National Republican Party as a loser and as the tool of the New England elite whom neither Anti-Masons nor Southerners could support."[7]

In the spring of 1834 a new party, the Whigs—named after the English opponents of the royalists during the English Civil War—emerged out of the National Republicans, supporters of the National Bank, and anti-Jackson Democrats. The latter came in four different groups. First were Southern states' rights supporters who believed in nullification—John C. Calhoun and his supporters. Second were states' rights supporters who opposed both nullification and the Force Bill—John Tyler and his supporters. Third were supporters of the Bank of the United States. Fourth and last were those who blamed Jackson for national economic problems or other reasons. What they all had in common was a dislike of a strong presidency. It was initially a party with more of a negative identity than a positive identity. Jackson was seen as the enemy.[8]

The Whigs only became competitive against the Democrats after 1837 when they used the tradition of state activity on behalf of the people during a depression. This was also the year that Calhoun, who had become one of the original Whigs after opposing Jackson during the Nullification Crisis of 1832, returned to the Democrats. After 1837 the Whigs had three main stars in Congress—Henry Clay and Daniel Webster (who, along with Calhoun, made up the Great Triumvirate that controlled the Senate through the power of their oratory) and former President John Quincy Adams in the House. Webster, a former Federalist from Boston who had opposed the War of 1812, and Clay, the War Hawk from Kentucky, were both bitten by "Potomac fever"; and in every election either one or both were running for president. Clay ended up running for president a total of five times: in 1824 as a Republican; in 1832 as a National Republican; and in 1840, 1844, and 1848 as a Whig. He only won the Whig nomination once—in 1844—but was a serious contender in 1840 and 1848 and did not run in 1852 only because he was too ill. Webster ran a total of three times: in 1836, 1848, and 1852. He was one of three official Whig candidates who ran in 1836 and did the worst both in terms of popular vote and electoral vote. At best, he could carry New England—at worst, only Massachusetts. In 1848 he lost the nomination to Taylor and in 1852 to Scott.

The Whigs were a party that believed in congressional supremacy with Congress rather than the executive as the most powerful branch. Clay seemed to think that he was entitled to the party's nomination as presidential candidate and entitled to behave as acting president if someone else won the nomination and the election. This was to cause friction with Harrison, divorce and rupture with Tyler, and rivalry with Taylor. Webster was more accommodating and served as secretary of state under three Whig presidents: Harrison, Tyler, and Fillmore.

The Whigs managed to elect two presidents and came close with a third candidate before the party collapsed in 1856. The one feature that all three of these candidates shared was that they were all popular war heroes; the two victorious ones were also Indian fighters.

The fortunes of the Whig Party, particularly in Massachusetts, were also closely intertwined with those of America's first political dynasty: the Adams family of Boston, Massachusetts. The founder of the dynasty, John Adams, was one of the members on the committee entrusted with drafting the Declaration of Independence in 1776, although Jefferson did most of the actual writing. Adams was one of the main negotiators of the peace treaty with Britain that ended the American Revolution. Adams served as the first vice president under Washington and, when the first parties began forming, became a Federalist. He was a rival of Alexander Hamilton for the leadership of the Federalists, with the latter more effective at controlling the caucus, but Adams was the only Federalist president. Washington is sometimes identified as a Federalist, but he considered himself to be a strictly nonpartisan figure and was elected without partisan support. Following the return of Adams to his law practice in 1801 and the death of Hamilton in a duel in 1804, the Federalist Party began to decline. But it was the Federalist Party that served as the forerunner of the National Republican Party when that party came together in 1824–28.

John's son, John Quincy Adams, grew up to become the country's leading diplomat in his early adult career. After helping to negotiate the Treaty of Ghent ending the War of 1812, he served as a minister (ambassador) to Russia. He then served as the secretary of state during the Monroe administration, becoming one of the most effective secretaries of state by developing the Monroe Doctrine and negotiating the purchase of Florida from Spain in the Adams-Onis treaty following the First Seminole War in 1818. After beating Jackson out of the presidency in 1824, Adams had a rather unremarkable presidency.

John Quincy Adams's most important public contribution, particularly as an elected official, was his service in the House from the seat of Plymouth from 1831 to 1848 where he was the most antislavery member of Congress. Adams despised Webster, who had worked to prevent the Massachusetts state legislature from electing Adams to the Senate. Adams had his revenge when he demolished Webster—to the delight of the Democrats who promptly dubbed him "Old Man Eloquent"—in a speech in the House on a defense appropriations bill that Webster opposed.

John Quincy Adams was the bane of the "slaveocracy" with his reading of antislavery petitions and his motions against the annexation of Texas. Southern congressmen dubbed him "the Madman of Massachusetts." By the mid-1830s he had seen that slavery was the root of all sectional divisions in the country. He began his fight against the "gag rule" on abolition petitions on December 16, 1835, and continued it for another six weeks. The "gag motion" passed the House on May 26, 1836, by a vote of 117 to

68. In 1839 he defended the "cargo" of the *Amistad* before the Supreme Court. (The *Amistad* was a Spanish slaver whose slave cargo revolted, murdered the crew, and ended up in America. Even Chief Justice Roger Taney—later the author of the infamous *Dred Scott* decision—voted with the Court to free the African defendants.) For eight years Adams opposed the annexation of Texas, and he balanced the final annexation with the rescinding of the gag rule on December 3, 1844, by a vote of 108 to 80. In May 1846 he led the forces in the House opposed to the war with Mexico. A month later he supported the deal with Britain that gave the United States control of Oregon. After suffering a stroke on November 20, 1846, he slowly recovered but was in poor health during his final year. He died from a stroke on the floor of the House on February 21, 1848, as he was opposing the peace with Mexico, because he was opposed to the new slave territory that the United States would acquire. Although he never considered himself to be an abolitionist and despised radical abolitionists who would break up the Union, John Quincy Adams was the closest thing to an abolitionist to serve in the antebellum Congress.[9]

Charles Francis Adams represented the third generation of the dynasty. Charles Adams began his political career, as did his father and grandfather, by writing political op-ed pieces for the Boston press. Adams began his career as an Anti-Mason in the early to mid-1830s when that party was quite powerful in Massachusetts. But he did not enter public office as an Anti-Mason. Initially horrified by the prospect of his father serving in the House, Charles later became an admirer of his father's antislavery stand and became a Whig. Charles Adams served for five years in the Massachusetts legislature as a Whig: three in the assembly followed by two in the senate, from 1841 to 1845. While in the legislature he became the leader of a faction of antislavery Whigs, known to history as the Conscience Whigs, who existed as a recognizable faction from roughly 1843 to 1848. Following his father's death in February 1848, Charles Adams was involved in the course of 1848 in leading his Conscience Whigs out of the Whig Party and to the creation of the first significant antislavery party, the Free Soil Party. He was the party's vice-presidential candidate in 1848. After running for Congress in 1850 as a Free Soiler and losing, Adams retired from politics for a number of years while he edited the papers of his grandfather, John Adams. Charles Adams played a role in the founding of the Republican Party in New England and campaigned on behalf of both Fremont and Lincoln. He was elected to Congress as a Republican in 1858 and again in 1860. He spent the Civil War as the ambassador to England where he performed valuable diplomatic services for the Union by keeping England neutral. Adams's role in the 1840s is narrated in greater detail in a later chapter as it is relevant to the story of the Whig Party and Zachary Taylor.

Some historians use the terms Cotton Whigs and Conscience Whigs as if they were interchangeable with Southern Whigs and Northern Whigs. Both were ideological divisions within Northern Whigs, and in the strictest sense, both factions existed only within the Massachusetts Whig Party, although each faction had its supporters within other New England states.

This is a good point to mention another Indian-fighter politician from Tennessee: David Crockett. Crockett was a literate but unschooled farmer and hunter who served as a scout with Jackson on a ninety-day enlistment at the beginning of the Creek War. He returned to his home near the Tennessee-Alabama border having been involved only in the Tallushatchee massacre. In late September 1814 he enlisted as a third sergeant in Major William Russell's Separate Battalion of Tennessee Mounted Gunmen during Jackson's expedition to Pensacola. The unit arrived the day after Jackson had already captured the town. Crockett's main job was hunting for the unit to supplement its inadequate rations. Crockett deserted in February 1815 when he learned that his wife was very ill; he later paid a neighbor to serve out the rest of his six-month enlistment.

In May 1815 Crockett was elected a lieutenant in the militia unit in Franklin County, Tennessee. The following year he moved to Lawrence County and became a justice of the peace, a town commissioner, and then in 1818 a colonel in the local militia. Starting in 1821 he served two terms in the state legislature. He was defeated in his first run for Congress in 1825 but was elected in 1827 as a Jackson Democrat, the same year that Houston was elected governor of Tennessee. Crockett served two terms in Congress but was defeated in a close election for a third term after breaking with Jackson over land reform and Indian removal. The secret to Crockett's political success was not his military reputation but his reputation as a hunter and marksman and his ability to tell tales and jokes. It was the same quality that got Lincoln elected in Illinois a decade later. Crockett's big congressional initiative was a land bill that would allow for transfer of the federal lands in Tennessee to state control and their sale by the state to the public in order to finance the building and operation of grammar schools. This bill was introduced repeatedly by Crockett in his three terms in Congress. It kept getting hung up in committee. During his first term Crockett denounced the Tennessee legislature in a congressional speech, claiming that it could not be trusted not to spend the money on universities instead of on public schools. For Crockett, universities were something only for the rich and a waste of taxpayers' money. During his second term he managed to have the bill transferred to a special committee that he chaired from the Public Lands Committee chaired by fellow Tennessean James K. Polk. But after the Tennessee delegation, with one exception, voted against a revised version of his bill, Crockett declared his independence from the delegation.[10]

Crockett came to national prominence at the beginning of the 1830s. He served as the model for Nimrod Wildfire, the hero of the play *The Lion of the West* by James K. Paulding, which opened in New York City in 1831. He had earlier served as the model for a secondary character, whose success inspired Paulding to write his play. "Crockett was then the lion of Washington," said one man after hearing him speak. But Crockett was too independent to be an effective politician. In the winter of 1830 he openly broke with Jackson, not only over Indian removal but also over the spoils system. On February 24, 1830, Crockett declared, "I shall insist upon it that I am still a Jackson man, but General Jackson is not; he has become a Van Buren man." This rhetoric helped to lose him the election as well as attract the attention of the National Republicans.[11]

Two years later a book of tall tales about him appeared. This sparked Crockett to write his autobiography with the help of fellow Congressman Thomas Chilton. He spent much of January and February 1834 writing the book. It was published with the help of the Whig Party in March 1834, two years before his death. In it he falsified his military record so that he was with Jackson throughout the Creek War and participated in all the battles except Horseshoe Bend, when he was supposedly off buying a horse. This is a telling fact—Crockett thought it was necessary to be an Indian fighter in order to be a successful national politician. Crockett's company commander during the Creek War, Francis Jones, served for three terms in Congress after the war. Crockett devoted a third of the book to his war experiences, one-third to hunting and other adventures before being elected to Congress, and the final third to his political career while reducing his first two congressional terms to an extended paragraph.[12]

Crockett lost his bid for a third term in August 1831 to William Fitzgerald by 586 votes out of 16,842. Crockett lost because of his opposition to Indian removal and his support for high tariffs and for internal improvements, all of which went against popular opinion in West Tennessee. He objected to the Indian Removal bill on the grounds that it gave Jackson a half-million dollars with no accountability, but he also professed a regard for many of the Indians whom he mainly regarded as peaceful.[13]

Crockett was elected once more to Congress in August 1833, beating Fitzgerald by a narrow 173 votes: 3,985 to 3,812. In April and May 1834 he went on a three-week turn of eastern cities sponsored by the Whig Party. The Whigs were talking of making him a presidential candidate. In the fall of 1833 members of a Mississippi state Whig convention wrote to Crockett wondering if they could place his name in contention for the 1836 nomination. Crockett by December 1834 saw Van Buren as unbeatable in 1836 and so hoped to run in 1840. So he supported most of the Tennessee delegation in asking Hugh Lawson White to run for president. Most of Jackson's Democratic colleagues in Tennessee disliked Van Buren and resented Jackson picking his own successor. The Whigs had an account of Crockett's tour, written in December 1834, published along with a very negative biography of Van Buren that appeared with Crockett listed as author. Crockett was dependent on these literary efforts not only as a means of political marketing but to raise money to pay debts and raise funds for campaigning. Crockett went on a second eastern tour from mid-June to mid-July 1834 and met with top Whigs including Webster and Adams. Crockett was seen as a good anti-Jackson candidate who would appeal to the common man. But his poverty and need to constantly borrow money hurt his chances of winning nomination.[14] Crockett was much in the same mold as the remade Harrison in 1836 and 1840.

Crockett's political career came to a sudden end when he was defeated by a peg-legged lawyer by some 252 votes out of nine thousand cast after being targeted by Jackson, James K. Polk, and Governor Carroll. The lawyer, Adam Huntsman, had lost his leg in the War of 1812 and was more of a genuine war hero than Crockett; plus he was more educated. Huntsman wrote in the local press in Tennessee under the pseudonym Blackhawk. Huntsman credited his victory to Crockett's support for high tariffs, a national bank, and personal attacks against "King Andrew" Jackson.[15]

Crockett then set off on a trip to Texas on November 1, 1835. His reaction according to popular legend was "The voters can go to hell, I'm going to Texas!" Crockett had met with Houston in Washington in the spring of 1834—some five years after he had last seen Houston on the day he resigned as governor—and Houston told him tales about Texas. Shortly after that, Crockett began talking about Texas for the first time. Crockett, then forty-nine, was thinking of restarting his political career in Texas. He still had dreams of possibly running for president in 1840. When he passed through the small town of Saint Augustine on his way to San Antonio, they offered to let him represent them at the Texas convention. He told them that he had come to fight—his first real mention of serving in the revolution. He was sworn in for six months as a volunteer and headed up a group of about twenty scouts, composed both of those who had followed him from Tennessee and those who joined him in East Texas. Because Houston, who was allied to Jackson, controlled eastern Texas, Crockett headed to San Antonio and the Alamo and his date with destiny. The consensus among historians is that he was not seeking martyrdom but joined the revolutionary struggle as a means of launching a new political career and accidentally found himself in a situation that he could not back out of without serious injury to his reputation.[16]

For Jeffersonian Democrats, the Republicans, access to land—the traditional mark of the aristocracy—became the key to political equality. This is seen in the careers of so many Republican politicians on the frontier, particularly Tennessee, who were land speculators. John Sevier, William Blount, and Andrew Jackson, the leading politicians in Tennessee at the turn of the eighteenth century, were all speculators. Later this land access became the centerpiece of Crockett's political career. And in this way much of "Jacksonian ideology" became a broad belief system that was shared by Whigs, and later by Free Soilers and Republicans as well. Daniel Webster and the Northern Whigs reinterpreted it in terms of equality of opportunity and of mobility.[17]

The Whigs realized by the end of 1834 that they could not hold a national convention without the danger of it "blowing apart" and damaging the party fatally. In 1836 the Whigs were unable to agree on a single presidential candidate and so ran three separate regional candidates in the hope that this would throw the election into the House by denying a majority to Martin Van Buren. Senator Hugh Lawson White of Tennessee became the candidate in the South, Daniel Webster was the New England candidate, and William Henry Harrison was the candidate in the West. The West actively disliked Webster, and Clay was still recovering from his 1832 defeat. Clay considered Harrison to be incompetent but electable. Clay preferred him to either White or Supreme Court Justice John McLean of Ohio. Clay determined that there should be two candidates, but Webster refused to drop out and so ran in New England.

Van Buren won 50.1 percent of the popular vote and fifteen states for 170 electoral votes compared with six states and 73 votes for Harrison, two states and 26 votes for White, and only one state with 14 votes for Webster. Richard Johnson, the hero of the Battle of the Thames, running as Van Buren's running mate, failed to win a majority of electoral votes but was confirmed by the House. Harrison received over thirteen times as many votes as Harrison did.[18]

The 1836 election was the first of three elections in which both parties had a prominent Indian fighter in one of the top two spots. The other two elections were in 1840 and 1848. By the time of the 1840 election, the "Indian problem" had been largely "solved" in the eastern United States through President Jackson's removal policy, which had by the end of 1838 removed most of the Five Civilized Tribes (Cherokee, Chickasaw, Choctaw, Creek, and Seminole), as well as most of the Northwest Territory's tribes to the West—across the Mississippi River. The Black Hawk War was an old memory, and only the Second Seminole War continued in the swamps of central Florida. Richard Johnson offended Southern sensibilities by living openly with his mulatto wife and their two children. He had also sold one former mulatto mistress down river after she abandoned him. Thus, he would have offended the sensibilities of both the religious and Southerners.[19]

That year James Hall wrote a campaign biography of Harrison that presented him as another log-cabin-born frontiersman and Indian fighter. At least the second part was true. This was the start of a process of tying presidential candidates to the frontier myth that had been created starting with Daniel Boone and with the fictionalized Boone, Nathaniel Bummpo (alias the Leatherstocking, the Deerslayer, the Pathfinder, etc.) created by novelist James Fennimore Cooper in 1823 and continued in a series of five novels that lasted until 1841. After Cooper the frontier myth was being reformulated by a class of entrepreneurs, journalists, politicians, writers, reformers, and intellectuals. Novelist Washington Irving, of *Legend of Sleepy Hollow* fame, wrote a series of multivolume histories of figures and movements that shaped American history. This trend continued until the end the Whig Party.[20]

Harrison had a minor political career after resigning his commission in May 1814. After settling in Cincinnati he became a trustee of Cincinnati College and represented the district in Congress from 1816 to 1819. After failing to be appointed ambassador to Russia in 1819, he served one term in the Ohio Senate from 1819 to 1821. After losing elections for both the governorship and seats in both houses of Congress, he was elected to the U.S. Senate in 1825. He served three years as a chairman on the committee of military affairs and the militia. In 1828 he was appointed ambassador to Colombia by John Quincy Adams but was recalled by newly inaugurated President Jackson a month after reaching Bogota in February 1829. He remained in place until September when his replacement arrived. He created a minor diplomatic incident by telling President Simon Bolivar that "the strongest of all government is that which is most free," after having been relieved of office. The controversy later proved useful to Harrison's political career. In 1834 he was forced to accept a position as the clerk of the court of common pleas in Hamilton County, Ohio, to pay his debts. The following year he began campaigning for the presidency by touring Illinois and Indiana.

Many Midwesterners and Anti-Masons considered Harrison to be the perfect candidate: he was a hero, a longtime resident of the West, and an anti-Jackson man. His similarities to Jackson in the 1820s made him attractive to both groups. The Boston *Atlas* editorialized on September 14, 1838: "What avail all other qualifications under Heaven, if the candidate be not popular." When the editor showed this to Webster at his home, Webster threw him out thinking that he was referring to him instead of to Clay. The Illinois Whigs endorsed Harrison after a convention in October 1839 in Springfield selected him as their candidate. Abraham Lincoln was selected as one of five Whigs to promote his candidacy, and the first series of Lincoln-Douglas debates took place during the 1840 presidential campaign. When the Whig convention met in Harrisburg, Pennsylvania, in December 1839 there were three presidential candidates. These were Harrison; Clay; and Major General Winfield Scott, the third popular hero of the War of 1812. On the first ballot Clay led with 103 votes to 91 for Harrison and 57 for Scott. After it was revealed that Scott had made an antislavery pitch to New York, the Southerners all abandoned him. On the final ballot, New York, Michigan, and Vermont abandoned Scott for Harrison. During the convention Clay suffered from poor timing, poor management, and poor attendance. The convention followed a string of Whig loses across the country for which Clay—as party leader—was blamed. Many of Clay's supporters refused to attend the convention on the grounds that they had campaigned against Van Buren because he had been nominated by a convention. As vice-presidential nominee the convention chose John Tyler of Virginia, a former states' rights Democrat who had broken with Jackson during the Nullification Crisis. He seemed to be a typical Clay supporter but in reality was not. The convention refused to adopt a platform.[21]

The 1840 campaign is more remembered for its songs than for its principles. The Whigs basically repeated Jackson's campaigns of 1828 and 1832 with Van Buren cast in the role of Adams. Van Buren, who was from a relatively modest background before becoming rich as a lawyer, was painted as a spoiled effete aristocrat; Harrison, the real aristocrat, was portrayed as a common man. Instead of hickory poles, the Whigs used log cabins and hard cider as their symbols. The last came from a swipe at Harrison by a Democratic newspaperman in Baltimore. "Give him a barrel of hard cider, settle a pension of two thousand dollars a year on him, and my word for it, he will sit for the remainder of his days in his log cabin by the side of a sea-coal fire, studying moral philosophy." The campaign slogan was "Tippecanoe and Tyler Too!" and Harrison was known as "Old Tippecanoe" or simply "Old Tip." Interestingly, Harrison chose to emphasize his lesser victory at Prophet's Town rather than his more strategic victory at the Battle of the Thames. Possibly, this was because the victory was his alone and did not have to be shared with others. Other slogans were "Down with Martin Van Ruin!" and "Van, Van, Van—Van's a Used Up Man."[22]

The 1840 campaign set the basic electoral strategy and voter coalition that would characterize the party until its demise. This was also true of the Democrats over the same period. It established the second-party system as stable. When Clay was reproached by Democratic colleagues in the Senate about the imbecility of the campaign, he blamed Jackson and the Democrats. Because a coon skin was part of the log-cabin image used in the campaign, the Whigs became known as "the coons" and Clay as "the Old Coon." This was an image used in many political cartoons of the day.[23]

Due both to his personal popularity and to the bad economic situation, Harrison won 52.9 percent of the popular vote to carry nineteen states and win 234 electoral votes compared with 46.8 percent and seven states for 60 votes by Van Buren. Harrison was content to continue recognizing Clay as party leader as long as Clay acknowledged that it was Harrison's administration. Clay told Harrison that he did not want a place in the cabinet when he hosted the president-elect at his country estate outside Louisville. Clay noted how old and tired Harrison looked when they met in November in Kentucky. Harrison offered Webster either treasury or state, and Webster chose the latter.

Harrison made a ninety-minute inaugural address in cold weather without a coat and caught a bad cold. Harrison's inaugural address was basically a summary of Whig philosophy, including the supremacy of the legislative branch, limited government, and shared authority. It included the view that the president should only serve for a single term. He stated that he expected Congress to come up with a plan for a national bank or another economic scheme and that it was not his duty to propose a solution. He promised to use the veto sparingly and spoke in favor of civil service reform—getting away from the Jacksonian spoils system. Harrison also stated that he wanted peace and harmony between the various branches of the government and the departments of the executive. This was the only major policy statement of his short administration.[24]

Clay seemed to have no voice in appointments, whereas Webster did—perhaps because he was more diplomatic in the way that he made suggestions and because he was a member of the cabinet. Harrison really wanted to end the Jacksonian spoils system of patronage but was under considerable pressure from Whigs to appoint Whigs to the civil service.

Clay demanded that Harrison call a special session of Congress to deal with the national bank question. Webster advised against this, and Harrison put it to a cabinet vote. The cabinet was deadlocked at 3-3 when on March 11 Harrison voted against it to break the tie. Harrison sent a letter to Clay explaining his reasoning and concluded, "I prefer for many reasons this mode of answering your notes to a conversation in the presence of others." Clay took this to mean a ban from direct meetings at the White House or on Capital Hill. As a result of this, Clay returned to Kentucky after the Senate adjourned on March 15. Harrison saw himself as "first among equals" in cabinet decision making having one vote like the others. Harrison probably would have grown restive at the cabinet and Congress trying to restrict his decision-making power, but there was not sufficient time for this to develop.[25]

During the early days of his presidency, Harrison was wont to walk around Washington in order to think—as Lincoln later did—and on one occasion was caught in a sudden downpour without a coat and became soaked. The cold developed into pneumonia and within three weeks he was confined to bed. On March 27, he was diagnosed with "bilious pleurisy with symptoms of pneumonia" and was confined to bed for a week. He seemed to improve and then had a sudden relapse and died on April 4, 1841. Harrison had been nominated by the Whigs because they expected him to be *both* pliable and electable. Now he was neither.[26]

Tyler was in Williamsburg, Virginia, when Harrison died and had not even officially been notified of his illness, although he had read reports of it in the press. No one knew exactly what the vice president's role should be if a president died in office. Justice Joseph Story in his famous *Commentaries*, published in 1833, held that a vice president should become president for the remainder of the term. But James Kent in his *Commentaries on American Law* held that the vice president was only "an acting president." On April 6 the cabinet decided that Tyler should take the oath and assume office. Adams never reconciled himself to Tyler being president and always referred to him as the "acting president," which was kinder than others who referred to him as "His Accidency" behind his back. Historian Arthur Schlesinger Jr. argued that the vice president was not provided mainly for the purpose of succession but to ensure a national ticket by forcing electors to vote for at least one man who was not from their state. Tyler set a precedent that held until it was enshrined in the Twenty-fifth Amendment to the Constitution in 1967.[27]

Tyler was sworn in as president. Unlike Harrison, he did not believe in legislative supremacy and made no mention of limiting himself to a single term. He soon began adopting policies that clashed with those of the party, particularly with those of Clay. At the Whig convention, Tyler was considered to be Clay's man. This quickly proved not to be the case. Tyler and Clay battled over a bank bill in the press. The pro-Tyler *Madisonian* saw cabinet officers as being in place to carry out the president's policies so that the executive could function as a single branch. The national Whig newspaper, *National Intelligencer,* dubbed this theory "an odious Jacksonian pretension." Tyler vetoed a National Bank bill that Clay had guided through the Senate in August 1841 over the objections of his cabinet. Everyone knew that there was no possibility of overturning Tyler's veto, so an open "war" existed between Tyler and the Whig Party. In a Senate speech Clay accused Tyler of "pride, vanity and egotism" in a speech that was "spiteful." This description could just as well apply to Clay himself.[28]

On September 3, 1841, the Senate approved the Fiscal Corporation bill 27 to 22 with only one Whig, a Tyler supporter, voting against it. Tyler vetoed it on September 9 but pleaded with Congress not to let differences over the bank bills enflame relations between the two branches of government. Tyler had given Congress little indication of what would cause him to veto a future bank bill after he vetoed the first bill, so his vagueness was in large part responsible for the feud with Clay and the national Whig Party.

Tyler named a new cabinet on September 11 with only Webster staying on because he was involved in delicate negotiations with the British government for a solution to a border problem. The negotiations resulted in the Webster-Ashburton Treaty of 1843, after which Webster resigned. Most of his cabinet members were states' rights supporters who were opposed to nullification. In little over a year a group of congressional Whigs had written him out of the party as Clay had in June 1842. The Whig Party printed up a manifesto restating its principles from the 1840 campaign and declared Tyler in violation of them, then distributed twenty thousand copies of it around the country. This was a de facto expulsion from the party.[29]

Tyler considered slavery to be a necessary evil rather than a positive good—as did the Calhoun "firebreathers"; and he both refused to praise it and made no effort to impede it or even free his own slaves. In this latter aspect he was just following the lead of both Jefferson and Henry Clay. He wished that "slavery would just go away somehow, quietly and without fuss." Despite not being an admirer of Calhoun, Tyler named him as his secretary of state to replace Webster in 1844, in order to accomplish the annexation of Texas.[30]

Clay was nearly a unanimous Whig candidate in 1844, but among the Democrats there was no lack of candidates: Lewis Cass of Michigan, James Buchanan of Pennsylvania, Richard M. Johnson of Kentucky, and several others were campaigning for the nomination. Some Southern Democrats even wanted to nominate Tyler if Calhoun did not run. Tyler wanted to run but lacked a party. He attempted to form his own party from states' rights supporters from the two major parties but was not successful. He finally withdrew from the race as an independent in August 1844 when it became clear that he had no chance to win. Tyler remarried on June 26, 1844, to a bride nearly thirty years younger than himself, his first wife having died in September 1843. This further alienated him from Washington society by making him an object of social gossip and ridicule.

The Democratic convention met in Baltimore in May 1844. A two-thirds majority rule was in effect meaning that the winning candidate would have to be supported by two-thirds or more of the delegates. Former President Martin Van Buren seemed to be the favorite before the convention, but he was opposed to the annexation of Texas. Former Tennessee Governor and House Speaker James K. Polk and Senator George Dallas of Pennsylvania were nominated. Polk was a "dark horse" who was a compromise choice to avoid Van Buren and Cass. Before the convention Jackson had announced that he supported both Van Buren and Texas, which everyone knew was simply illogical. Polk won on the ninth ballot. Polk claimed that Texas had been part of the original Louisiana Purchase of 1803 and that Adams had then renounced American rights to it when he purchased Florida in 1819. So his slogan was that the United States should "reannex Texas."[31]

In 1844 the Tyler administration negotiated an annexation treaty with the Republic of Texas, but the Senate voted against ratification on June 8, 1844, 35 to 16. Only a single Whig, from Mississippi, voted in favor of annexation. The Texas Senate also voted against ratification. The rejection of the annexation caused problems for President Sam Houston in Texas. Mexican dictator Santa Anna vowed vengeance on Texas and anyone who would aid her. There was a presidential election in Texas in September 1844 with Houston barred from reelection. Anson Jones, who was opposed to annexation, was elected president. Houston wanted to turn to Britain for assistance as a means of pressuring the United States, whereas Jones wanted to wait and see what Washington would do.[32]

Clay was hurt in both the South and the North when he tried to stay neutral on slavery. Southerners distrusted him when the Southern emancipationist Cassius M. Clay (a distant relative) endorsed him and some Northern Whigs deserted him for the new abolititionist Liberty Party. Webster dutifully campaigned for the Whig ticket without often mentioning his rival, Clay, by name. The Native American Party grew rapidly in 1843–44 in the major cities in the first wave of American nativism.

The two main issues in the campaign were Texas and the border dispute with Britain over Oregon. There was a popular slogan "54 40 or fight" referring to the location in degrees of the American proposal for the border with British Canada. To Catholics and immigrants the Whig Party seemed bigoted and hostile, whereas to nativists it seemed too moderate and restrained. Many in the South and West voted for the Democrats in 1844 because of the lure of cheap land in Oregon and Texas.

Polk narrowly beat Clay by about forty thousand votes—1.34 million to 1.30 million for an electoral vote lead of 170 to 105. Polk carried seven free and eight slave states and lost Tennessee by a very narrow margin of 113 votes and lost Kentucky only because of Clay's local popularity there. Clay carried eleven states for 105 electoral votes, eight fewer states than Harrison carried in 1840. The only Western states he carried were Ohio, Kentucky, and Tennessee. Polk beat Clay by only a little over five thousand votes in New York, which decided the election. The antislavery Liberty Party polled 15,814 votes in New York, thereby deciding the election. Texas had affected the outcome. Had Texas not been an issue, the Democrats probably would have nominated Van Buren whom Clay could probably have beaten. The Whigs lost both the immigrant vote in the North and the states' rights vote in the South when Clay waffled on annexation.[33]

The election was a major turning point for the Whig Party. Clay's loss exacerbated sectional differences within the party, and there was even talk of dropping the Whig label after 1844. Webster publicly declared that Clay had been defeated by Southern determination to expand slave territory. But privately he told friends that Clay's vindictive and obstinate opposition to Tyler had cost him the election. Daniel Howe wrote, "Though never president, he was often right; and he would have been right even more often had he wanted to be president less. . . . Clay was a victim of his own ambition." Leslie Coombs, a Kentucky friend and supporter of Clay, believed that resistance to annexation had cost Clay the election.[34]

Tyler took the election as a referendum on annexation and decided to push for a joint resolution of Congress in favor of annexation before he left office. This was accomplished in December 1844.

Traditionally American presidential historians have placed Tyler along with Taylor and Fillmore (all Whigs) and others in the low-average to below-average category. In a 1962 poll, seventy-five historians relegated Tyler to below-average status.[35]

NOTES

1. Robert V. Remini, *Andrew Jackson and His Indian Wars* (New York: Viking, 2000) (hereafter *Indian Wars*), pp. 184, 207; Remini, *The Life of Andrew Jackson* (New York: Harper Row, 1988)(hereafter *Life of*), pp. 111, 130; Remini, *John Quincy Adams* (New York: Times Books, 2002) (hereafter *JQA*), pp. 64–65.

2. Remini, *Indian Wars*, pp. 212–13, 216; Robert V. Remini, *Martin Van Buren and the Making of the Democratic Party* (New York: Columbia University Press, 1959) (hereafter *MVB*), pp. 43, 48; Remini, *JQA*, p. 66.

3. Remini, *Indian Wars*, pp. 212–13, 216; Robert V. Remini, *MVB* (New York: Columbia University Press, 1959), pp. 43, 48; Remini, *JQA*, pp. 69–71, 74.

4. Remini, *MVB*, op. cit., pp. 28, 37.
5. Ibid., pp. 124 n. 4, 125, 131, 146.
6. Ibid., pp. 171–72, 184, 185, 189, 190, 192, 195, 197; Remini, *Indian Wars*, p. 225; Remini, *Life of*, pp. 166, 169; Remini, *JQA*, p. 116.
7. Michael F. Holt, *The Rise and Fall of the American Whig Party* (New York: Oxford University Press, 1999), pp. 12–14, 17, 39; Remini, *JQA*, p. 133.
8. Norma L. Peterson, *The Presidencies of William Henry Harrison & John Tyler* (Lawrence: University Press of Kansas, 1989), pp. 15–16.
9. Remini, *JQA*, pp. 136, 138–41, 148, 151–55.
10. "Crockett, David, *"The Handbook of Texas Online* at www.tsha.utexas.edu/handbook/online; Mark Derr, *The Frontiersman* (New York: William Morrow, 1993); pp. 73, 75; William C. Davis, *Three Roads to the Alamo* (New York: Harper Collins, 1998), pp. 138, 172–74.
11. Davis, pp. 176–77, 180, 183–84.
12. Davis, pp. 320–22.
13. Derr, pp. 65, 71; Davis, pp. 176, 186.
14. Davis, pp. 313–14, 393–95, 398, 399.
15. Ibid., p. 406.
16. William C. Davis, *Three Roads to the Alamo* (New York: Harper Collins, 1998), pp. 389, 414–16.
17. Richard Slotkin, *Fatal Environment* (New York: Harper Perennial, 1994), pp. 112, 114.
18. Robert V. Remini, *Henry Clay: Statesman for the Union* (New York: W. W. Norton, 1991), pp. 474, 479, 490.
19. On Johnson see Holt, op. cit., p. 43 and Major L. Wilson, *The Presidency of Martin Van Buren* (Lawrence, KS: University of Kansas, 1984), p. 18.
20. Slotkin, op. cit., pp. 117, 119, 123–34.
21. Stephen B. Oates, *With Malice Toward None: The Life of Abraham Lincoln* (New York: Harper Row, 1977), pp. 50–51; Holt, op. cit., pp. 101, 103, 104; Merrill D. Peterson, *The Great Triumvirate* (New York: Oxford University Press, 1987), p. 283.
22. Remini, *Clay*, op. cit., p. 562; Holt, op. cit., pp. 105–107.
23. Remini, *Clay*, pp. 563–64.
24. Norma Lois Peterson, *The Presidencies of William Henry Harrison & John Tyler* (Lawrence: University Press of Kansas, 1989), p. 35.
25. Ibid., pp. 37, 39, 41.
26. Ibid., pp. 41–42.
27. Ibid., pp. 42, 46–47, 48, 50.
28. Ibid., pp. 70–71, 77–78.
29. Ibid., pp. 84–85, 87–88, 90, 92; Remini, *Clay*, p. xxi.
30. N. Peterson, p. 205.
31. Ibid., pp. 224–25, 236; Van Deusen, op. cit., pp. 184–85.
32. N. Peterson, op. cit., p. 233.
33. Ibid., pp. 241–44; M. Peterson, op. cit., p. 366; Van Deusen, op. cit., pp. 188–89; Holt, op. cit., pp. 206–207.
34. N. Peterson, pp. 244, 262–63.
35. Ibid., p. 261.

5

The Mexican Fighters and the Collapse of the Whig Party

INTRODUCTION

The 1848 election was a critical election and turning point in the history of military leadership in American politics during the nineteenth century. It was the first election in which the candidates of both the major parties were Indian-fighter politicians. It was also the first in a series of several presidential elections lasting through 1860 in which there were more than two important candidates. The period from 1848 to 1860 was the only period in which America had a multiparty system. Unlike the 1990s, when Ross Perot made significant inroads into the popular vote in several states as the Reform Party candidate but failed to win a single electoral vote, these minority candidates won electoral votes—significant amounts in 1860. This period also had viable party structures that elected many candidates to Congress and to state legislatures and governors' mansions across the country. This compares very favorably to Governor Jesse Ventura of Minnesota—who ended up breaking with the Reform Party. This chapter examines two of these temporary parties, the Know-Nothing Party and the Free Soil Party, as well as the Republican Party, which became the permanent replacement for the Whig Party.

Zachary Taylor, the second and final Whig candidate elected president, was a transitional figure—he was the last Indian-fighter president and the first Mexican-fighter president. In total there were four Mexican-fighter American presidents: Taylor, Franklin Pierce, and Ulysses S. Grant of the United States and Jefferson Davis of the Confederate States. Grant was another transitional figure between the Mexican-fighter presidents and the Civil-War-veteran presidents with three more following him.

The Taylor administration also saw the beginning of the road to the Civil War with major talk of secession by the Southern states in 1850. This was halted by threats from Taylor to use force to prevent it and the 1850 Compromise engineered by "the Great Pacificator" Henry Clay and "Godlike Daniel" Webster, the two leaders of the Whig Party. The deaths of John Quincy Adams in 1848, of John C. Calhoun and Zachary Taylor in 1850, and of Henry Clay and Daniel Webster in 1852 left both the Congress and the Whig Party without seasoned leadership. This was the era of the passing of the baton of leadership to a new generation that had not taken part or experienced the War of 1812.

COTTON AND CONSCIENCE WHIGS

The Northern Whigs were divided after 1844 over the degree to which they were willing to alienate their Southern colleagues by opposing slavery— or its expansion. One of the most successful state Whig parties was the Massachusetts Whig Party, which from 1834 to 1848 in every year but one controlled both branches of the state legislature and in every year but two had a Whig governor. Whigs had an advantage over the Democrats because of their economic control and the wealth of their leaders. The Massachusetts Whig Party opposed all movements from 1834 to 1854 that would alienate Southern Whigs.[1]

Abolitionism became an important movement in New England after 1831, particularly in the Boston area. Between 1831 and 1838 abolitionists formed over two hundred antislavery societies. Abolitionists split into two wings: a radical anticonstitutional wing led by William Lloyd Garrison and a political wing led by Samuel Sewall; the latter organized the Liberty Party in 1840. That year the Liberty Party won only 1 percent of the vote and at its peak in 1846 won only 9 percent of the vote.[2]

Whigs opposed the abolitionists because of their attack on property rights. Many Whig leaders had slave-owners as personal friends, business associates, and political allies. The Whig Party in Massachusetts in the 1840s was led by the Cotton Whigs—men who were tied to the large textile industry in eastern Massachusetts and who had made their fortunes in the preceding two decades. The two most prominent of these were Abbot Lawrence and Nathan Appleton. Lawrence did business in the mid-1840s with such Southern Democrats as John C. Calhoun and James K. Polk. Opposing them were a handful of prominent Massachusetts Whigs who believed that the party must take an antislavery stand. Most of these antislavery Whigs were young men with little or no connection with the textile industry and who were not in a commanding position in either the party or the social aristocracy. Several of them were from prominent Boston families who had been politically influential in previous generations. Most prominent of these was the group's leader, Charles Francis Adams, son of John Quincy Adams and grandson of John Adams. These men eventually became known as the Conscience Whigs. They saw themselves as the guardians of morality and republican values. They believed that the Liberty Party was too weak to be effective. The two terms—*Cotton Whigs* and *Conscience Whigs*—arose during a series of debates in the Massachusetts legislature in April 1846.[3]

Both the Cotton and Conscience Whigs were antislavery, meaning that they opposed the spread of slavery and saw it as a system that should eventually die out. Both wings opposed the annexation of Texas, and both opposed admitting the territories captured in the Mexican War as slave states. They were divided about the extent of their resistance to these moves. In the 1840s the terms *antislavery* and *abolitionist* had very different meanings. Abolitionists took a moral stance on slavery and considered it a moral evil to which opposition was more important than the Constitution or avoiding civil war. The distinction is somewhat analogous to the mainstream Pro-Life movement that is abolitionist, as opposed to those constitutional lawyers who object to *Roe v. Wade* as bad constitutional law or those politicians who see abortion as being bad social policy.[4]

The Conscience Whigs established the Texas Committee to oppose annexation of Texas in September 1844. The Committee had a membership of between thirty-five and forty-five members, mostly from eastern Massachusetts of whom about two-thirds were abolitionists, during its few months of existence. It had few Whigs or Democrats in its membership. Adams had been responsible for the state legislature passing a series of anti-annexation resolutions by a large majority, but these had little effect on Congress. On October 2, 1845, Adams informed the Whig state committee that he would not run for reelection. Henry Wilson took over the leadership of the group from Adams in 1846. Many antislavery Whigs won election to both houses of the legislature in 1845. The political abolitionists led by Sewall kept trying to lead the Conscience Whigs out of the party to get them to combine with the Liberty Party.[5]

Adams and historian John Palfrey decided in early 1846 that the Conscience Whigs must establish their own Whig paper to give a voice to their views. In May 1846 they acquired the *Boston Whig* (or *Daily Whig*). Adams, who had received a large inheritance from his father-in-law, supplied 40 percent of the purchase price and became the editor. The paper remained in financial difficulty throughout Adams's tenure as editor from 1846 to February 1848. It received institutional support not from either the antislavery Liberty Party or the Whig Party but from individuals in both parties. Initially the editorial content of the paper was quite subdued but picked up as the battle with the Cotton Whigs escalated during 1846 as elections neared.[6]

The Texas question and the Mexican War gave the antislavery Whigs a chance to assert themselves. The Whig leadership wanted to appease the antislavery Whigs while suppressing antislavery excitement in Massachusetts. The antislavery sentiment increased in Massachusetts as the fights over Texas and Mexico took place in Congress. The Cotton Whigs were faced with the tough choice of either giving into the demands of the Conscience Whigs—and thereby splitting the party nationally—or driving them out of the Massachusetts Party.[7]

Fourteen Whigs voted against declaring war on Mexico in 1846—five of them were from Massachusetts. Only two senators voted against the war bill in the Senate—one of these was from Massachusetts. The Cotton Whig newspapers all opposed the war in Mexico. The Cotton Whigs wanted to appease the Conscience Whigs at the 1846 Whig convention for fear of driving them into the Liberty Party. At this time there were no substantive issues separating the two wings of the party as Texas was already part of the country and both opposed the war with Mexico. The Cotton Whigs dominated the Whig state convention of 1846, and their candidates were elected to office in November 1846. After the convention the Conscience Whigs turned their focus to national issues—the war. They wanted to deny Polk any support for the war effort. "No territory" became the official policy of the conservative Whigs, this later being modified to "no slave territory." This meant that any territory that the United States gained from the war should become free rather than slave territory.[8]

ZACHARY TAYLOR AND THE 1848 ELECTION

The early presidential speculation in the Whig Party in 1846–47 focused on Winfield Scott. Leading Senate Whigs declared Clay to be *hors de combat* (out of action). Suddenly, in February 1847, General Zachary Taylor won the Battle of Buena Vista after the national press had prepared the country for a disaster at the hands of Santa Anna. Overnight he became presidential material; no one knew if he was a Democrat or a Whig. (This was a similar situation to Eisenhower in 1948 or Colin Powell after the Gulf War.)

With the prospect of a major victory in Mexico, slavery was becoming a major national issue for the first time since 1820. The Whig Party was split between the Northern Whigs and Southern Whigs. Northern Whigs in New England and New York were opposed to the spread of slavery. Southern Whigs were opposed to any limitations on slavery. A Northern Whig from Pennsylvania, David Wilmot, had introduced a proposal in Congress known as the Wilmot Proviso prohibiting any territory acquired from Mexico to be slave territory. This became a litmus test for Conscience Whigs, even though it failed to pass in Congress.[9]

By the end of 1846 the dominant group of Cotton Whigs in Massachusetts had decided that Taylor rather than Clay or Webster should be the party's candidate for president in 1848. The victory at Buena Vista merely strengthened their conviction. But Webster was prepared to make another run at the presidency. The Conscience Whigs believed that this split among the Cotton Whigs gave them leverage. Webster supporters backed the Wilmot Proviso and Webster backed it in an attempt to win the support of the Conscience Whigs, which hurt him with the Southern delegates at the Whig convention in 1848.

Zachary Taylor was born in November 1784 in Virginia. His father, Colonel Richard Taylor, was a hero of the American Revolution who was given six thousand acres of land in Kentucky as a war bonus. The Taylor home was located six miles northeast of Louisville, Kentucky. Richard Taylor helped to write the state laws for the new state in 1792 and joined the legislature afterward. In May 1808 Zachary Taylor was commissioned a first lieutenant in a new infantry regiment, which was the beginning of a forty-year career in the military. In November 1810 he was promoted to captain. His older brother William was killed in an Indian attack while serving in the army one month after Zachary joined. Taylor had the misfortune to be away testifying at the trial of General James Wilkinson in New York City when Harrison attacked the Prophet at Tippecanoe. After briefly becoming a national hero for his defense of Fort Harrison in September 1812, he settled back into obscurity. It would be twenty-five years before he became famous again. Taylor resigned from the army briefly in disgust in 1815 when reductions briefly cost him his rank but returned in May 1816 after President Madison, a distant cousin, managed to have him reinstated as a major.[10]

Taylor spent most of his career on the frontier: in posts in Indiana, Illinois, Wisconsin, and along the Mississippi River; in Florida; and finally in Texas. Other than the two actions against Indians from the War of 1812 already mentioned, he fought two other battles against Indians. During the Black Hawk War of 1832 he commanded the Sixth Infantry Regiment, a command he assumed in May 1832 upon his promotion to colonel, as well as four hundred Illinois militiamen. He did a very bad job of commanding the militia, leading about half of his militia force to desert by July. He fought at the Battle of Bad Axe on August 3, 1832, although he arrived after Brigadier General James Henry had already basically won the battle. In the battle 150 Indians were killed, 50 surrendered, and up to 300 escaped. Taylor had spent the war in pursuit of Black Hawk. Scott, who had been ordered west by President Jackson at the outbreak of trouble in Illinois, spent the war transiting from New York to Illinois with a ship full of cholera-infected soldiers. He ended up missing out on the war completely. But he was put in charge of mustering out the Illinois militia and of signing a peace treaty with the Sauk and Fox. He put Black Hawk's rival, Keokuk, back in charge of the tribe.[11]

Taylor's next and last Indian battle came on December 25, 1837, when he fought the Battle of Lake Okeechobee against the Seminole in central Florida.

He led an assault on the enemy's main camp and had 48 killed and 192 wounded compared to Seminole losses of as few as 11 to 14 killed. The Indians had carefully prepared the battlefield ahead of time building rifle rests on tree trunks. The battle lasted 2.5 hours. Taylor made little effort to pursue the Indians once they left. He was later severely criticized by Senator Thomas Hart Benton for his conduct of the battle but was promoted to brigadier general after the battle nonetheless.[12]

Taylor was the senior officer commanding in Florida for three years from May 1837 to May 1840, after which he requested a transfer for health reasons. Taylor was no more productive or successful as a commander than were his predecessors—Thomas Jesup, Winfield Scott, and Walker Armistead. But his willingness to share the discomforts of his troops earned him the affection of his men and the nickname "Old Rough and Ready." Taylor developed the "squares plan" as a counterinsurgency concept that was similar to French concepts in the twentieth century in Indochina. He thought that the Floridians could contribute much more to their own defense than they had been willing to do. Because of sickness, only about 10 percent of his force was fit for duty at any one time.[13]

Taylor was sent to Texas to protect against invasion from Mexico in 1843, as the United States prepared to annex Texas, in command of an "army of observation." By September 1845 there were almost four thousand soldiers in Corpus Christi, Texas—about half of the regular American army. Taylor himself had spoken out against the annexation. In April 1846 he moved his army south to the Rio Grande frontier where it clashed with Mexican cavalry. In May 1846 two major battles ensued as Taylor moved to defend himself from attack in the disputed zone between the Nueces River and the Rio Grande. Texas claimed the Rio Grande as its southern border with Mexico, dating back to the treaty signed by Santa Anna after the Battle of San Jacinto, whereas Mexico recognized Nueces as being its northern border. Taylor used his artillery to defeat the Mexican cavalry and overnight became a new Andrew Jackson.

Polk wanted to win the war as quickly and cheaply as possible without, however, producing a new Whig president. When the war started, Polk offered the army's command to Scott but the latter was not expecting this and so had no campaign plan prepared. Scott wanted to train the one-year volunteers in the United States during the Mexican rainy season and then send them to Mexico in September. But Polk relieved Scott of the command in Mexico for writing a pair of letters that Polk considered treasonous when they were circulated by the recipients. Polk wanted to use military pressure along the Mexican border to force Mexico to sell California to the United States rather than conquer Mexico itself. Some twenty thousand volunteers arrived, mostly from the western and Southern states. Taylor sent home short-term units from Kentucky, Louisiana, and Missouri because they lacked equipment, discipline, and a taste for training. He also faced immense logistical problems. Polk made Taylor a brevet major general for Palo Alto and Reseca de la Palma on May 30, 1846. But Taylor played down talk of himself as a presidential candidate as long as the war continued.[14]

Scott was a known Whig, having campaigned for the Whig presidential nomination against Harrison in December 1839. But Taylor was an unknown quantity, not even having voted in his life before 1848. Polk felt comfortable putting Taylor in charge. Taylor set September 1 as the date for the beginning of the campaign to capture Monterrey in northern Mexico. He captured the city that month, although the defenders outnumbered his own forces. He signed a truce with the Mexican commander allowing him to withdraw his forces without pursuit.

When he did this, Taylor was not aware that Polk had just changed his war policy from one of military pressure to one of conquest. Washington then revoked the truce and ordered Taylor to pursue the enemy. Polk felt personally betrayed by Taylor, and this was the beginning of a personal feud between the two. Scott wrote to Taylor that Polk was attempting to build up a Democratic general as a presidential or vice-presidential candidate. By November 1846 Polk wanted to fire Taylor because he thought that he was not intelligent or experienced enough for the task; but because of Taylor's three military victories and the popularity that they had brought him, Polk could not fire Taylor for political reasons. Taylor captured Saltillo in mid-November and planned to prepare to march south toward Mexico City. But Washington ordered him not to move southward, as an amphibious expedition under Scott would land at Veracruz and march inland to capture Mexico City.[15]

Taylor was upset that about half of his regular troops and veteran volunteers were being taken from him and transferred to Scott's army. Taylor began to perceive Scott as being in league with Polk against him. If Polk could not immediately create a Democratic war hero, he had at least succeeded in pitting the two Whig generals against one another, hopefully weakening both to the point that neither would be a viable candidate in 1848. The Whigs took control of Congress in the 1846 election; and Taylor decided that if he was not allowed to play a major role in the war, he would resign and run for president in 1848 in order to have his revenge against Polk and the Democrats.[16]

At this point General Antonio Lopez de Santa Anna, who was in and out of power nearly a dozen times between 1833 and 1855 as either president or dictator, returned to the scene. Santa Anna was in exile in Cuba at the beginning of the Mexican War. He persuaded the American Navy to let him pass through the American blockade of Mexico by arguing that he could return to power and make peace with the United States. Upon arriving in Mexico City he returned to power and declared that he would drive the United States from Mexico. He started north with an army to attack Taylor at Saltillo and Buena Vista. En route to Taylor's position, across the open desert, Santa Anna lost some three thousand men to death or desertion. He had lost hundreds marching north to put down the Texas rebellion in 1836 and was completely indifferent to the fate of ordinary soldiers. In February 1847 he arrived at Buena Vista ranch and threatened Taylor with about twice as many men. In a single day's fighting Santa Anna lost about 20 percent of his army: 594 killed, 1,039 wounded, and 1,854 missing of whom some 321 had been taken prisoner. The hero of the battle was Taylor's former son-in-law, Jefferson Davis, a former congressman from Mississippi and former lieutenant under Taylor at Fort Crawford in Wisconsin. Davis formed a V formation with his own First Mississippi Rifles on one side and Colonel James Lane's Third Indiana Infantry on the other. Davis was wounded in the fighting but continued on.[17]

The press made much of Taylor's seeming miraculous victory. Taylor failed to pursue the retreating Mexican army but remained in place. This was Taylor's last major battle of the war. He continued to battle guerrillas who attacked his lines of supply, often in response to atrocities and crimes such as robbery, rape, and murder carried out by racist American troops. The Texas troops were notorious for their poor conduct in Mexico.

In March 1847 Scott landed at Veracruz on the east coast of Mexico and began to make his way inland as other units of volunteers arrived throughout the spring to join the expedition. Scott's army entered Mexico City on September 14, 1847. After a few weeks of fighting, the war was basically over. The American army remained in occupation both in Mexico City and in northern Mexico. Taylor was granted six months leave in late November 1847, although he remained in nominal command in Mexico. In July 1848 he took over the Western Division based in Louisiana. He remained in that position until he became president in March 1849. Scott, as opposed to Taylor, was so good at keeping his army discipline that he suffered from few guerrilla attacks against his lines of supply. In fact, after the war a group of Mexican notables offered to make Scott dictator of Mexico for six to eight years until the Mexicans could learn "peaceful habits." But Scott turned them down—after the Treaty of Guadalupe Hidalgo was signed in 1848.[18]

In what was intended as a campaign biography, author Henry Montgomery published in 1847 his *The Life of Major General Zachary Taylor*. This fictionalized the real Indian fighter by giving him a childhood on the frontier in which his home had to be barricaded against Indians and in which Indians threatened even his path to school. This continued the process begun by Crockett in 1834 and Hall in 1836 when real frontier figures were given a complete frontier life. The process reached its peak in 1852 with a campaign biography that linked Winfield Scott to Indian fighting, even though his entire experience of Indian fighting was in the Battle of Queenstown in which a few Indians fought on the British side. But Scott was being linked to Jackson, Harrison, and Taylor. Like Hollywood producers in the late twentieth century who kept producing sequels of a winning formula, campaign biographers stressed repetition of a winning formula. This demonstrates that much of politics is just another form of marketing.[19]

Taylor positioned himself as a nonpartisan candidate and refused to commit himself publicly on the Wilmot Proviso. As noted earlier, the Proviso was a litmus test for antislavery Northern Whigs and for Southern Whigs. To take a position on it either way would have risked alienating a major section of the party. Taylor owned a plantation in Louisiana and a home in Mississippi and had over a hundred slaves, making him one of the major slave-owners in the country. In the South his supporters claimed that as a slave-owner and Southerner he was more trustworthy than a Northerner, no matter what the latter's policy. In the North his supporters claimed that he offered a less proslavery policy than his Democratic opponent. Clay positioned himself as "a Southern man with Northern feelings." John Jordan Crittenden, the "king-maker" in the Whig Party, wrote Clay that he was unelectable. Crittenden had Taylor sign a statement that the former authored, declaring that he was a Whig "but not an ultra-Whig" and that "if elected, he would be the President of all the people, not simply the Whig President" and would be "independent of party domination."[20]

In June 1846 the first mass meeting in support of Taylor for president was held on the Trenton battlefield in New Jersey. Local Taylor or "Rough and Ready" clubs were formed in support of his candidacy. In December 1846 fourteen Whig congressmen known as the Young Indians formed a Taylor club. They included both Alexander Stephens of Georgia—the future Confederate vice president—and Abraham Lincoln. By March, fourteen Northern Whig congressmen had joined the club and Taylor had become the leading candidate. Most were Clay supporters who had decided that he was simply not electable. Clay's own equivocation and hesitation throughout the fall of 1847 did not help his candidacy. In May 1847 Taylor was endorsed by John Bell of Tennessee. The leading alternative candidates were Scott; Daniel Webster; and Justice John McLean of Ohio, who had been postmaster general under Jackson. One Taylor supporter simply concluded that he was their best chance to win and that they would lose with the other candidates. Even some Democrats wanted to nominate Taylor as their candidate.[21]

Taylor was one of the largest slave-owners in the country with some 150 slaves before the war, then 300 while he was president, which made him a problem for some antislavery Northern Whigs. At this time there were fewer than eighteen hundred planters throughout the country who owned more than a hundred slaves. Taylor declared that he would support whatever Congress decided regarding tariffs, internal improvements, and the currency. In other words, he had no interest in economics.

The three major candidates at the Whig national convention in Philadelphia in June were Scott, Taylor, and Clay; there were also three minor candidates: Thomas Clayton, John McLean, and Webster. Taylor led on the first ballot with 111 votes to 97 for Clay, 43 for Scott, and only

22 for Webster. Clay's support was concentrated in the East and Taylor's in the South. The Northern Whigs split their support among three different candidates. Taylor's New York manager, Thurston Weed, told younger delegates that Clay had all kinds of older supporters across the country that he would give his patronage to if elected. This caused Clay's younger delegates to begin to defect. His congressional supporters had gone throughout the state delegations telling them that Clay had no support in the deep South, while talking up Webster as an alternative to Scott among the New England delegates. The Southern Whigs were solid for Taylor, whereas the Northern Whigs were divided among Clay, Scott, and Webster. Scott's supporters began to quickly defect to both Taylor and Clay, and Webster lost his support after the second ballot. On the second ballot Taylor led with 118, to 86 for Clay, 49 for Scott, 22 for Webster, and 4 for Clayton. The third ballot was: Taylor 133, Clay 74, Scott 54, Webster 17, and Clayton 1. Taylor won on the fourth ballot when New England abandoned Webster and Scott and went for him. The nomination had been made by "gunpowder popularity." Clay ended up with fewer votes than Scott did. Clay sulked, "I fear that the Whig Party is dissolved"; but many considered him to be the party's chief problem. In the final tally Taylor had a clear majority with 171 to 63 for Scott and 35 for Clay, while Webster held on to his loyal supporters—13; Taylor had the nomination.[22]

The convention easily elected Pennsylvania native Millard Fillmore as the vice-presidential candidate to give the ticket geographic balance. Clay's support at the convention was from districts that were solidly Whig, whereas Taylor had support from areas that were either marginal or Democratic. For these delegates Taylor was the best prospect to win the Democratic defectors that the Whigs needed to win in November. The Whigs needed a "brave old soldier" to win, and Taylor won the nomination because he was politically more astute than was "Old Fuss and Feathers" Scott, who had little appeal as a populist.[23]

Opposing him on the Democratic ticket were Lewis Cass, who had fought at the Battle of the Thames in October 1813, and General Benjamin O. Butler, who had fought in the War of 1812 and in the Mexican War. The Democrats needed a war hero to run against Taylor and one who could carry the North. So they nominated Cass with Butler to give the ticket two war heroes. Cass led from the very first ballot at the Democratic convention in Baltimore in May 1848. James Buchanan of Pennsylvania and Levi Woodbury of New Hampshire were his only competition. He secured the nomination on the fourth ballot.[24]

Cass's father was a career military officer who retired from the army in 1800 to farm and moved to Ohio. Cass, not wanting to be a farmer, passed the bar, opened a law practice, and was elected to the Ohio legislature in 1806. He became a colonel of Ohio volunteers in 1812 and served with General William Hull at Detroit. Exchanged after the surrender, Cass testified against Hull at the latter's court martial. Cass then became a colonel in the regular army and was eventually promoted to brigadier general before the war ended. Harrison left Cass in charge of the northwest as provisional governor with a thousand men to defend Detroit when he departed for Buffalo following the Battle of the Thames.

From 1815 to 1831 Cass served as territorial governor of Michigan. He also served as secretary of war for Jackson for six years and had been in charge during the Black Hawk War, before becoming ambassador to France in late 1836. Jackson's regard for Cass was so high that he kept a bust of him at the Hermitage. Cass returned to New York from France in December 1842. In May 1844 he was a candidate for the Democratic nomination at the convention in Baltimore. With the two-thirds rule in effect, he failed to win the nomination, but he was ahead of Van Buren on the fifth ballot, 107 to 103. Polk became the dark-horse candidate, and Cass bowed out in order to preserve his chances of winning in 1848. In 1848 he was a senator from Michigan. He, like John Quincy Adams, had much better qualifications for the presidency.[25]

Webster gave Taylor a very tepid and halfhearted endorsement in September 1848; Clay declined to endorse Taylor and did not even vote for him as he was sick on election day. But all the pro-Webster press in Massachusetts endorsed Taylor. Taylor, like Jackson, refused to campaign, only making appearances in the two states in which he owned homes. Southern Whigs said that a Southern slave-owner like Taylor was trustworthier on slavery than a Northerner like Cass. Democrats made the mirror reverse of this argument in the North. It was the beginning of the country splitting along sectional rather than partisan lines.

Whigs had to capture at least two of the three largest states in 1848. In the end the race came down to a single state—Pennsylvania, Fillmore's home state. Cass lost the state because of the Walker tariff, which was popular with voters in the state but was opposed by the Democrats. Cass favored "popular sovereignty," a term later made famous by Stephen Douglas of Illinois, as a solution to slavery. Between the 1844 and 1848 elections four states shifted from the Democrats to the Whigs: Georgia, Louisiana, New York, and Pennsylvania. Ohio moved in the opposite direction. On election day, Taylor carried eight slave and seven free states and Cass won in fourteen states in the West and South including Virginia, Alabama, and Mississippi. Cass lost the popular vote by only 138,625 votes. Taylor won in the electoral college 163 to 127, figures that would have been reversed had he lost in New York. In Illinois and Wisconsin, if the Black Hawk War was even a factor in 1848, Secretary of War Cass was given more credit than Colonel Taylor was for the victory.[26]

THE FREE SOIL PARTY

Charles Adams had been thinking of a split from the Whig Party since 1844 when he organized the Texas Committee. But the time never seemed right. The Conscience Whigs had become steadily less loyal to their party over time. They opposed the election of Congressman Robert Winthrop of

Massachusetts, a Whig, as speaker of the House in 1847 because he refused to commit himself to the Wilmot Proviso. Adams wrote to Palfrey, "I think the election of Winthrop means the victory of the Slavepower among the Whigs, the granting of supplies, the smothering of the Wilmot Proviso . . . Of course, if such be the result, those of us who will not subscribe to these terms must prepare the way for a separation from the Whig Party." Ironically, John Quincy Adams provided the one-vote margin for Winthrop's victory in order to pay back an old debt of honor to Winthrop's father. In 1847 the Van Buren wing of the New York Democratic Party, "the Barnburners," adopted the Wilmot Proviso as part of its program. The Barnburners boycotted the polls in 1847, and the Whigs swept the state. This gave the Conscience Whigs a possible partner if they decided to bolt the Whig Party. In February 1848 Charles Sumner, one of the Conscience Whig leaders, was ready to bolt the Whig Party.[27]

In March 1848 the Massachusetts Whig Party chose delegates to the June national Whig convention. Individual districts chose two Conscience Whigs, although the faction as a whole had been banned from participation. By this time the Cotton Whigs were no longer afraid of a split in the state party. Webster promised the Conscience Whigs that come what may, he would not support Taylor for president. The battle for the nomination was among Clay, Taylor, Scott, and Webster—all of the party's heavyweights. Neither Scott nor Webster had any real chance of winning the nomination. Before the convention the Conscience Whigs had met at Adams's office in Boston and decided to bolt the party if a Southern slave-owner was nominated as presidential candidate. This decision applied to both Clay and Taylor, the only realistic candidates.[28]

Conscience Whig delegate Charles Allen told the convention: "I declare to this convention my belief that the Whig Party is here and this day dissolved." He was premature by about eight years in his prediction. Henry Wilson declared: "But the convention have [sic] seen fit to nominate a man who is anything but a Whig. And sir, I will go home, and, so help me God, I will do all I can to defeat the election of that candidate."[29]

Antislavery Whigs held a meeting in Philadelphia, the site of the convention, following the convention. On June 9 Adams sent a letter to all Conscience Whigs inviting them to a meeting in Worcester, Massachusetts, on June 28 to organize a national convention in Buffalo in August. On June 28, 1848, some seven thousand anti-Taylor Whigs, mostly Conscience Whigs, assembled at Worcester, Massachusetts, to decide on a course of action. The group was led by Charles Francis Adams, son of John Quincy; by Senator Charles Sumner; and by Charles Allen. The group adopted the principles of the pro–Van Buren "Barnburner" meeting in Utica, New York, and the slogan "free soil, free labor and free men."[30]

This was the beginning of the Free Soil Party, the first major antislavery party. The party was formed in August in Buffalo where Adams was chosen president of the antislavery convention. There were ten thousand people attending the three-day convention from four basic groups:

- Massachusetts Conscience Whigs;
- New York Barnburner Democrats;
- Ohio Whigs and Democrats opposed to slavery; and
- Liberty Party members.

There were only two candidates for the presidential nomination: former President Martin Van Buren, the "Silver Fox"; and John P. Hale of New Hampshire, the leader of the Liberty Party. The Whigs decided the nomination by voting for Van Buren, who won 244 to 88. Ohio nominated Adams for vice president. Adams proposed a Western candidate, but Ohio insisted upon his nomination. Adams personally voted for Joshua Giddings, thereby alienating neither major faction. Adams did not like Van Buren and did not campaign with him.[31]

The common wisdom among historians is that at the convention, "the dissident Democrats got the presidential nomination, the Conscience Whigs got the vice presidency, and the Liberty Party got the platform." But according to Garrison biographer Henry Mayer, "Liberty Party ideas did not register much in this platform." The new party promised not to interfere with slavery where it already existed but was still tepidly welcomed by Garrison and the purist abolitionists.[32]

In the election Free Soilers took Northern votes away from both parties' candidates and was not decisive in determining the election although it did increase Taylor's margin. Van Buren won 10 percent of the popular vote, compared to 2 percent for the Liberty Party in 1844, but no electoral votes. In seven Northern states the Free Soil total exceeded the margin by which the state was won, and Van Buren outpolled Cass in a couple of states including New York. The party also elected nine congressmen, which gave it a pivotal role in a Congress divided by only three votes. Lincoln stumped New England in September 1848 on behalf of Taylor arguing that "a vote for Van Buren, is a vote for Cass." Earlier Lincoln had argued that "Mr. Clay's chance for an election is just no chance at all."[33]

Taylor died suddenly of gastroenteritis on July 9, 1850, after less than sixteen months in office. Neither Clay nor Webster had wanted to serve in a Taylor cabinet, and Taylor's friend wanted to serve as governor of Kentucky. President Polk had only negotiated a treaty with Mexico before Taylor was elected. This left the issue of whether or not the new territories would permit slavery. Every Northern Whig congressman had supported the Wilmot Proviso, and the Southerners were dead set against it. Clay spent his remaining strength crafting a compromise proposal, the Compromise of 1850, that combined a prohibition of slavery in the new territories and an end to the slave trade in the District of Columbia with a strengthening of the fugitive slave measures. It also settled the border dispute between Texas and the New Mexico Territory and had the federal government assume the debt of Texas. Because Taylor was jealous of Clay's role in Congress, he opposed the Compromise and it was defeated as an omnibus bill. Taylor threatened to send federal troops to deal with the border dispute after Texas threatened to invade New Mexico. But after Taylor's death, Douglas helped to shepherd a series of separate bills that encompassed the Compromise through the Senate. Millard Fillmore, a Clay supporter from Buffalo, New York, was made president. Webster returned after a seven-year absence to become secretary of state. And the Fillmore administration became a real Whig administration.[34]

WINFIELD SCOTT, FRANKLIN PIERCE, AND THE 1852 ELECTION

Winfield Scott rose to high rank and prominence in the army at a young age. He joined the army in 1808, the same year as Taylor, after graduating from college. He was captured in the Battle of Queenstown in October 1812, already a lieutenant colonel. He was exchanged and by 1814 had risen to the rank of brigadier general when he was involved in two major battles, Lundy's Lane and the Battle of Chippewa. He was the favorite officer of Major General Jacob Brown, who invaded Canada in July 1814. Chippewa was a major American victory over British regulars—the first in the war. At Lundy's Lane Scott was wounded in the shoulder with a musket ball ending both the battle and the war for him. Although the battle was a draw, his wounding while directing his troops under fire made him a popular war hero. It also won him command of the Tenth Military District, consisting of Maryland and northern Virginia. There was even talk of making him secretary of war, although he discouraged it himself.[35]

With Jackson's victory over the British at New Orleans, the public had a new war hero. Jackson became the "undisputed darling of the American people." Scott was left to pursue a professional military career and a lifelong rivalry with Edmund Gaines, who had successfully commanded Fort Erie during a British siege in August 1814 that cost the British more men than at Lundy's Lane. The two officers had parallel careers and promotions until Gaines finally died in 1841, leaving Scott undisputably in charge as commander of the army. Scott had been involved in a military board that reorganized the army in the spring of 1815, leaving it with two major generals, Jackson and Brown, and four brigadiers brevetted to major general. Scott and Gaines were two of the four. Scott was challenged to a duel by Jackson because of a remark by Scott in a private conversation that Jackson had been mutinous; the remark had been overheard by a reporter and passed on to Jackson. Scott sensibly declined the challenge and patched up his feud with Jackson while visiting Washington in December 1823 while Jackson was a senator.[36]

Unlike Taylor, Scott was a professional interested in his own military development as a tactician. During the War of 1812 he carried with him a French manual on tactics from the Napoleonic wars. Scott missed out on command in the Black Hawk War because of a cholera outbreak on the ship carrying him and his troops to the war theater. But he arrived in Columbia, South Carolina, on January 31, 1836, to take command of the troops for an invasion of Seminole territory in Florida in March. Scott left Florida only two months later under orders to deal with a Creek uprising in Georgia and Alabama. Brevet Major General Thomas Jesup attacked the Creek rebels in June 1836 and captured the rebel chief and six hundred of his men. A court of inquiry tried Scott, who had failed to encounter any concentration of Seminole to attack, for his conduct of the Seminole and Creek wars. He was acquitted. Scott requested reassignment to Florida, but the war department turned him down so as to avoid friction between him and Jesup.[37]

In 1838 Scott was involved in supervising the removal of the Cherokee from Alabama, Georgia, North Carolina, and Tennessee. Scott divided the Cherokee territory into three sectors and arranged to march the Indians to rivers and move them by flatboat to the West. He had three thousand troops under him to carry out the move. Scott issued an order to his troops calling on them to carry out the removal in a humane manner, but local militia who hated the Indians and coveted their lands carried out most of the removal. Scott escorted one of the first groups to proceed west as an observer. He was recalled to Nashville in late October and then ordered to proceed to Canada to negotiate another border dispute with the British. In 1841 Alexander Macomb died and Scott was made general in chief of the army.[38]

Scott's role in the Mexican War has already been discussed sufficiently—suffice it to say that he was the commanding general that ended the war by capturing Mexico City. In early 1855 he was promoted to lieutenant general retroactive to March 29, 1847, when he had accepted the surrender of Veracruz and begun his campaign in Mexico.[39] This is now a good point to review the career of one of Scott's subordinate generals in Mexico and his rival in the 1852 campaign.

Franklin Pierce was born in a log cabin in New Hampshire in 1804 but soon moved to much better accommodations. His father was a veteran of the Revolution and Franklin had two brothers and a brother-in-law who fought in the War of 1812. Pierce attended Bowdoin College in Maine, where he became friends with future novelist Nathaniel Hawthorne. Pierce was not a very diligent student. He was admitted to the bar in 1827 after studying with a family friend. Pierce was elected to the state legislature in the late 1820s while his father was governor. In 1831 Franklin Pierce was elected speaker of the state house of representatives at the age of twenty-six. The following year he was elected to Congress. He was elected to the Senate in 1837. Pierce had been a strong supporter of states' rights since his youth and he despised Northern Whigs as hypocrites. A close friend of his, Democratic Senator Cilley of Maine, had been killed in a duel in 1838 for which Pierce blamed the Whigs. He retired from the Senate in 1842, after less than a full term, because his wife disliked Washington.[40]

Pierce had formed a law partnership with Asa Fowler in Concord in 1838. Upon returning to Concord in 1842 he devoted himself to his law practice and to the state Democratic Party. He became chairman of the State Central Committee of the Democratic Party that year. He also gave up drinking, which he had engaged in heavily since his student days, and joined the temperance society. Pierce campaigned vigorously on behalf of Polk and the Democratic ticket in 1844. For carrying the state for Polk he was rewarded the following year with an appointment as federal district attorney for New Hampshire. The year after that Polk offered him a cabinet post as attorney general, but Pierce declined. Pierce was quite content to remain in New Hampshire and practice law. At this time the leading Democrat from the state was Senator Levi Woodbury.[41]

When the army was expanded in February 1847 in preparation for Scott's landing in Veracruz, Pierce was made a colonel of volunteers and then soon promoted to brigadier general and made a brigade commander. As Pierce had no military experience, except for a militia command in which he did little, it was a purely political appointment.

Pierce's unit sailed from Boston to Veracruz on May 27, 1847. It arrived in the Mexican port a month later and did not leave the city until July 12. The brigade experienced its first combat on July 19. The unit reached Puebla on August 6. He was thrown off of his horse during a charge at San Agustin and suffered a wrenched knee and a groin injury. Pierce insisted on leading his brigade in the attack but injured his knee and fell unconscious; and as a result of being left leaderless, his unit failed to take its objective. Pierce fought in the capture of Molina del Rey but did nothing heroic. He was sick in bed with dysentery during the Battle of Chapultepec in September 1847. He dragged himself from his sick bed to participate in the final assault, but the Mexicans surrendered first and deprived him of his chance for glory. He returned to the United States on December 28, 1847, after a seven-month absence. But while in Mexico he made important friends in the army who helped his political career later on.[42]

Pierce returned to his legal practice and to local politics. In 1848 he did not even attend the Democratic national convention, as he was busy with legal cases and not terribly interested in national politics. Woodbury died in 1851, which made Pierce the favorite presidential hopeful of Democrats in New Hampshire. The Democrats searched desperately for a presidential candidate in 1852 who would be able to beat either President Millard Fillmore or General Scott. Four main candidates were discussed: General

William O. Butler of Kentucky, who had been a general in Mexico and had also fought in the War of 1812; James Buchanan, a professional politician and diplomat from Pennsylvania; Stephen A. Douglas of Illinois, "the little giant" and a master orator in the Senate; and William Marcy of New York. Butler dropped out of nomination contention in March. Prior to this a group of Democratic Mexican War generals, led by Caleb Cushing and Gideon Pillow, had gotten together to choose a candidate with Mexican War experience to run against Scott. They decided upon Pierce and found support for this choice in Washington. New Hampshire nominated him as a favorite-son candidate in January 1852.[43]

At the Democratic national convention in Baltimore in June 1852, Cass was the favorite to be the nominee. He led on the first ballot, with Buchanan in second, Marcy a distant third, and Stephen Douglas close behind Marcy. Cass had been on the Senate committee that crafted the compromise resolutions in 1850, and this more than made up for his loss in 1848. Cass remained the leading candidate through forty-eight ballots that lasted for five days. By this time it had become evident to the delegates that they needed to select a compromise choice that was not one of the four candidates. They chose Pierce and he won as a "dark horse" on the forty-ninth ballot. Pierce had appeal as "a Northerner with Southern sympathies." He was considered a moderate who had campaigned on behalf of the 1850 Compromise after it was passed. Pierce said that the Fugitive Slave Law was wrong but insisted that it be strictly enforced. When questioned about this contradiction he claimed that he had been misquoted but declined to indicate on which part, leaving both sides to believe that the contradiction that they disapproved of was a result of the misquote.[44]

Among the Whigs there were three serious candidates. Clay finally decided not to run because of his advanced age—which is just as well as he ended up dying in June 1852. He would have been too sick to attend the convention. Webster decided that this was his last chance to be elected president and ran. Scott believed that it was his turn, as he was the only surviving Whig general. And Millard Fillmore believed that he should be nominated because he was the incumbent president. By the end of 1851 Fillmore and Webster were the only presidential candidates seriously considered by Southern Whigs. Webster's role in reaching the 1850 Compromise was appreciated by Southerners, and Fillmore was considered sound. But many Southern Whigs revered Scott's military achievements and referred to him as "Old Chippewa" or "Old Chapultepec" to commemorate his two great victories. Scott's supporters wanted a candidate who had taken no public position on the 1850 Compromise and thus could appeal to as many people as possible and win Democratic support. They believed that the North held the key to victory in 1852 and that it could be won only by winning support from Democrats. Webster was anathema to most Northern Whigs—as insufficiently sound on slavery—and not considered seriously by most Southern Whigs.[45]

The 1852 Whig convention was the most rancorous in the party's history. Fillmore and Webster could have controlled the convention if they had worked together; but Fillmore was too proud to ask for Webster's assistance to beat Scott, and Webster was too proud to offer it without being asked. The Scott men dominated in nine state conventions—all in Northern states—and California was divided but leaned toward Scott. Fillmore dominated fourteen slave states and Iowa. Webster controlled only New Hampshire and Massachusetts—the two states that he had lived in. Another three New England states were split between Webster and Fillmore. At the end of the first ballot the tally was: Fillmore 133, Scott 131, and Webster 29. The first two were both within reach of the nomination if they could attract enough delegates away from Webster. Webster despised Scott as another general without political experience like Taylor. Webster refused to meet with Fillmore out of pride and resentment—he thought that the nomination should have been his by right. Both men were ready to withdraw and support the other, but their delegates would not necessarily have obeyed them. Finally, on the fifty-third ballot, Scott won with 157 votes to 114 for Fillmore and 21 for Webster. Webster had majority support only in the two New England states and in Wisconsin. William Graham of North Carolina, Fillmore's secretary of the Navy, was chosen as vice president.[46]

The 1852 campaign focused on the personalities of the candidates more than any election had since 1836. Northern Whigs were disgusted with a party platform that failed to make a clear antislavery stand. Many of them voted for the Free Soil Party in November or stayed home. Former Governor John Quitman of Mississippi nearly endorsed Scott for president. Webster refused to endorse Scott. Webster died on October 25, 1852. Although Scott won a record number of votes for a Whig candidate, he won only 44 percent of the popular vote compared to 50.9 percent of the vote for Pierce. The latter won with over a 200,000-vote margin, 1.6 million to 1.39 million. Scott managed to carry only four states: Kentucky, Tennessee, Massachusetts, and Vermont, although he did come close in Delaware, Louisiana, and North Carolina. The first two states had been solidly Whig for two decades in presidential elections, and the other two were areas of strong antislavery sentiment. Pierce won on the basis of new Democratic voters—he was able to attract more first-time voters than was Scott. Most of these new voters were in the major cities of the Atlantic coast that were controlled by Democratic party machines.[47]

Scott was the last presidential candidate to run solely on the Whig ticket. Before Scott, the Whigs had only been able to win the presidency with a famous general as candidate. Now they were unable to win even with one. Four years later Millard Fillmore ran as a joint candidate of the Whig Party and the Know-Nothings.

Whig internal differences widened after 1848 as interparty differences lessened. Through 1848 most politicians in the two main parties were motivated more by party loyalty than by sectionalism. After 1850 politicians became increasingly motivated by sectional loyalties as the Southern states' rights supporters moved increasingly to reject any limits on slavery. After the death of John C. Calhoun in 1850, the new leader of the "fire-eaters" was Jefferson Davis.

The next major turning point was the Kansas-Nebraska Act of 1854 introduced by Davis's main opponent for leadership of the Democratic Party in the Senate—Stephen A. Douglas. Douglas was the chairman of the Senate Committee on Territories that was in charge of shepherding new territories into the United States and taking them through the process to statehood. Douglas was a bit of a demagogue, a great orator who appealed to men's baser instincts rather than to their finer ones. In 1850 he had declared that the Missouri Compromise of 1820, which put a Northern limit on slave territory, was "canonized in the hearts of the American people" and that "no ruthless hand would ever be reckless enough to disturb it." Douglas provided the hand himself four years later. In January 1854 he introduced the concept of "popular sovereignty" and proposed that the inhabitants of any territory vote as to whether that territory be free or slave, regardless of the limitations of the Missouri Compromise. Pierce signed the Kansas-Nebraska Act into law on May 30, 1854, enshrining "popular sovereignty" into law. Pierce was a weak president who had no ideas of his own on how to solve the slavery crisis and keep the country together—so he grabbed at those of Douglas, who had become the real leader in the Senate following the deaths of Calhoun, Clay, and Webster. Pierce had also always regarded the Missouri Compromise as unconstitutional because it limited some states' right to own slaves. His acting vice president, Senator David Atchison of Missouri, wanted the Missouri Compromise repealed. The Pierce Administration had gone all out in favor of the bill, pressuring congressmen and postponing eighteen bills that stood ahead of it for a hearing.[48]

The law had two immediate effects. First, it tore apart the Whig Party as Northern antislavery Whigs got together with Free Soilers and Democrats to form the Republican Party. The Whigs had only half as many congressmen as the Democrats following the 1854 election, and in the Senate the Democrats had thirty-seven senators to twenty-two for the Whigs and two Free Soilers. Second, it turned Kansas into a battleground as the state was flooded by committed abolitionists from New England and Ohio and proslavery Missourians. In Kansas there were two competing state legislatures based in Lecompton and Topeka and each vied for recognition by the federal government as the legitimate government of the territory. The state became "bleeding Kansas" in 1855 and 1856 as proslavers raided Lawrence and John Brown carried out the Pottawatamie Creek massacre on May 24, 1856. Two days before this Congressman Preston Brooks beat Charles Sumner severely on the floor of the Senate over a perceived insult to his uncle. Pierce was suspected by both Northerners and Southerners of favoring the other side in Kansas.[49]

The Whig Party began to split apart in the 1850s, due not only to the different electoral and economic interests of its two geographic wings but also to the social differences. The Southern Whigs consisted not only of planters like Taylor but also of the professional class of bankers, doctors, small businessmen, and lawyers who supported the planters. This is similar to the business wing of the Republican Party or the lawyers who support the Democratic Party. The Northern Whigs were more based on the church-going, Protestant middle class who were vulnerable to appeals from prohibition, antislavery, and nativist parties, much more so than were the Democrats. They are comparable to the Christian wing of the Republican Party today. Conservative Whigs could defect to either the Democrats or the Know-Nothings, who had exploded in popularity in 1853 and 1854 taking over the state governments of Pennsylvania and New York. The more antislavery Whigs joined the Republican Party. By 1854 the Northern Whig Party was decimated and had lost much of its electorate.

The Whig Party elected 117 congressmen in 1854–55, its best total since 1846–47, but many of these Whigs soon left to join other parties. The Know-Nothings gained power by secretly infiltrating other parties and then defecting after obtaining positions of power. In 1856 there were four major parties: the Democrats, the Republicans, the Know-Nothings, and the Whigs. In the North the Whigs were split into pro- and anti- Know-Nothing factions. The remaining Whig leadership in 1856 decided not to hold a national convention but to wait until the other three parties had held their conventions and then see what to do. Fillmore was nominated by the Know-Nothing Party along with Jackson's nephew, Andrew Jackson Donelson. A rump Whig convention of 144 delegates, almost half from New York, nominated the Know-Nothing ticket. So it now became the common ticket of two parties or one-and-a-half.[50]

Pierce began focusing on foreign affairs in 1854 as a diversion from his domestic woes. In addition to the division within the country, his young son had been killed in a train crash in January 1853. His wife blamed him for the crash: she saw the death as God's price for her husband's election. She became withdrawn.

Pierce appointed Buchanan as ambassador to England in order both to rid himself of a potential opponent and to have a skilled diplomat in a key foreign capital. Pierce carried out an expansionist policy in both the Caribbean and the Pacific. He authorized the acquisition of the Gadsden Purchase in southern Arizona and New Mexico from Mexico for $15 million. But the Senate reduced the price to $10 million so Mexico had to settle for that. This was after a failed filibustering expedition by William Walker to Sonora, Mexico, made the Mexicans see that maybe they would be better off selling the area. Secretary of State William Marcy attempted to buy Cuba from Spain and Alaska from Russia. Pierce's expansionist policy met opposition from both Europe and Congress. Britain and France united to oppose

American policy in Central America, and Congress refused to authorize the money to buy Cuba. This was tied up with the slavery question as the South wanted Cuba as a new slave territory. Pierce tried to raise the money for the Cuban purchase from European loans, but Spain canceled the sale once word had leaked out; Spain feared it made her look weak. Britain and France opposed the annexation of Hawaii, so the treaty was sent back to Hawaii for revision to make it acceptable to the European powers. The king who approved it died, and his successor opposed annexation.[51]

JEFFERSON DAVIS

Pierce named another Mexican War veteran, Jefferson Davis, as his secretary of war in 1853. Pierce wanted to have a sectionally balanced cabinet with three Northerners and three Southerners. To balance William Marcy of New York in the senior cabinet position as secretary of state, he needed a prominent Southerner as secretary of war. Davis as a former West Point graduate and Southern Senate leader fit the bill.

Davis graduated from West Point in 1828. He spent his entire military service after graduation serving in two frontier posts in Wisconsin, then part of Michigan Territory: Fort Crawford outside Prairie du Chien on the Mississippi River, and Fort Winnebago located between the Wisconsin and Fox Rivers. Lieutenant Davis served as Zachary Taylor's personal aide during 1832. Davis was on leave in Mississippi when the Black Hawk War broke out in April 1832. Davis returned to his unit sometime in July, although official records indicate later because he reported to it in the field rather than returning to Fort Crawford to sign back in. He was in time to participate in the Battle of Wisconsin Heights on July 21, 1832, and in the final battle at Bad Axe on August 3. After the war he escorted the defeated Black Hawk to prison in Saint Louis. Davis sympathized with his captive and considered him to be a skilled commander.[52]

Davis fell in love with Taylor's young daughter. Taylor forbade them to marry, as he did not want his daughter to marry an officer, as he knew first hand what hardships the lifestyle imposed on family life. Davis left with the daughter and married her at a relative's plantation near Louisville in June 1835. He then resigned his commission effective from the end of the month. She died of malaria in September on Davis's plantation in Mississippi. Davis then became a planter and made himself busy improving his plantation and working in local affairs.

Davis ran for the Mississippi state legislature in the fall of 1843 at age thirty-five as a Democrat. He lost but soon became a Democratic star in Mississippi. Davis never held any state offices in Mississippi. He was a delegate to the Democratic state convention in Mississippi in 1844. He was a strong supporter of John Calhoun and was opposed to repudiation of state debts. Davis remarried in February 1845. The day before his second wedding he reconciled with Taylor during a chance meeting aboard a steamboat. Davis was sworn into Congress in December 1845 at age thirty-seven.[53]

There is no record that Davis ever ran on the basis of his participation in the Black Hawk War. His status as a former army officer was well known and in the South would have been considered an asset. But Davis was primarily respected and elected because of his political skills: his intellect, speaking ability, and defense of states' rights. Sam Houston had wanted Davis as his secretary of war in Texas. They had met in a store in Arkansas in 1834 when Houston was returning to Texas. Davis spoke out against war with Britain over Mexico in his first major congressional speech on February 6, 1846, but said that the United States should be prepared to go to war with Mexico over Texas if necessary. Adams remarked after hearing the speech, "That young man, gentlemen, is no ordinary man. Mind me, he will make his mark yet. He will go far."[54]

Davis resigned from Congress in June 1846 to command the Mississippi Rifles Regiment (also known as the First Mississippi Rifles) as a colonel under Taylor in Mexico. The regiment was equipped with a brand new type of rifle from the armory at New Haven, Connecticut. Polk might have offered Davis a general's commission, but Davis wanted to command the regiment. The Mississippi Rifles Regiment was considered to be the best volunteer unit in Taylor's army.

Davis took a fort at Monterrey by assault and began to establish a reputation for himself. At the Battle of Buena Vista, Davis was wounded in the heel but remained in action. Henry Clay's son, a lieutenant colonel, was killed in the battle. Davis returned to Mississippi, leaving Mexico on May 29, 1847, when the one-year enlistment of the unit expired. Polk offered Davis a commission as a brigadier general of volunteers, but Davis declined on the ground that the president did not have the constitutional authority to appoint volunteer officers. Because of his fervent belief in states' rights, this should be accepted as the true reason rather than as an excuse by someone who was tired of the war and absence from home. Taylor, however, suspected Polk of trying to keep Davis out of the Senate.[55]

In August 1847 Governor Brown of Mississippi nominated Davis to fill a vacancy in the U.S. Senate caused by the death of General Jesse Speight. Davis took the Senate oath on December 6, 1847, while still on crutches recovering from his wound received at Buena Vista. Davis was appointed to the Senate Committee on Military Affairs because of his military background. Davis voted and campaigned for Cass as a loyal Democrat but was happy when Taylor was elected president. In this he set a precedent for Senator Thomas Hart Benton when his son-in-law ran for president on another party's ticket eight years later. Davis was one of three people put in charge of the arrangements for the national inauguration ball in 1849, showing his prestige within Washington.[56]

In December 1849 Davis was voted chairman of the Military Affairs Committee. This was the same month that Henry Clay returned to the Senate after a seven-year absence. With the deaths of Calhoun in 1850 and Clay and Webster in 1852, Davis soon became an influential leader in the Senate inheriting Calhoun's camp of Southern Democrats. Davis was elected to a full six-year term in December 1850. But the following year he was persuaded to quit the Senate and run for governor of Mississippi when Unionist Henry Foote looked likely to beat John A. Quitman, Davis's former brigade commander in Mexico. Davis ended up losing the race to Foote. But Davis was quite content to run his plantation until he could be reelected to the Senate.[57]

Pierce had to beg Davis to accept the position of secretary of war in his cabinet. Davis was one of the more innovative secretaries of war of the nineteenth century as he modernized the army. He introduced slightly more modern light infantry tactics based on the Mexican experience; rifled muskets—like those used by his own unit in Mexico; and the Minie ball, a conical bullet invented by a Frenchman, which was to prove deadly during the Civil War. Davis got along very poorly with the commander of the army, General Scott, possibly because of their different partisan affiliations. Davis was an enemy of Scott—the latter was probably his greatest personal enemy—and opposed him at every turn as secretary of war. This later benefited Scott in 1860–61 by making him appear that much more loyal to the Union to have been such an enemy of Davis. But by then Scott's military career was virtually over. Davis also played an important role within the cabinet and as a personal friend of Pierce. Davis recommended to Pierce sending James Gadsden of South Carolina to negotiate with Santa Anna for the purchase of territory lying south of the Gila River. This then became known as the Gadsden Purchase.[58]

John Quitman was himself a Mexican fighter with a fascinating career. He was born in New York in 1798, the son of a Lutheran minister. He was educated by his father for the ministry and briefly taught English at a college in Pennsylvania in 1818. After discovering that he had no wish to be a minister, he moved to Ohio where he studied law. In 1821 he was elected a lieutenant in the local militia and admitted to the bar. He then moved to Natchez, Mississippi, where he established his own law practice. In 1827 he was elected to the state legislature and in 1834 to the state senate. He became president of the state senate on December 3, 1835, and because of a quirk in state law served as temporary governor for a month.

In April 1836, having already lost a race for Congress, he organized a "company" of volunteers (seventeen men—half a platoon) and crossed the Sabine River and marched into Nacogdoches, Texas. Initially they volunteered to protect the town; but discovering that there was no immediate threat, they marched to meet up with Houston. They failed to meet up with Houston until two days after the battle of San Jacinto. Houston offered to make Quitman the presiding judge in a trial of Santa Anna, but Quitman convinced him to allow the general to return to Mexico. Two weeks later Quitman returned with his volunteers to Natchez, the expedition and some aid given to refugees in East Texas having cost him ten thousand dollars—a small fortune at the time.

Quitman spent the next decade practicing law. He spoke out in favor of the annexation of Texas in 1844. Upon returning to Natchez, Quitman had been appointed a brigadier general in the militia. On July 1, 1846, he was commissioned a brigadier general of volunteers in Taylor's army. Quitman served first in Taylor's campaign and was brevetted to major general in late September for his role in the Battle of Monterrey. In April 1847 he was given a regular promotion to major general and he switched to Scott's army. He fought at both Veracruz and Puebla and then led the assault on Chapultepec. After the fall of Mexico City, he was appointed governor during the American occupation. On July 20, 1848, he was discharged from the army. That year he was a strong candidate for the vice-presidential nomination at the Democratic convention in Baltimore but lost it to General Butler.

A strong advocate of states' rights and nullification, Quitman was elected governor in 1849. As an advocate of annexation of Cuba, Quitman entertained revolutionary leader Narciso Lopez in Jackson in 1850 and turned down his offer to lead his filibusterers' army. But a federal court indicted him for violating neutrality laws in favor of the insurrectionists and he was forced to resign as governor in 1851. The charge was finally dropped and Quitman ran and was elected to Congress in March 1855. Reelected in 1857, he fell ill and died at his plantation in July 1858.[59]

Filibustering was all the rage in the South in the 1850s and appears to have been a by-product of the Mexican War. A corruption of the Dutch term for "free booter" or free agent, a *filibuster* was a mercenary who attempted to take control of a foreign territory through a private campaign financed by politicians of the target country. An earlier series of filibuster expeditions to Texas followed the War of 1812.[60] Lopez's army in 1849–50 was basically composed of Southerners who had been recruited as adventurers, many of them hoping to annex Cuba to the United States as another slave state. The height of the movement came in 1854 when a group of American diplomats in Europe, including future president James Buchanan, issued the Ostend Manifesto in support of filibustering.

Only one filibuster was even temporarily successful—William Walker—who took power in Nicaragua and ruled for three years before being overthrown. Walker was unique in that he was a Tennessean with Free Soil politics. Born in Nashville in 1824, Walker was educated as a doctor while still a teenager, then trained as a lawyer. He went out to the gold fields of California in 1852 to seek his fortune. He became a journalist in Sacramento advocating Free Soil policies. In 1853 he organized a filibustering expedition to Sonora, Mexico. The expedition failed because Walker failed to bring enough food for the men and they were forced to surrender.

But the expedition had the practical effect of expediting the sale of the Gadsden Purchase to the United States, although Walker had no direct connection with either Jefferson Davis or Gadsden. Because of this expedition and his reputation as a liberal, Walker was approached by financier Cornelius Vanderbilt, who ran an overland stage company in Nicaragua and wished to build a canal. Nicaragua was torn apart by a political rivalry between the Liberal and the Legitimist parties, each based in the two main cities of the country at the time—Leon and Granada, respectively. In 1854 Walker was able to take control with about two hundred Americans and establish himself as the head of the army. Walker had a Legitimist leader who was trying to organize Central American opposition to his rule shot. He then fell out with the Liberals and took direct control of the country himself in 1856. He then overturned the country's antislavery laws and made slavery legal. At this time he made a tour of the United States and visited New Orleans looking for new volunteers. He was well received there and feted. In 1857 he was overthrown by a pan-Central American army backed by the British. Besieged in his capital in Granada, Walker ordered the destruction of the city before he left. The main buildings were dynamited. Walker then retreated overland to the port of Rivas. His army began to desert, and Walker surrendered himself to an American naval officer, abandoning his remaining supporters. This left him with a ruined reputation and little remaining support.

Instead of just abandoning his Central American dreams and practicing one of his three professions—medicine, the law, and journalism—Walker continued to dream. He wrote *The War in Nicaragua*, which was published in 1860. Walker was invited in 1860 to prevent the return to Honduran rule of a small island off the coast of Honduras. Walker planned to use the island as a base for conquering Honduras and eventually Nicaragua. Believing that lightning would strike twice, he recruited a small force of adventurers and landed on the island. After landing in Honduras, Walker's force was besieged in Trujillo. He surrendered to a British naval captain who promptly turned him over to the Hondurans; they put him against a wall and shot him. Walker was dead at thirty-six, and an era died with him. Walker was a symptom of American expansionism and its tie to slavery, rather than an independent force in American politics. The only place in America where he had personal political influence was in California in 1852–54. But he was a symbol, an icon—the Southern counterpart to John Brown as the country was preparing to tear itself apart.[61]

BLEEDING KANSAS, JAMES AND JOSEPH LANE, AND THE 1856 CAMPAIGN

The other half of Colonel Jefferson Davis's famous V formation at the battle of Buena Vista was led by Colonel James Henry Lane and consisted of the Third Indiana Infantry. Lane was born in Indiana in June 1814.

Upon returning from Mexico he was elected the lieutenant governor of Indiana. He then served one term as a congressman from the fourth district in Indiana from 1853 to 1855, voting in favor of the Kansas-Nebraska Act. In Indiana he was a Democrat. But in reality he was a political opportunist who was indifferent to ideology. He was a spellbinding orator who was ambitious and without scruples. He moved to Kansas in 1855 with the early settlers and served as the commander of the volunteers during the defense of Lawrence in the "Wakarusa War" of late October to early November 1855. He managed to negotiate a truce with the leader of the "border ruffians" that had invaded Kansas, after having deterred their attack, thereby avoiding bloodshed. He agreed that the Free Staters would abide by the territorial laws. An early assessment of him from a newspaper in Missouri declared, "Lane is hot-headed, rash, regardless of consequences, but not wanting in bravery; just the man to carry out plans and directions. . . . Lane looks only to the present, acts only for today, never gives a thought about how his acts will appear in history. . . ."[62] He presided over the Topeka convention that elected an extralegal Free State legislature and governor, Charles Robinson. Previously, "border ruffians"—proslavery inhabitants of the border counties of Missouri—had invaded Kansas to illegally vote in elections in the fall of 1854 and in the spring of 1855.

When an active guerrilla war began in Kansas in May 1856 following the proslavery "sacking" of Lawrence and John Brown's retaliatory raid, Lane emerged as the leader of the Free State militia. Lane was known as the "grim chieftain" more for his words than for his actions. By then the Free State forces had some three thousand Sharps rifles—"Beecher's Bibles"—as well as thousands of pistols, swords, and knives. Lane went on a tour of the North speaking on behalf of the Free State settlers in Kansas in the summer of 1856. Lane's "Army of the North" came streaming through Iowa and Nebraska to Kansas—a collection of idealists and mercenaries with heads full of visions of plunder. In Iowa City, Iowa, the abolitionists raided the local armory for weapons, possibly with the connivance of local politicians. One of those riding south with Lane was a man named John Brown. Lane returned to Kansas on August 7, 1856, and immediately began eliminating proslavery strongholds along the Kaw (Kansas) River. This secured peace for Lawrence and the main Free State settlements until the beginning of the Civil War in 1861. But border raids continued along the border with Free State "jayhawkers" entering into western Missouri on slave liberation and plundering raids. An election of a new legislature was finally held on October 6, 1857, and Governor Robert Walker courageously threw out fraudulent ballots from a few areas. The final outrage of the informal civil war in "bleeding Kansas" was the Marias des Cygnes massacre in May 1858 in which eleven Free State settlers were lined up in a shallow ravine along the river and shot down. Six were killed, four were wounded, and one emerged unscratched after feigning death. On June 3, 1858, Lane killed his neighbor and rival militia leader, Gaius Jenkins, with whom he had feuded for two years. Jenkins had invaded Lane's property after being repeatedly warned; as a result Lane was acquitted of the killing, but it impacted on his political future and he became unpopular.[63]

When Kansas finally became a state under a Free State, Free Soil constitution in January 1861—after having rejected independence under the Lecompton slavery constitution recognized by President Buchanan—James Lane was one of the first two U.S. senators. He pooled his support in the state legislature with rival Sam Pomeroy to ensure that both would be elected. Lane then politically "assassinated" Governor Charles Robinson by having him investigated and tried for the illegal sale of state bonds, something done by Robinson because the state was broke. Lane arrived in Washington in April 1861 and promptly organized a 120-man volunteer company of guards for the White House. The volunteers slept on the carpeted floor of the White House while off duty. As a result, Lane became good friends with Lincoln and was able to use the friendship to dispense federal patronage in Kansas.

In the summer of 1861, without resigning his senate seat, Lane raised three regiments of volunteers in Kansas and was commissioned a brigadier general. The brigade spent the war fighting in Missouri and along the border. The Battle of Wilson's Creek in Missouri on August 6, 1861, was proportionately the costliest of any major battle in the Civil War with 23 percent of all participants ending up as casualties. Kansas had the highest rate of participation and the highest casualty rate of any Union state in the Civil War. On September 23, 1861, Lane led the brigade to sack the defenseless town of Osceola, Missouri. Lane took a thousand dollars in gold, several silk dresses, and a piano as his share of the loot. Lane was the first Union commander to enlist black troops—many of them liberated Missouri slaves—and his troops were the first black casualties in the Civil War in 1862. Lane was in Lawrence on August 21, 1863, when Quantrill sacked the town. Lane snuck out of his house, hid in a cornfield, and then organized pursuit of the raiders. Lane played a key role in leading the militia in the defense of Kansas during a Confederate invasion by General Price in October 1864. This feat won him reelection—which until then had seemed beyond his grasp—the following month.

Lane was instrumental in winning Lincoln's nomination as the Republican candidate in 1864 when many in the party wanted to go with someone else. This won him Lincoln's gratitude. In 1865 following Lincoln's assassination he gave up his support for the Radical Republicans and supported Andrew Johnson and his policy of reconstruction in tribute to the slain president. This lost him much support in Kansas and resulted in his loss of friends and prestige. In July 1866 he committed suicide. Lane, like Houston, was able to build successful political careers in two different states that were separated by a long distance. Like Houston, he cut his first political career short for personal reasons—his support of abolitionism. Lane could well have built a successful political career in Kansas through the cow town era if he had been mentally more stable.⁶⁴

Incredibly, there was another prominent Lane who was a Mexican War veteran from Indiana who afterward built a political career. Joseph Lane was born in North Carolina in 1801 and moved to Kentucky at age three. He was raised and educated there before moving to Indiana as a young adult and settling along the Ohio River where he made a living as a farmer and merchant. He had a quarter-century political career in both houses of the state legislature starting at age twenty-one. When the Mexican War began he volunteered and was elected colonel of his regiment. Polk then gave him a commission as a brigadier general. As Lane had no previous military experience, this was purely a political appointment as in the case of Pierce. Polk was desperate to create a crop of Democratic generals. Initially Lane fought under Taylor, commanding a two-regiment brigade of Indiana volunteers. Lane played a major role at Buena Vista. For this he received favorable attention in the American press. In September 1847 he was transferred to General Scott's army and played a major role in the battles at Puebla and Huamantla in September and October. He was promoted to major general.

In August 1848 Polk appointed Lane territorial governor of Oregon for his military service. In 1850 he was replaced as governor by President Taylor. He was elected to Congress from Oregon in 1850 and served in the House from 1851 to 1859 and then in the Senate from 1859 to 1861. In 1853 he was commissioned a brigadier general to deal with an Indian uprising and was wounded in the decisive battle of Table Rock. He then negotiated a peace with the Indians. In 1860 he was chosen as the vice-presidential running mate of former Whig John C. Breckenridge to run on the Southern Democrat ticket. This ended his political career.⁶⁵

The main electoral issues in the 1856 presidential campaign and election were slavery and Kansas. This was the third presidential election in a row with a Mexican fighter running on the top of a major party ticket. The next presidential election would only feature a Mexican fighter on the bottom half.

The new Republican Party, which held its first organizing meeting in Ripon, Wisconsin, in the spring of 1854, held its first presidential nominating convention in Philadelphia in June 1856. There it selected as its candidate another Mexican fighter and popular American hero, the "Pathfinder of the West," John Charles Fremont; and William Dayton of New Jersey was chosen as his running mate.⁶⁶

Fremont was born in Savannah, Georgia, the bastard son of an émigré Frenchman who worked as a French teacher at private academies in the South. As a baby sleeping in the Nashville Hotel in September 1813, he was almost killed by stray bullets from his future father-in-law, Thomas Hart Benton, and the future president as they engaged in their famous brawl.

Several shots penetrated the room where he was sleeping. Fremont was raised in Charleston where he studied law but was an indifferent student. He was a handsome young lad and developed a reputation as a heartbreaker. He served as a math instructor aboard a navy warship for three years and then became a civil engineer and an army officer. He then spent two years surveying in the Northwest territory. On October 17, 1841, he eloped with Jesse Benton, the seventeen-year-old daughter of Senator Thomas Hart Benton of Missouri.[67]

In 1842 Fremont began his career as a western explorer that he would pursue for the next decade. His first expedition was to Oregon to explore the region; he was led by Kit Carson, who was then an unknown mountain man. In 1843 he led a second major expedition—this one overland to California—for which he was promoted to captain. His third expedition was to northern California in 1845–46. Fremont arrived there in March 1846 and was promptly ordered out of the territory by General Juan Castro of the Mexican army, who had de facto control over northern Alta California. Fremont raised the American flag outside San Juan Bautista Mission and staged a three-day standoff before he was convinced that American honor—and his own pride—had been satisfied. He had nearly started the Mexican War two months before it began in Texas.[68]

Fremont then headed up to Oregon with his approximately twenty-man expedition. Kit Carson led Fremont's men on a massacre of 175 peaceful Indians in northern California in April; Fremont was not involved. Klamath Indians attacked Fremont's camp one night after Fremont neglected to post a sentry. Three men were killed and one wounded, and one Klamath chief was killed in the attack. The expedition retaliated by attacking a Klamath camp on Upper Klamath Lake on May 12, 1846, and killed more than twenty Indians. In one encounter Fremont saved Carson's life. Violence and vengeance had become a way of life for Fremont as he absorbed the values of the mountain men.[69]

General Castro ordered all noncitizens out of California on April 17, 1846. As the Americans outnumbered the Mexicans in northern California—they had been arriving in a steady stream for a decade—he ended up setting off a revolution. In late May Fremont sent Marine Lieutenant Gillespie, who had traveled overland from Mexico City to reach Fremont, to get supplies including gunpowder and shot from a navy warship in San Francisco bay. There was no mention of California and certainly not of seizing it in the orders that sent Fremont on his third expedition, but he may have received oral encouragement from his father-in-law. Castro had stirred up the local Indians against the American settlers—he had separatist dreams for his own independent republic in the area and feared competition from the Americans. Fremont ordered a preemptive strike against a village of peaceful Maidu Indians, fearing that they would later attack if left alone.

A group of some thirty-three adventurers among the settlers had formed a group that they called the *Osos,* Spanish for Bears, and Fremont encouraged them to attack the Spanish post at the village of Sonoma. The Bears captured the post without firing a shot—but suffered from hangovers the next morning from the hospitality of the commander. On June 15, 1846, the Bears proclaimed the California Republic and hauled up a flag resembling the state flag of California. Unlike the Republic of Texas, the California Republic never actually ruled. It was purely a revolutionary movement that seized territory that was then taken over by the U.S. government and ruled under a military government until California became a state in 1850. It was as if the United States had annexed Texas in May or June of 1836. Fremont threw in his lot with the Bears five days later when he learned that Castro was moving against them.[70]

On July 23 Commodore Stockton, the navy commander in San Francisco Bay, promoted Fremont to major and gave him command of the California Battalion, which consisted of his own men, the Bears, and various sailors and marines from a couple of warships in the bay. It was to operate like horse marines as an amphibious force. The battalion was about three hundred men strong. Proceeding by ship down the coast they managed to capture the coastal towns or villages without a struggle.[71]

Fremont sent Carson and a few men east to meet with General Stephen W. Kearny who was advancing westward from Fort Leavenworth, Kansas. In October Carson met up with Kearny just south of Socorro, New Mexico, about half the distance to California. Carson told Kearny that California had already been conquered. So Kearny sent his army back to Santa Fe and proceeded to California with 110 men led by Carson. Twenty-five American volunteers captured San Diego in October and built a fort above the town to protect it. At the end of that month Stockton promoted Fremont to lieutenant colonel. A month later the battalion had grown by nearly 50 percent to 430 men as it swelled with sailors, mountain men, freed blacks, and emigrants. Kearny's force arrived in early December 1846 and engaged in the Battle of San Pascual where it was cut apart by Mexican Californio lancers. The general was severely wounded in the battle. A relief force from the California Battalion then rescued Kearny's force.[72]

Fremont had a policy of pardoning captured Californios provided that they promised not to take up arms against him. This facilitated the surrender of the Californios—native Mexican Californians—to Fremont on January 13, 1847. At this point Commodore Stockton and General Kearny became involved in a dispute over who was in command in California. The two men were of equal rank but belonged to different services. Fremont, who owed his appointment to Stockton, refused to obey orders from Kearny until the two had worked out who was in command. He even traveled north from Monterey to San Francisco to meet with Kearny and attempt to work out their differences.[73]

After Fremont and his expedition marched back with Kearny's force to Fort Leavenworth in August 1847, Kearny had Fremont "arrested" for mutiny and disobedience of orders. Fremont was sent to Fort Monroe, Virginia, to be tried by a court martial composed of senior army officers. Senator Thomas Hart Benton defended him. After demonstrating that Fremont was not being willfully disobedient and that there was a basic conflict over command, the court found him guilty and sentenced him to dismissal from the service in January 1848 but ruled that there were extenuating circumstances. This meant that President Polk had considerable leeway. Polk upheld the conviction but ruled that Fremont should remain in the service. Fremont, having cleared his name in his own opinion, then resigned from the service. His fourth expedition from California was a disaster, as the men became snowed in in the Sierra Nevada mountains. A dozen men died of starvation and others suffered from frostbite before they finally made their way out into northern New Mexico and were nursed back to health by Kit Carson on his ranch.[74]

Fremont returned to California and began to work a ranch that he had staked out during the rebellion. When California was admitted as a new state in 1850, Fremont was one of its two U.S. senators. But he was given the short term and failed to win reelection in 1851. He spent 1851–52 developing his ranch and mining for gold. In 1853–54 his final expedition was a disaster—a repeat of his previous one. Caught in the mountains of Utah, the expedition survived by eating mule meat; and one man died before they were rescued and nursed back to health by Mormon settlers.[75]

Fremont rejected Democratic offers to run as a candidate for high office as he thought that the party was too proslavery. He was persuaded to compete for the Republican nomination because the new party was antislavery. Northern liberals, who believed that Fremont could bring along many Know-Nothings from the North, backed him. They thought he might be able to bring along a few Democratic voters as well. William Seward, a former governor of New York and leader of the Whig Party in that state and one of the party's main sources of strength in the Northeast, was convinced that the party could not win the election on its first time out and so he was content to have Fremont nominated. Fremont and the Republicans ran on an antislavery ticket with the slogan: "Free Soil, Free Labor, Free Speech." Fremont had established his antislavery credentials by advocating admission of California as a Free State in 1850. William Lloyd Garrison refused to endorse Fremont or the Republicans, but many other abolitionists supported the new party as the first crack in the hold of slave-power over the party system. Garrison conceded that Fremont was preferable to either Buchanan or Fillmore on the issue of slavery—a major concession for a purist like Garrison. Garrison in fact gave more respect to the Republicans than he had previously to either the Liberty Party or the Free Soil Party.[76]

There were three main candidates for the Democratic nomination at the convention in Cincinnati that year: incumbent Franklin Pierce and former candidates Stephen Douglas of Illinois and James Buchanan of Pennsylvania. The two-thirds rule was in effect. Pierce was supported by the New England states, Douglas by the South, and Buchanan by the mid-Atlantic and border states. The real contest was between Buchanan and Pierce through the first fourteen ballots, which were held on the first day. That night Pierce's supporters dropped him in favor of Douglas, but Douglas failed to win any more votes on the next ballot than Pierce had. Buchanan won on the seventeenth ballot after Douglas withdrew in order to preserve his chances for 1860. On the previous ballot, Buchanan had a 2:1 lead in delegates in all regions except the South where Douglas had a 2:1 lead. Buchanan had an advantage in that having been in England for the previous three years, his views on slavery were not well known.[77]

The Democratic platform supported "popular sovereignty" and the 1850 Compromise, whereas the Republicans ran on Kansas and the vow to bring to justice those guilty of the crimes committed there. Pierce was implicated in those crimes in their belief. Ironically, Buchanan had first brought Fremont to the attention of the wide public by convincing the Senate to print thousands of copies of the official report from Fremont's first expedition. Both the Democratic and Republican press carried quotations from Republican leaders. As there were 3.5 times as many newspapers in circulation in the North as in the South, the Republicans benefited from this free publicity.

Fillmore was deliberately chosen as the candidate of the Southern Know-Nothings and the remaining Whigs because he was bland and uncontroversial. He ran without a platform that election with his strength being only in the border slave states. He appealed to the conservative Unionist voters who lived in these states, which had previously been Whig states. Lincoln campaigned vigorously in Illinois on behalf of Fremont, attempting to convince former Whigs that a vote for Fillmore was really a vote for Buchanan. But his efforts were in vain: Fremont lost Illinois to Buchanan by about nine thousand votes.[78]

The Democrats carried Pennsylvania by only a small margin in the state elections on October 15, 1856. The sons of both Henry Clay and Daniel Webster, the two Senate giants of the Whig Party and perennial presidential candidates, spoke in support of Buchanan at a rally in Lancaster, Pennsylvania, a week before the November election. On election day Buchanan won 1.93 million votes compared to 1.34 million for Fremont and .93 million for Fillmore. Buchanan received 174 electoral votes, compared to 114 for Fremont and only 8 for Fillmore. Fremont took this as another failure, but it was actually a stunning success for a new party. The Republicans had carried eleven out of sixteen free states and won 56 percent of the popular vote in the North and West, compared to Buchanan who won most of the slave states (except Maryland, which Fillmore won) and five of the free states. Buchanan was elected president with the lowest percentage of the popular vote—45 percent—of any president since John Quincy Adams in 1824. The Whigs did not win until their second time out, and this is in spite of their previous existence as the National Republicans.[79]

Fremont was only forty-three when he lost. He returned to his ranch and threw off claim jumpers and began serious mining for gold. By 1859 he was clearing $100,000 a month from the mines in revenue. So he soon became a very rich man.

In July 1861 Fremont was appointed a major general in charge of the Department of the Missouri. As his only previous military command experience beyond about thirty men had been as commander of the California Battalion in 1846–47, this was clearly a political appointment. He lost the battle of Wilson's Creek and then committed the sin of emancipating black slaves prematurely. Lincoln promptly revoked the order. After only a hundred days Lincoln removed him as commander in October. In March 1862 he was appointed commander of the Mountain Department consisting of western Virginia (future West Virginia), eastern Kentucky, and part of Tennessee. He was saddled with bad troops who were miserably equipped; and he was up against the best tactical commander in the Confederate army, Thomas "Stonewall" Jackson. He was put under General Pope's command in the spring of 1862. Jackson defeated the dispersed Union troops in the Shenendoah Valley one after another in his classic campaign. Fremont asked to be relieved of his command after this, and Lincoln obliged. Fremont never held another command, and he resigned from the army in June 1864.[80]

A convention in Cleveland nominated him to run as a Radical Republican against Lincoln in 1864. But he declined this as well as overtures to form a new party consisting of Radical Republicans, War Democrats, and Unionist Germans. This was the height of Fremont's career, and it slowly went into free fall after this. After going bankrupt and being arrested for failure to pay off debts in France, he finally made a modest recovery. In October 1878 he was appointed territorial governor of Arizona and served for three years until October 1881. He died in 1890.[81]

By 1856 Jefferson Davis wanted to get back into the Senate. The Democratic Party controlled the state legislature in Mississippi, so whomever the caucus selected would be elected to the Senate without a fight. Davis faced an opponent from northwestern Mississippi who had a similar ideology and social standing. Davis ended up winning by the tie-breaking vote of the presiding officer.[82]

THE ROAD TO WAR

After 1856 both the Whigs and the Know-Nothings disappeared as coherent parties. Both their voters and their politicians drifted to either the Republican or Democratic parties. The Republican Party, as a purely

Northern party, need not fear splitting, but the Democratic Party remained divided along sectional lines.

Many leading Republicans spoke in favor of either dissolution of the Union or using force to suppress slavery—this included Seward, who by 1858 had become the leading figure in the new party. The abolitionists held a convention in Worcester, Massachusetts, in January 1857 where they proposed to secede from the Union. They ended up influencing many Republican politicians in the Northeast.

Buchanan, like Pierce before him, was a doughface: "a Northern man with Southern principles." So his actions on Kansas were disturbingly similar to those of Pierce. In October–November 1857 the recognized legislature at Lecompton drafted the Lecompton Constitution that was designed to bring Kansas into the Union as a slave state. The constitution was presented to the electorate of Kansas in December 1857, and the Free Soilers boycotted the election. President Buchanan urged Congress to admit Kansas as a slave state under this constitution, and the Senate complied, voting on a strictly partisan basis. But the House, under the urging of Senator Stephen A. Douglas, refused and the constitution was resubmitted to the voters in a second referendum in August 1858. This time the proslavery forces boycotted the election and the constitution was defeated. Kansas refused statehood on the basis of the Lecompton Constitution on August 2, 1858. This stand by Douglas lost him the support of the South, which he had enjoyed up until then. Douglas dreamed of building a transcontinental railroad and wanted Chicago to be its hub. He needed Southern support to accomplish this. So he obliged them by ditching the Missouri Compromise in 1854 with his "popular sovereignty" doctrine. But he did not wish to see the doctrine abused by squatters like the "border ruffians" from Missouri. And his railroad bill was defeated by Southern opposition, freeing him from any obligation to the South. The *Dred Scott v. Sanford* decision in March 1857 by the Supreme Court held that "the Negro has no rights that the white man is bound to recognize." This made it difficult for Douglas to reconcile his "popular sovereignty" concept with the new ruling. It also served to embolden the South and make it less open to compromise on slavery.[83]

In 1858 the Senate seat held by Douglas was up for election again by the Illinois legislature. From mid-August until mid-October 1858 Abraham Lincoln, who at this point held no office, and Douglas engaged in a series of seven debates in towns around Illinois from Freeport in the north to Jonesboro in the south. The Republicans took control of the state legislature in 1858, but Democratic holdovers in the state senate ensured the reelection of Douglas to the Senate by a vote of 54 to 46. But the debates brought Lincoln national exposure and fame as he proclaimed that "this country cannot long endure half slave and half free, it will soon be completely one or the other." Lincoln was afraid that Douglas was becoming acceptable to Republicans in the East, so he emphasized his own moral opposition to slavery to the indifference of Douglas to the institution. Douglas accused Lincoln of changing his views so that he was pure white in the southern part of the state and then mulatto as he moved north until he was pure black in Freeport.[84]

Seward echoed Lincoln's language within weeks of the debates by stating on October 25, "It is an irrepressible conflict between opposing and enduring forces, and it means that the United States must and will, sooner or later, become entirely a slave-holding nation or entirely a free-labor nation." That same year Charles F. Adams, in his active return to politics, was elected to Congress from Massachusetts. The Republicans controlled the Congress. John Sherman of Ohio lost the speaker's post to a nonentity from New Jersey in 1859. There was increasing talk in the South of secession as fear grew that Seward would be the Republican nominee in 1860 and might actually win.

John "Ossowatomie Brown," the instigator of the Pottowatomie Creek massacre of May 1856, invaded Harper's Ferry, Virginia, on October 16, 1859, with a force of twenty-one men in an attempt to seize the armory there and distribute the weapons to local slaves. The ultimate aim was to organize another slave revolt similar to the Nat Turner revolt of 1831. The attempt was secretly financed by a group of influential abolitionists in New England. The attempt failed when a force of Marines led by Lieutenant Colonel Robert E. Lee and Lieutenant James "Jeb" Stuart captured Brown's force. Brown was taken to the nearby county seat of Charleston, Virginia, where he was tried and hanged in December 1859. The South was alarmed by the raid, and talk of secession increased.

In 1860 there were four separate party tickets running for president. The Democratic convention, held in its perennial spot in Baltimore in June, split when the Southerners walked out. By the time of the convention both sides thought that a split would be to their advantage as a three-way election would force the issue into the House where a compromise would be made on their terms. Both sides wanted compromise—but only on their terms. There had in fact been an early convention in Charleston in April that broke up when delegates from the Gulf states walked out. The two-thirds rule was in effect, and the rules committee ruled that Douglas needed to win two-thirds of all the delegates, not just two-thirds of those that remained. This Douglas was unable to do.

Douglas towered above all his competitors on every basis: speaking ability, voter appeal, erudition, and record of accomplishment. Douglas worked to win the replacement of the bolters who had left with his own Southern moderates. The Douglas men voted to seat both the bolters who agreed to return when the convention reconvened in Baltimore and moderate new delegates from Alabama and Louisiana. This led to a second and final walkout. This time it was not only delegates from the Gulf states leaving but from the entire South.[85]

The Southerners stayed in Baltimore long enough to choose John C. Breckinridge of Kentucky along with Joseph Lane of Indiana as their ticket. They also wrote a slave-code plank that made all territory that was not already free territory open for slavery. This was the issue that split the two conventions, as the delegates from the Gulf States were under instructions from their state legislatures to walk out if there was no slavecode.[86]

The Republican convention in Chicago was a lively affair. Chicago then had a population of over 100,000 and was only a generation old. A brand new auditorium, the Wigwam, had been built specially for the convention. Lincoln was only one of many favorite sons at the convention; and Seward, the best-known Republican in the country, was expected to walk away with the nomination. Two statements by Seward had labeled him as a radical or even an abolitionist. In the debate on the 1850 Compromise he declared that there was a law higher than the Constitution that he must obey, and then he made his divided-country speech in 1858. The Republican Party—like most democratic political parties—was a loose coalition of many different interests. Missouri was the only slave state in which it had any support—and there only in the Saint Louis area. The loss of New York alone, or Pennsylvania and any other state, would lose the party the election.

Lincoln had three advantages over the other anti-Seward hopefuls. First, he had a home court advantage. Second, he had skilled political managers working the crowd in the auditorium to exploit that advantage. Third, Lincoln had no sworn enemies—he had always taken principled moderate stands. And his rail-splitter populist image was perfect for the campaigns of those days.[87]

On the first ballot Seward led as expected with 173.5 votes to Lincoln's 102, with Simon Cameron having 50.5 and Salmon Chase trailing at 49. In the second ballot Seward led with 184, with Lincoln only three votes behind after Cameron dropped out. On the third ballot there was a mass wave of delegates flowing to Lincoln and he was easily put over the two-thirds limit. Hannibal Hamlin of Maine was chosen as his running mate.[88]

A new party, the Constitutional Unionists—basically the remaining rump of the Whig Party in the border states along with Southern Know-Nothings, met in Baltimore in May and nominated John Bell of Tennessee and former Secretary of State Edward Everett of Massachusetts as its ticket. Its sole platform was "the Constitution, the Union, and enforcement of the laws," and its sole support was in the border states where support for slavery was combined with a loyalty to the Union. This then gave the country four separate tickets in 1860, each regional in support.[89]

Lincoln misestimated Southern sentiments, confusing the Old Northwest—those Kentuckians who had moved to Indiana and Illinois—for the South. Davis had tried to unite the Democrats and the Constitutional Unionists behind a single candidate—probably himself—but Douglas refused to obey the advice of his old adversary and withdraw from the race. Some 4.7 million Americans—two-thirds of the potential electorate—voted on election day. Lincoln had 180 electoral votes compared to 72 for Breckenridge, 39 for Bell, and only 12 for the unfortunate Douglas, who carried only Missouri and part of Vermont. But Douglas had some 30 percent of the popular vote, more than that of Bell and Breckenridge combined. Lincoln would have won with 169 electoral votes if he had had a straight shot at any of his three opponents. Douglas and Bell were both devout Unionists and would remain loyal. Even Breckenridge was not a wild secessionist: "not every Breckenridge man was a secessionist, but every secessionist was a Breckenridge man."[90]

South Carolina seceded on December 20, 1860. By February 1, 1861, it had been followed by: Mississippi, Florida, Alabama, Georgia, Louisiana, and Texas. The seven states constituted a solid contiguous belt of territory from Charleston to Austin. The Gulf-state delegates and South Carolinians met in Montgomery, Alabama, at the beginning of February and drew up a constitution and unanimously elected Jefferson Davis president and Alexander Stephens vice president. The "ticket" was balanced with a former Democrat and a former Whig. The delegates wanted to choose a president with stature and few enemies, eliminating the radical secessionists of South Carolina. Davis was the only candidate who combined legislative, executive, and military experience. The constitution was modeled on the American Constitution but with explicit guarantees for slavery, more states' rights, and cabinet members being allowed seats in Congress. For the moment the more northerly slave states of Tennessee, Arkansas, North Carolina, and Virginia remained within the Union. Douglas advocated that the United States withdraw all of its federal posts in the South except for two coaling stations.[91]

By mid-December Davis was convinced that the issue was no longer one of Union or secession but rather one of war or peace. On January 10, 1861, he made an eloquent plea for peace in his final address to the Senate. President Buchanan, after sleeping through the crisis for nearly four years, finally decided to act. He stood firm on Fort Sumter remaining in federal hands. Lincoln was powerless to do anything until he was sworn in as president. Davis took his oath of office exactly two weeks before Lincoln did. In his inaugural address in March 1861 he gave the South three assurances. First, the administration would not disturb slavery in the slave states. Second, he would faithfully enforce the fugitive slave law. Third, he would impose no hindrance to the domestic slave trade. Lincoln inherited his policy of resistance to secession from Buchanan. He sent a supply ship to Fort Sumter to replenish its food supply. Davis and his cabinet interpreted this as an act of aggression and voted to fire on Fort Sumter. Only his secretary of state, Robert Toombs, dissented from this decision.[92]

This ended the era of the Mexican fighters in the United States, but it continued for another four bloody years in America.

NOTES

1. Kinley J. Brauer, *Cotton versus Conscience* (Lexington: University of Kentucky Press, 1967), pp. 18–19.
2. Ibid., p. 21.

3. Ibid., pp. 23–24, 159; Henry Mayer, *All On Fire: William Lloyd Garrison and the Abolition of Slavery* (New York: St. Martin's Press, 1998), pp. 343–44.

4. Mayer, p. 364 for the distinction. The analogy is this author's.

5. Brauer, op. cit., pp. 133, 143–44, 160, 162, 164; Francis Russell, *Adams: An American Dynasty* (New York: American Heritage Publishing, 1976), p. 248.

6. James T. Adams, *The Adams Family* (New York: Literary Guild, 1930), pp. 240, 242.

7. Brauer, op. cit., pp. 27–28.

8. Ibid., pp. 200–209.

9. Russell, op. cit., p. 249.

10. David R. Collins, *Zachary Taylor: 12th President of the United States* (Ada, OK: Garret Educational Corp., 1989), pp. 5, 10, 12, 16, 25, 32–36.

11. K. Jack Bauer, *Zachary Taylor: Soldier, Planter, Statesman of the Old Southwest* (Baton Rouge: Louisiana State University Press, 1985), pp. 58, 60, 62, 63–64; John Eisenhower, *Agent of Destiny* (New York: Free Press, 1997), pp. 128, 130–31.

12. Bauer, pp. 81–82; Collins, op. cit., pp. 49–52; John K. Mahon, *History of the Militia and the National Guard* (New York: Macmillan, 1983), pp. 89–90.

13. Bauer, pp. 90–91, 94.

14. Bauer, op. cit., pp. 165, 167–70; Collins, op. cit., pp. 71–72.

15. Bauer, pp. 184–86, 188–89; Collins, p. 78.

16. Bauer, p. 192; Collins, p. 78; Don C. Seitz, *The Also Rans* (Freeport, NY: Books for Libraries Press, 1968), p. 96.

17. Bauer, op. cit., pp. 195, 202–203, 205–206.

18. Eisenhower, op. cit., pp. 298, 307.

19. Richard Slotkin, *Fatal Environment* (New York: Harper Perennial, 1994), pp. 124–25.

20. Merrill D. Peterson, *The Great Triumvirate* (New York: Oxford University Press, 1987), pp. 431–32, 435, 439; Robert V. Remini, *Henry Clay: Statesman for the Union* (New York: W. W. Norton, 1991), p. 705.

21. Bauer, op. cit., pp. 218, 220–21, 222, 223.

22. See Hudson Strode, *Jefferson Davis: American Patriot Vol. 1: 1808–61* (New York: Harcourt Brace & Co., 1955), p. 196 on Taylor's slaves. Peterson, pp. 440–41; Glyndon G. Van Deusen, *The Jacksonian Era* (New York: Harper Torchbooks, 1959), pp. 255–56; Remini, *Clay,* p. 706; Michael F. Holt, *The Rise and Fall of the American Whig Party* (New York: Oxford University Press, 1999), pp. 324–25.

23. Holt, pp. 329, 330; Eisenhower, op. cit., p. 320.

24. Seitz, op. cit., p. 102.

25. Van Deusen, op. cit., p. 248; Seitz, op. cit., pp. 99–101.

26. Peterson, pp. 442–43; Remini, *Clay,* p. 712; Holt, op. cit., p. 372; Van Deusen, op. cit., pp. 260–61; Hudson Strode, *Jefferson Davis: American Patriot Volume 1: 1808–61* (New York: Harcourt Brace, 1955), p. 205; Seitz, pp. 103, 105.

27. Brauer, op. cit., pp. 220, 222, 223–24.

28. Adams, op. cit., p. 241.

29. Ibid., pp. 230, 232–33.

30. Ibid., p. 238; Merrill D. Peterson, *The Great Triumvirate* (New York: Oxford University Press, 1987), p. 442.

31. Brauer, pp. 240, 242–43.
32. Mayer, op. cit., pp. 381–82.
33. Ibid., p. 384; Stephen B. Oates, *With Malice Toward None: The Life of Abraham Lincoln* (New York: Harper Row, 1977), pp. 81, 83.
34. On the Taylor presidency see David R. Collins, *Zachary Taylor: 12th President of the United States* (Ada, OK: Garret Educational Corp., 1989), pp. 95–111; Remini, *Clay*, pp. 728–52 passim.
35. Eisenhower, op. cit., pp. 84, 93, 97–98, 103.
36. Ibid., pp. 103–104, 114, 118.
37. Ibid., pp. 125–28, 132, 152, 158, 161, 164, 173, 184.
38. Ibid., pp. 184–86, 193–94, 209.
39. Ibid., p. 333.
40. Fern G. Brown, *Franklin Pierce: 14th President of the United States* (Ada, OK: Garret Educational Corp., 1989), pp. 4, 6, 8, 13–14, 17, 20, 29, 35, 38, 40.
41. Ibid., pp. 41–43.
42. Ibid., pp. 43, 46, 49–52.
43. Ibid., pp. 54, 58, 59.
44. Ibid., p. 60.
45. Holt, op. cit., pp. 672, 680–83.
46. Ibid., pp. 712, 720–24.
47. Ibid., pp. 732, 756; Eisenhower, op. cit., pp. 328, 329.
48. Seitz, op. cit., pp. 172–75; Brown, op. cit., pp. 78–79, 81–82.
49. Brown, pp. 76, 78, 81.
50. Holt, op. cit., pp. 957, 959–62, 972–73, 977.
51. Brown, op. cit., pp. 63–64, 84–85, 88.
52. Strobe, op. cit., pp. 46, 52, 61, 67, 71–73, 75.
53. Ibid., pp. 95, 121, 133–34, 136, 145.
54. Ibid., pp. 145, 147, 149–50.
55. Ibid., pp. 157, 163, 165, 179, 182, 185, 188, 189.
56. Strode, op. cit., pp. 190, 195, 205, 209.
57. Ibid., pp. 215, 222, 232; William and Bruce Catton, *Two Roads to Sumter* (New York: McGraw-Hill, 1963), p. 87.
58. Strode, op. cit., pp. 250, 260–62, 275, 287; Eisenhower, op. cit., pp. 332, 350.
59. "Quitman, John Anthony (1798–1858)," *The Handbook of Texas Online* at www.tsha.utexas.edu/handbook accessed in October 2002; "Quitman, John Anthony," *The Columbia Encyclopedia, Sixth Edition, 2001* at www.bartleby.com accessed October 2002. According to Richard Slotkin, *Fatal Environment* (New York: Harper Perennial, 1994), p. 244, Quitman planned an expedition to Cuba but it never left New Orleans.
60. Jim Bowie's brother Reza was one of those who took part in a filibustering expedition in 1818.
61. Slotkin, *Fatal Environment*, pp. 244–61. Walker's career invites comparisons with the more successful career of French mercenary leader Bob Denard who after serving in the Congo and Yemen, took control of the Comoros in 1978 and ruled for eleven years as the man behind the throne. But Denard had the backing of first France and then South Africa. Walker's career also compares unfavorably with that of Fremont who was successful in California and retained his Free Soil politics.

62. *Parkville (MO) Weekly Southern Democrat*, April 24, 1855, quoted in Thomas Goodrich, *War to the Knife: Bleeding Kansas 1854–61* (Mechanicsburg, PA: Stackpole, 1998), p. 50.

63. Bauer, op. cit., pp. 202–203; "Lane, James Henry," *Grolier's Multimedia Encyclopedia 1995*; Kenneth S. Davis, *Kansas: A Bicentennial History* (New York: W. W. Norton, 1976), pp. 48, 50, 52, 60, 63–64, 69; Goodrich, op. cit., pp. 96, 143, 209–210.

64. Davis, pp. 79, 80, 81–82, 84–86, 88.

65. "Lane, Joseph," *Webster's World Encyclopedia 2000*; and excerpts from his campaign biography found on the Web, "Biographical Sketch of General Joseph Lane, of Oregon," *Illinois Historical Digitization Projects* at www.lincoln.lib.niu.edu accessed on October 1, 2002.

66. Seitz, op. cit., p. 161.

67. Ibid., pp. 144–46; Ferol Egan, *Fremont: Explorer for a Restless Nation* (Garden City, NY: Doubleday, 1977), p. 6.

68. Seitz, op. cit., pp. 146–47; Egan, p. 320.

69. Egan, pp. 330, 333–34.

70. Egan, pp. 344, 349, 353.

71. Ibid., pp. 365–69, 371.

72. Ibid., pp. 374, 379, 384, 386, 392, 396.

73. Ibid., pp. 401, 404, 408.

74. Ibid., pp. 431, 461–62; Seitz, op. cit., pp. 158–59.

75. Seitz, pp. 160–61.

76. Ibid., pp. 196–97; Philip S. Klein, *President James Buchanan* (University Park, PA: Pennsylvania State University Press, 1962), p. 256; Egan, op. cit., pp. 507–509; Mayer, op. cit., pp. 454–56.

77. Klein, p. 255; Brown, op. cit., pp. 101–102.

78. Catton and Catton, op. cit., pp. 126–27.

79. Klein, op. cit., p. 260; Seitz, op. cit., p. 161; Mayer, op. cit., p. 469.

80. Seitz, pp. 163–65; Egan, op. cit., pp. 514–18.

81. Egan, pp. 520–22, 524.

82. Catton and Catton, op. cit., pp. 131–32.

83. Seitz, op. cit., pp. 174, 178–79; "Lecompton Constitution," *Grolier's Multimedia Encyclopedia 1995*.

84. "Lincoln, Abraham," *Grolier's Multimedia Encyclopedia 1995*; Seitz, op. cit., pp. 181–82.

85. Catton and Catton, op. cit., pp. 202–207.

86. Ibid., pp. 202, 208.

87. Ibid., pp. 216–20, 222.

88. Ibid., pp. 224–25; Seitz, op. cit., pp. 200–201.

89. Catton and Catton, pp. 230–31.

90. Ibid., pp. 235, 238, 243–44.

91. Ibid., pp. 247, 262–64, 266–67.

92. Ibid., pp. 260, 269, 272, 278.

John Sevier, ca. 1795.
© Hulton/Archive.

Andrew Jackson.
© Library of Congress.

Currier & Ives lithograph. *Death of Tecumseh: Battle of the Thames,* October 18, 1813. © Library of Congress.

Colonel Crockett, engraved by C. Stuart from the original portrait by J. G. Chapman. © Library of Congress.

Henry Clay. © Library of Congress.

Currier & Ives lithograph of William Henry Harrison. © Library of Congress.

Major-General Zachary Taylor, ca. 1848.
© Library of Congress.

Jefferson Davis, ca. 1890.
© Library of Congress.

Portrait of George Crook by Matthew Brady. © National Archives.

Portrait of Nelson Miles, October 21, 1865. © Library of Congress.

Israeli Brigadier Uzi Narkiss, left, walks with Defense Minister Moshe Dayan, center, and Yitzak Rabin, Israeli Chief of Staff Major General, right, through the Lion Gate into the Old City of Jerusalem, in this June 7, 1967 photo. Narkiss, who was then commander of Israel's Central Front, and who led Israeli troops in the battle for Jerusalem's Old City, including the capture of the Wailing Wall in the Six-Day War of 1967, died Wednesday, December 17, 1997, at the age of 72, according to Israeli media reports. © AP/Wide World Photos.

Portrait of William Carroll by Matthew Brady. © Library of Congress.

Sam Houston in civilian dress, ca. 1850. © Library of Congress.

Richard M. Johnson, ca. 1837.
© Library of Congress.

When a Democratic editor suggested sarcastically that Harrison would be satisfied to retire to a log cabin with a barrel of hard cider, the Whigs countered by making log cabins and cider barrels their party symbols. The Whigs won the popular vote and captured 79 percent of the electoral votes. © Library of Congress.

George Washington, portrait by John Trumbull, 1796. © Library of Congress.

John Sullivan, ca. 1785. © Hulton/Archive.

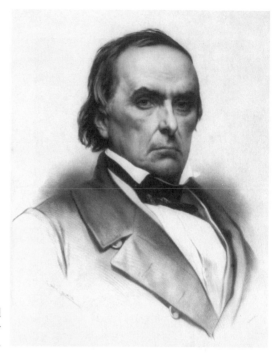

Undated print of Daniel Webster. © Library of Congress.

Portrait of James Lane by Matthew Brady. © National Archives.

6

Indian and Mexican Fighters as Presidents

INTRODUCTION

This chapter examines the main Indian, foreign, and defense policies of the four most important Indian-fighter and Mexican-fighter presidents: George Washington (1789–97), Andrew Jackson (1829–37), Zachary Taylor (1849–50), and Jefferson Davis (1861–65). William H. Harrison was in office for too short a time for his presidency to be worth examining separately. Franklin Pierce's presidency was examined in the chapter on Mexican fighters. Jefferson Davis's term as the president of the Confederacy is examined in depth because he had more military experience than did Pierce and was the last Indian fighter to hold high office. The purpose of this chapter is to see if there are any common themes or characteristics of the Indian-fighter presidents. Those discovered can then be compared to the common characteristics of Arab-fighter prime ministers discussed in the Appendix.

GEORGE WASHINGTON (1789–97)

When Washington became president in April 1789, his biggest challenge—and opportunity—was serving without any precedent or model and hence writing on a blank slate. He could become an elected king or monarch or a simple governor on a national scale. He had individuals address him as "Mister President" rather than as "Your Excellency" or "Your Majesty" or other royal forms of address. Washington lived well on his plantation at

Mount Vernon, Virginia, and intended to live well in the new national capital of Philadelphia. He had both white servants and slaves to serve him and a luxurious coach as his mode of transport.¹

Washington began the tradition of small limited cabinets that remained the norm throughout the nineteenth century. He had only five members: secretary of state, secretary of war, secretary of the treasury, vice president, and attorney general. In fact Washington invented the concept of a cabinet when he began holding collective meetings of the department heads in 1793 in his second term rather than meeting with them individually, as had been the case up until then. Later presidents would add a secretary of the navy, and a postmaster general. Washington believed in using his patronage to reward talented officers from the Revolution and even nonmilitary figures from the Continental Congress who had aided the Republic. He also wanted to collect the best political talent of his day in his cabinet. For these reasons he chose Thomas Jefferson as his secretary of state, Alexander Hamilton as secretary of the treasury, Henry Knox as secretary of war, and Edmund Randolph as attorney general. John Jay was made chief justice of the Supreme Court, which was a very weak branch of government at the time.²

With no modern defense department with its huge office complex in the Pentagon, and even no real standing army to speak of, the war department was one of the weaker departments. The most important offices were those of secretary of state and secretary of the treasury. The treasury combined the functions of the various economic cabinet posts today, such as commerce. Hamilton's job was to determine national economic policy. Jefferson was in charge of foreign policy, which basically meant policy toward the European powers. The vice presidency, as it remained until the late twentieth century, was a weak office. John Adams did not have much input into policy and felt underappreciated. Because of his low salary he had to live relatively frugally.

Jefferson and Adams were good friends and remained so until they became political rivals to succeed Washington. By contrast, Jefferson and Hamilton were enemies from the start. By 1791 two distinct political parties were forming: the Federalists led by Adams and Hamilton and the Republicans led by Jefferson. The Federalists believed in a strong federal government, a federal economic policy designed to protect and promote domestic industry, and a strong foreign policy that tended to be pro-British. Hamilton wanted the federal government to assume the debts of the various states, which was opposed by Virginia because it had already taxed its citizens to pay off its debt. Hamilton also wanted to charter the Bank of the United States to serve as a source of capital for business development. The Federalists as a party were strongest in the large cities of the East Coast. The Republicans believed in a rural republic made up of farmers, skilled artisans, and laborers and was the party of states' rights. The Republicans were strongly pro-French during the French Revolution, much more than the Federalists were pro-British, and wanted an alliance with France.

Washington considered himself to be above factions but was in ideology and practice a Federalist.[3]

In the spring of 1792, Washington told James Madison that he was thinking of retiring—he was then sixty—at the end of his first term. Both Madison and Jefferson urged Washington to run for a second term. Madison argued that the rise of factionalism and party spirit was an argument in favor of, rather than against, a second term. Washington ran for a second term, and the Republicans voted for him but opposed Adams. Adams was, however, easily elected vice president. In December 1792 Hamilton admitted to having had an adulterous affair with a woman whose husband was trying to blackmail him. A congressional committee investigated the allegations against Hamilton and cleared him of any wrongdoing.[4]

Washington's major foreign policy problems were in the West. In the Northwest, American expansion had to contend with both the British who had seven forts in the Great Lakes region south of Canada and the Indians. In the Southwest, Americans had to contend with the Indians, mainly the Creek and Cherokee, and the Spanish. Both the British and Spanish intrigued with the Indians and encouraged them to resist the Americans. A flood of new immigrants settled in Kentucky and began settling in Ohio in the Northwest Territory and in Tennessee and northern Georgia and Alabama in the Old Southwest. In order to make those settlers safe and secure, Washington needed to rid the Northwest of the British presence and keep the United States neutral in any future European war.

By the end of 1791 it was apparent that a great European war was about to erupt. This was due to the reaction of the absolute monarchies of Europe to the French republic, which had not only overthrown the monarchy but executed the monarchs. Meanwhile, an inter-Indian war between the Chickasaw and the Creek kept the latter occupied so that they were not inclined to attack American settlers.

Washington was inclined to use force to back up American expansionism in the Northwest. In 1790 he sent an army led by General Josiah Harmer into Ohio. But Harmer split his army in two, violating a basic rule of warfare, leading one part himself and giving command over the second part to Colonel John Hardin of Kentucky. Chief Little Turtle of the Miami, leader of a large Indian confederation, caught the two forces by surprise in sequence and defeated them in succession. In the fall of 1791 a second force led by General Arthur St. Clair invaded Ohio. It consisted of 1,650 regulars and 350 militia. St. Clair allowed the army to become strung out and the Indians attacked, causing panic among the militia troops in the vanguard, and killed some nine hundred men. This was the greatest American defeat at the hands of the Indians. A congressional inquiry was held to investigate the disaster, and Washington cooperated fully, turning over all correspondence related to the expedition. General St. Clair was cleared of charges of cowardice, but his career suffered as a result of the defeat.

Congress reacted to the defeat not only by investigating it but also by authorizing funds to raise a four-thousand-man army, the Legion of the United States. Washington considered all the top officers from the Revolution to determine whom to appoint to lead it. He narrowed it down to a choice of two individuals: Colonel "Light Horse" Harry Lee (the father of General Robert E. Lee) and General Anthony Wayne. Washington decided in favor of Wayne for three reasons. First, Wayne had commanded larger units in the Revolution than had Lee. Second, Wayne was older and more experienced. Third, Wayne had experience in Indian warfare fighting the Cherokee in northern Georgia. Wayne was then suffering from a scandal that had caused him to resign his House seat after less than one term.

While Wayne was raising and training the army, Washington sent former General Benjamin Lincoln, Timothy Pickering, and Beverly (a man) Randolph to negotiate with the Indians as commissioners. Lord Dorchester, the British governor of Canada, told the Indians, however, that Britain would support them against the Americans and encouraged them to resist American demands.[5]

Alexander Hamilton had declared an excise tax on whiskey production as a means of raising revenue in order to pay off the national debt. This tax was unpopular with farmers living in the West as they tended to live in a barter economy and whiskey was a basis of barter. Whiskey was also popular as a recreational drug with the rural population who did not drink large amounts of other types of alcohol sold in the East. Four counties in western Pennsylvania were in revolt against the federal government, refusing to pay the tax. Revenue collectors were initially threatened and then a few were tarred and feathered when they persisted. In September 1792 Washington threatened to take legal action against those who refused to pay the tax. In June 1794 there was a riot in Washington County, Pennsylvania, and a revolutionary veteran, Major James McFarlane, was shot and killed by federal troops after taking charge of the rioters. After this, David Bradford, the prosecuting attorney of the county, occupied Pittsburgh with several thousand men in August. Washington decided to use force to put down the insurrection; he considered it to be especially dangerous as he saw it as linked to both Jefferson's Republican Party and French ambassador, Edmond Charles Genet, who was stirring up pro-French sentiment in America. Washington sent emissaries offering the rebels amnesty if they complied with the law.

So in 1794 Washington set two armies in motion: Wayne's army into Ohio against the Indians and an army of militia led by himself and Hamilton, who was temporarily acting as secretary of war in Knox's absence. The two rode with twelve thousand militia from four states. On the second day of march Washington received news of Wayne's victory at Fallen Timbers in Ohio. After riding a distance with the army Washington headed back to Philadelphia as Congress was about to come into session and he expected the return of a treaty from Britain. Washington left "Light Horse" Lee, who was riding in charge of the Virginia militia, in charge of the entire army. When they arrived at Pittsburgh, two of the Whiskey Boys were killed when they resisted and twenty were taken prisoner for trial in Philadelphia. Bradford, one of the few individuals who were not offered a pardon, fled to Spanish Louisiana. Two of the prisoners were eventually convicted of treason and hanged.[6]

The biggest challenge in Washington's second term was presented by the French Revolution and the pan-European war that it provoked. France declared war on both Austria and Prussia in the spring of 1792 and repelled armies of invasion sent by those two countries. Britain joined the anti-revolutionary coalition in February 1793 after France invaded Belgium. Spain and the Netherlands then joined the coalition. But Prussia and Spain left the coalition in 1795.

Initially most Americans sided with the French republicans, both out of gratitude for French assistance during the American Revolution and because of a natural ideological identification with other republics. But when the French Revolution turned anti-Christian and began creating its own religion, Federalists were deeply offended. Federalists were based on the establishment churches of New England: the Congregational Church, the Presbyterian Church, and the Episcopalian Church. They found this anti-Christianity offensive. This was particularly the case with John Adams who was deeply religious.

The French had already cast the Americans in the role of their client state, assisting France with trade, privateering, and possibly protection of French Caribbean colonies. Genet gave letters of marquis, which recognized the holders as privateers in the service of France, to American captains. They began seizing British merchant vessels on the high seas. Washington was determined to remain neutral in the European war and issued a proclamation of neutrality prohibiting Americans from taking part in hostilities on either land or sea. Washington regarded the various Democratic clubs and Republican clubs, modeled on French societies, as a threat because of their violent rhetoric. Washington had decided, with the unanimous approval of the cabinet, in the summer of 1793 to demand that Paris recall Genet. But Paris had already decided to do so and the demand proved unnecessary.

Britain began impressing men on American ships that they took to be British. Britain also seized American merchant ships bringing foodstuffs in violation of its blockade of Europe. These actions combined with French actions led to clamor in Congress for action against both Britain and France. The Federalists advocated preparation for war and sending an envoy to London to warn off the British. Britain decided to withdraw its blockade from American trade with the French Caribbean as a concession.

Washington appointed John Jay, a veteran diplomat from the American Revolution, to negotiate a treaty with Britain to resolve the outstanding issues between the two countries. Washington knew that Hamilton was too pro-British to appoint as negotiator—the Republicans would automatically reject anything negotiated by him. He did not want to send a Republican, as the Republicans were too pro-French and unlikely to successfully resolve the dispute. Jay was a moderate Federalist whom Washington deemed acceptable. Washington also changed American ambassadors in France, replacing the aristocratic Gouverneur Morris with James Monroe, a supporter of Jefferson. Morris had been too aristocratic for the French republicans. And Washington sent Thomas Pinckney to Madrid to attempt to open up the lower Mississippi River to American navigation and resolve boundary disputes between American and Spanish territories. These three powers (Britain, France, Spain) and the Netherlands were the only countries with which American diplomacy concerned itself in the late eighteenth century. America had limited funds with which to conduct its foreign relations—maintaining embassies and negotiating treaties—so it concerned itself only with the leading European powers in the Western Hemisphere, specifically in North America and the Caribbean.

Jay signed a treaty with Britain on November 19, 1794, which required evacuation of the seven British forts in the Northwest during 1796 in exchange for American concessions on trade. The Jay treaty was very unpopular in the United States with the public and the Republicans. Washington even temporarily went against the treaty in the summer of 1795; but he concluded that the top American priority was getting the British out of the Northwest and opening up the territory for settlement. Washington announced at a cabinet meeting in August 1795 that he would sign the treaty. For this he was severely criticized by the Republican press. The Jay treaty passed the House by a vote of 50 to 49 with the Republican speaker sacrificing his political career in order to break the tie. Wayne quite happily took the surrender of Fort Miami in Ohio in 1796, a fort he had wanted to assault in 1794.

In his farewell address in 1797, Washington warned against both permanent hostilities and permanent alliances, stating that the United States had only permanent interests. He had enshrined in American consciousness the concept of national interest.[7]

ANDREW JACKSON (1829–37)

Andrew Jackson's presidency is remembered by historians mainly for four things: the nullification crisis, the Bank of the United States battle, Indian removal, and the two Indian wars that occurred during his presidency. I review these four issues, concentrating on the latter two.

Secretary of the Treasury Alexander Hamilton created the original Bank of the United States in 1791. It was a private bank, with the government owning some of the stock, and was chartered for a twenty-year period. It was designed to issue currency and stimulate the economy by granting loans. It was resented by Westerners, such as Senator Thomas Hart Benton, for supposedly granting special favors to powerful men; and its charter was not renewed. For the next five years currency issue was in the hands of state banks that tended to overissue, thereby fueling inflation that was detrimental to savings. So in 1816 a second Bank of the United States was chartered for another twenty years. This second bank was again unpopular with Westerners and with middle- and lower-class Americans. The opponents claimed that it had a virtual monopoly over currency and credit and that it served the interests of a privileged few. The bank was well managed; but as it was designed mainly to serve industry, ordinary Americans resented it. Jackson as a candidate campaigned against it. Jackson used the bank as a leading issue in his campaign for reelection in 1832.

During his second term, in September 1833, Jackson ordered that no more government money be deposited in the bank and that money already deposited with the bank be withdrawn gradually in order to meet the operating expenses of government. Carefully chosen state banks then became a substitute for the Bank of the United States as a source of deposit of national funds. This unregulated system helped to fuel western expansion but also kept the country subject to periodic panics and depressions, such as the panic of 1837 that crippled Jackson's successor.[8]

Near the end of Jackson's first term, a protective tariff was passed that was unpopular in South Carolina, as the planters there saw it as benefiting Northern manufacturers while making them poorer. John C. Calhoun, who had been Jackson's vice president up until 1832, led the local battle against the tariff. In 1828 he had written in his *South Carolina Exposition and Protest* that states had the right to declare tariffs null and void within their borders. South Carolina adopted an ordinance of nullification that declared both the 1832 tariff and a steeper 1828 tariff to be null and void within state borders. The state also passed measures to enforce the ordinance by appropriating money for raising and equipping a military force.

In response Jackson dispatched seven small naval vessels and a major warship to Charleston in November 1832. On December 10 he issued a proclamation against the nullifiers that declared them to be on "the brink of insurrection and treason." He appealed to the citizens of the state over the heads of their government to be loyal to the Union.

When the issue of tariffs again came before Congress, it became evident that only National Republican Henry Clay, the champion of tariffs, could steer a compromise measure through Congress. This he did. Clay's tariff bill quickly passed Congress in 1833. It specified that all tariffs in excess of 20 percent of the value of the good would be gradually reduced so that by 1842 all tariffs would be at the level of the moderate tariff of 1816. Nullification was not supported by any other state, which greatly disappointed South Carolina. Both sides claimed victory: South Carolina got what it desired and the United States defeated the doctrine of nullification.

Calhoun established himself as the champion of states' rights in the South for the rest of his life—another eighteen years.[9]

The Adams Administration was in favor of Indian removal as a solution but was never able to implement it. Secretary of State Henry Clay told the cabinet that Indians were inferior and predicted that they were destined for extinction and that "their disappearance from the human family will be no great loss to the world." No member of the cabinet objected to Clay's remarks. One might think that it would be natural for slave-owners such as Clay to consider humans of another race to be naturally inferior, but the derogatory attitudes toward Indians crossed party, sectional, and socio-economic lines.

In 1828 Adams shot himself in the foot politically when he declared that the Treaty of Indian Springs between Georgia and the Creek Nation was "null and void" on the grounds that the Creek had never properly ratified it. Adams called for a survey and a renegotiation of the treaty. The Senate appointed a committee headed by Senator Thomas Hart Benton of Missouri to investigate the issue. The committee criticized the administration for interfering in the internal affairs of Georgia. This lost Georgia for Adams in 1828 and probably several other states as well. Jackson advised his friend John Coffee and John D. Terrill, appointed commissioners to negotiate the treaty, not to make promises they could not "religiously perform" when negotiating with Indians. The negotiations failed and the matter soon became academic.[10]

On December 20, 1828, the Georgia legislature passed a law stating that all Indians within its borders would fall under its jurisdiction within six months. Alabama and Mississippi seemed likely to soon follow Georgia's lead. Jackson sent two Tennessee militia generals, John Coffee and William Carroll, to try to persuade the Creek and Cherokee to relocate voluntarily. Carroll served as governor of Tennessee from 1821 to 1827 and was a veteran of the War of 1812.

National security was Jackson's prime concern, and the welfare of the Indians was a secondary concern. Jackson had a paternalistic attitude toward the Indians, much like the attitude of white Afrikaners toward the mixed-race Coloreds in South Africa. Jackson saw removal as a means of preventing annihilation. Interestingly enough, Sam Houston, who had lived with the Cherokee as an assimilated white, was also an advocate of removal and had assisted in it following the War of 1812 when he convinced several bands to move to Arkansas. Basically Jackson had four choices in dealing with the Indians. First, extermination—the Indians were obviously opposed to this, as were most Americans. Second, assimilation—neither whites nor Indians wanted this. Third, enforcement of existing treaties—Indians wanted this, but this was very unpopular with whites and so would have been difficult to implement. Fourth, removal—Indians were opposed to this, but it was very popular with whites.[11]

Jackson appointed Thomas L. McKenney, the official in charge of Indian affairs and an Adams supporter, to mold public opinion in favor of removal. McKenney was noted for his humanistic attitude toward the Indians but was himself in favor of removal as a solution to the problem. Jackson's State of the Union address in December 1829 addressed the Indian question and gave the Indians the choice of voluntary transfer or assimilation and possible extinction. By February 1830 bills were ready for debate in both houses of Congress. On April 26, 1830, the Senate passed a removal bill on a strictly partisan basis. Jackson's opponents accused him of unconstitutional interference in congressional business. The Indian Removal Act was signed into law on May 28, 1830, after passing the House. The act allowed the president to exchange land in the West, across the Mississippi River, for land in the East. An Office (later Bureau) of Indian Affairs was established in 1834 in order to oversee the removals. Jackson had an interesting attitude toward federal treaties with the Indians—he believed that they could be overridden at will by the states. This means that he had one attitude toward nullification that affected Indians and another toward nullification that affected whites.[12]

The Choctaw agreed to move between 1831 and 1833. The Chickasaw agreed to move in 1832. The Seminole agreed to move in May 1832—provided that the land in the West was suitable. The Creek agreed to move in March 1832. By the end of Jackson's first term the Cherokee were the only holdout among the Five Tribes. In March 1831 the Supreme Court had ruled that the Indians were not sovereign nations but rather domestic dependent nations—wards of the federal government—not subject to actions by individual states. By the spring of 1832, as a result of the Supreme Court ruling and the success in getting the Five Tribes to agree to move, it was Jackson administration policy to remove all eastern tribes.[13]

The Cherokee divided into a treaty party, led by a Major Ridge and his son, who was the editor of the Cherokee newspaper *Phoenix,* and a resistance party. Many of the treaty party were later mysteriously murdered for their stand in favor of removal. Cherokee Chief John Ross was heartily disliked by Jackson as a "half-breed" and a "great villain." Whenever Jackson encountered problems with forcing his views on Indians, he blamed this on the influence of half-breeds, who he considered to be corrupted, unlike the pure Indians of the forest—who of course had no use for courts.

The Cherokee Nation approved a removal treaty by a vote of 79 to 7 on December 28, 1835; but about 94 percent of the Cherokee population boycotted the meeting in protest. By this time about half of all Cherokee households had someone who was literate in Cherokee, English, or both. This enabled them to follow the debate. In 1835 there was a tribal census that arrived at the following population figures for the Cherokee: 8,946 in Georgia; 3,644 in North Carolina; 2,528 in Tennessee; and 1,424 in Alabama for a total of 16,542 eastern Cherokee. The ratification of the treaty in the

U.S. Senate passed by only a single vote on May 23, 1836. The Cherokee took the Jackson administration to court over the removal policy and lost.[14]

After constant badgering from a Jackson in retirement, the Van Buren administration ordered the use of militia to execute the removal of the Cherokee from Georgia. By June 1838 all the Cherokee tribe was out of Georgia. More than eighteen thousand were removed and at least four thousand—and possibly as many as twice that figure—died along the way to the West. It was a very harsh winter, and the militia forcing the Indians to leave with little chance to prepare exacerbated this. Ross won permission for the Cherokee to proceed westward without a military escort. General Winfield Scott accompanied one of the first groups to leave as an observer. Scott had considerable sympathy for the Cherokee and ordered his troops to treat them kindly during the removal. But in late October he was recalled to Nashville and ordered to proceed north to deal with another border dispute with Canada. Only a small group of Cherokee remained in the mountains of western North Carolina, as no one wanted their land.[15]

As part of the removal process Jackson acquired about 100 million acres of land in the East in exchange for $68 million and 32 million acres in the West or about 68 million acres net for $68 million or about $1.00 per acre. This was a good price for the government but not nearly so cheap as some of the land bought earlier from the Indians or the French or the Spanish.

By the time Jackson became president, the population of the United States had tripled from at the time of the revolution and the number of states had increased from thirteen to twenty-four. During this same period the number of Indians had steadily diminished. By 1800 there were 700,000 whites living west of the Appalachians and 100,000 Indians. The number of whites in the transmountain area had continued to increase since then. Only about nine thousand Indians were without treaty stipulations for removal when Jackson left office. As one recent historian has concluded, "frontier whites did not want Indians civilized. They wanted them out."[16]

The fate of the Cherokee leader, Major Ridge, who supported going along with the removal, is ironic. He, then known as The Ridge, had been one of a party that assassinated Chief Doublehead in July 1807 for selling land to whites without permission in 1805–06. This left the Cherokee only in possession of the southeastern corner of Tennessee—about 5 percent of the total area of the state. After this most Cherokee land was in North Carolina and Georgia. In 1808–10 the Cherokee passed a series of measures prohibiting individual land sales and recognizing the supremacy of the council. The penalty for defying these laws was death. This was the beginning of the Cherokee Nation, a legal entity recognized by the United States. In 1827 the Cherokee Nation was formally instituted with a constitution based on the American Constitution. The Ridge and Elias Boudinot, editor of the *Phoenix*, were murdered in Oklahoma shortly after John Ross arrived there.[17]

A small group of Cherokee living in the mountains of western North Carolina was allowed to remain. The price for this concession was that they executed four Cherokee who resisted the expulsion by killing two soldiers and wounding a third. (They today live in Quallatown.) During the Civil War they provided two 110-man companies, known as the Thomas Legion, for local defense to North Carolina. In Indian Territory in Oklahoma there was a mini civil war among the Five Civilized Nations during the Civil War. Some fought with the Union and some fought with the Confederacy. It was a choice between fighting for the government that deported them or for the people who instigated the deportation.[18]

The final Indian wars in the East were fought during the Jackson and Van Buren administrations. First, there was the Black Hawk War with four thousand soldiers and militiamen chasing after two thousand Indians—the number was only a quarter of that by the final battle. Jackson wanted to make Black Hawk an example and gave orders to ensure that he was captured. Jackson also personally ordered General Winfield Scott out to direct the war effort. Scott was too late to take part in the war, but he did remain to negotiate a new treaty with the Sauk and Fox. Scott promoted the return to power of Chief Keokuk, who had been in power until shortly before the war. They were forced to give up about 6 million acres—most of present day Iowa—and received about four hundred square miles on the Iowa River; and the Winnebago were forced to cede 5 million acres—most of Wisconsin—even though they sided with the government.[19]

The Second Seminole War began in December 1835 with the ambush of a company of troops providing escort for civilians moving through Seminole territory. The Seminole had found the territory allotted for them in the West to be unacceptable. The war lasted for over six years and involved some forty-one thousand federal troops at different times. It cost the lives of thirteen hundred regulars and cost the treasury nearly $120 million. It was the most difficult Indian war ever fought by the United States. General Scott, who had no previous experience, arrived in Augusta, Georgia, to take command at the end of January 1836. On his way through he had stopped off in Washington to get personal advice from Old Hickory on the techniques of Indian fighting. Scott conducted a two-month campaign through Seminole territory without encountering any resistance. In May 1836 he was ordered from Florida to Georgia to deal with a Creek uprising in the Chattahoochee Valley of western Georgia. Major General Thomas Jesup put down the rebellion in July. Jesup managed to catch the Seminole leader, Chief Osceola, through an illegal ruse—when the latter was under a white flag of truce—and imprison him. Osceola died in prison on January 31, 1838, and the war continued for another four years. Brigadier General Zachary Taylor did much to end the war by overseeing the deportation of about four thousand Seminole to the West. Taylor ended his period as commander of Florida in April 1839 but remained for about another year as an Indian commissioner to negotiate with the Seminole. Several hundred Seminole escaped by hiding in the Everglades, and a third war was fought in the late 1850s (1856–68) during the Buchanan administration.[20]

ZACHARY TAYLOR (1849-50)

Zachary Taylor was in office as president for only sixteen months. He came into office with no political experience or even any great interest in politics. Taylor believed in a very limited rather than an activist presidency. He suggested no policies or programs in his short inaugural address. He relied upon advice from Thomas Crittenden, a prominent Whig senator from Kentucky and longtime personal friend who had functioned as his campaign manager. Crittenden himself refused to join the administration out of fear that there would be rumors of a "corrupt bargain" similar to that between Adams and Clay in 1824. His cabinet selections were "generally respectable, solid appointments" and included some from the Harrison-Tyler administration. Thomas Ewing, Harrison's secretary of the treasury, was made secretary of the interior.

Taylor simply ignored the main Whig leaders like Clay, Webster, and John Bell of Tennessee, both in choosing his cabinet and in determining his policy. Clay complained in 1850, "I have never before seen such an Administration. There is very little cooperation or concord between the two ends of the avenue (i.e., the White House and Congress). There is not, I believe, a prominent Whig in either House that has any confidential intercourse with the Executive."[21]

Taylor took a tour of the Northeast as a vacation in the summer of 1849. In Ohio Taylor met with a group of Northern Whigs and told them, "The people of the North need have no apprehension of the further expansion of slavery." Taylor at this point may have been thinking of forming a new party or of changing the alignment of the Whig Party. His main domestic problem during his administration was the controversy over the spread of slavery and the status of the new territories won from Mexico. A group of secessionist Calhoun supporters met in South Carolina in May 1849 and urged making common cause with like-minded people in other Southern states. The governor suggested putting the state on a "military footing." In October a large unofficial meeting took place in Jackson, Mississippi, and called for a convention of dissatisfied Southerners at Nashville on June 3, 1850. These Southerners saw the Wilmot Proviso, prohibiting territory won from Mexico from coming into the Union as slave territory, as "a deliberate act of aggression against our legal rights." States' rights and free soil were bipartisan or multipartisan issues in the South and North, respectively. By December 1849 when the thirty-first Congress opened there was open talk of secession.[22]

His aide, Colonel William Bliss, carried Taylor's only integrated policy statement, the State of the Union message, to Congress on Christmas Eve.

After a review of foreign relations with Europe and Latin America, Taylor discussed domestic affairs. This was mostly devoted to tariffs and a discussion of military reforms, something dear to Taylor's heart. Taylor thought secession was anathema but did not suggest any proposals to deal with the crisis. But others in the Whig Party did.

Henry Clay and Daniel Webster worked out a series of compromise proposals, later the basis of the 1850 Compromise, at Webster's home on January 21, 1850. The two came up with six proposals:

- Organize territories without regard to slavery.
- California would have a free choice over slavery.
- The federal government would assume Texas' debt in exchange for relinquishment of its claims to New Mexico.
- Abolish slave trade in the District of Columbia.
- Pass a stronger fugitive slave law.
- Prepare a declaration of freedom of interstate slave trade.

These proposals were presented as a package in an attempt to settle the national controversy over slavery. Clay gave a three-hour speech in support of the proposals in the Senate on February 5 and then spoke again for almost two hours the next morning. On February 28, 1850, Senator John Bell offered an alternative compromise that was closer to Taylor's ideas than to Clay's. Calhoun, who was dying of consumption, appeared in the Senate and had Senator Mason of Virginia read a speech for him putting forward the rejectionist Southern position. On March 7, 1850, Webster gave a three-hour epic speech pleading for tolerance and compromise. The speech earned him praise everywhere except for in his own New England.[23]

Stephen A. Douglas was chair of the Committee on Territories in the Senate. He worked with Southern leaders to develop a compromise on territorial admissions. Douglas reported a bill on March 25, but before discussion could start Calhoun died. This removed a restraining influence on Southern fire-breathers who were advocating secession. On April 17 Senator Henry S. Foote of Mississippi pulled a pistol on Senator Thomas Hart Benton and claimed that Benton had threatened him. The next day a thirteen-man executive committee was created to secretly work out the California constitution and all of the slavery proposals. It consisted of three Northerners and three Southerners from each of the two main parties with Clay as the chairman. Five of the members had been or would be presidential candidates (Bell, Cass, Clay, Douglas, and Webster). The final compromise, which was worked out on May 8, 1850, was very close to the original Clay-Webster proposals.

Taylor was ill-suited for leadership at such a delicate time. He was quick to take offense, tended to hold grudges, and was jealous of those who were more talented than he. Taylor opposed the Clay proposals, probably for three reasons: first, out of a desire to show his independence from the Whig leadership; second, to demonstrate that his administration was capable of managing the country on its own; and third, because of personal pique at Clay for opposing his nomination. After a debate, the Senate was split with nineteen each supporting the Clay proposals and the administration's proposals, five supporting the Wilmot Proviso, and four wanting to extend the 1820 Missouri Compromise line to the Pacific.

Taylor announced that he was prepared to use force to stop secession, not aware of the political impact that such use of force could have. Alexander Stephens of Georgia, the future vice president of the Confederacy, threatened to impeach Taylor if he used force against Texas in its border dispute with New Mexico. The Nashville Convention met June 3–12, 1850, with nine states sending delegates. But the convention could not agree on a single definition of states' rights. Vice President Millard Fillmore told Taylor that he intended to vote for Clay's compromise proposals in order to break the tie. The Clay proposals had been reintroduced as a series of separate bills rather than as a single measure, after failing as a package proposal in July. Stephen Douglas shepherded the proposals through the Senate with the support of President Fillmore.

The House was preparing to investigate Secretary of War George Crawford for an affair before he joined the administration. A major cabinet shake-up was planned with Crittenden replacing Crawford at state, John Bell becoming attorney general, and Governor Hamilton Fish of New York becoming secretary of the treasury. Then Taylor suddenly died of dysentery or diarrhea after eating lots of fresh vegetables and drinking buttermilk during the Fourth of July weekend. Webster returned to the cabinet as secretary of state shortly after Taylor's death.[24]

American foreign relations were in good shape when Taylor took office. Taylor was not directly involved in either foreign policy formulation or diplomacy. He abandoned control of this field to his secretary of state. The administration greeted the wave of European revolutions in 1848–49 with cautious support. Taylor instructed a diplomat in Paris to secretly visit Hungary and assess the prospects for success of the revolution. The revolution was crushed by Austrian and Russian troops before the diplomat could make his trip. The German revolutionary government was in the process of collapse when Taylor took power. Taylor did not embrace the Monroe Doctrine with great enthusiasm, but his administration adhered scrupulously to international law and its treaty obligations.[25]

Taylor and Jackson were Southerners, planters, and nationalists, but Jackson was too much of a populist for Taylor's taste. Taylor was very stubborn once he set his mind on something and would not be moved. Taylor was a poor public speaker who tended to stammer. Even a recent biographer referred to him as "a man of limited emotional and intellectual capacity." Another recent biographer conceded that he was remembered more as a military leader than as an effective president. James Buchanan's secretary of war, William Marcy, wrote:

I thought well of him as a general but never for a moment regarded him as a great one. His knowledge of military affairs beyond the details in which his life had been spent was very limited. . . . His bravery and steadfastness of purpose are the summary of his high qualities as a commanding officer.[26]

JEFFERSON DAVIS (1861–65)

Jefferson Davis took the oath of office as president of the Confederate States of America in Montgomery, Alabama, in late February 1861, exactly two weeks before Abraham Lincoln—the proximate cause of the Southern secession—took his oath of office in Washington. Only two other candidates were even considered by the delegates, Robert Toombs and Howell Cobb, and Davis ended up as the unanimous choice as Washington had been. This was because he combined in a single individual legislative, executive, and military experience. At this time there were only seven Confederate states—the states bordering the Gulf of Mexico, Georgia, and South Carolina. But Virginia, North Carolina, Tennessee, and Arkansas followed suit in March 1861.[27]

Davis modeled his cabinet on the American cabinets of his day: a secretary of war, secretary of state, secretary of the treasury, attorney general, secretary of the navy, and postmaster general. Representation in the cabinet was more a matter of balancing the states, as in the United Nations Security Council, than it was a matter of picking the best talent. Nine states out of eleven were at various times represented in the cabinet—only Tennessee and Arkansas were never represented, and Kentucky, which never joined the Confederacy, was represented by John C. Breckenridge.

Davis worked hard but concentrated on the big picture—important issues of strategy and state—leaving details for his aides and cabinet secretaries to take care of. Davis, like Lincoln, often acted as his own secretary of war—consulting with generals directly. Because of his own experiences as a West Point graduate, officer, commander in Mexico, and secretary of war under Pierce, this was natural. Davis had in fact wanted to serve as a general at the beginning of the war but had to be persuaded that he could be more effectively used in a political than in a military capacity.

Davis was both a militarist and a constitutionalist—he believed in both force and constitutional legitimacy. Throughout the four years of the Confederacy, the individual states remained stronger than the central government, which moved from Montgomery to Richmond, Virginia, in the spring so as to be closer to the center of fighting. This was the fatal flaw of the Confederacy. Davis had a deep sense of dignity and always defended the prestige of the presidency, not only for his own sake but for that of the office. He was a deeply religious man who set aside days of prayer for the Confederacy. Davis's vice president was Alexander Stephens, a former moderate Southern Whig who was not a secessionist but like Lee went along with secession out of a sense of regional patriotism. Stephens was a greater defender of individual liberty than of collective independence and in turn opposed all major steps taken to increase the power of the Confederacy: conscription, impressment of property, and the increased power of the military.[28]

Three great problems were to confront Davis during his time as president: first, keeping the armies of the North from overrunning the South and suppressing his government; second, raising enough revenue to pay for the defense of the South and its government and keep the economy solvent; and third, winning foreign recognition so as to aid in the first two goals.

Other than by his experience as a planter, Davis was not an economist or businessman with a profound understanding of economics and commerce. So he let his secretary of the treasury handle the economy. The three weak offices in the cabinet were postmaster general, attorney general, and secretary of the navy. Communications depended more upon the military situation than they did on the policies of the postmaster general. The attorney general, Judah Benjamin, made a few legal rulings but was not otherwise greatly occupied, as crime was generally left to the states and local governments to investigate and punish. With the exception of a handful of commerce raiders, like the *CSS Alabama* and the *CSS Florida* and a few ironclads, the South never really had a navy.

Once he had given a few general guidelines to his secretaries, Davis spent most of his time occupied with grand strategy and with relations with the prickly state governments. Davis wanted Braxton Bragg as his secretary of war, but Bragg opted to become a general commanding in the West. He came to Richmond in February 1864 to serve as a personal military aide and advisor to Davis. Davis suffered—or benefited, depending on how one interprets his true wishes—from a string of weak inexperienced secretaries of war.

The first secretary of war, William H. Russell, had no military training or experience but held a commission as brigadier general in the Alabama militia. Next came Attorney General Judah Benjamin, who became acting secretary of war in September 1861 and remained for six months. His first action upon taking command was to conduct a survey of war needs. He concluded that there was an insufficient supply of saltpeter—needed for making gunpowder—and not enough small arms for the army or the ability to produce them locally. He was unfairly blamed for Confederate reversals in the West, the fall of Forts Henry and Donelson to General Grant, and the loss of Roanoke Island off the coast of Virginia to the federal navy. George Wythe Randolph, who had served as a midshipman in the American Navy for six years in the 1840s as a teenager before becoming a lawyer, followed him in

1862. He briefly commanded an artillery unit until February 1862 when he resigned from the army for reasons of health. Randolph lasted only two months longer than Benjamin had.[29]

On November 22, 1862, James A. Seddon took over as secretary of war. Seddon remained as secretary of war for twenty-six months before resigning for health reasons on February 7, 1865—by which time the war was lost. Seddon was ill for much of 1864 and often absent from his office for health reasons. Seddon was a close personal friend of Davis, but his influence over Davis on military policy began to fade from the summer of 1863 following the Confederated defeats at Vicksburg and Gettysburg. Seddon was a Richmond lawyer who had served two terms in the U.S. House. He had no military experience. His most important decision was appointing Joseph Johnston commander in the West.

The final secretary of war was John C. Breckenridge, who had been Buchanan's vice president, a Southern Democratic presidential candidate in 1860, then served as a senator in 1861 until he decided that his usefulness to the South in Washington was finished. He then joined the Confederate army as a general. He wanted to surrender in February 1865 but failed to persuade Davis. He spent most of his tenure as secretary in the field conferring with the commanders of the Confederate armies. He was briefly involved in surrender negotiations with Sherman in April 1865.[30]

For the first year of the war General Robert E. Lee served as the chief engineer of the Confederacy constructing defensive works in Virginia. He also served as personal military advisor to Davis, and the two of them developed war plans together. When General Joseph Johnston was severely wounded during the Seven Days' Battles in May 1862, General Lee was appointed to replace him as the commander of the army of Northern Virginia. The South's best chance to win the war was in the beginning at the First Battle of Bull Run (First Manassas) in July 1861 when the Union army retreated in panic. Had the Confederate army followed up in pursuit, they might have captured the capital and forced the North to sue for peace by recognizing Southern independence. By the time that Davis decided to invade the North in September 1862, the North was too strong and well organized to defeat. Lee lost the bloody Battle of Antietam fighting on nominally Northern soil in Maryland. This was against the tactically incompetent and timid commander General Phillip McClellan. Against General George Meade in July 1863, Lee lost on an even bigger scale.

By mid-1863, halfway through the life of the Confederacy, at any one time one-third to one-half of the Confederate army (including the state armies) was away without leave. Armies of deserters roamed the countryside robbing farmers and waging guerrilla warfare against the Confederacy. This meant that valuable state troops were used for local defense. The depreciated currency made people reluctant to sell to the Confederate government. The problems of the South could only have been solved through the recognition and support of a foreign power. To this end the South directed its foreign policy.[31]

The first Confederate secretary of state was Robert Toombs, a Georgia lawyer and Whig who served in the state legislature. He was elected to Congress in 1844 and to the Senate in 1851. His selection was popular. Toombs sent Confederate envoys to Belgium, Britain, France, and Spain. The general strategy was to win foreign recognition on the basis of virtual free trade and liberal navigation laws. All he won from Europe was recognition of belligerent rights under international law and that Southern privateers would be considered that and not pirates. Spain was told that the South no longer had any territorial designs on Cuba, as those designs had been based on a desire to balance the free states within the United States with the creation of more slave states. As independence had occurred, there was no longer any necessity to annex Cuba. Spain was not entirely convinced by this argument.

The problem for the South was that the Europeans did not want to antagonize the United States by intervening in a civil war, and the United States played on that fear by threatening legal sanctions against any power that recognized the South. The South's plans were centered upon Britain and France, the two leading European powers. But Napoleon III, the emperor of France during the Civil War, took his clues from Britain. The able Charles F. Adams, the former Conscience Whig and Free Soil candidate, represented Washington in London. Adams had diplomacy both in his blood and in his upbringing; he was a child in Russia when his father was ambassador there. Adams prevented the *CSS Alabama*—the South's most successful commerce raider—from being armed in Britain, although a British ship managed to rendezvous with it at sea and provide it with its armament. In order to win European recognition, the Confederacy had to win a big victory on the battlefield to convince Europe that it was capable of winning the war. It made no sense to the Europeans to risk reprisals from Washington in exchange for commercial treaties with a country under blockade and with no hope of winning independence. Realizing that he had done all he could, Toombs resigned as secretary of state and became a brigadier general in the army. He resigned from the army after Antietam and returned to his plantation. Toombs's only previous military experience had been as a militia captain during the Creek rebellion of 1836.[32]

Robert Mercer Taliaferro Hunter was Toombs's successor. Hunter was a planter-lawyer who served in the U.S. Congress and the Senate from Virginia. Hunter amended Toombs's instructions and sent them to the envoys. The main change was that in exchange for recognition he was offering long-term (twenty-year) commercial treaties with low tariffs, combined with a legal defense of the South's right to secede under the Constitution. Hunter personally wrote out the diplomatic guidelines/instructions for his envoys and had Davis approve them. His instructions said that the Confederacy would make peace with the North in exchange for independence and a referendum on independence in the border states. This was a pipe dream. Hunter resigned in order to strengthen the Confederate Senate as a senator from Virginia on February 22, 1862, and was replaced by William M. Browne.

After Benjamin resigned as acting secretary of war in March 1862 he became secretary of state and Browne became a presidential aide. Benjamin continued as attorney general and remained in both cabinet posts until the end of the war. Benjamin's appointment was unpopular with the public, who still blamed him for Confederate reversals, but was supported by the press. Benjamin concentrated his diplomatic efforts totally on Britain and France and did not even bother explaining the South's position to lesser powers such as the Netherlands and Russia, which were considered unimportant. Benjamin directed James Monroe, the Confederate envoy to England, to demand British recognition or the South would withdraw its legation. He thought that this threat might shock Britain into acting. Mason saw no chance of getting recognition and so withdrew from London to Paris on October 1, 1863. By early 1865 Benjamin was so desperate that he offered the abolition of slavery in exchange for recognition—something that might have worked in 1861 or 1862. But London refused to take the bait, as it knew that this would not end the war. Paris followed London's lead. The closest Benjamin ever got to winning foreign recognition was a letter from the Pope, at a time before the Vatican was an independent state, addressed to "the President of the Confederate States of America." But this was a meaningless gesture. On October 7, 1864, Benjamin issued a decree stripping the British consuls in the Confederacy of their powers. Formally he was expelling them, but in reality the South merely stopped recognizing their status.

Davis let Benjamin run the Confederate state department as he saw fit, while Benjamin kept Davis well informed of his efforts. Benjamin, a non-practicing Jew married to a Catholic, was the president's alter ego and chief confidant. He was probably the most important secretary in the cabinet throughout his four years because of his personal relationship with Davis.[33]

Davis enjoyed about one good year as president. Outnumbered nearly 2.5:1 or 22 million to 9 million, the South was also dependent on a few cash crops such as cotton and tobacco. Northern agriculture was more devoted to raising food crops, so it was much better able to feed its population. The South had few manufacturing centers, with Charleston and Atlanta being the largest. By the spring of 1862 the Union was on the march in the West. From this point onward the South's perimeter began to shrink. The United States went on the offensive in the spring with Grant capturing Forts Henry and Donelson on the Cumberland and Tennessee Rivers. These victories guaranteed Union control of Kentucky and opened up these two rivers to Union penetration as far as northern Alabama. The North was able to cut off the South's only East-West railroad link. In April 1862 Generals Buell and Grant defeated Albert S. Johnston at Shiloh, and Johnston, possibly the South's most able general, was killed.

In May 1862 McClellan invaded Virginia and fought his way to within about thirty miles of Richmond. He was defeated by Generals Johnston, Lee, and Jackson and forced to retreat out of Virginia. But General Burnsides returned in early 1863 to fight the battle of Fredericksburg. The Union army could penetrate Virginia at will, even if it could not yet capture Richmond. In January 1863 New Orleans was captured by Union troops. The fall of this city helped to make the federal blockade effective cutting off Southern exports of cotton to Europe and Southern imports of food, arms, and medicine. Federal troops began moving to take control of the Mississippi River, moving in both directions. This forced the South to fight where the North chose. In July 1863, as the Confederates were failing in their offensive in Pennsylvania, Grant captured the port of Vicksburg, effectively cutting the Confederacy in two and cutting Arkansas and Texas off from the other states. This resulted in a further loss of manpower.

By the summer of 1863 the Southern armies were suffering major deprivations in the form of worn-out boots, ragged uniforms, and food shortages. Davis could do little to remedy these problems. In the fall of 1863 Grant advanced through Tennessee. In March 1864 he replaced Meade as commander in the East and began actively coordinating his efforts with those of General Sherman, who took his place as commander in the West. By June 1864 Grant had driven to Petersburg and Richmond was under siege. For the remaining ten months of the war Davis could do little except surrender or free the slaves, which was anathema to Southern secessionists. Sherman captured Atlanta and marched to Savannah and the sea. He then marched up into South Carolina.

Davis's main jobs and roles were the promotion, demotion, and replacement of field commanders. Davis would sometimes give advice to Confederate commanders, who might follow it or might not. Many often complained about his interference. Davis, because of his West Point education and experience in Mexico, considered himself a tactical genius. This resulted in disputes with commanders. The war ended with him being much lower in repute than most of the generals, largely because the South preferred to blame its politicians rather than its generals. This is probably a correct judgment because it was the politicians who were rash and foolish enough to secede and go to war in the first place. But this is a problem with the aristocratic culture of the South, with its exaggerated notion of honor and quickness to take insult.

THE INDIAN-FIGHTER PRESIDENTS: A COMPARISON

The first common trait of these four presidents that sticks out is their interest or even obsession with national security. And this interest is directed in the words of an oath that soldiers take, "against all enemies of the Constitution, foreign and domestic." Two of these presidents dealt with

Indian threats. Both supervised the conduct of the wars against the Indians by choosing the generals to lead the military effort.

Two of them, Washington and Davis, faced foreign threats—the latter's threat was foreign by the definition from which Davis was operating. Washington avoided his threat by an astute policy of neutrality and negotiation. Davis, however, created his problem by a rash policy of secession that was opposed to making concessions. Washington aided his nation; Davis hurt both of his nations—the United States and the Confederate States. Washington is still remembered as the "father of his country." Davis is remembered today usually either as a villain or as an unfortunate actor but was for generations remembered as the leader of a heroic lost cause. This belief changed when integration occurred in the South and support for racists was no longer seen as respectable.

All four were involved in national expansion or preservation. Washington's foreign policy was concerned with opening up the trans-Appalachian West to settlement by removing British forts from the Northwest and allowing navigation on the Mississippi. During this period the United States doubled or even tripled its territory by expanding to the Mississippi River. Jefferson, a "civilian" president, also expanded the United States with the Louisiana Purchase in 1803, again doubling the territory of the United States.[34] Jackson expanded the United States by encouraging Houston to go to Texas and by recognizing the government of Texas after the revolution. He then worked after his presidency to replace Van Buren with Polk as the Democratic candidate for president in order to put someone in the White House who favored annexation of Texas. Taylor ended this period by overseeing the integration of the captured territories from the Mexican War into the United States. Davis supported war with Mexico as a representative in Congress but was not able to support the expansion of the Confederacy while its only president, as this was not practical. But the fact that Davis volunteered for service in Mexico demonstrates that he was an expansionist by inclination.

There is in fact a chain of expansion that connects the careers of the Indian-fighter politicians. Washington favored expansion into Ohio. This gave William H. Harrison his first experience fighting Indians in Ohio in 1794 and the beginning of his administrative-political career. Jackson as president gave Taylor a chance to develop his reputation as an Indian fighter by participating in the two Indian wars during his administration. Davis also saw his only spell as an Indian fighter during this first war in 1832. Taylor then gave Davis an opportunity to earn his reputation as a commander by commanding him in the Mexican War. This accelerated the latter's political career through an appointment to the Senate and his selection to the cabinet as secretary of war under Pierce, a fellow Mexican fighter. But Davis as president of the Confederacy, a lost cause, did not have the opportunity to further anyone's career for the postwar era. The chain came to an end.

NOTES

1. John R. Alden, *George Washington* (Baton Rouge, Louisiana State University Press, 1984), p. 237.
2. Ibid., pp. 238–39.
3. Ibid., pp. 242, 243–45, 247.
4. Ibid., pp. 250–52.
5. Alden, op. cit., pp. 248–49, 254–58.
6. Ibid., pp. 262–65.
7. Ibid., pp. 266–88.
8. "United States History, Battle of the Bank," *Webster's World Encyclopedia 2000*.
9. "American History Nullification Crisis," *Webster's World Encyclopedia 2000*.
10. Robert Remini, *Andrew Jackson and His Indian Wars* (New York: Viking, 2001), pp. 222–24.
11. Ibid., pp. 227–29, 279–80; John Finger, *Tennessee Frontiers* (Bloomington, IN: Indiana University Press, 2001), p. 288.
12. Ibid., pp. 232–35, 237, 242; Finger, op. cit., p. 304.
13. Remini, op. cit., pp. 249–55.
14. Ibid., pp. 261–63, 267, 269–70; Finger, op. cit., pp. 298, 309; John R. Fingers, *The Eastern Band of Cherokees* (Knoxville, TN: University of Tennessee Press, 1984), p. 16.
15. John S. D. Eisenhower, *Agent of Destiny* (New York: Free Press, 1997), pp. 193–94; Finger, op. cit., p. 310. Eisenhower gives 2,000 as the number of Cherokee dead on the Trail of Tears. Finger gives the total number of Cherokee in the United States at the time of removal as 16,542. Eisenhower's figure of 18,000 Cherokee possibly included those who were already in the West from earlier removals.
16. Remini, op. cit., pp. 278–79; Finger, op. cit., p. 322.
17. Finger, op. cit., pp. 221, 223, 275, 311; Finger, *Eastern Cherokees*, p. 8.
18. Finger, *Eastern Cherokees*, pp. 23–27, 82–100.
19. Hudson Strode, *Jefferson Davis: American Patriot Volume 1: 1808–61* (New York: Harcourt Brace & Co., 1955), p. 77; Miriam Gurko, *Indian America: The Black Hawk War* (New York: Thomas Crowell, 1970), p. 131; Eisenhower, op. cit., pp. 128, 130–32.
20. Remini, *Indian Wars*, pp. 272–77; Eisenhower, op. cit., pp. 147, 152, 158, 161, 164; David R. Collins, *Zachary Taylor: 12th President of the United States* (Ada, OK: Garret Educational Corp., 1989), pp. 49–52.
21. K. Jack Bauer, *Zachary Taylor: Soldier, Planter, Statesman of the Old Southwest* (Baton Rouge: Louisiana State University Press, 1985), pp. 254–55, 257, 262, 265. Quote is from a letter from Clay to James Harlan quoted on p. 265.
22. Ibid., pp. 268–69, 296–97.
23. Ibid., pp. 298, 301–305; Robert Remini, *Daniel Webster: The Man and His Time* (New York: W. W. Norton, 1997), pp. 463–65.
24. Ibid., pp. 306–307, 309, 310–11, 312, 315; Remini, *Webster*, p. 478; see David Collins, *Zachary Taylor: 12th President of the United States* (Ada, OK: Garret Educational Corp., 1989), pp. 110–11 for an alternate theory of the cause of his death. The belief that Taylor was poisoned was discounted when his body was dug up in the 1990s and an autopsy performed to check for traces of arsenic. No evidence of poisoning was found.

25. Bauer, op. cit., pp. 273–75, 278, 325; Collins, op. cit., p. 116.
26. Ibid., pp. 323, 327.
27. William and Bruce Catton, *Two Roads to Sumter* (New York: McGraw-Hill, 1963), pp. 263, 266–67, 269.
28. Rembert W. Patrick, *Jefferson Davis and His Cabinet* (Baton Rouge, Louisiana State University Press, 1944), pp. 29, 31, 34, 36, 41, 49.
29. Ibid., pp. 104–105, 121, 158, 164, 168, 177–78.
30. Ibid., pp. 132, 138, 140, 147, 148, 149, 152–54.
31. Ibid., pp. 126, 142–43.
32. Ibid., pp. 77–78, 81–83, 86, 90, 92–93, 95–97, 99, 101.
33. Ibid., pp. 101, 182–90.
34. Richard Slotkin, *Fatal Environment* (New York: Harper Perennial, 1994), pp. 109–138.

7

Indian Fighters on the Frontier: Kentucky, Ohio, Tennessee, and Texas

INTRODUCTION

As the Indians were pushed back from the Atlantic seaboard in front of encroaching white settlement and civilization, Indian-fighter politicians increasingly became a feature of the politics of the new frontier states. During the American Revolution and immediate post-revolutionary period there were Indian-fighter politicians from the original thirteen colonies in Virginia, New Hampshire, and Georgia. There were probably other minor Indian-fighter politicians in the Carolinas as well. As the frontier moved westward the focus shifted first to Kentucky and then to Tennessee. Daniel Boone's period as a politician was over before Kentucky gained statehood, and Isaac Shelby was the main Kentucky Indian-fighter politician. The period of Indian fighting was over in Kentucky by the early 1790s as the Shawnee were driven north into northern Ohio. The Treaty of Greenville following the Battle of Fallen Timbers kept the Shawnee and other northern tribes well away from Kentucky.

In order for a state to become a center for Indian-fighter politicians the Indian threat must remain in place for a number of years, possibly for decades. Such a place was Tennessee where the Indian threat remained alive from the time of early white settlement in the late 1780s until the Creek War of 1813 destroyed the power of the last of the southern tribes that were aggressively resisting white encroachment on their lands. Tennessee gave rise to more prominent Indian-fighter politicians than any other state. These included at least three governors, a number of congressmen, one senator, and a president. By name these individuals included: John Sevier, the hero of the Battle of King's Mountain; Andrew Jackson, the hero of New Orleans; William Carroll, Jackson's second-in-command at New Orleans; and Sam Houston, a hero of the Battle of Horseshoe Bend and the future hero of San Jacinto.

Ohio was the home of a number of prominent Indian-fighter politicians. Its territorial governor before statehood was General Arthur St. Clair, who had the misfortune of having half his troops flee in battle to suffer the worst defeat in battle at the hands of Indians of anyone in American history. William Henry Harrison served as General St. Clair's secretary and then, after serving as territorial governor of Indiana, returned to represent Ohio in Congress and to make his home in the state where he also served as a town clerk before being elected president.

The Black Hawk War of 1832 was the final Indian war of the East, except for the last two Seminole wars in central Florida in 1835–42 and 1856–58. But the regular army rather than the militia fought these last two wars. The Black Hawk War was the last Indian war in the East in which militia played a major role; and it produced three governors in Illinois, a future secretary of the interior under Lincoln, and a future governor of Wisconsin.

Texas was the last major center of Indian-fighter politics in the United States. It had an Indian problem longer than any other state: about half a century. Indian raids were a problem from the beginning of white settlement in east Texas in the early 1820s, and Indians remained a threat in the hill country of central Texas until the end of the Red River War of 1874–75. The U.S. Army did the bulk of the fighting in the Red River War. The last Indian battles were fought in west Texas against the Apache during Victorio's War of 1880–81, which was mostly fought by the U.S. Army in New Mexico. Texas had its own militia—a mounted militia: the famous Texas Rangers. They would produce the bulk of Texas' Indian-fighter politicians. They were of influence in the period up until the Civil War and afterward.

KENTUCKY AND OHIO

Kentucky was the first frontier state—the first transmountain state. The name comes from a Cherokee word, "Ken-tah-te," meaning "tomorrow." In the mid-eighteenth century the American population entered a growth phase that had it doubling every twenty-five years. While it took some 170 years to populate the East Coast of America and reach the Appalachian Mountains, it took only a century once the mountains had been crossed to conquer the rest of the country. After Pontiac's Conspiracy of 1763 the British moved quickly to make peace by prohibiting further settlement, with the border being a line drawn along the crest of the Appalachian Mountains. A series of peace meetings with Indian tribes led in 1768 to the Fort Stanwix Treaty. This treaty drew a line from Fort Pitt (Pittsburgh) to the confluence of the Ohio and Tennessee Rivers with the whites kept to the south of the line and the Indians to the north.[1]

Starting in the 1760s after the French and Indian War, parties of "long hunters" numbering up to ten in a group would move into Kentucky and Tennessee and stay for up to two years at a time hunting and trapping. These hunters were in danger of having their pelts "confiscated" by local Indians or even of being killed for invading the local hunting grounds. In 1766 there were at least four parties of "long hunters" in Kentucky. Kentucky was hunting territory for both the Cherokee, the predominant tribe of the Southeast, and the Shawnee, who inhabited southern Ohio. There was no permanent Indian population in central Kentucky due to a mineral deficiency in the water and diet that was fatal to residents. Daniel Boone, who had heard about Kentucky from John Finley, chief scout for General Braddock during the French and Indian War, was not the first explorer or settler in Kentucky. Boone, Finley, Boone's brother-in-law John Stewart, and three others went on a long hunt in Kentucky on May 1, 1768, that lasted for two years. Boone and Stewart were captured by Shawnee and forced to turn over all of their pelts. Stewart was later killed by Indians, another man starved to death while fleeing Indians, and Boone and his brother Squire—who had brought fresh supplies to the party from North Carolina—had many close escapes from the Indians. In May 1771 Boone, on another long hunt, was robbed of his pelts by a party of Cherokee.[2]

In June 1773 a party led by Captain Thomas Bullitt surveyed sites for settlement at the sites of present-day Frankfort and Louisville. In September 1773 Boone led the first party of settlers into Kentucky, but shortly after entering Kentucky the whole party was killed by Indians while Boone was off getting supplies. Harrodsburg, the first permanent settlement, was founded in the spring of 1774 but not really settled until March 1775. Richard Henderson, a lawyer in North Carolina involved in land speculation, hired Boone to make treaties with the Indians and lead a settler party into Kentucky for the Transylvania Company. The next twenty years were marred by repeated clashes between Indians and whites over the land. Boone founded Boonesboro (also spelled Boonesborough) in April 1775 just as the American Revolution was beginning in Massachusetts. On May 23, 1775, representatives of all the settlements in Kentucky—three main settlements—met and agreed to a constitution that entailed company rule with settler representation. George Rogers Clark arrived in the summer of 1775. He returned to Virginia for the winter and then returned to Kentucky in the spring of 1776. In June 1776 Clark and another man were elected as delegates to represent Kentucky in the Virginia assembly. Clark continued to represent Kentucky for at least two terms—coinciding with the period during which he pursued a war against the British in the West. Kentucky County was created in December 1776 with the county seat at Harrodstown.[3]

Indian raids had depopulated Kentucky by 1777 so that only about 150 settlers remained in three settlements. In the fall of 1777 a hundred Virginia militiamen reinforced them and then were joined by some Carolina troops from the Yadkin Valley, where many of the settlers had come from. Harrodstown had 217 residents in 1778 including 24 women. Boonesboro was besieged by Indians led by Shawnee Chief Blackfish for several weeks in September 1778. Boone had escaped from captivity in Ohio, where he was treated as the adopted son of Blackfish, in order to warn Boonesboro of the coming attack. He had been taken captive at Blue Licks in February 1778 while getting salt for the settlement. He was later tried by court martial and found innocent of treason.

A relative peace prevailed from 1778 to 1781 between the Indian alliance of Shawnee, Mingo, and Wyandotte and the settlers. There was major immigration to Kentucky in 1780. Many of the new settlers were probably loyalist refugees from the East, but nobody cared in Kentucky as long as they were anti-Indian and willing to fight.

There were major battles between Indians and whites in 1782 as the British tried to secure control of the Ohio Valley. The last major battle of the Revolution was fought at Upper Blue Licks in August 1782 when Indians ambushed white militia. Boone counseled caution and was taunted with cowardice. He paid the price of giving into that taunt by losing a son.[4]

The population of Kentucky went from a few hundred whites in 1780, to twelve thousand in 1783, to one hundred thousand by 1792 when statehood was achieved. At the time of the first census in 1790 there were 12,430 slaves. Kentucky politicians—that is to say wealthy landowners—first began organizing in favor of statehood in 1784. It took them eight years to achieve that goal in June 1792. Leading advocates of statehood included: James Wilkinson, intriguer with the Spanish and commander in chief of the American army before the War of 1812 who was involved in Aaron Burr's conspiracy; Green Clay, a former surveyor who became a wealthy landowner and served as a state legislator from Madison County for two decades before serving as commander of the state militia in the War of 1812 under General Harrison; and Isaac Shelby, the son of Indian fighter Evan Shelby and himself a hero of the Battle of King's Mountain and the first governor of Kentucky.[5]

The last Indian fights took place in the early 1790s before the Battle of Fallen Timber brought permanent peace to Kentucky. From the 1790s until the War of 1812 there was no opportunity to produce new Indian fighters. During the War of 1812 a number of new Indian fighters arose, as the state militia was very active in the war. The Kentucky frontiersman became an American folk legend from Daniel Boone to the Battle of New Orleans to John Wayne's movie *The Fighting Kentuckian*. The Whig Party was very influential in Kentucky, the home of one of its primary statesmen, Henry Clay. Kentucky—in addition to Boone, who retired from politics in 1791—had three main Indian-fighter politicians.[6]

Kentucky Indian-Fighter Politicians

As mentioned previously, Isaac Shelby was a hero of the American Revolution as co-commander of troops with John Sevier at King's Mountain. Before that he had defeated British troops led by Major Patrick Ferguson in several battles in the Carolinas, but General Cornwallis's victory at Camden forced him to retreat across the Appalachians to the Watauga settlement. He was also involved with his father Evan in various battles against the Cherokee. His family had moved to East Tennessee in 1773, then part of Virginia, from Maryland, and a decade later he moved to Kentucky after marrying a Boonesboro woman the previous year. Shelby began his political career in the Virginia legislature in 1779 representing Washington County. Three years later, after King's Mountain, he was elected a member of the North Carolina legislature. In 1792 he was elected the first governor of Kentucky and served a single four-year term. He became a leading bourbon whiskey distiller, and his only political involvement after leaving the governor's mansion was to participate in the constitutional convention of 1799. In 1812 he was again elected governor for four years. During this time he commanded troops under General Harrison at the Battle of the Thames in October 1813, for which Congress gave him a gold medal. After turning down an appointment as secretary of war by President James Monroe, he became a commissioner for peace treaties with the Chickasaw Indians. He died in July 1826 at age 76.[7]

Green Clay came to Kentucky in 1780 as a surveyor after having served as a soldier in the Continental Army during the Revolution. In 1788–89 he was elected to the Virginia state legislature to represent Kentucky; he was elected to the state legislature in 1793–94; and from there he was elected to the state senate in 1795–98 and again in 1807. He was a delegate to the Kentucky state constitutional convention in 1799. In the War of 1812 he served as a brigadier general in the Kentucky militia under General Harrison commanding some twelve hundred troops. He participated in the capture of Fort Meigs in May 1813 and then held the fort while Harrison advanced in pursuit of Brigadier General Procter and Tecumseh. Thus, Clay was a politician who became an Indian fighter rather than the reverse. He died in October 1826 a few months after Isaac Shelby. He was the father of Cassius Marcellus Clay, the leading abolitionist in the South, who served as a major general in the Union Army during the Civil War.[8]

The final Indian-fighter politician was Richard Johnson. Johnson was born in Louisville in 1781—a first-generation Kentuckian. After studying law at Transylvania University he was admitted to the bar in 1802 and became a state legislator in 1804. Johnson, a Democrat, served for three decades in both houses of Congress beginning with the House in 1807, where along with Henry Clay he was a leading war hawk. In 1812 he resigned to fight in the war, commanding a regiment of mounted Kentucky riflemen that he raised himself. He was a leading hero of the Battle of the Thames and claimed to have killed Tecumseh himself in the battle, a claim that most historians dismiss. He was severely wounded in the battle by the chief he killed, who he claimed was Tecumseh. Several British officers captured in the battle identified the body as Tecumseh's, but Indians report that Tecumseh's body was removed from the battlefield and buried in a swamp by fellow Indians.

After the war Johnson returned to the House where he served until 1819 when he was elected to the Senate. He served in the Senate for a decade before returning to the House. He was a loyal supporter of President Jackson. His main political issues were opposition to imprisonment of debtors, opposition to the elimination of Sunday mail service, and support of public education. He established an academy for Indians. He was Martin Van Buren's running mate in 1836, when he failed to win a majority in the electoral college and so was elected by the Senate, the only time in American history when a vice president was chosen by the Senate. Johnson returned to Kentucky in 1841 to once again sit in the state legislature, after Van Buren lost to Harrison. Johnson died in 1850. He was hurt as a national politician by openly living with a mulatto mistress that offended both the religious and the racists in the South. He was accused of having sold one former lover into slavery after she left him.[9]

Ohio

Before white settlement began in the mid-1780s, there were about fifteen thousand Indians living in Ohio from five different tribes: the Miami, the Shawnee, the Ottawa, the Wyandotte, and the Delaware. Hunters and trappers began going to Ohio in the 1760s, the same period as the "long hunters" in Kentucky and Tennessee. George Washington went to the Ohio Valley in 1760 to survey land for distribution to veterans of the French and Indian War. When he died, Washington had forty-one thousand acres of Ohio Valley land listed in his will. In councils at Fort Stanwix in 1784 and Fort McIntosh in 1785 some of the western chiefs "sold" away title to parts of Ohio. This was the beginning of a thirty-year process of buying up Indian land titles. White squatters began illegally moving onto land on the north side of the Ohio River in 1785. Fort Harmar was established at the junction of the Ohio and Muskingum Rivers that year in order to evict illegal white squatters—the only fort in American history established for that purpose. Most squatters either ignored the orders to evacuate or merely shifted to another location in the Valley. Between October 1786 and June 1788, 631 boats with some 12,205 passengers passed Fort Harmar; most were probably heading down the Ohio to Missouri and New Orleans. In 1787 the Northwest Ordinance was passed that prescribed laws for the new territory, which encompassed present-day Ohio, Indiana, Michigan,

Wisconsin, and Illinois. One of the thirteen ordinances or rules involved in the law was the requirement of four days of military service annually for each adult white male resident. The first official legal settlement began in 1788 with forty-eight men from the Ohio Company from Massachusetts and Connecticut.[10]

There was a substantial threat from the native population until 1795. Three separate expeditions were sent by the U.S. Army into Ohio to deal with this threat: General Harmar in 1790—he was forced to retreat; General Arthur St. Clair in 1791—he lost over half his command—some 700 men—in the greatest defeat by Indians of an American military force in American history; and General "Mad" Anthony Wayne in 1794—who defeated the Indians at the Battle of Fallen Timbers. The following year a former white Indian, William Wells who had lived among the Miami, translated at the Treaty of Greenville, which gave the United States control of the southern two-thirds of Ohio.[11]

Ohio produced only one prominent Indian-fighter politician: William Henry Harrison. Harrison was born and raised in Virginia and did most of his Indian fighting outside of the state, but he did serve both the territory and the state in the House and Senate and was the first of eight presidents from Ohio. Following his period as territorial governor of Indiana, Harrison made Ohio his home. Harrison's political career is dealt with elsewhere.[12]

Grant was probably the only other president from Ohio that was elected due to his own accomplishments rather than due to the geographic importance of Ohio as being in the geographic center of the nation following the Civil War. The first five of these presidents were generals—four of them in the Civil War. The state also produced three vice presidents, thirty-five cabinet officers, three chief justices of the Supreme Court, and eight associate justices. Another Ohio Indian fighter was the father of a leading U.S. senator, John Sherman, and of a future commander of the army, William T. Sherman. The "T" is for Tecumseh, with whom Captain Sherman was very impressed.[13]

TENNESSEE

The Cherokee

Tennessee was the home of the Cherokee, the most powerful Indian people in the Southeast who at the height of their power ruled about forty thousand square miles in the western Carolinas, western and West Virginia, northern Georgia and Alabama, eastern Tennessee, and Kentucky. In the early years of the eighteenth century they expelled the Yuchi, the Creek, and the Shawnee from Tennessee. Speaking an Iroquoian language, but not part of the Iroquois Confederacy of the Northeast, the Cherokee had a principal (or paramount) chief and a war chief; but political power centered on the towns each with its own "king" and war chief. Each town was centered around a public square and a council house. The Cherokee usually supported the British against the French and Spanish but played all three powers off against each other. They were officially neutral during the French and Indian War. In the middle of the French and Indian War they were provoked by settlers into going to war against colonists in Virginia and the Carolinas in 1758–60. This led to open warfare between the British and the Cherokee in 1760, and the latter lost half of their five thousand odd warriors. They were enthusiastic allies of the British during the Revolution.[14]

A tree in East Tennessee bears the inscription "D Boon cilled a bar 1760," but it is not known if it is authentic. But the first white hunters were actively hunting in the state after the French and Indian War. The first permanent white settlement, in what is today Tennessee, began in the Watauga settlement of East Tennessee in what was then Virginia in 1769. In 1776 the settlers appealed to both North Carolina and Virginia for annexation in order to win protection from Indian attacks. North Carolina advised the settlers to elect delegates to North Carolina's constitutional convention in November 1776. Five delegates were elected—but only four attended—including John Sevier. Sevier was elected to the lower house of North Carolina's assembly.[15]

In late September 1776 a militia army of eighteen hundred troops from Virginia and North Carolina invaded Cherokee territory and the Cherokee were forced to abandon their towns and sue for peace in the summer of 1777. In the peace treaty the Cherokee ceded all the land already occupied in Virginia and East Tennessee. The treaty was supposed to be "for all generations" and to be kept by the settler's "children's children." This treaty kept the supply road open to Kentucky and allowed the settlements there to hang on. A group of Cherokee led by Chief Dragging Canoe, a leading war chief, refused to accept the peace and split off to form the Chickamauga, named for their place of abode along the Chickamauga Creek. They remained a threat to white settlers until the War of 1812. Colonel Evan Shelby led an expedition against the Chickamauga in April 1779 and destroyed several of their towns. For this he was appointed a brigadier general in the Virginia militia.[16]

In October 1780 John Sevier and Isaac Shelby, militia commanders of two North Carolina counties, with one thousand men attacked forces under British Major Patrick Ferguson at King's Mountain. The British suffered 157 killed and 153 wounded to 28 Americans dead and 62 wounded. This was the turning point of the Revolution in the South and caused Cornwallis to retreat across the mountains to Virginia. Shelby and Sevier aided General Francis Marion (the famous "Swamp Fox" who was played by Mel Gibson in a very thinly disguised character in the movie *Patriot*) in "mopping up" operations in South Carolina at the head of an army of six hundred men.[17]

Sevier then organized an expedition that defeated the Cherokee in December 1780. The following year he led another expedition against the Middle Cherokee. In 1782 he led another force against the Chickamauga, but a Cherokee guide pressed into service diverted Sevier away from five Chickamauga towns. The Chickamauga continued to raid settlements in Middle Tennessee (the Nashville area); but in three Indian campaigns from 1780 to 1782, Sevier's volunteers destroyed more than thirty-one Indian towns.[18]

The State of Franklin

Sevier was leader of the Franklin scheme that involved the secession of the Watauga settlement area from North Carolina after the latter ceded lands to the federal government in 1783. The following year in November North Carolina revoked the cession because it did not receive what it wanted from the United States in exchange. In August 1784 a convention met in Jonesboro and urged formation of a new state. A third convention in December 1784—unaware of the revocation of the cession—approved a constitution for the State of Franklin. From March 1785 when Sevier was elected governor by the new state assembly until the summer of 1788, this area in what is today East Tennessee had two rival state governments. Sevier was both the commander of the militia for the Washington District of North Carolina and the governor of the State of Franklin, which consisted of four counties—one named after the governor. In 1786 residents of Washington and Sullivan counties held rival elections on the same day with more voting in the Franklin election than in the North Carolina election. This led to two sets of rival office holders. In 1787 the Franklinites participated in a North Carolina assembly election and Sevier claimed that he was elected from Washington County. But he did not attend sessions of the assembly.

In 1787 the Constitutional Convention in Philadelphia prohibited the secession of areas from existing states to form new states without the consent of the former. As a result of this, by the spring of 1788 support for Franklin had pretty much collapsed. In 1787 Franklin had gone to war against the Cherokee and Sevier had led an expedition into Cherokee territory in retaliation for an Indian massacre. A relative of those killed in the massacre murdered several Indian chiefs during a parley when Sevier was absent. Many Americans blamed Sevier for the murders, hurting the image of the state. In 1788 there was almost a state of civil war between the supporters of Sevier and those of political rival John Tipton, who was backed by North Carolina. Tipton seized several of Sevier's slaves to satisfy a court judgment against Sevier, which resulted in a battle between the two sides and the death of a North Carolina sheriff. Sevier was charged with treason by North Carolina, and Tipton arrested him in October 1788 and brought him across the mountains to Morganton for trial. One of Sevier's fellow commanders from King's Mountain, General Charles McDowell, signed his bail bond and obtained his release. The trial was never held, and his friends and sons escorted him home. The following year Sevier took an oath of loyalty to North Carolina and in August was elected to the state senate and reconfirmed as brigadier general of the state militia on the basis of an appointment from 1784. The western counties of North Carolina were ceded by the state for a second time in 1789 and in 1790 were organized by the United States into the territory of Tennessee.

Sevier possibly conspired with Spain in 1788 to obtain Spanish protection against the Indians, supported by Spain. But the Spanish preferred to deal with James Wilkinson in Kentucky. Sevier sent an envoy, Dr. James White, to New Orleans to negotiate on his behalf with Spanish Governor Miro. Miro offered the Franklinites the chance to colonize Louisiana but under similar terms to those later offered immigrants to Texas. The negotiations came to nothing. Settlers in the Cumberland area intrigued with the Spanish in order to win protection against the Indians and recognition from North Carolina.[19]

Tennessee Politics

President Washington appointed a North Carolinian who had served as a paymaster during the Revolution, William Blount, as governor of Tennessee. Blount negotiated a treaty with the Cherokee and then turned a small existing settlement into the territorial capital at Knoxville. But in 1792 John Watts, the war chief of the Chickamauga led a combined army of six hundred Cherokee, Creek, and Shawnee warriors against the whites. Sevier pursued the Indians with an army of several hundred militia in September 1793 and defeated them in the Battle of Etowah (near present-day Rome, Georgia). He also destroyed several Cherokee and Creek towns. Spain was encouraging Indians to attack Americans as a check on American expansionism. Wayne's victory over the northern Indian confederation in 1794 had the effect of pacifying the southern Indians.[20]

At this point there were no real political parties in the modern sense in Tennessee but, rather, only political factions organized around personalities. This remained the case until the late 1820s or early 1830s. The Federalist Party never became effective in Tennessee, due to its opposition to statehood, and after the War of 1812 the country was divided among different factions of the Republican Party until the Democrats and the Whigs emerged. The factions were then organized around the personalities of William Blount and John Sevier. Blount wanted statehood both in order to protect his personal land-speculation schemes and to protect settlers against Indian attacks. Blount had national ambitions and planned to go to the Senate, allowing Sevier, his only real rival for power, to be elected governor. The first census in 1795 gave Tennessee a population of 66,649 free inhabitants and 10,613 slaves. Normally the minimum population level for statehood was seventy thousand, but a state could be admitted with fewer inhabitants if it could argue that this was in the national interest. Blount and Sevier were business associates and good personal friends, and both benefited from the relationship.[21]

A rising star in the Blount faction at this time was a young Nashville attorney who had migrated from South Carolina in 1789—Andrew Jackson. Jackson also began to establish his reputation as an Indian fighter at this time. Shortly after moving to Nashville he took part in his first battle with Indians. Jackson had inherited a hatred of Indians from his mother, who died during the Revolution, and acquired a hatred of the British during the Revolution when he was cut with a sword by an arrogant young officer for refusing to shine his boots. At the Constitutional Convention in 1796, Jackson played a minor role. When Tennessee became a state, he was appointed the only congressman, Blount and William Cooke were elected the two U.S. senators, and Sevier was elected governor. Blount was forced to step down from the Senate, avoiding impeachment, when he was caught intriguing with the Spanish. Jackson took his place in the Senate, but Blount remained the head of the faction.[22]

The most famous feud in Tennessee politics—and possibly in early American politics anywhere on the frontier—began in 1796 when Jackson challenged Sevier over militia elections in 1796. Initially the feud was felt much more strongly on Jackson's part than on Sevier's as the latter appointed Jackson to a position on the superior court, Tennessee's highest court, after he resigned from the Senate. Sevier's biographer attributes the origin of the feud to the first gubernatorial election. There is no record of the election, but it was doubtful that Sevier was a Tennessee Washington, elected by acclaim. Possibly Jackson challenged Sevier for the governor's mansion or backed his opponent. But the feud began in earnest once Jackson beat Sevier, then no longer the governor, for head of the militia in Tennessee in 1802. Sevier had relied on his military reputation, whereas Jackson had carefully campaigned for the job for years. In the election they were tied and Governor Roane, from the Blount faction, appointed Jackson.[23]

As a result of the acrimony over the elections, Jackson dredged up information about an impropriety on Sevier's part in a land deal. Jackson published a lengthy attack on Sevier in the *Tennessee Gazette* of Nashville in July 1803. He claimed that "no honest man" would vote for Sevier. He gave this information to Roane after Sevier beat Roane for reelection in 1804. Roane gave the evidence to the legislature and recommended an investigation, which the legislature declined to do. The "fraud" was over whether transfer of land titles by Sevier to North Carolina Secretary of State James Glasgow amounted to a bribe for an illegal act or reasonable payment for a legal service that Glasgow had rendered as Sevier maintained. Modern historians disagree about whether or not the affair constituted fraud. But in any case, the "fraud"—if it was such—was not serious enough to hurt Sevier's reputation with the electorate, probably because it was not all that unusual.[24]

The public name-calling that followed the affair led to the famous Sevier-Jackson "duel" in Indian territory. Jackson came off second best in public opinion as most Tennesseans refused to believe that the hero of King's

Mountain and thirty-five Indian "battles" was a coward. Jackson's conduct of attacking an unarmed man goes against the dueling code and itself was an example of cowardice. Two years later Jackson was involved in another duel in which he killed a man who had wounded him. The man he killed was the son-in-law of planter Andrew Erwin, who succeeded Sevier as leader of his faction following Sevier's death in 1815. Erwin, unlike Thomas Hart Benton, was disinclined to forgive Jackson.[25]

In the summer of 1803 Sevier was ordered to provide a regiment of troops to go to Natchez for service in New Orleans if the French government refused to evacuate the city in terms of the Louisiana Purchase agreement. Sevier sent five hundred men from West Tennessee with a commander from East Tennessee. This kept Jackson from commanding the troops. Ultimately they were forced to mobilize another fifteen hundred men, which was very unpopular in the state. The sectional animosities were a result of the Sevier-Jackson feud, rather than the reverse.[26]

The Tennessee constitution limited a governor to serving three successive two-year terms in any eight years. This allowed someone else to replace a popular governor, like Sevier or later William Carroll, and campaign as an incumbent against the popular former governor. Sevier was forced to step down after serving six years in 1802 and then served again from 1805 to 1809 before giving way to Willie Blount, the half-brother of William and leader of the Blount faction after William's death. Sevier pushed to buy new lands from the Cherokee in 1807–1809 during his final term as governor. There had been previous major government purchases in 1803 and 1805.

Sevier then moved to the state senate in 1809. In 1811 Sevier was elected to Congress from East Tennessee and served two terms until his death in 1815. Along with Henry Clay, John Calhoun, and Richard Johnson, he was a leading War Hawk in 1811–12. Sevier was a frequent dinner guest of President Madison, and his importance can be gauged by the fact that he served as a pallbearer at the funerals of two vice presidents. He served on the Military Affairs Committee of the House and supported Clay on a measure to increase the size of the army as a result of the War of 1812. He was purely a state and regional politician, interested in national ideas and debates only to the extent that they affected the West. On his tomb is the inscription: "35 battles—35 victories."[27]

The War of 1812 was very popular in Tennessee, as it was also in Kentucky; and the popular response of young males to the call for volunteers earned the state its motto—the Volunteer State. Tennesseans were expansionists and looked toward territory in Canada and Florida as booty from the war. The ruling political class was full of land speculators like William Blount, Sevier, and Jackson. Tennesseans also believed that both the British and the Spanish were conspiring to unite all Indians on the frontier against the settlers. So the war was popular with both the politicians and the settlers.

Jackson offered twenty-five hundred volunteers for the war effort, but after the Pensacola expedition was canceled in the fall of 1812 there was no further call for volunteers. After the Fort Mims massacre in August 1813 the Tennessee legislature called for thirty-five hundred volunteers and the response was enthusiastic. Two armies were organized: one under Jackson in Middle Tennessee and one under General John Cocke in East Tennessee. The Creek War of 1813–14 produced the second generation of Tennessee Indian fighters, the first generation having been produced in the Revolution and the fighting with the Cherokee in the late 1780s and early 1790s. If the first generation produced men like Sevier and Jackson, the second produced three major Indian-fighter politicians who served as governors of the state throughout the 1820s and a man who served as a U.S. senator during this time. It also produced the Congress' most eccentric member in the 1820s and early 1830s, David Crockett, who was a leading Jackson opponent in Tennessee.[28]

William Carroll, John Williams, and Sam Houston all established their reputations at the Battle of Horseshoe Bend in March 1814. Carroll, whose duel with one of the Benton brothers had led to Jackson's feud with the pair and his severe wound before the Creek War, was a Pennsylvanian native who became a Nashville merchant and part owner of the first steamboat to reach Nashville. During the Battle of New Orleans he was in charge of the troops that bore the brunt of the British attack and led to the British defeat with their cool reaction under fire.[29]

In 1821 Carroll ran for governor. Both Carroll and his opponent, William Ward—a wealthy planter, were friends of Jackson. The Blount faction decided to back Ward, and the Sevier faction backed Carroll, now led by Erwin. Ward lacked experience in frontier campaigning and was soon painted by Carroll as an effete Federalist. Ward had suffered from a business failure in 1819 so that he was portrayed as a "poor rich man." Carroll emerged from the campaign as governor and no longer a friend of Jackson. He served a total of twelve years as governor in the 1820s and 1830s running unopposed in 1823, 1825, and 1829 and with little difficulty in 1831 and 1833.[30]

In 1827, when Carroll was prohibited by law from running again, Sam Houston, a Jackson protégé, followed him. Houston had the good fortune of being supported by both Carroll and Jackson. Houston had made a meteoric rise in the early 1820s after being practically adopted by Jackson as a son. After qualifying as a lawyer in only eighteen months after retiring from the army in 1818, Houston became state attorney general in 1819, then general of the militia in 1821, and finally a congressman in 1825. Willie Blount, who was making a comeback attempt, opposed Houston. Houston was inaugurated on October 1, 1827. In early 1829 he fell in love with a beautiful young woman. They married, but within months the marriage went sour as she still seemed to be in love with a previous suitor. She returned to her wealthy parents to live; and Houston, distraught, suddenly resigned the governorship and started drinking heavily. He went off to live with the band of Cherokee that he had lived with as a teenager before the War of 1812. During the next three years he fished, hunted, drank quite heavily—acquiring the name of "Big Drunk" among the Cherokee—and occasionally represented the band on diplomatic missions with other Indians or with the federal government. In December 1831 he went off to Washington on a diplomatic mission for the Cherokee. While there he assaulted a congressman who had insulted him. As a former member of the House, he elected to be tried by that body. After a brilliant oration he was let off with a mild reprimand. While in Washington he spent much of his time at the White House in discussions with Jackson. In November 1832 he left for Texas, probably as Jackson's agent in winning its independence and annexation. When the Texas Revolution began at Gonzales in October 1835, Houston was appointed head of the army. He allied himself with both Stephen Austin and Jim Bowie—another Indian fighter—and after Texas declared independence in early March 1836 began to raise an actual army. After retreating across Texas before Santa Anna for several weeks, Houston made a stand at San Jacinto, just east of the city that bears his name—at present day Deerfield, and won a miraculous victory in a surprise attack on April 21, 1836. Houston served for the next quarter-century as president of the Texas republic, senator from Texas, and governor of Texas. He owed his entire subsequent political career to San Jacinto and his appointment as head of the Texas army to Horseshoe Bend and his rank of major general in the militia.[31]

The man who served out Houston's term as governor was William Hall, speaker of the state senate, who had served under Jackson in the War of 1812 and risen to the rank of brigadier general. He served for 5.5 months as governor. It seemed that service as an officer in the War of 1812 under Jackson was a requirement for the governor's mansion in Tennessee in the 1820s. Carroll returned to the governor's mansion in 1829.[32]

John Williams brought a regiment of volunteers on short enlistment to Jackson's aid during the Creek War in 1813. He turned around and brought the regiment back to Tennessee at the end of its three-month enlistment. Williams split with Jackson after Jackson had him tried by court martial for disobeying an order that Williams considered illegal. Williams was elected to the U.S. Senate by the state legislature in 1815 as a war hero. He was very critical of Jackson's invasion of Florida during the First Seminole War, earning for himself Jackson's eternal enmity. Williams served for many years in the Senate, becoming a leading founder of the Whig Party in Tennessee in 1834 along with Congressman Newton Cannon, Andrew Erwin, and Congressman David Crockett.[33]

The last famous Indian-fighter politician from Tennessee was David Crockett, always known in folklore as Davy but who preferred David. Crockett served two separate six-month enlistments in the Tennessee militia during the War of 1812: first as a scout during the Creek War in 1813 and then as a member of a mounted rifle unit during the Pensacola occupation of West Florida in 1814. Crockett was only involved in one major fight with Indians, but he doctored his war record in his campaign autobiography so that it would look like he was present throughout the entire Creek War.[34]

Crockett was a literate but unschooled farmer and hunter, born in East Tennessee in 1786 to John Crockett, who had fought with Sevier at King's Mountain and had been a Franklinite. John was constable of Greene County in East Tennessee in 1783, 1785, and 1789—the gap because of his support for the State of Franklin. Crockett's grandfather David was killed by Creek raiders in 1778, and an uncle was a prisoner of the Creek for years. So, like Jackson, he should have grown up with a frontier racial hatred of Indians. If he did, it was less powerful than his later dislike of and rivalry with Jackson. As a youth Crockett was hardworking, at least when compared to his political contemporaries like Clay, Houston, and Jackson. His father often hired out Crockett as labor to their neighbors. As a youth Crockett aspired only to being an innkeeper or farmer and was resigned to living in poverty.[35]

Crockett had been planning on sitting out the War of 1812 on his farm in West Tennessee when the Fort Mims massacre occurred. Crockett was one of the first ninety-day volunteers to sign on, despite his wife begging him to stay home. He returned to his home near the Tennessee–Alabama border having been involved only in the Tallushatchee massacre. He was released on furlough for two weeks along with many other men, and they were to meet up again in Huntsville. But after Crockett reported, a wave of newly released men passed through the town spreading mutiny among the returnees. They were released, and Crockett was officially discharged on December 24, 1813. In late September 1814 he enlisted as a third sergeant in Major William Russell's Separate Battalion of Tennessee Mounted Gunmen during Jackson's expedition to Pensacola. The unit arrived the day after Jackson had already captured the town. Crockett's main job was hunting for the unit to supplement their inadequate rations. This was a common problem for the Tennessee militiamen throughout the war; in fact, Crockett had returned to the burnt village of Tallushatchee after the battle to forage for food—some meat and a few potatoes. Crockett deserted in February 1815 when he learned that his wife Polly was very ill—she later died of the illness. He later paid a neighbor to serve out the rest of his six-month enlistment. During the war Crockett developed a dislike of officers and the planter class, after Colonel John Coffee refused to believe a report of his after a scouting expedition but believed a major who reported the same thing the next day. Jackson accused the short-termers of being unpatriotic, which may have spurred Crockett's later dislike of Jackson.[36]

In May 1815 Crockett was elected a lieutenant in the militia unit in Franklin County, Tennessee. The following year he moved to Lawrence County and became a justice of the peace, a town commissioner, and then in 1818 a lieutenant colonel in the local militia. This enabled him to use the title "Colonel" for the rest of his career. Starting in 1821 he served two terms in the state legislature. He was elected by using humor as a weapon, appearing as an ignoramus to appeal to the truly ignorant, and bribing voters with free drinks and tobacco. He was defeated in his first run for Congress in 1825 but was elected in 1827 as a Jackson Democrat, the same year that Houston was elected governor of Tennessee. Crockett served two terms in Congress but was defeated in a close election for a third term after breaking with Jackson over land reform and Indian removal. The secret to Crockett's political success was not his military reputation but his reputation as a hunter and marksman and his ability to tell tales and jokes. It was the same quality that got Lincoln elected in Illinois a decade later. Crockett's two real pleasures in life were hunting and campaigning—which he compared to hunting for votes. Whenever he lost an election—three times—he would console himself by going on a prolonged hunting trip.[37]

Crockett's company commander during the Creek War, Francis Jones, served for three terms in Congress after the war. This is possibly what inspired Crockett to go into politics. Or, it may have been the ease with which he was elected a "colonel" in the militia in Lawrence County in 1818.[38] Crockett was a minor entrepreneur who owned a flourmill, which was managed by his second wife Elizabeth while he was off hunting or politicking. She had been widowed in the Fort Mims massacre of 1813. Despite his projected image during his political campaigns, Crockett was an independent and spirited legislator who took his job seriously. His mill was swept away during a flash flood, and Crockett was forced to declare bankruptcy. His land was sold off to pay his debts, and he was forced to move. In the winter of 1823 his only income was from hunting and trapping. During this time he resembled Boone in the 1780s: a small entrepreneur, dogged by debt, who had a minor political career. After moving within Tennessee from Lawrence County to Carroll County, he ran again for the legislature in the summer of 1823 and was again elected. That year he supported John Williams for the U.S. Senate against Jackson when the legislature voted on the appointment. This earned him the lasting enmity of the Blount faction. Crockett tended to be independent for its own sake and often confused his pride with his conscience. When he ran for Congress for the first time in the summer of 1825 against incumbent Adam Alexander, he made a good show, losing by only 267 votes out of 5,645 cast. Alexander was well connected and was supported by the Blount faction.[39]

That winter and spring Crockett built a pair of flatboats to take barrels down the Mississippi for sale in New Orleans, but his efforts went to economic waste when he insisted on lashing the two boats together and they were wrecked in a rapids near Memphis. But there he made the acquaintance of a local merchant, Major Marcus Winchester, who outfitted him with new clothes and loaned Crockett a hundred dollars to pay for "entertainment expenses" in campaigning for Congress the next year. Crockett also became famous in Memphis merely for surviving the wreck of the flatboats. So the episode may have destroyed Crockett the entrepreneur, but it established Crockett the politician.

The congressional district in West Tennessee was physically the second largest district in the country at the time. Crockett learned from his mistake and rhetorically aligned himself with Jackson for the rematch in 1827. A third candidate, militia General William Arnold, ran in the race helping to divide the "respectable vote" between him and Alexander. During debates, Crockett ran on his wit rather than on his record or the issues. Crockett polled 5,868 votes to 3,647 for Alexander and 2,417 for Arnold. Crockett had more than doubled his vote while Alexander's had risen only by eight hundred. Crockett openly admitted to lying about his opponents, claiming that this was in exchange for their lies about him. This endeared him to the voters who distrusted politicians naturally.[40] Crockett stayed aligned with Jackson through his reelection campaign and then began to reassert his independence from Jackson and the Blount faction/Democratic Party. He criticized Jackson for the spoils system and openly opposed him on the Indian Removal bill. The social life in Washington was much more tempting than it had been in Nashville. Crockett began conducting an active social life and partying with the result that he missed many roll call votes. In the end he was hurt by his combination of lack of diligence and independence, which his populism was not enough to make up for. This was his undoing in his fourth congressional election, costing him his seat by a narrow margin.[41]

Crockett has gone down in history not only for his populism and his death at the Alamo but also for his being one of the few frontier politicians to oppose Indian removal. He opposed it on three grounds. First, the Indians in the East had done what the whites had for decades said they should do—become farmers—and now that the whites wanted their land they were to revert to hunters. Second, the policy was coercive. Third, the half-million dollars appropriated to finance removal should be spent under congressional, rather than executive, supervision.[42]

In 1834 when the Whig Party was organized nationally it ended the faction era of politics in Tennessee and began the political party era. Several Tennessee politicians were important members of the new Whig Party: John Bell, who was considered to be the party founder in Tennessee; Hugh Lawson-White, who ran as a Whig presidential candidate in 1836 while claiming to remain a Democrat in Tennessee; Newton Cannon, a future governor; Andrew Erwin, leader of the Sevier faction; and Crockett, the leading anti-Jackson Democrat in Tennessee. To these were added such national figures as: Senators John Calhoun and Henry Clay of South Carolina and Kentucky; Senator Daniel Webster of Massachusetts; and Representative John Quincy Adams, the former president.

Senator Hugh Lawson-White was one of three regional Whig candidates for president in 1836. He did worse than Harrison did but better than Webster in terms of electoral and popular vote. Lawson-White considered himself to be a Democrat even though Jackson had had him written out of the state Democratic Party after he accepted the Whig nomination. Inside Tennessee his supporters were considered anti-Jackson Democrats, but nationally they were considered Whigs. Newspaper editorials pointed out rationally that Lawson-White was not on the ballot in enough states to win an electoral victory over his Democratic opponent; thus the election would have to go to the House to be decided if he was to win—and there his fellow Whig candidates had more support. But he carried Tennessee anyway. By 1837 the Whigs were on equal terms with the Democrats in Tennessee and remained so until the collapse of the Whig Party in the 1850s. For the next two decades there was a period of "partisan fury" in Whig politics.[43]

Jackson had favored James K. Polk over John Bell for speaker of the House in 1834. Bell emerged victorious after ten ballots. But Polk went on to have the more illustrious career: he was elected governor in 1839 and president in 1844, after Jackson used his influence to have Martin Van Buren replaced as the Democratic nominee because he was neutral on the annexation of Texas. Polk was the only Tennessee Democrat in Congress to be unscathed by the Whig victories in 1836–37. After Carroll announced that he would not run for governor in 1839, Polk ran and beat Cannon by twenty-five hundred votes with his margin coming from Middle Tennessee. But he lost to James "Lean Jimmy" Jones, a candidate in the Crockett mold who served for two terms.[44]

The last Indian-fighter politician in Tennessee history was William Trousdale, a veteran of the Creek War, who was elected governor in 1849 as a Democrat. He was beaten by Whig candidate Judge William B. Campbell, a Mexican War veteran, in 1851, symbolizing the changing of the era from the Indian fighters to the Mexican fighters.[45]

In 1852 Winfield Scott carried Tennessee—the last Whig victory in the state. The Whigs had carried the state in every presidential election starting in 1836; Polk lost his own state in 1844 by 113 votes. By 1855 the "Know-Nothing" or American Party had replaced the Whigs as the opposition party with six out of ten congressmen and control of the state legislature. The party had two main principles: it was anti-Catholic and anti-immigrant. Andrew Jackson Donelson, Jackson's nephew, was the Know-Nothing candidate for vice president in 1856. The Democrats carried Tennessee in the presidential election for the first time since 1832. A Know-Nothing candidate was defeated for governor the following year, and the party quickly collapsed in the state leaving the Democrats as the only organized political party in the state.[46]

During the period under discussion here, the slave population of Tennessee was between one-fifth and one-quarter of the total population and most prominent populations were slave-owners. The Kansas-Nebraska Act served as a death blow to the Whig Party by intensifying the split between its two regional wings to a point beyond repair. But John Bell, leader of the Whigs in Tennessee, became the presidential candidate of the Constitutional Union Party, the party of former Southern Whigs and moderate Southern Democrats, in November 1860. His loss to another former Whig, who was born in neighboring Kentucky, precipitated the Civil War.[47]

TEXAS

Texas had four separate governments during most of the Indian-fighter period. First, it was an independent republic from October 1835 (or March 1836 depending on whether one dates the republic from the beginning of the Texas Revolution or from the declaration of independence) until December 1845 when it became an American state. The Texas Republic resembled the later Boer republics of South Africa—especially the South African Republic or Transvaal Republic: it was dirt poor, had minimal government, and had a severe native problem that produced many native-fighter politicians. It was during this period that Texas was most vulnerable to Indian raids. Texas was part of the United States until 1861 when it seceded to join the Confederate States of America. During this period the Rangers shared responsibility for protecting the frontier with the U.S. Army. During the Civil War the frontier once more became dangerous as most men joined up to fight for Confederate independence and the Rangers again became responsible for protecting the frontier. After the war Texas, like the rest of the South, was practically occupied territory under the control of the reconstruction administration. The Rangers were disbanded and only reformed in 1874 just before the start of the Red River War. Former prominent Confederate officials were banned from office during this period. It was only with the end of reconstruction in 1877 that those who played prominent roles in the Confederate government or in the army of the Confederacy were allowed to enter or reenter politics. The period of the Indian-fighter politicians came to an end in Texas during the 1880s when a number of former Indian fighters finished out their careers. Thus the period of the Indian-fighter politician came to an end about a century after it began on the East Coast.

The Texas Rangers

The term *ranger* is an old American term meaning someone who "ranges" ahead—a scout. It was first used by Major William Rogers who organized the Rogers Rangers scout unit in the French and Indian War. In Texas it was first used by Stephen Austin, the entrepreneur who began American settlement in Texas, in the early 1820s when he hired a force of ten "rangers" to protect the colony against Indian attacks. He paid for these rangers out of his own pocket. The term *ranger* came to mean a paid citizen soldier. Until the end of the Red River War in mid-1875, the Texas Rangers were more of a paramilitary mounted militia than a law enforcement organization. The men were paid but were expected to furnish their own mounts and arms. The first official governmental Ranger unit, consisting of three, fifty-six-man companies was created in October 1835 in order to protect the colony's rear during the Texas Revolution. During the "runaway scrape" between the fall of the Alamo and the Battle of San Jacinto, the Rangers protected the rear of the Texas army during its retreat eastward. The Indians caused no problems during the revolution, but the Rangers had their first scrape with the Comanche rescuing a kidnapped child at Walnut Creek, ten miles from Austin.[48]

Most of the Ranger captains who became famous during the period of the Republic and afterward either arrived after the Texas Revolution was over or fought with the regular army at San Jacinto. Most of these Ranger captains were quite young: in their twenties or early thirties. They tended to be soft-spoken quiet men who won election to the job because of their intelligence, energy, and bravery. They tended to be utterly fearless rather than courageous—this allowed their brains to figure out solutions to tactical problems in a fix. Most of these were either killed, left the Rangers while still young and never went into politics, or moved out of state. But a few remained and supplied the top Indian-fighter politicians. These included Peter Bell, John Salmon "Rip" Ford, and Lawrence "Sul" Ross. Other Indian-fighter politicians emerged from the fighting of the late 1830s and happened to also be major figures in the Texas Revolution such as Edward Burleson, Thomas Rusk, and Francis Lubbock.

Texas experienced three major Indian wars over a thirty-year period: in 1839–40, in 1858–60, and in 1874–75. The first post-revolution Ranger unit was authorized in December 1838 and formed in January 1839. It consisted of eight companies of mounted volunteers who were authorized for six months duty. The first major battle with the Comanche was on February 15, 1839, when Rangers commanded by Captain John Moore attacked a Comanche village near the San Saba River. On May 26, 1839, 240 Comanche surrounded thirty-five Rangers and killed seven including the leader, Captain John Bird. About a week previously, details of a Mexican-Indian plot against the Republic were found on the body of a Mexican killed by Rangers in a fight with between twenty and thirty Indians and Mexicans. This was all the excuse that the Texans needed to rid the Republic of all the Indians in the area controlled by the Republic. Several eastern Indian tribes that had been expelled from the United States by the Jackson and Van Buren administrations took up residence in Texas. Edward Burleson led the Texas army against the Cherokee on July 15, 1839, after the Cherokee leader, Chief Bowles, refused to evacuate the

Republic immediately. The Cherokee band had arrived in Texas in 1824, before most of the whites that wanted to expel them. A two-day battle was fought and by the end of the month the Cherokee and eight other tribes had been evicted from Texas and chased into either Arkansas territory or Indian territory in present-day Oklahoma. This ended Indian fighting in East Texas.[49]

Texas really had no standing army but, rather, just a commander who could command the militia units when they were called up as they were in 1839–40. The commander of the army was a hothead, Felix Huston, who, when Sam Houston tried to replace him with Albert S. Johnston, provoked a duel with the latter that ended up deferring Johnston's appointment due to the wound he received. Eventually Johnston became secretary of war for the Republic and Huston remained as commander of the army. But Houston furloughed the entire six-hundred-man army while Johnston was recovering. The Rangers fought beside the militia during the 1839–40 war.[50]

The war began with clashes between the Rangers and the Comanche after heavy raids in late 1838 had led to the mobilization of the Rangers. The war culminated in three major battles and a major Comanche raid, all in 1840. As a result of the Ranger actions, three Peneteka Comanche chiefs rode into San Antonio on January 7, 1840, and said that they wanted to make peace between their band and the Texans. They met with the Ranger leader, Colonel Henry Karnes, who instructed them that they must return with all of their white captives in order to make peace. They promised to do so within twenty days. Finally two months later on March 19, 1840, a group of Comanche led by twelve chiefs rode into San Antonio. They had only a single captive, a teenaged girl whose nose had been burned nearly off and who had suffered from repeated rape and maltreatment. The girl told the white negotiators that there were many more captives among the tribe but that the Indians intended to ransom them one at a time in order to extract the maximum price from the whites. One chief rather arrogantly confirmed this, at which point the military commander ordered the chiefs seized as hostages. A scuffle broke out and seven Texans were killed and eight wounded compared with thirty-four Comanche killed and twenty-seven captured in what became known as the Council House fight. The Comanche then murdered thirteen white captives in retaliation.[51]

In August 1840 a Comanche army of between four hundred and one thousand warriors led by Chief Buffalo Hump, the leading war chief of the Peneteka Comanche, raided deep into Texas and sacked the town of Victoria and burned the tiny port settlement of Linnville on the Guadulupe River. The population of Linnville took refuge on a boat in the harbor while the Indians burned the town. Flush with success the Comanche made the mistake of taking the same route back that they had taken in. An ad hoc mounted force of Rangers from Victoria and other towns commanded by Ben McCulloch, Adam Zumwalt, and John Tumlinson, numbering about a hundred, met up with the Indians at Plum Creek. After prolonged skirmishing, Huston, who took command of the force, was persuaded by Ed Burleson and Ben McCulloch to allow the Rangers to attack. In a running battle between sixty and eighty Comanche were killed for the loss of a single Texan. The Comanche were preoccupied with recovering their captured horse herd that the Texans had stampeded. On October 23, 1840, Lipan scouts found a Comanche village and in a thirty-minute fight a Ranger unit led by Captain Moore killed 125 and suffered only one dead and one wounded. This battle and the Battle of Plum Creek took the fight out of the Peneteka Comanche and in the mid-1850s they were put on a reservation at Camp Cooper at the Clear Fork of the Brazos River.[52]

The leading Ranger captain of the Republic period was John Coffee Hays, known as Jack Hays. Hays was on nearly continuous duty from 1840 to 1848 fighting for the Republic or for the state of Texas in the Mexican War. Hays trained the other outstanding Rangers of the period: Ben McCulloch, "Big Foot" Wallace, and Sam Walker. Hays was from Tennessee near where President Jackson lived. In fact, Hays's grandfather had sold Jackson the Hermitage and his paternal grandmother was related to Rachel Harmon, whom Jackson married. Hays came from Tennessee shortly after the Revolution and distinguished himself as a Ranger in the late 1830s serving under Deaf Smith and Henry Karnes. Hays fought at Plum Creek but was not a major figure there. Joining the Rangers as a private at age twenty-one he was a captain by twenty-three, a major at twenty-five, a colonel in Mexico at thirty-one, and an ex-soldier at age thirty-four.[53]

Originally the Rangers were at a considerable disadvantage facing the Plains Indians, as they were equipped only with the long rifles that they had brought with them from Kentucky, Tennessee, and elsewhere. These woodland arms were not designed for use on horseback. Even the single-shot horse pistols were no match for the rapid-fire bows of the Comanche and Kiowa. But relief arrived in the form of Samuel Colt's five-shot revolver, which went into production in late 1836. Much of the first run of a thousand made its way to Texas, so that it became known as the Texas Paterson. The Texas navy purchased 180 Colts from an agent of Colt for use by boarding parties. When Houston returned as president for his second term he tried to sell off the Texas navy, but the citizens of Galveston prevented him from seizing the four small ships of the navy. But in January 1844 Houston authorized Hays to requisition the whole lot of revolvers, spare cylinders, and bullet molds from the navy. Hays had privately purchased a revolver in 1839, and it had saved his life in a fight with Comanche at "Enchanted Rock" when Indians surrounded him atop a small hill in 1841 or 1842. The Colt, which fired five shots rather than the six in later versions, had its official baptism of fire with the Rangers on June 8, 1844, in a fight with about sixty-five to seventy Comanche. It was an instant success.[54]

Texas Politics

There were no formal party politics in the Texas Republic. Rather there were two informal factions organized around the two leading political figures: Sam Houston and Mirabeau Buonaparte Lamar. Stephen Austin had died of natural causes in December 1836. The conservative planter class who owned the cotton plantations that were the backbone of the economy supported Houston. Lamar was a Georgian by origin that had quickly risen through the ranks of the Texas army to lead the cavalry during the Battle of San Jacinto. In the first election Houston was elected president and Lamar was elected vice president. The first presidential term was for two years, and the president was not allowed to succeed himself. Lamar was supported by ordinary Texans, as he was a populist who had his finger on the pulse of Texas. After two years Lamar was elected president after the Houston faction failed to find a serious candidate to oppose him. The presidential term had been lengthened to three years. The capital was also moved from Washington-on-the-Brazos to Houston to Austin.[55]

Houston spent his time making peace with the Indians and attempting to preserve the peace with Mexico. Texas was basically bankrupt from 1837 to 1841 when the French agreed to buy up a bond issue that the United States had rejected. Lamar spent his term expelling Indians and sending a filibustering expedition to Santa Fe. During his second term, from December 1841 to December 1844, Houston had to deal with a Mexican invasion of southern Texas and occupation of San Antonio and Goliad. The Texas army was sent to recapture San Antonio and expel the Mexicans, which they did. The Rangers played an important role in this battle in which sixty Mexicans and only one Texan were killed. The commander, Alexander Somervell, then returned to San Antonio. But a few hundred men proceeded to remain and invade the Mexican border town of Meir. There they were captured and every tenth man executed. Ed Burleson served as Houston's vice president during his second term and ran against Anson Jones in December 1844 for the final term.[56]

The government of Texas was based on that of the United States: three branches of government, a bicameral Texas Congress with a house and senate; and a small cabinet consisting of the president, the secretary of war, the secretary of state, and the secretary of the treasury. The job of the secretary of war was to oversee the militia system and Rangers; the secretary of state strived to win foreign recognition and negotiate trade treaties; and the secretary of the treasury drew up the budget to be voted upon by the congress. Congress authorized the mobilization of Rangers or the militia.

President Jackson recognized Texas on his last day as president. On September 12, 1843, he declared that the United States must annex Texas "peacably if we can, forcibly if we must." The force was to be used against Mexico, with which Texas had a border dispute, rather than against Texas.

The final two years of the Republic were focused on the issue of annexation. By April 1844 a treaty of annexation had been negotiated between Texas and the United States, but it failed to win approval from either the U.S. Congress or the Texas Congress. A lame-duck President Tyler organized the annexation of Texas by a joint resolution of Congress during his final weeks in office in March 1845. The resolution was on more generous terms to Texas than those originally negotiated, and the terms were overwhelmingly accepted by a referendum in Texas in October 1845. President Polk, a protégé of Jackson who backed annexation, signed the annexation into law on December 29, 1845, and the flag of the Republic of Texas was lowered for the last time in February 1846.[57]

The Mexican fighters of the revolution dominated the politics of the Republic. Those of them who were Indian fighters had been Indian fighters before the Republic or had participated in the war of 1839–40 against the Cherokee and the Comanche. Two of the Republic's potentially most successful politicians, both Indian fighters, were killed at the Alamo: David Crockett and James Bowie. Bowie had successfully countered a Comanche attack in 1832 while searching for silver mines near the San Saba River and had left tens of Indians dead. He had also been a hero of two major battles of the Bexar campaign in the fall of 1835. Crockett had fought Indians in one battle during the Creek War. This left Houston, Burleson, Rusk, and John S. Jones as Indian-fighter politicians.

The population of Texas began to increase exponentially after independence. The Republic had thirty thousand Texans settled on 62.6 million acres in 1836. By 1850 this had increased to over 200,000—and it continued to grow rapidly. In 1836 the largest town was San Antonio with a population of two thousand. In 1860, on the eve of the Civil War, Texas had an urban population of only twenty-eight thousand in the five largest cities. San Antonio was still the largest city with a population of 8,235. With a population that was 95 percent rural, politics was the realm of a relative handful of professional politicians who came from the professional class or from the war heroes of the Revolution.[58] Houston became a U.S senator upon annexation and remained the only national figure in Texas until 1863 when Governor Francis Lubbock went off to Richmond to join Jefferson Davis as an aide. Lubbock was more of a regional politician for the South than a national politician. Texas did not have a national political figure after Houston until Sam Rayburn and Lyndon Johnson in the 1950s.

The major issue in Texas politics before, during, and immediately after the Civil War was frontier defense. The United States took over the protection of Texas' frontier with Comancheria in 1846. A string of forts was constructed along the ninety-eighth meridian on a north-south line, from Fort Worth in the north to Fort Inge in the south, along the edge of the Great Plains. The United States treated the Comanche and Kiowa as wards to be administered and tolerated rather than as enemies to be vanquished and defeated. Initially the U.S. Army lacked a cavalry arm that could pursue and fight the Plains Indians. The Dragoons were mounted infantry that could ride but preferred to fight dismounted. In practice this amounted to providing the Indians with a secure sanctuary from which to raid Texas. In its declaration of secession in February 1861 the Texas state legislature listed dissatisfaction with the federal government's failure to protect the frontier as a prime reason for secession second only to the issue of slavery and states' rights.[59]

The Texas Rangers did not mount a single major campaign from 1848 to 1858, being mobilized only in reaction to Indian raids. They served mainly to bury the dead and chase the Indians out of the area. Five, seventy-nine-man companies were authorized in 1850, with "Rip" Ford as senior captain and "Big Foot" Wallace, J. B. McGown, Henry McCulloch, and R. E. Sutton as the other captains. On May 12, 1850, Ford and fifteen Rangers clashed with fifteen Comanche and killed four and wounded seven while suffering only one wounded and a horse killed. But Ford suffered a scratch on the back of his right hand and within six years his arm was paralyzed—the scratch was probably due to an arrow dipped in rattlesnake venom. But the Rangers were mustered out of service in the fall of 1851.[60]

Texas Indians

There were three classes of Indians in Texas during the Republic: those who were native to the area, those who had moved in from the East, and those who migrated into the state. The latter two groups were dealt with in July 1839 leaving only the first group. There were seven main tribes of Indians that the Texans dealt with: the Caddo, the Karankawa, the Wichita, the Waco, the Tonkawa, the Lipan, the Kiowa and Kiowa-Apache, and the Comanche. The first two tribes were the main tribes resident in East Texas when the first Anglo settlers arrived. The Karankawa, who were rumored to be cannibals and were fiercely territorial, caused most of the problems with the whites until they were basically exterminated about 1860. Sam Houston made peace with the Caddo, the Lipan, and the Tonkawa. The Lipan, a group of eastern Apache who had been displaced by the Comanche, and the Tonkawa, a traditional enemy of the Comanche, became traditional allies of the Texans during the Indian wars of the frontier period. The Wichita and Waco were gradually displaced from the edge of the Great Plains by white settlement, put on reservations in the mid-1850s and then expelled from Texas. The Lipan, Tonkawa, and Wichita all lived on the edge of Comancheria—Comanche territory.[61]

The Comanche were an Indian tribe that used to live in the Yellowstone River region of the Rocky Mountains in Wyoming and Montana. With the coming of the horse culture to the Great Plains in the late seventeenth century they split off from their Shoshone relatives and migrated down into

Oklahoma, Texas, and New Mexico. From about 1750 onward they ruled Central Texas and the Staked Plain of the Texas Panhandle, accepting tribute from the Spanish in exchange for relative peace. But they kept the Spanish from colonizing north of San Antonio and east of Santa Fe and Taos. Eventually they became allies of the Kiowa and Kiowa-Apache who also lived in the Staked Plain (Llano Estecado). The Kiowa tended to raid north into Kansas. The Kiowa-Apache were a small Apache tribe that had adopted the culture of the Kiowa upon coming into contact with them but continued to speak their native tongue.

The Comanche, who like other Amerindian tribes referred to themselves as "the people," were known as "the lords of the Plains" for their skilled horsemanship and ferocity. Various partisans will claim that the Lakota, the Cheyenne, or the Comanche were the best warriors among the Plains Indians. The Comanche managed to delay white advancement for an entire generation in Texas, whereas the Cheyenne and Sioux were almost like speed bumps that slowed white advancement down but did not delay it. There were five bands of Comanche: the Peneteka (Honey Eaters), the Noconi (Wanderers), the Kotsoteka (Buffalo Eaters), the Yamparika (Yap Root Eaters), and the Quohadi/Kwahadi (Antelope), all named after some feature of their diet. The divisions were similar to those among the various bands of the Lakota/Teton Sioux or the Apache. Warriors would frequently switch their allegiance from one band to another—those favoring war leaving the band of a chief pursuing peace to join one favoring war. The Peneteka lived in Central Texas along the Colorado River valley. The Noconi lived between the Brazos and Trinity Rivers. The Kotsoteka lived along the Canadian and Washita Rivers of the Indian Territory in Oklahoma. The Yamparika lived north of the Cimarron River, and the Quohadi lived in the Staked Plain. At their peak the Comanche numbered some twenty thousand. But their numbers started to dwindle rapidly in the mid-nineteenth century due to disease, increased warfare with whites, and finally the demise of the buffalo.[62]

During the 1830s political instability in Mexico led to the end of treaty payments to the Comanche and the Mexicans encouraged other Indian tribes to attack the Comanche. The Comanche came into conflict with the Texans when they raided Parker's Fort in May 1836 and killed seven and took five captives including Cynthia Ann Parker, the mother of Quanah Parker, the last great Comanche war chief. Houston attempted to make peace with the Comanche, but the Texas Congress refused to fix a border between Texas and Comancheria, preferring to claim territory all the way to the Rio Grande. The Texas Congress had even claimed both Californias for Texas in 1843. Lamar pursued an aggressive policy vis à vis the Comanche. In December 1841 Houston reinstated his peace policy but the Comanche were suspicious and, although an agreement was reached in 1844, by the following year relations were again strained. Austin, on the edge of Comacheria, was raided in the mid-1840s. Whites continued to encroach on Indian territory as Texas' population exploded. In 1854, 350 Peneteka Comanche were moved onto a twenty-three-thousand-acre reservation that was established on the Clear Fork of the Brazos River in what is today Throckmorton County. But five years later they were moved to Indian Territory after Texans blamed them for participating in raids.[63]

In 1840 five tribes made peace under the sponsorship of trader William Bent at Bent's Fort, Colorado Territory. These five tribes were: the Southern Cheyenne, the Arapaho, the Kiowa, the Kiowa-Apache, and the Comanche. Together they made a formidable barrier to white settlement in the Southern Plains. This alliance was really a grand alliance of two smaller alliances: that between the Cheyenne and Arapaho on one hand; and between the Comanche, the Kiowa, and the Kiowa-Apache on the other. The Kiowa had moved from the Black Hills of South Dakota where they had come into collision with the Teton Sioux moving west from Minnesota. In the late eighteenth century they migrated down to the Southern Plains. A Spanish missionary helped to arrange an alliance between the Kiowa and the Comanche.[64]

The Final Indian Wars, 1858-75

Hardin Runnels defeated Sam Houston for the governor's office in December 1857 by nearly nine thousand votes—the only politician to defeat Houston in an election. Runnels had been elected partly on the basis of his advocacy of a vigorous defense policy. In 1853, when Jefferson Davis had become secretary of war, the Second Cavalry Regiment had been brought to Texas to guard the frontier. In 1857 it had been moved to Utah. This left the frontier unguarded. Severe Comanche raids had resulted. Runnels appointed John Salmon Ford, a member of the Texas state legislature and a veteran Ranger and adjutant to Jack Hays in the Scott campaign in 1847, as senior captain to lead a Ranger force against the Comanche. On May 12, 1858, Ford led his troop of a hundred Rangers in an attack on a Comanche village and killed seventy-six Indians for the loss of only two Rangers.

On August 9, 1858, the Second Cavalry was ordered into action against the Comanche. Four companies under Major Earl Van Dorn attacked a Comanche village of 120 lodges (about 500 Indians) accompanied by friendly Tonkawa led by Lawrence "Sul" Ross on October 1, 1858. Ross was the son of Indian Agent Shapley Ross and was working on the Brazos Reservation while on vacation from college in Alabama. Ross led a force of 125 Tonkawa auxiliaries that Van Dorn had encouraged him to recruit. In a thirty-minute battle fifty-six Comanche were killed and five whites were killed and ten or eleven wounded including both Van Dorn and Ross.[65]

Ross, who historian Charles Robinson III designated "the last great Ranger leader of antebellum Texas," had his first Indian fight as a boy. In 1859 he graduated from college and spent much of the year recovering from his battle wounds. He also adopted a former captive girl who had remained unclaimed after being recovered from the Indians. In March 1860 he joined a Ranger company from Waco and soon became a lieutenant and then the captain after the former commander was promoted to major.

In the fall of 1860 Chief Peta Nacona led a war party into Parker County, Texas, near the old fort. As they withdrew, Ross raised a force of sixty mounted volunteers to pursue them accompanied by Tonkawa scouts, twenty American soldiers, and some seventy militia. On December 17 the Tonkawa scouts found a Comanche camp along the Pease River. While the men were off hunting, the Texans raided the camp and recovered a number of Mexican slaves and a blond-haired, blue-eyed Comanche woman. The woman was taken around to various settlements to be shown to relatives of those missing kin. Isaac Parker arrived at Camp Cooper and questioned her through an interpreter—she could no longer speak English. She described a childhood home similar to the Parker Fort. Parker told the interpreter, "If this is my niece, her name is Cynthia Ann." The woman slapped her chest and said "Cynthia Ann." The mystery of the missing girl had finally been solved after twenty-four years. But she was so assimilated into Comanche society that she was completely lost among the whites. She tried to escape back to the Indians and had to be kept as a virtual prisoner. Her daughter died at age five, and Cynthia Ann slashed her breast in mourning and began to starve herself to death. In 1870, in a weakened state, she died of influenza.[66]

Rip Ford was involved in putting down an insurrection by the followers of Mexican nationalist bandit Juan Cortina in the Rio Grande area from December 1859 to March 1860. It was this period of activity from 1858 to 1860 that established Ford as a Ranger legend.

In December 1859 Sam Houston was elected governor of Texas, the final political office he held in nearly a forty-year career. Texas was a virtual one-party state controlled by the Democrats. The Whig Party had died at the Alamo with David Crockett. Houston was a Unionist—that is, he supported the maintenance of the United States through a compromise solution to the slavery issue. The Democratic Party split nationally between the Northern wing led by Stephen Douglas and the Southern wing. A Constitutional Union Party had been established, and Houston competed with John Bell of Tennessee for the presidential nomination. Bell outpolled Houston 67 to 57 votes on the first ballot and won the nomination on the second ballot. Houston supported Bell's candidacy, but most Texans supported John C. Breckenridge of Kentucky, the candidate of the Southern Democrats. Unionist sentiment was restricted to a number of German towns in Central Texas around Austin and Fredericksburg.

In the midst of all this Houston came up with a scheme to raise a combined Ranger, militia, and Indian force from Texas to invade Mexico and conquer it for the Union. He corresponded on this scheme with Col. Robert E. Lee of the Second Cavalry and used former Ranger Ben McCulloch as an intermediary with bankers out East in an attempt to win financial support for the venture. Historians are divided about the motive for this quixotic filibustering scheme. His critics see it as a bid for the presidency through conquest. Others see it as a desperate attempt to avoid a civil war and the shedding of American blood by shedding Mexican blood instead. Houston took pains not to implicate the United States in the scheme, which failed to win financial support.[67]

In February 1861 the state legislature of Texas overwhelmingly declared its independence of the United States. The following month Houston was forcibly removed from the governor's office in Austin after he tried to argue that after declaring independence Texas should revert to its republican status. He died two years later in exile in Huntsville, Texas.[68]

He was replaced by Francis Lubbock, a longtime civil servant and politician who had briefly served in the army in the late 1830s and possibly saw action in the Indian expulsion of July 1839. Lubbock appointed Rip Ford, Ben McCulloch, and Henry McCulloch to organize the defense of the state. Ford was in charge in the Rio Grande area and the border with Mexico; Ben McCulloch was in charge of the San Antonio area; Henry was in charge of the northwest frontier. A force of ten companies of Rangers was organized for defense of the frontier. Ben McCulloch eventually joined the Confederate States Army and was killed at Pea Ridge, Arkansas, in 1862 as a general. Albert Johnston, the former secretary of war, was killed fighting against Ulysses S. Grant at Shiloh.[69]

Some four hundred Texans were killed, captured, or wounded by Indians during the Civil War. This was a small fraction compared to the number that died fighting against federal troops in the battlefields of the West and East. But the frontier was driven back a hundred miles in many places, all the way to Fort Worth in the northwest. In 1870 the fortified frontier was where it had been in 1850. Rip Ford led a Confederate force against Union invaders in May 1865 in a dramatic victory at Palmito Ranch in the last battle of the Civil War. Upon being informed that Lee had surrendered more than a month previously at Appomatox, an armistice and an end to the war was quickly arranged.[70]

For the next nine years the frontier remained vulnerable as the federal government implemented the peace policy with the Plains Indians. One-hundred-sixty-three settlers were killed, forty-three kidnapped, and twenty-four wounded in the first thirty months after the Civil War—and these figures were incomplete. Governor Throckmorton authorized the raising of a thousand veteran Rangers in 1866 but General Sheridan, in charge of the Department of Texas, vetoed this. Quakers were put in charge of the reservations in the Indian Territory. In 1867 Sherman met with Plains Indian leaders at Medicine Lodge in southern Kansas to sign a peace treaty. But after this, half of the Comanche and a majority of the Kiowa failed to even show up on the reservations set aside for them in Indian Territory. The Quahadis had not participated at Medicine Lodge and did not consider themselves bound by the treaty. The Comanche and Kiowa considered the Texans as a separate people from the Americans—dating back to when the Republic had been independent—and, although they remained at peace with the United States, they remained at war with Texas. Army officers actually had a freer hand to operate against Indians raiding out of Mexico than raiding out of Indian Territory. Evidence for this is the raid into Mexico by Colonel Ranald Mackenzie's Fourth Cavalry against the Kickapoo in 1872. The following year the Kickapoo were forcibly transferred from Mexico to Oklahoma with the approval of the Mexican government. Indian Agent Laurie Tatum on the Comanche Reservation admitted that reservation Indians had murdered a hundred whites and stolen a thousand horses during 1872 and he was powerless to stop them.[71]

This peace policy did not begin to change noticeably until 1871 when General William Sherman was present to witness the recovery of the bodies of a group of teamsters massacred by Kiowa raiding into northern Texas on May 19, 1871. Sherman was very nearly killed himself by the same Indians. Sherman had war chiefs Satanta, Satank, and Big Tree arrested on the Kiowa Reservation. Satank died in an escape attempt on a train after seriously wounding a guard. Satanta and Big Tree were tried for murder in Texas and sentenced to life imprisonment. They were pardoned by Governor Davis in October 1873. Davis was under pressure from opponents and hoped to win favors from Washington for the gesture. Satanta soon went on the warpath again and was arrested in 1874. In a fit of depression he committed suicide by jumping head first from the second story of a building, thereby breaking his neck. Big Tree converted to Christianity and never went to war again.[72]

The senior leadership of the army did not consist of Indian lovers: neither Sherman nor Sheridan had ever been accused of that. But Sheridan had decided that the best way to destroy the power of the southern tribes was to destroy the southern buffalo herds. Sheridan spoke out against a bill in the Texas legislature to protect the bison. He explained that the way to destroy the way of life of the Indian tribes—which included raids against white settlements—was to destroy their source of food and construction material. The destruction of the buffalo herd began in 1870 in Kansas with the hunters gradually moving south as the buffalo were depleted there. By 1874 the only remaining buffalo in the southern herd to be found were on the Staked Plain of the Texas Panhandle.[73]

The first post–Civil War Ranger units were organized in 1870, including one in El Paso. But this was similar to the Ranger units of the 1850s and quickly faded away. In April 1874 the legislature authorized the creation of the first permanent Ranger force: a Frontier Battalion of six, seventy-five-man companies. On May 2 Major John B. Jones, a former Civil War officer, was chosen to lead the unit. Jones was forty. Jones had five companies in the field within a month and the sixth by July 10. Jones thought like a theater commander or strategist rather than as a mere Ranger captain. He thought of the front as a whole.[74]

In 1874 a Quahadi medicine man, Isa-Tai (later known as White Eagle), began preaching that if the Indians submitted to white rule they were doomed but that if they resisted and drove the whites away that the buffalo would return. In the spring of 1874 a war council of the five allied tribes of the Southern Plains (Arapaho, Cheyenne, Comanche, Kiowa, Kiowa-Apache) was held. A decision was made to go to war to save the buffalo herd of the Staked Plain by attacking and killing all the buffalo hunters and driving them from the plains. The coalition could raise only seven hundred warriors among the five tribes. The Quahadi war chief Quanah Parker, the son of Nocona and Cynthia Ann Parker, led the Comanche.

The war began with an attack on the main camp of the buffalo hunters at Adobe Walls in the Panhandle—the site of a battle between Kit Carson and the Navajo and Arapaho ten years before. The attack began at first light in the morning on June 27, 1874, with the charging horde of warriors being spotted by accident by one of the hunters. From the cover of their two bunkers the hunters blasted at the Indians with their long rifles, driving them off. The attackers suffered fifteen killed and many wounded in the first battle.

The army did not go on the offensive against the Plains Indians until August 1874 when five separate task forces began converging upon the Staked Plains. In the interim the Frontier Battalion was responsible for security and maintained a role for the first six months of the war. Jones and twenty-five Rangers were trailing a group of Indians in the Lost Valley when about a hundred Kiowa jumped them. The Rangers holed up in a thicket and prepared for a long siege while one Ranger volunteer was sent to get help from Jacksboro, the nearest settlement. Once the Indians failed to stop the relief rider, they broke off the attack in the knowledge that help would come for the Rangers. The Rangers lost only two men: one ambushed while getting water from a spring and one who died from wounds. The Rangers claimed to have killed three Indians and wounded three, although the Kiowa claimed that they never lost a single life. This was not only the first but the biggest and most intense engagement of the war. In the first six months the Rangers had fifteen engagements with fifteen Indians killed, ten wounded, and one captured. During the next six months the Frontier Battalion had five engagements with five Indians killed and one wounded. From September 1875 to February 1876 no Indians were reported on the border.[75]

Rangers patrolled the border during the Victorio Apache campaign of 1880. After Victorio was killed by Mexican federal troops in October 1880, a group of survivors infiltrated into the Rio Grande valley and began raiding. On January 29, 1881, a group of Rangers ambushed the group in camp killing four warriors, two women, and two children. Most of the warriors fled, leaving the women behind to suffer the burden of the attack. It was the last Indian battle on Texas soil.[76]

The Indian-Fighter Politicians in Texas

The *Lone Star Junction* website lists forty-six "Notable Texans Before 1900." If we eliminate the Spanish conquistador Francisco de Coronado, French explorer Seiur de La Salle, ragtime composer Scott Joplin, and Mexican general Santa Anna, we are left with forty-two individuals. A further three are women, who were not likely to be military figures. This leaves us with thirty-nine figures. Of these, twenty-seven participated in the Texas Revolution (including Susana Dickenson who was present at the Alamo with her husband), nineteen in Indian fights, fifteen in the Mexican-American War, and fifteen in the Civil War. Several participated in several of these wars, including five that participated in all four categories. From these numbers it would appear that Indian fighters rank behind heroes of the Texas Revolution in importance but ahead of figures from the Mexican War and the Civil War in the Texas hierarchy of heroes. Most of the military figures who participated in the Mexican War were also Indian fighters, although there were more who participated in Indian fights and sat out the Mexican War (or died before it) than the reverse.[77]

The high amount of overlap between the two categories is not surprising when one considers that the Texas Rangers were the primary protection against Indians on the frontier in Texas after 1835 and played a prominent role in the Mexican War. Because many more Texans fought in the Civil War, there are more who were not Indian fighters than is the case with the Mexican War. But many of the senior officers in the Texas units that fought in the Civil War either fought as privates in the Texas Revolution or fought Indians and Mexicans with the Rangers or both.

Texas Indian-fighter politicians can be grouped chronologically into about three different periods: those who came as Indian fighters or participated in Indian fights before independence and became politicians as heroes of the revolution; those who gained Indian-fighting experience after the revolution and had their political careers before the Civil War; and finally, those who had their political careers after the Civil War.

The first group consisted of men born in the eighteenth century in the South and who saw action in the Creek War or elsewhere in the War of 1812 or in the Creek Rebellion of 1836 in Georgia. After Houston, the most prominent member of this group was Edward Burleson.

Burleson served as private in his father's company as part of Perkin's Regiment during the Creek War and took part in the Battle of Horseshoe Bend, where according to legend he first met Sam Houston—although this seems unlikely. After the war he moved to Missouri Territory and was married. He was appointed a captain of militia in Howard County in

October 1817. In June 1821 he was commissioned a colonel of militia in Saline County. He then moved to Tennessee and served as the colonel of militia in Hardeman County. In May 1830 he moved to Texas. After being given a land grant in April 1831 he became part of the ruling *ayuntamiento* (council) for the counties of Austin, Bexar, Goliad, and Guadalupe—basically the settled portion of Texas. From 1830 to 1842 he was involved in numerous engagements with hostile Indians—or those he mistook for hostile Indians. Like many settlers, Burleson did not often distinguish between Indians of one tribe and those of another.

Burleson was elected a lieutenant colonel of infantry in Stephen Austin's army in October 1835. The following month he replaced Austin as head of the army and two days later commanded at the Grass Fight outside San Antonio along with Jim Bowie. On December 1, 1835, he was commissioned commander in chief of the volunteer army by the provisional government. Five days later he entered Bexar (San Antonio) after Ben Milam led the capture of the town. Two weeks later the volunteer army dissolved. Burleson raised a company of volunteers and went to Gonzales in February 1836. In March he was officially elected colonel commanding the First Infantry Regiment, which he commanded at the Battle of San Jacinto in the storming of the Mexican defenses a month later. During the second half of 1836 he was commander of the Rangers. In 1837 he was engaged in surveying for key roads and then appointed brigadier general of militia. In September 1837 he was elected a representative to the Second Texas Congress and served on several committees including as head of the Indian Affairs Committee, which rejected Houston's treaty with the Cherokee in December 1837. In 1838 Burleson served as commander of the First Infantry Regiment in the Texas army and defeated a Mexican insurrection in April. He was elected to the senate of the Third Texas Congress but shortly afterward resigned to take control of the Frontier Regiment at the request of President Lamar. In that capacity Burleson led the Texas forces in battle against the Cherokee in July and against a small remnant force in December. He played a major role at the Battle of Plum Creek against the Comanche on August 12, 1840—although Felix Huston was in nominal command. In December 1841 Burleson was elected vice president under Houston. In the spring of 1842 volunteers at San Antonio elected Burleson to take command of Texas forces to move against General Rafael Vasquez. But Houston appointed Alexander Somervell to command instead. In the fall Burleson raised troops to defend against another Mexican invasion, this time by Adrian Woll, but again yielded command to Somervell. In December 1844 Burleson was defeated for the presidency by Doctor Anson Jones. But the following year Burleson was elected to the state senate of Texas and elected unanimously president pro tem of the state senate. He served in that capacity until his death from pneumonia in December 1851. He was probably the fifth most prominent Texan in the Republic after Houston, Lamar, Jones, and Rusk.

The next most prominent member of this first group is George T. Wood. Born in Georgia, he raised a company that fought at Horseshoe Bend in 1814 and, according to tradition, met both Burleson and Houston at the battle. Wood became a merchant and served in the Georgia state legislature in 1837–38. The following year he moved to Texas and settled on the Trinity River. He represented Liberty County in the Texas Congress in 1841 and at the Convention of 1845. He then became a state senator after annexation. Wood resigned from the senate to form a company of mounted volunteers for the Mexican War. He served as colonel of the Second Texas Mounted Volunteers (or Rifles) from July to October 1, 1846, when Zachary Taylor disbanded the unit—presumably due to its lack of discipline. Wood became involved in a dispute with Governor Pinckney Henderson who had taken leave to command the unit at the Battle of Monterrey. The dispute was over the conduct of the battle. This dispute helped Wood to defeat James Miller for governor the following year. But Wood was defeated for reelection by Peter Bell in 1849. Wood was viewed as Houston's man, and the anti-Houston forces supported Bell. Wood lost a second bid for reelection in 1853 and retired to his plantation and the life of a planter. He died in 1858.[78]

The last prominent member of this group was James Smith. Smith was born in South Carolina and fought in the Creek War and at New Orleans as a lieutenant under Jackson. In 1819 Smith moved his family to Tennessee and became a colonel in the state militia and led a vigilance committee against Indians. Smith moved to Texas in March 1835 and settled at Nacogdoches where he became a planter. He then went to New York with a letter of introduction from Houston to buy weapons for the revolution. He bought one hundred rifles and shipped them to Nacitoches, Louisiana. He served as captain of cavalry of the Nacogdoches Mounted Volunteers at San Jacinto. After the battle he was appointed inspector general of the army with the rank of colonel. He served with Rusk at army headquarters in Victoria until September 1836 when Smith went to Nacogdoches to build forts and organize militia for a defense of the area. Smith commanded the second battalion of Rusk's regiment at the Battle of Neches in July 1839. In March 1840 he was elected a brigadier general and took command of the Third Brigade on the northwest frontier with Mexico. Smith served in the Texas House of Representatives from February 1846 to December 1847 representing Rusk County. He died on December 25, 1855.[79]

Thomas Jefferson Rusk was the most prominent member of the second group. He came to Texas from Georgia in 1834 in pursuit of the officers of a mining company that had embezzled the money of the company in which Rusk had invested. He never recovered the money but did decide to stay on in Texas. He was appointed inspector of the army in the Nacogdoches District by the provisional government in December 1835. The revolutionary government appointed him secretary of war following the declaration of independence from Mexico. Following the Battle of San Jacinto, in which he participated, he was named commander in chief of the Texas army. He was appointed secretary of war in Houston's first cabinet but resigned shortly afterward to take care of personal problems. Rusk represented Nacogdoches in the Second Texas Congress. In the summer of 1838 he commanded the Nacogdoches militia in suppressing the Cordova Rebellion. In October he helped to defeat the Caddo, and the following month he captured marauding Caddo and crossed over into Louisiana to turn them over to an American Indian agent at Shreveport. Rusk commanded part of the troops at the Battle of Neches against the Cherokee in July 1839. In December he was elected chief justice of the supreme court of Texas. He served in this post until June 1840 and then resigned to become a lawyer in private practice. In 1845 he was involved in establishing Nacogdoches University and became its president in 1846. He served as president of the Texas Constitutional Convention of 1845, which fixed the terms for annexation. Upon annexation he along with Houston became a U.S. senator. He had a successful career in the Senate and was urged to run for president in 1856 but declined. President Buchanan offered him the position of postmaster general. In 1857 he was elected president pro tem of the Senate, but on July 29, 1857, he committed suicide due to depression over his wife's death the previous year and the discovery of a tumor on his neck.[80]

The most prominent Indian fighter who was not a hero of the revolution was probably John S. Ford. Ford came to Texas from a new medical practice in Tennessee in 1836 just after the Battle of San Jacinto. After serving briefly in the Texas army he moved to San Augustine and practiced medicine there for eight years. During this time he participated in the Battle of Neches against the Cherokee. He was elected to the Ninth Texas Congress in 1844 and moved to Austin. In Congress he worked for annexation by the United States. In Austin he became editor and co-publisher of the *Texas Democrat* in partnership with another man. He served as Jack Hays's adjutant in the First Texas Mounted Rifles and commanded a scout company during the Mexican War. In 1849 Ford was appointed a captain in the Rangers. In 1852 he was elected to the Texas state senate and served two terms. While in the senate he founded a new paper, the *State Times*, which he also edited. In 1858 he returned to the Rangers to fight first Comanche and then Mexicans. Ford served as a member of the Secession Convention in 1861 and negotiated a trade agreement between the Confederacy and Mexico. He served as colonel of the Second Texas Cavalry in the Rio Grande district and between 1862 and 1865 was commandant of conscripts. In May 1865 he successfully commanded the Texas forces in the Battle of Palmito Ranch in the last battle of the Civil War. In 1868 he moved to Brownsville to edit the *Sentinel*. In January 1874 he led a mob on the capital to help oust the Union-appointed Governor Edmund J. Davis and replace him with Governor Richard Coke. This marked the effective end of reconstruction in Texas. In 1874 Ford served as mayor of Brownsville. He served as a member of the Constitutional Convention in 1875, which wrote the present state constitution and restored the Democratic Party to power. He also served again in the state senate from 1876 to 1879. He was later appointed superintendent of what eventually became the Texas School of the Deaf.[81]

Rip Ford's biggest opponent for the title of leading Indian-fighter politician of this period was Peter Bell. Bell fought at San Jacinto as a private under Henry Karnes. Bell was appointed inspector general of the army in January 1839. He joined the Rangers under Jack Hays in 1840 and served as a major in the Somervell expedition against the Mexicans in 1842. In 1845 Bell served as captain of a company of Rangers and then resigned the following year to enter the U.S. Army at the beginning of the Mexican War. He won distinction serving at the Battle of Buena Vista under Zachary Taylor. Bell eventually became a battalion commander in Jack Hays's First Texas Mounted Rifles. Returning to Texas as a war hero Bell was elected to two terms as governor. He resigned during his second term in 1853 to serve a vacancy in Congress caused by the death of David Kaufman. Bell served in Congress for two terms. After marrying the daughter of a wealthy North Carolinian planter, Bell moved to Littleton, North Carolina. He refused to serve in the Civil War. He remained in North Carolina until his death.[82]

Another leading Indian-fighter politician of this period was Ben McCulloch. McCulloch and his brother Henry came from Tennessee in early 1836 after meeting Crockett there and being persuaded to go to Texas. Crockett left before them, to their great fortune, but they arrived in time to take part in the Battle of San Jacinto. Ben McCulloch was elected to the Second Texas Congress in 1837. His opponent, Alonzo Sweitzer, accused him of cowardice for refusing to debate during the campaign. Following the election there was an Indian attack and Matthew Caldwell called both McCulloch and Sweitzer up to serve as Rangers. They quarreled as to who should have credit for discovering the Indian trail. After the trail was lost and the pursuit was declared over, McCulloch challenged Sweitzer to a duel in camp. Sweitzer declined and McCulloch declared him to be a coward and not a gentleman. Sweitzer challenged McCulloch to a duel when they had returned to town, but McCulloch refused to accept it and ended up fighting a duel with Sweitzer's second, Reuben Ross, with whom he had no quarrel. McCulloch was severely wounded in the arm in the duel and took some months to recover. McCulloch was charged with dueling, which was as illegal in Texas as in the United States, but the district attorney declined to prosecute.[83]

After a prominent role in the Battle of Plum Creek in 1840, McCulloch served as a Ranger for several years and then was elected to the first Texas state legislature in 1845. McCulloch served as a scout at the beginning of the Mexican War before joining Hays's regiment as a company commander. In 1849 McCulloch left for the gold fields of California and served as sheriff of

Sacramento County from 1850 to 1852 when he returned to Texas. McCulloch was prominent in the formation of state defense at the beginning of the Confederacy in 1861 and then led a division at the Battle of Pea Ridge in Arkansas in March 1862. He was killed on the second day of the battle.[84]

Like McCulloch, Jack Hays also went to California—leading a wagon train; but he decided to stay. Hays served for four years as sheriff of San Francisco County. President Franklin Pierce, who possibly had known him in Mexico, then appointed him surveyor general of California in 1855. Hays laid out the city of Oakland and became quite rich and a leading figure in the California Democratic Party. In 1876 he was a delegate to the Democratic National Convention.[85]

The last prominent Indian-fighter politician of this period may have been Francis R. Lubbock. His *Handbook of Texas Online* biography does not list any Indian fights, but he is checked on the *Lone Star Junction* website page of famous Texans for having participated in Indian fights. He moved to Texas shortly after the revolution and entered public service as a clerk of the house of representatives of the Texas Congress. Houston named him comptroller, but Lubbock then transferred to the frontier as the adjutant of a command to protect the frontier. He was possibly involved in the Battle of Neches against the Cherokee or in actions against other Indians during this time. In 1841 he was again appointed comptroller but again resigned to become district clerk of Harris County. He served sixteen years as district clerk and then became lieutenant governor under Governor Runnels. He was very active in Democratic politics during this period, fighting the Know Nothing Party during the mid-1850s. In 1861 Lubbock was elected governor of Texas to replace Houston by only 124 votes. In that capacity Lubbock vigorously supported conscription of all able-bodied men but passed an exemption for counties on the frontier. He organized the residents of the frontier into a militia for self-defense. He was so effective on behalf of the Confederacy, unlike many Confederate governors, that President Jefferson Davis invited him to Richmond to serve as his aide in August 1864. From December 1863 to August 1864 he functioned as a Confederate staff officer in the Trans-Mississippi Command.

In April 1865 Lubbock fled with Davis from Richmond and was arrested. He was confined for eight months before being paroled. He returned to Texas where he ranched briefly and then went into business in Houston and Galveston. He served as a tax collector in Galveston and from 1878 to 1891 was a treasurer of Texas. He lived in Austin from 1891 until his death in 1905. His political career stretches from the period of the first group to that of our last group.[86]

Another member of this second group was David Kaufman. Kaufman was very unusual for a Texas politician in that he was both a Northerner by birth and a Jew. Born in Pennsylvania he graduated with honors from Princeton University at age seventeen and then went to study law in

Natchez, Mississippi. After being admitted to the bar, he moved to Natchitoches, Louisiana, in 1835 to practice law. Two years later he moved to Nacogdoches, Texas, where he practiced law. He participated in the Battle of Neches against the Cherokee in July 1839 and was wounded. He represented Nacogdoches in the house in the Third through Fifth Texas Congresses and was speaker in the latter two. He represented three counties in the Texas senate from December 1843 to June 1845. After annexation he represented the eastern district of Texas for three terms. He was the last Jew to serve in Congress from Texas until the 1970s. Kaufman died in Washington in April 1851. His main claim to fame was a role in helping to win national assumption of Texas' debts in the 1850 Missouri Compromise agreement.[87]

An example of a minor politician who was probably fairly common in Texas, and probably earlier in other frontier states, was Daniel Montague. Montague arrived in Texas in 1836 to fight in the Revolution but was too late for San Jacinto. He returned to Louisiana and settled his affairs before returning to Texas permanently the following year. He settled at Old Warren in the Fannin Land District along the Red River in northern Texas. He participated in a number of Indian fights including the final one in Grayson County in 1843. During the Mexican War he served as a captain in the Third Texas Mounted Rifles Regiment. In 1849 he moved to Cooke County and worked as a surveyor. He was elected district surveyor in 1854, county commissioner in 1858 and 1862, and state senator in 1863. After the Civil War he moved to Mexico and thus avoided being tried for his involvement in the Great Hanging at Gainesville, where local Unionists were hanged. Montague returned to Texas in September 1876 and died three months later.[88]

A similar figure is Jerome Robertson. Having moved to Texas from St. Louis in 1836 following the revolution, Robertson served for a year in the Texas army. Robertson settled in Washington-on-the-Brazos in late 1837 and begin practicing medicine. For the next six years he served in every military campaign against either Indians or Mexicans. He was elected coroner of Washington County in 1838–39 and mayor of Washington-on-the-Brazos the following year. From 1841 to 1843 he served as postmaster of the town. In 1847 he was elected to the state house of representatives and in 1849 to the state senate. In 1861 he was elected to the Secession Convention. Robertson became one of the first men in the state to raise a company of volunteers to fight for the Confederacy, which became part of Thomas Hood's Fifth Texas Infantry Brigade. Robertson quickly rose through the ranks to the rank of brigadier general and command of Hood's brigade after Hood was promoted. His son, Felix Huston Robertson, was also a brigadier general during the war. A court martial in 1863 tried Robertson after he attracted the displeasure of Gen. James Longstreet in the East Tennessee campaign. Robertson returned to Texas and assumed command of state reserve forces. After the war he served in a number of minor posts while continuing to practice medicine until his death in 1890.[89]

The primary Indian-fighter politician after the Civil War was Lawrence Sullivan "Sul" Ross. As mentioned previously, Ross took part in campaigns against the Comanche while quite young. In 1861 he joined the company raised by his older brother, Peter, that was part of the Sixth Texas Cavalry. By early 1864 Ross had risen to the rank of brigadier general and the command of the Texas Cavalry Brigade after participating in numerous western campaigns. He spent the eight years of reconstruction farming and recovering his health. In 1873 he was elected sheriff of McLennan County. He organized the Sheriffs' Association of Texas and then helped to rewrite the post-reconstruction constitution of Texas in 1876. In 1880 he was elected to the state senate. In 1886 he was easily elected governor and served two terms. Immediately after stepping down as governor in 1891 he assumed the presidency of the Agricultural and Mechanical College of Texas (later Texas A & M University). He turned the institution around and helped build many new buildings and attracted new students. In 1893 he assumed command of the Texas war veterans association. Ross died suddenly in 1898.

The other two primary Indian-fighter politicians of the post–Civil War period were the Baylor brothers: John Robert and George Wythe. John R. Baylor was born in Kentucky in 1822 but moved to Indian Territory with his parents at a young age. After his father died in 1834 he was sent to live with his uncle in Fayette County, Texas. John participated in the Dawson expedition in 1842 to avenge the seizure of San Antonio by General Woll, but John managed to avoid the massacre of the party. In 1851 he was elected to the state legislature, despite being wanted as an accomplice for murder in Indian Territory. In 1853 he was admitted to the bar. In September 1855 he was appointed Indian agent at the Comanche reservation on the Clear Fork of the Brazos. But two years later he was dismissed for accusing reservation Comanche of participating in raids against settlements. He had also quarreled with his superior, Robert Neighbors. For the next four years John Baylor traveled throughout North Texas preaching hatred of the Comanche. He addressed mass meetings; organized a vigilante force; and even edited a newspaper, *The White Man,* to spread hatred of Indians. In June 1860 he led a posse of residents to defeat a small party of Comanche in the Battle of Paint Creek that had killed and scalped nine residents.

Baylor was made a lieutenant colonel following secession and put in command of the Second Texas Mounted Rifles. He was ordered to occupy a chain of forts protecting the route between Fort Clark and Fort Bliss. Baylor reached Fort Bliss in July 1861 and then moved to occupy the Mesilla Pass in eastern Arizona. Baylor proclaimed the Confederate Territory of Arizona with himself as military governor. In December he was promoted to colonel. He led a raid into the Chihuahua mountains of Mexico and killed a large number of Apache. In March 1862 he ordered the extermination of Apache in the area. When Davis heard of this he removed Baylor from command and revoked his rank. In 1863 Baylor was elected to the Second Confederate Congress from Texas. In late March 1865 he was reinstated as colonel. In 1873 he competed unsuccessfully for the Democratic nomination for governor. He dabbled in various third parties of the populist varieties and was involved in several violent confrontations. He reputedly killed a man in a livestock feud in the 1880s. He died in 1894 with no further political success.[90]

John's younger brother George was more successful. George Baylor was born in 1832. He took part in the Indian fight led by his brother in June 1860. At the outbreak of the war he was commissioned a first lieutenant in Company H of his brother's Arizona Brigade. He resigned in August or September 1861 to become aide-de-camp to Gen. Albert S. Johnston. After Johnston's death at Shiloh in April 1862, Baylor returned to Texas and was elected lieutenant colonel of the Second Battalion of Henry Sibley's Western Army. The battalion merged with the Second Cavalry regiment of his brother's Arizona Brigade, and George Baylor was elected its colonel. He commanded a cavalry regiment during the Red River Campaign of 1864. On April 6, 1865, he killed a fellow officer in a quarrel over the reorganization of the Trans-Mississippi Department. Baylor shot the unarmed man after the man slapped him on the face.

After the war Baylor became a lieutenant in Company C of the Frontier Battalion of Texas Rangers, established in 1874. Throughout 1879 and 1880 Baylor campaigned against Victorio and his band of Mescalero Apache raiders but was unable to catch the Apache. In September 1880 Baylor was promoted and transferred to command of Company A. In 1882 he was promoted to major and given command of several Ranger companies. Baylor resigned from the Rangers in 1885 and was elected to the Texas house of representatives from El Paso. He served as clerk of the district and circuit courts for a number of years. He died in 1916.[91]

Probably the most unusual and atypical Indian-fighter politician for Texas was Albert J. Fountain. Fountain grew up in New York City and attended Columbia University before heading out to California in the 1850s. He worked as a reporter for the *Sacramento Union*. He journeyed to Nicaragua to cover the filibustering expedition of William Walker. In 1861 he enlisted in the First California Infantry Volunteers and rose to the rank of lieutenant. The unit helped drive General Sibley's Confederate force out of Arizona. Fountain participated in the relocation of the Mescalero Apache to Bosque Redondo in 1862 and commanded volunteer New Mexico cavalry against the Mimbreno and Chiricahua Apache. He was severely wounded in the campaign and sent to El Paso, then occupied by the Union Army, to recover. After recovering he was discharged and decided to make El Paso his home. He established a law practice and became a civic leader and the leading organizer of the Republican Party in West Texas. He was appointed collector of customs and county surveyor in El Paso.

Fountain's oratory at the 1868 Radical Republican Convention in Corpus Christi led to his being elected vice chairman of the convention. As a result he played a major role in drafting the political platform for the Texas Radical Republicans. In 1868 the military government permitted the first postwar elections in Texas; and Radical Republican Edmund Davis was elected governor, and Fountain was elected to the state senate representing El Paso. He helped to draw up much of Davis's program for reconstruction and advocated the reactivation of the Texas Rangers, sponsoring the "frontier protection bill" to that effect. Political enemies regularly challenged him, and he killed one enemy in a duel after the man insulted him in a saloon. He was elected president of the state senate in one session and minority leader the following session. He introduced bills in favor of female suffrage—defeated—and the incorporation of El Paso—approved.

In 1873, with reconstruction coming to an end in Texas as more former Confederates regained the franchise, Fountain suffered from a shrinking political base. So he moved his family back to Mesilla, New Mexico Territory, where he had met his wife in 1862. He emerged as Republican leader in the New Mexico house of representatives. In 1879 he became captain of the Mesilla Scouts, a militia unit formed to protect the town against Indian raids. He published the *Independent* in Mesilla and became one of the most prominent attorneys in the territory. He was particularly successful in winning convictions against rustlers. In February 1896 he and his eight-year-old son disappeared while traveling between two towns in New Mexico. The bodies were never found, but they were presumed to be murder victims.[92] Fountain was unusual for a Texas politician in three ways: he was a Northerner by origin, he was a Union veteran, and he was a Republican. He could only have flourished during reconstruction and he was most successful in a frontier town near where his Indian fighting had taken place.

John B. Jones is a person who had a chance to have the last successful Indian-fighter political career in Texas politics. Born in 1834 in South Carolina and raised in Texas from age four, Jones served as a staff officer during the Civil War and finished the war as a major. After the war he scouted possible locations in South America and Mexico for a Confederate colony but reported to his superiors that no site was suitable. In 1868 he was elected to the state senate but denied his seat by Radical Republicans. Jones was appointed a major in command of the Frontier Battalion of the Texas Rangers when they were reconstituted in 1874. That year he saw action in the Red River War, being the last major Ranger commander to do so. In January 1879 he was appointed state adjutant general, the official in charge of the military resources of the state. But in July 1881 he died of natural causes. Most of the senior captains of the Rangers resigned that same year.[93] The Frontier Battalion remained as an anachronism. Had Jones lived he might have followed Ross as governor and prolonged the period of the Indian fighter in Texas politics. Jones was probably the best Ranger commander since Rip Ford, if not since Hays.

The Texas experience mirrors the American national experience. The heroes of the major battles of Texas inherited the largest prizes: those who were heroes of San Jacinto, the Grass Fight, the major battles of the Mexican War, and the major Texas campaigns of the Civil War. Those who fought only the Comanche or the Cherokee or other Indians probably received some boost but benefited to the degree of their natural political gifts. Those who were charming, good orators, and analytical thinkers or good organizers went the farthest. That means that the successful Indian-fighter politicians either came from the professional class or from the planter class. They were doctors, lawyers, or planters. In the United States this was the same: Washington, Taylor, and Jefferson Davis were planters; William H. Harrison was a medical student when he became an officer; Jackson was a lawyer and land speculator; Houston was a lawyer; Crockett was an entrepreneur. The pages of *The Handbook of Texas Online* are full of the short biographies of Indian fighters who either had no political careers or very minor ones. This is because they fought in countless minor skirmishes, lacked political skills, or opted for commercial careers.

But in one simple respect the Texas experience was different: the Mexican fighters came before the Indian fighters and not after as occurred nationally. Thus, most of the Indian fighters up until Ross and the Baylor brothers had been Mexican fighters before they became Indian fighters or their fighting was intertwined. Such was the experience of the early Texas Rangers from 1835 to 1860: they would fight Indians one year and Mexicans the next, or vice versa.

Texas had Indian-fighter politicians later than any other state for a simple reason: it had Indian fights later than any other state. The last Indian war in Texas occurred some forty years after the Black Hawk War in Wisconsin, in which the Illinois militia participated. The wars in Florida and in the American West were prosecuted by the professional army rather than by state militias. Even though the Red River War was largely conducted by the U.S. Army, rather than the Texas Rangers, and no Rangers who participated had major political careers afterward, militia organizations were fighting with Indians on a regular basis from 1858 to 1870 and the "Red peril" was a potent political issue until the end of the Buffalo War. John Baylor was successful preaching hatred in the late 1850s because it was such a potent issue. Had Florida been left to conduct the Seminole wars by itself, a similar climate would have prevailed in that state. Leading Indian-fighter army officers could probably have had successful political careers in Oregon, Idaho, Montana, South Dakota, New Mexico, and Arizona in the 1880s and 1890s had those places been states and not territories and had the officers been willing to give up their military careers.

Nelson Miles no doubt could have had a successful career in either Montana (where he had a city named after him) or in Arizona following the final Geronimo campaign. George Crook could have had a successful career in Arizona in the early 1880s, before Geronimo broke out of the reservation for his final fling, or in South Dakota. Ranald Mackenzie could possibly have had a successful career in Texas or in Arizona. But their ambitions were primarily military and not political. Crook and Mackenzie both died in the military—Crook of a heart attack and Mackenzie from the effects of insanity, possibly brought about by syphilis. When Miles finally decided to run for president in 1904 after being forcibly retired by President Theodore Roosevelt, he had passed his political expiration date.[94]

NOTES

1. Steven A. Channing, *Kentucky: A History* (New York: W W Norton, 1977), pp. 4, 6, 7, 11.
2. Ibid., pp. 12, 15, 24.
3. Ibid., pp. 16, 17, 19, 20, 21, 25, 26, 27.
4. Ibid., pp. 29, 30–33.
5. Ibid., pp. 39, 46, 53, 64.
6. Ibid., p. 21.
7. "Shelby, Isaac," *The Columbia Encyclopedia, Sixth edition, 2001* online at www.bartleby.com/65sh/Shelby-I; and "Isaac Shelby 1750 to 1826," at www.shelbysvolunteers.org/Isaac. Both accessed in August 2002.
8. "Clay, Green (1757–1826)," at www.politicalgraveyard.com/bio accessed in August 2002; and Channing, op. cit., p. 48.
9. "Richard M. Johnson," *Encyclopedia Americana: The American Presidency* at www.gi.grolier.com/presidents/ea/vp/vpjohn accessed in August 2002; Derr, op. cit., pp. 256–57.
10. Walter Havighurst, *Ohio: A Bicentennial History* (New York: W. W. Norton, 1976), pp. 3, 10, 12, 21–22, 26.
11. Ibid., p. 23,
12. See Chapter 2.
13. Havighurst, op. cit., pp. 154–56.
14. Stanley Folmsbee et al. *Tennessee: A Short History* (Knoxville: University of Tennessee Press, 1969), pp. 22, 39, 42, 69; John R. Finger, *The Eastern Band of Cherokees 1819–1900* (Knoxville: University of Tennessee Press, 1984), pp. 4, 5.
15. Folmsbee, op. cit., pp. 50–52, 61.
16. Ibid., pp. 69–70.
17. Ibid., The producers used a fictional name for Marion because Marion was a slave-owner, something that they did not want to deal with in the film.
18. Mark Derr, *The Frontiersman* (New York: William Morrow, 1993), p. 39.
19. Folmsbee, op. cit., pp. 80–92; 94–96.
20. Ibid., pp. 98, 103, 105.
21. Ibid., pp. 106, 126; Carl Driver, *John Sevier: Pioneer of the Old South West* (Chapel Hill, NC: University of North Carolina, 1932), pp. 111, 116.
22. Ibid., pp. 109–110, 112; Remini, *The Life of Andrew Jackson,* op. cit., p. 29. Folmsbee claims that Jackson played a major role at the convention, but his

biographer, Remini, writes that he played only a minor role. I am inclined to believe Remini. See Remini, . . . *Indian Wars,* op. cit., pp. 12–24, for Jackson's early life.

23. Driver, op. cit., p. 170.

24. Folmsbee, op. cit., pp. 132–33; Driver, pp. 149–50, 166.

25. Folmsbee, pp. 133, 179; Remini, . . . *Life of,* op. cit., pp. 45, 53–54 for Remini's accounts of the two duels.

26. Driver, op. cit., pp. 191–92.

27. Folmsbee, op. cit., pp. 134–35, 185; Driver, op. cit., pp. 198–200, 203, 205, 209, 213, 217.

28. Ibid., pp. 136–37.

29. Ibid., pp. 137, 142.

30. Ibid., p. 163.

31. Jean Fritz, *Make Way for Sam Houston* (New York: G. P. Putnam's Sons, 1986), pp. 19–40; Davis, op. cit., p. 29. Bowie won a notable victory over a group of about 125 Tawakoni, Caddo, and Waco that attacked him and a small party when they were treasure hunting in December 1832. This gave him a reputation that gave him a major military role at the beginning of the revolution and probably would have given him a good political career had he survived. See Davis, op. cit., pp. 298–304.

32. Folmsbee, op. cit., p. 170.

33. Ibid., pp. 178–79.

34. Derr, op. cit., p. 71.

35. Ibid., pp. 37, 39, 40, 42–43, 50–51.

36. Davis, op. cit., pp. 27, 31–32; Derr, p. 64.

37. "Crockett, David," *The Handbook of Texas Online* at www.tsha.utexas.edu/handbook/online; Derr, op. cit., pp. 73, 75; Davis, op. cit., pp. 70–73, 80, 116, 310–11.

38. Derr, pp. 65, 71.

39. Davis, op. cit., pp. 114–15.

40. Davis, pp. 117–19; Derr, op. cit., p. 139.

41. Derr, pp. 144–45; see Chapter 3 in this text on the election and the remainder of Crockett's career.

42. Ibid., pp. 174–77.

43. Ibid., pp. 189, 193.

44. Ibid., pp. 196, 203.

45. Ibid., pp. 228, 230.

46. Ibid., pp. 207, 231, 234–35, 238.

47. There were four major candidates in 1860 as both the Whigs and Democrats had split into regional wings.

48. See Walter P. Webb, *The Texas Rangers: A Century of Frontier Defense* (New York: Houghton Mifflin, 1935), pp. 17–25; Charles M. Robinson III, *The Men Who Wear the Star* (New York: Random House, 2000), pp. 20–38.

49. "Cherokee War," *The Handbook of Texas Online* at www.tsha.utexas.edu/handbook/online on August 18, 2002; Webb, op. cit., p. 47.

50. David Nevin, *The Texans* (New York: Time-Life Books, 1975), p. 205.

51. T. R. Fehrenbach, *Lone Star: A History of Texas and the Texans* (New York: Macmillan, 1968), p. 459; "Council Hill Fight," *The Handbook of Texas Online* at www.tsha.utexas.edu/handbook/online on August 18, 2002.

52. Fehrenbach, op. cit., pp. 59, 61; "Plum Creek, Battle of," *The Handbook of Texas Online* at www.tsha.utexas.edu/handbook/online on August 18, 2002.
53. Webb, pp. 67, 69, 80; Robinson, op. cit., pp. 56, 59–60.
54. Fehrenbach, op. cit., pp. 470, 475; Robinson, pp. 61, 63, 70.
55. Fehrenbach, pp. 254, 260; Nevin, op. cit., pp. 184–85.
56. Nevin, pp. 214, 216.
57. Nevin, p. 243; Fehrenbach, op. cit., pp. 265–66.
58. Nevin, pp. 156, 179.
59. Fehrenbach, op. cit., pp. 495, 497.
60. Webb, op. cit., pp. 141, 143; Robinson, op. cit., p. 110.
61. Fehrenbach, op. cit., pp. 13–17; Webb, pp. 6, 20.
62. Based on a map found at "Comancheria," *Comanche Lodge* at www.comanchelodge.com on August 10, 2002.
63. Fehrenbach, pp. 32–36; "Commanche Indians," and "Kiowa Indians," *The Handbook of Texas Online* at www.tsha.utexas.edu/handbook/online on August 18, 2002.
64. "Kiowa Indians," op. cit.
65. Fehrenbach, op. cit., pp. 499–500, 503; Webb, op. cit., pp. 151, 154, 155–56, 160.
66. Robinson, op. cit., pp. 117–18, 120.
67. Fehrenbach, op. cit., pp. 339–40, 346, 349; see Webb, op. cit., pp. 197–217 for details of the plot.
68. "Sam Houston 'The Raven'," *Lone Star Junction* at www.lsjunction.com/people on July 15, 2002.
69. Robinson, op. cit., pp. 139–40; "Peter Bell," *Lone Star Junction* at www.lsjunction.com/people on July 15, 2002.
70. Fehrenbach, op. cit., pp. 390–91, 529–30; Robinson, op. cit., p. 151.
71. Fehrenbach, pp. 530, 533–34.
72. Ibid., pp. 539–42.
73. Ibid., pp. 535–36.
74. Robinson, op. cit., pp. 168–70; Webb, op. cit., p. 309.
75. Fehrenbach, op. cit., pp. 543, 546, 549–50, 587; Robinson, op. cit., pp. 177–78; Webb, p. 318.
76. Webb, pp. 403–406; "Baylor, George," *The Handbook of Texas Online* at www.tsha.utexas.edu/handbook/online on August 18, 2002.
77. "Notable Texans Before 1900," *Lone Star Junction* at www.lsjunction.com/people on July 15, 2002.
78. "Wood, George Tyler," *The Handbook of Texas Online* at www.tsha.utexas.edu/handbook/online on August 18, 2002.
79. "Smith, James," *The Handbook of Texas Online* at www.tsha.utexas.edu/handbook/online on August 18, 2002.
80. "Rusk, Thomas Jefferson," *The Handbook of Texas Online* at www.tsha.utexas.edu/handbook/online on August 18, 2002.
81. "Ford, John Salmon," *The Handbook of Texas Online* at www.tsha.utexas.edu/handbook/online on August 18, 2002; Fehrenbach, op. cit., pp. 431–32, 434.
82. "Bell, Peter Hansborough," *The Handbook of Texas Online* at www.tsha.utexas.edu/handbook/online on August 18, 2002.
83. "Dueling in the Republic of Texas," *The Handbook of Texas Online* at www.tsha.utexas.edu/handbook/online on August 18, 2002.

84. "Ben McCulloch," *Lone Star Junction* at www.lsjunction.com/people on July 15, 2002.

85. "John C. 'Jack' Hays," *Lone Star Junction* at www.lsjunction.com/people on July 15, 2002.

86. "Francis R. Lubbock," *Lone Star Junction* at www.lsjunction.com/people on July 15, 2002; "Lubbock, Francis Richard," *The Handbook of Texas Online* at www.tsha.utexas.edu/handbook/online on August 18, 2002.

87. "Kaufman, David S." *The Handbook of Texas Online* at www.tsha.utexas.edu/handbook/online on August 18, 2002.

88. "Montague, Daniel," *The Handbook of Texas Online* at www.tsha.utexas.edu/handbook/online on August 18, 2002.

89. "Robertson, Jerome B.," *The Handbook of Texas Online* at www.tsha.utexas.edu/handbook/online on August 18, 2002.

90. "Baylor, John Robert," *The Handbook of Texas Online* at www.tsha.utexas.edu/handbook/online on August 18, 2002.

91. "Baylor, George," *The Handbook of Texas Online* at www.tsha.utexas.edu/handbook/online on August 18, 2002.

92. "Fountain, Albert J.," *The Handbook of Texas Online* at www.tsha.utexas.edu/handbook/online on August 18, 2002.

93. "Jones, John B.," *The Handbook of Texas Online* at www.tsha.utexas.edu/handbook/online on August 18, 2002. See also Robinson, op. cit., pp. 169–245 passim; Webb, op. cit., pp. 309–339 passim, 374–91 passim.

94. He only received a couple of votes at the Democratic Convention that year. This was before the advent of primaries where candidates could demonstrate their viability by running in elections for delegate votes.

8

The End of the Indian-Fighter Era

INTRODUCTION

The era of the Indian fighters ended for four main reasons. First, the Black Hawk War and the Third Seminole (1856–58) War were the last eastern Indian wars in which the militia played a major role. The Second Seminole War (1835–42) was fought almost exclusively by regular troops and volunteers. Generals Thomas Jesup and Taylor were the major military heroes of the second war. Jesup, who put down a Creek rebellion in Georgia in 1836, remained in the army. The use of professional troops broke the electoral relationship between the commanding general and the troops he commanded. A new era of Indian wars in the West began in the mid-1850s, but it was fought with professional troops and immigrant enlistees. This new era lasted for thirty years until the last Apache campaign ended in 1886. After the War of 1812 the connection between foreign enemies and the Indians was also broken; this meant that Indian fighters had less chance of tying their campaigns to a larger war.

Second, as Indian warfare moved west of the Mississippi, it moved away from major population centers. The last time Indians threatened any large number of civilians was when the Sioux invaded New Ulm, Minnesota, in the summer of 1862 during the Sioux rebellion. Henry H. Sibley, who led the Minnesota militia in putting down the Sioux rebellion, was governor of Minnesota *before* the rebellion and was actually picked to lead the rescue effort by his personal friend and political rival who was serving as governor.[1] Henceforth, it would be the army that would threaten Indian civilians.

Civilian settlers were killed in large numbers in Kansas in 1868 and 1874, in Oregon in 1873 and 1877, in the Dakota Territory (where they were illegally) in 1876, and in Arizona in the 1870s and 1880s. But they were dependent on the army for their security. In the West, large-scale settlement came after conquest, not before. Arizona and New Mexico did not become states until 1912. Minnesota suffered its ravages from Indians during the Civil War, when the losses were comparatively miniscule compared with what was happening in the East.

Third, the heroes of those Indian wars were professional career army officers. The top Indian fighters were "boy generals" in the Civil War who then competed to regain their Civil War rank of general in a much smaller army. The only one to seriously consider a run for the presidency was Nelson Miles, who retired from the army when Roosevelt was president. He would have run as a hero of the Spanish-American war (he commanded the invasion of Puerto Rico) rather than as an Indian fighter. There were relatively few of these successful Indian fighters. George Custer died in combat; Ranald McKenzie went insane after years on the frontier; George Crook died as a major general after failing to end the last Geronimo campaign.

Fourth, no political party after the Civil War was dependent on generals as candidates as the Whigs had been. After the Civil War there was no slavery issue to split the political parties into two sectional wings. And the Republicans and Democrats learned how to balance their presidential tickets geographically. For the first twenty years after the Civil War the main candidates from the Republican Party were former Civil War generals from Ohio. The Democrats actually began the Civil War veteran era in politics by nominating George B. McClellan, the Union commander in 1861–62, as their candidate in 1864. He was followed by a string of Republican and Democratic generals. The remainder of this chapter elaborates on these causes.

THE INDIAN WARS

Indian warfare resumed after a nearly fifteen-year hiatus with wars in the Pacific Northwest and Florida in 1856. There were wars against the Bannock (Paiute) in Oregon and Idaho starting in 1855. There was also a minor Indian war against the approximately three hundred remaining Seminole in the Everglades of Florida. This began in 1856 and finally ended in 1858 when the Seminole leader, Chief Bowlegs, was successfully bribed along with 122 of his followers to go into exile in Arkansas and forty-one Seminole who had been captured joined them.[2]

There were also the first clashes with the Lakota (Teton Sioux) and Cheyenne on the Great Plains, but these remained isolated. A few Indian campaigns were fought in the West during the Civil War, but they were limited because most of the troops were in the East fighting the Civil War. The

Sioux Uprising or Sioux War in Minnesota began on August 18, 1862, with the murder of five whites by young braves. Crop failures had produced hunger among the Indians; and this, combined with deductions from their annual allotment due to questionable charges from merchants, led to anger and the uprising. The war lasted for five weeks; and the casualties were 413 white civilians, 77 soldiers, and 71 Indians including the 38 hanged in Mankato on December 26, 1862. There were three major battles in the war. A relief column was ambushed on the first day and nearly wiped out with forty whites killed. At Birch Coulee the Dakota were victorious, and in the final battle at Wood Lake the Indians were defeated and fled to Dakota Territory and Canada. Most of the white casualties came when the Indians attacked nearby settlements such as New Ulm and were finally driven off after furious battles. While these losses were quite heavy, they paled beside the losses that Minnesota experienced during the Civil War.[3]

A massacre by Colorado militia led by the notorious Colonel Chivington in November 1864 of a peaceful Cheyenne village led by Chief Black Kettle at Sand Creek, Colorado, led to a war in Colorado, Kansas, and Nebraska by the Lakota, Cheyenne, and Arapaho against the local white settlers. They even sacked the town of Julesburg, Colorado, in the extreme norteast corner of that state in January 1865.

This war began a decade of Indian warfare in Kansas that did not end completely until the Red River War of 1874–75. Scores of settlers were killed in the late 1860s, and captives were tortured to death. Between two peace treaties in 1865 and 1867, some two hundred settlers were killed. Another two hundred were killed by the end of 1868, when the Sheridan-Custer winter campaign of 1868–69 finally brought the killing to an end. The peace then lasted for five years until the outbreak of the Red River War in the summer of 1874. In this last war twenty-six Kansans were killed and thousands fled. A like number were killed during the Cheyenne revolt of September–October 1878, which was the final raid in Kansas history. Responsible for keeping the settlers protected were the Seventh Cavalry under Lieutenant Colonel George A. Custer and the Sixth Infantry under Colonel Nelson Miles. Custer and the Seventh Cavalry departed for reconstruction duty in Kentucky in 1871.[4]

Red Cloud's War broke out in the summer of 1866 as Oglala Lakota Chief Red Cloud led the Lakota and Cheyenne in attacks against miners and settlers traveling north through Wyoming to Montana. The U.S. Army established a series of forts to protect the road north. The Fetterman "massacre" of December 1866 when Captain Fetterman and eighty of his men were wiped out by the Indians in an ambush initiated a period of twenty years of continuous warfare involving the army. In 1868 the Indians won when the government agreed to evacuate the Bozeman Trail—they could reach Montana through an alternate route. It was the last time that the Indians won a war.

Most of the Indian wars were guerrilla conflicts with few pitched battles. The Indians waged wars of ambush against long supply lines, isolated travelers, and inexperienced commanders. The few notable exceptions to this rule were in the Great Sioux War of 1876–77 when Crazy Horse fought two large conventional battles against Custer's Seventh Cavalry and George Crook at the Little Bighorn and Rosebud respectively. Custer was wiped out in the largest army defeat in more than eighty years against Indians. Crook was left in possession of the battlefield but refused to advance, leaving Custer to his fate. The war was brought to a conclusion by a very aggressive campaign by Colonel Nelson Miles harassing the Indians throughout the autumn and winter of 1876 and 1877. Colonel Ranald Mackenzie led a raid against Dull Knife's Cheyenne village in November 1876, taking the Cheyenne out of the war.

After the Great Sioux War the Nez Perce War broke out in the summer of 1877 in Oregon with massacres of white settlers by young braves as the tribe was preparing to move to a new reservation in Idaho from its ancestral homeland. The war lasted until early October when Miles cut the retreating Nez Perce off just short of their successful escape into Canada. Another conventional battle was fought that lasted several days, and a shortage of ammunition compelled the Indians to surrender. This was the last major Indian war fought on the Great Plains. The following autumn was the breakout of the Northern Cheyenne from their reservation in Oklahoma and their attempt to return to their traditional homeland. The Indians were interned at Fort Robinson, Nebraska, and then broke out again during a blizzard. This was the final campaign with fighting. Another revolt involving the Ute Indians in Colorado was ended without bloodshed.

Earlier there had been a guerrilla war fought in the lava beds south of Lake Klamath on the California-Oregon border. The Modoc were being moved out of their traditional lands to a reservation to make room for white settlement. A small group led by a leader called Captain Jack by the whites resisted. The Modoc retreated into the treacherous passages of the lava beds, which were well known to them, and were able to wage a defensive war from a position with home ground advantage. The army suffered embarrassing reversals before the war was finally ended. This was also the only Indian war in which an American general was killed. The Modoc murdered General Edward Canby while he was negotiating. This led to a determination by the army to avenge his death. The casualties at the beginning of the Nez Perce War matched the casualties at the beginning of this war.

The 1880s saw Indian resistance reduced to the American Southwest—the Apache in New Mexico and Arizona. Both territories were sparsely populated, mostly by ranchers and miners. The army was free to deploy in strength to deal with the rebellions. Victorio's band of Mescalero Apache were forced into Mexico in October 1880, and he was killed and his band wiped out by the Mexican cavalry in a battle that month. This left only Arizona as a problem.

Arizona had experienced problems with the Apache for twenty years—from 1866 to 1886—off and on. Colonel George Crook ended a war by Cochise in 1873 for which service he was promoted to brigadier general. The Apache wars were finally ended by employing loyal Apache mercenaries against the renegade Apache warriors by Crook and Miles. Although this was a major problem for the army, it was not a great issue for the nation as a whole.

THE INDIAN FIGHTERS OF THE WEST

Most historians of the American West see three individuals as competing for the title of most successful Indian fighter: George Crook, Ranald Mackenzie, and Nelson Miles. In fact, one of Mackenzie's two biographers concedes that Crook and Miles had superior records as Indian fighters. He rates Crook as number one and Miles as number two, the latter making up for his lack of imagination with his drive and determination to overcome obstacles. Stan Hoig, a historian of the Southern Cheyenne and chronicler of Custer's southern campaigns, rates Mackenzie as first among Indian fighters.[5] Partisans are generally divided over which was the superior figure. The two National Park Service historians concerned with the West and the Indian wars, Robert M. Utley and Jerome Greene, are fair-minded partisans of Crook and Miles respectively.[6] All accept that Custer fell into a lower category of Indian fighter.

Crook spent almost thirty years on the frontier—interrupted only by the four years of the Civil War. He started out fighting Indians in northern California and Oregon in the late 1850s. In the Civil War he started out as a colonel of volunteer infantry and ended the war as a brevet major general in charge of a corps. He played a particularly important role in the final two weeks of the war. After the Civil War he fought the Paiute of Idaho for two years as a lieutenant colonel, before retiring to San Francisco for a time to sit on a board determining which officers to retain in the army.

Crook then spent four years in Arizona as the commander of the Department of Arizona, after initially turning down the offer but being persuaded by the Arizona governor who lobbied for Crook, in the Division of the Pacific. Crook was successful in his campaign against the Tonto Apache and the Yavapai by doing three things. First, he organized Apache from other bands—primarily the White Mountain Apache—into companies of scouts and auxiliaries to fight the renegades. Second, he organized a system of pack mules to keep the units supplied in the field. Third, he raised the morale and self-reliance of his men. In 1873 he was promoted over forty colonels to brigadier general in recognition of his success in pacifying the territory.

In 1875 Crook was sent to head the Department of the Platte in preparation for the campaign against the Lakota (Sioux) and the Cheyenne of the northern plains. A week before the Battle of the Little Bighorn, he fought

Crazy Horse to a tactical draw—although it was a strategic victory for the Lakota—at the Battle of the Rosebud. Crook conducted a forced march—the "horseflesh march"—through eastern Montana and western Dakota Territory in the late summer of 1876 in pursuit of the Indians. He organized Mackenzie's attack on Dull Knife's village on November 25, 1876, that knocked many of the Cheyenne out of the war. He used a system of auxiliary Cheyenne and Lakota to help bring in the remaining hostiles in the spring of 1877, and he oversaw the surrender of the main groups of hostile Indians. He remained in charge of the Platte for seven years, then returned to command in Arizona in July 1882 for three years during the end of the Apache wars.

Crook organized the Chiricahua Apache at San Carlos into auxiliary units to pursue their fellow tribesmen, and he teamed them with able officers. He led a campaign with a force of 193 scouts accompanied by one troop of cavalry into Mexico. After successfully storming the camp of Chato, one of Geronimo's leading partners, they convinced Geronimo—or rather let Geronimo convince them to allow him—to return to the reservation. Geronimo returned to the reservation in March 1884 after being met at the border by scouts and escorted there.

Fourteen months later Geronimo organized his final breakout from the reservation with forty-two men and ninety-two women and children. Crook organized two columns of scouts and cavalry to pursue Geronimo into Mexico, while he remained in command in Arizona and had three thousand troops patrolling the border. In October 1885 the columns recrossed the border and went to Fort Bowie to refit. In January 1886 the troops penetrated into Geronimo's stronghold and just missed catching him. Mexican troops then fought the hostiles, and the troop commander was "accidentally" shot dead by the Mexican troops. The troops returned to Fort Bowie with an offer from Geronimo to meet with Crook at San Bernardino in "two moons." On March 25, 1886, Crook met with Geronimo in Canon de los Embudos, twelve miles south of the border, and Geromino agreed to surrender. After Geronimo betrayed Crook by going back on his surrender and Washington repudiated his terms, Crook asked to be relieved of command. But the surrender did not prevent him from being promoted to major general in 1888. He had at least twice if not three times as much experience fighting Indians as his nearest competitor, Nelson A. Miles.[7]

Miles joined the army as a volunteer officer in October 1861 after raising his own company of infantry. He served as an aide under General Oliver O. Howard. Miles was wounded four times during the war; he fought in every major campaign in the East and ended the war as an infantry division commander and brevet major general. Miles arrived in the West in April 1869 as commander of the Fifth Infantry Regiment and spent the next two decades there and was continually involved in Indian fighting and peace making for three years from August 1874 to October 1877 and again in

1886 and in January 1891. He first saw combat against Indians in late August 1874. He was the last commander to return from the field during the winter campaign of the Red River War in February 1875. Miles arrived at the Tongue River Cantonment in September 1876. After preparing a base for the winter, Miles prepared for a winter campaign against the hostile Indians with the order of special winter clothing. Never having even five hundred men under his command, Miles kept the men marching throughout the winter in the bitter subzero temperatures and roaring winds of the northern plains. The men of the Fifth Infantry Regiment kept Sitting Bull and Crazy Horse harassed throughout the winter. Miles fought Crazy Horse to a standstill in early January until a blizzard finally ended the battle. Finally in May 1877 Crazy Horse surrendered to Crook, and Sitting Bull fled into Canada with his Hunkpapa Lakota followers. In May 1877 Miles set out to bring in the last major Indian chief still holding out, Chief Lame Deer of the Minneconjou Lakota. Lame Deer was killed when he opened fire on Miles during the start of negotiations, and his war chief was also killed. The Fifth Infantry overran the village and the band was knocked out of the war as a factor.[8]

In late September 1877 Miles marched his men some three hundred miles to cut off the escape route of Chief Joseph and his Nez Perce into Canada. Miles kept the village pinned down until General Howard, who had been pursuing them since the start of the war in July, could arrive, and Miles scattered the horse herd of the Nez Perce. Miles then conducted surrender negotiations with Joseph and convinced him to surrender, thereby sparing any further army and Indian casualties. Miles was the only army hero of the Nez Perce War, but his taking Joseph hostage during the negotiations tarnished his reputation. For the next several years he engaged in an unbecoming battle with Howard over who should get credit for ending the war. "General Miles pounced upon and captured a game which had been chased to death by Howard and Sturgis," allegedly said Division of the Missouri Commander General Philip Sheridan.[9]

Mackenzie, the son of a career naval officer and writer, graduated from West Point in 1862 near the top of his class. He spent the next two years serving as an engineering and staff officer. Finally in June 1864 he was given a combat command with the rank of colonel in the regular army commanding an infantry brigade of Connecticut volunteers. He ended the war as a brevet major general in charge of a cavalry division. Along with George Custer, he quickly became one of Sheridan's favorite cavalry officers on the frontier. In 1869 he was given command of an infantry regiment in Texas. In February 1871 he was transferred to command of the Fourth Cavalry Regiment, the unit he would command until promoted to brigadier general in 1883. Mackenzie spent most of his service in Texas, serving either to patrol the border with Mexico or at Fort Concho. Mackenzie fought in the one decisive action of the Red River War, the Battle of Palo Duro Canyon in September 28, 1874, when he defeated a combined Comanche, Cheyenne, and Kiowa force and destroyed their village with only one person killed in his command. The destruction of the horse herd and the village left this great concentration of Indians destitute on the plains.[10]

After the Civil War the army had been reduced from a force of hundreds of thousands to only about twenty-five thousand regulars. Officers who had risen to command divisions and corps during the Civil War found themselves commanding regiments as they were reduced in rank from major general to lieutenant colonel or colonel. Competition arose among the most promising officers for choice commands and the chance to serve in the field and thus advance. All of these officers played politics, using connections with the top leadership of the army formed during the Civil War or political connections to promote themselves. Miles married into the Sherman family, which gave him a senator and the commander of the army as uncles-in-law. Miles was continually firing off letters to his uncles after every success in the field promoting himself and blowing his own trumpet. He seemed to annoy General Sherman more than he mobilized him in support of his schemes. Mackenzie had attracted the attention of both Sherman and Grant during the Civil War, with the latter declaring that Mackenzie was "the most promising young officer in the army." Custer was regarded as Sheridan's favorite cavalry commander, both during the Civil War and on the frontier. Only Crook lacked a favorite patron. After Crook was promoted to brigadier general, taking the commission of Edward Canby who was murdered during negotiations with the Modoc in 1873, Custer, Mackenzie, and Miles were in a race for the next brigadier slot to open up. Miles, a personal friend of Custer, did not regard him as competition as much as he regarded Mackenzie. After Custer's death, the two were the leading competitors for promotion.[11]

Mackenzie was transferred with the Fourth Cavalry to Camp Robinson, Nebraska, in August 1876. When he arrived, Mackenzie discovered that half the Indians normally resident at the post had gone to join the hostiles. Red Cloud had moved his band of Oglala Lakota thirty miles from the agency, partly to keep them away from those attempting to subvert them. But it was feared that Red Cloud, the successful war leader from 1866 to 1868, would join the hostiles. Mackenzie used the Fourth Cavalry and two companies of the Fifth Cavalry to force Red Cloud to return to the reservation by surrounding his village.

On November 25, 1876, Mackenzie led a combined cavalry force with companies from several regiments into the village of Northern Cheyenne Chief Dull Knife. Mackenzie claimed twenty-five Indians killed in the battle compared to his own six killed and twenty-six wounded. Sheridan was planning a further campaign for the northern plains that proved unnecessary when the Indians began surrendering in large numbers. In November 1877 the Fourth Cavalry was transferred to the Nueces region of Texas on the Mexican border. Mackenzie twice led raids into Mexico and was often in the field between 1871 and 1878. Two years later the Fourth Cavalry was moved to Colorado to deal with problems with the Ute. Mackenzie resolved the problem at the last minute a year later when the Indians refused to move and he told them he would move them by force if necessary. In September 1881 the Fourth Cavalry was moved to Fort Apache, Arizona, after an outbreak of Indian trouble.

When General Ord was forced to retire in 1880, opening up a brigadier position, Mackenzie was recommended for the slot by Crook, Pope, Sheridan, and even Sherman. But Miles, through his own political connections, received the promotion. Mackenzie became commander of the District of New Mexico in September 1881. Mackenzie was finally promoted to brigadier when the next slot opened up in October 1882. Both Sheridan and Grant recommended him for the promotion. Mackenzie was given command of the Department of Texas in 1883; and only a few months after moving to take up the position, he was diagnosed with mental illness at the age of forty-three. At the end of the year he was admitted to an asylum, after being forced out of the army. He died in January 1889 at age forty-eight. His condition was possibly syphilis or some sort of condition brought on by acute stress over the years.[12]

George Armstrong Custer graduated bottom of his class at West Point in 1861, just as the Civil War was breaking out. Custer spent the first two years of the war as a staff officer, serving on the staffs of both Brigadier General Kearny and Major General George McClellan, who was in charge of the Army of the Potomac. Custer was then transferred in 1863 to the staff of Brigadier General Alfred Pleasonton, who was in charge of the Union cavalry for the Army of the Potomac. In June 1863 Custer was jumped three grades from captain to brigadier general. At age twenty-three he was the youngest general in the Union army. He fought recklessly in the Battle of Gettysburg and during Grant's Virginia campaign in May 1864. He ended the war as a brevet major general in charge of a cavalry division of Michigan volunteers operating under General Sheridan. Custer's division played a very important role in the final week of the war. As recognition of his outstanding war record, Custer was demoted back to lieutenant colonel instead of captain at the end of the war.[13]

Custer served in Texas on reconstruction duty for a year from 1865 to 1866 and then was posted to Fort Riley, Kansas, to take effective command of the Seventh Cavalry. The actual commander, Colonel Samuel Sturgis, was away on periods of extended leave in Washington and elsewhere. Custer served in the spring of 1867 in Hancock's war against the Sioux as the only force to be pursuing the Indians, but he failed to ever close with them. Sentenced to one year's absence without pay for being absent without leave, Custer was suddenly recalled before the sentence had been fulfilled in September 1868. Custer led the Seventh Cavalry south from

Fort Dodge. After making camp at Camp Supply in northern Oklahoma, Custer set out with the Seventh Cavalry trailing hostile Indians who had been raiding into Kansas. The trail was followed into the village of Black Kettle, a peace chief of the Southern Cheyenne, whose village had been attacked by Colonel Chivington and the Colorado volunteers in November 1864. On November 27, 1868, the Seventh Cavalry charged into the village to the accompaniment of a band playing "Gary Owen." Custer directed the action from a small knoll on the battlefield while his men went through the village crushing any resistance. A Major Elliot wandered off with a platoon of cavalry and was wiped out by Indians from the surrounding village. Custer supervised the burning of the village and the stores and then ordered a countermarch out of the village in the late afternoon so that the unit could get back to its supplies before being cut off. Custer later claimed 103 warriors killed; the actual figure is unknown, and estimates vary from three dozen including women and children to almost three hundred. Custer campaigned in the field until April 1869.[14]

The Washita campaign was successful in pacifying the Cheyenne and Arapaho for the next several years. In 1871 the Seventh Cavalry was reassigned to reconstruction duty in Kentucky. In 1873 the Seventh Cavalry was part of the Yellowstone Expedition, a surveying trip for a new railroad to be built through the area. Custer fought two actions against the Lakota that summer, which tested his military skill much more than the Washita campaign did. The following summer he led a surveying expedition into the Black Hills, which discovered gold. This led to a gold rush in the Black Hills in 1875–76 and the planning of the Great Sioux War after no credible Lakota chiefs were willing to sell the Black Hills to the federal government. In June 1876 Custer, with General Alfred Terry, led one of three columns into Lakota territory in the Yellowstone region. On June 25, 1876, Custer split the Seventh Cavalry into three separate "battalions" and led them in converging attacks on a massive combined Lakota and Cheyenne village on the Little Bighorn River. Custer's "battalion" was completely destroyed, and the other two battalions under Major Reno and Captain Benteen fought a defensive action, suffering many dead and wounded, until help arrived. It was the greatest American disaster in an Indian war since 1791, when General Arthur St. Clair lost seven hundred men in Ohio. The battle immortalized Custer by making him a figure of controversy that still continues over a century after his death.[15]

Following the Indian wars in the East, Indian commissioners appointed by Washington carried out negotiations with the defeated tribes or tribal coalitions. In some cases, these included the commanders in the wars. Jackson had enough personal popularity that he could dictate his own terms for negotiations with the Indians. Harrison used deceit—including alcohol—as his preferred tool in negotiations. Jackson preferred intimidation and fear, but he was not above using bribery. Bribery was particularly effective in combination with coercion, as the bribed leaders felt that they were succumbing to the coercion, and accepting an inevitable result.

In the western Indian wars after 1866 the commanders in the field might have negotiated surrender terms, but they did not negotiate peace treaties. The peace treaties had already been negotiated with leaders that were either more corrupt, more cowardly, or more realistic about the balance of power than the resistance leaders. After the conquest of the Great Plains had been accomplished through the winter campaign of 1868–69, the Red River War, and the Great Sioux War, most Indian resistance was driven by desperation caused by mismanagement of the reservations. Repeatedly Miles and Crook found themselves negotiating what they considered to be honorable surrender terms only to see these same terms repudiated by civilian authorities. The authorities cared neither enough about their personal honor nor about the effect that this would have on future negotiations to give them strict negotiating instructions.

Only one Indian leader, Red Cloud, was able to outnegotiate the federal government after 1866. This is because he was fighting on remote territory, used superior generalship, and had limited aims. And Washington realized that it was able to accomplish its goal by simply bypassing Red Cloud's territory. By the 1870s Red Cloud realized that he would not be able to repeat this success, and he very carefully negotiated the location of the reservation, keeping in mind the balance of power.[16]

The ambition of these "boy generals"—who got used to being addressed as "General" while still in their twenties—was to return to a status where that was their actual rank, rather then merely a brevet rank and honorary title. This consumed both Custer and Mackenzie. Crook died while still in the army. By the time that Miles ran for president, he was too late to win elections on the basis of his fame as an Indian fighter and had not sufficiently paved his way by a public relations campaign. Miles and Crook both had good chances of making it as successful politicians at the state level, either in their native states, Massachusetts and Ohio respectively, or in one of the states in which they had their most important Indian campaigns—Montana, South Dakota, Oregon, or Arizona. Miles had a small city—established on the site of his camp in 1877, Miles City—named after him in Montana. Montana and both the Dakotas became states in 1889. Miles could probably have been elected to the legislature and eventually possibly the governor's office or become a U.S. senator from Montana. The fact that John Sherman, a powerful senator from Ohio, was an uncle certainly would have helped him. Miles probably also could have made a political career in Arizona following the final Geronimo campaign. But Miles was more interested in being commander of the army.

Likewise, Crook probably could have made a political career in either South Dakota—where he made his "mud march" in the summer of 1876 to rescue the gold miners at Deadwood—or in Arizona. Arizona might have been a bit more difficult, as his policy of using Indians to defeat other Indians was very controversial. But he was popular in the state in the decade from 1873 to 1883. Had he quit the military sometime during this period to go into politics there, he might have been quite successful. But nationally, the Civil War veterans whose reign we now consider blocked both of these figures.

THE CIVIL-WAR-VETERAN PRESIDENTS

Former Civil War generals served as president from 1869 to 1893, with a break from 1881 to 1889 of "civilian" presidents. The first, Ulysses S. Grant, was born and raised in Ohio and from there went to West Point where he graduated in 1843 in time for the Mexican War. He served with Scott's army in Mexico as a lieutenant. After the war he was sent to serve in various frontier posts, including California; and isolation and boredom led to drinking that led to his exit from the army. In 1861 he became colonel of a volunteer unit in Illinois; and for whipping the unruly volunteers into shape, he was promoted to brigadier general. He won his first major battle in November 1861 and continued to win battles throughout 1862 and 1863 when the Union was starved for victories. This led to his steady promotions to commander in the West and then in March 1864 to commander of the Union forces. In May 1864 he began his Wilderness campaign in Virginia that led eventually to the siege of Petersburg, Virginia. When he finally crushed the Confederate army in Virginia in April 1865, he was the most revered man in the Union, a change from being considered a drunk and a butcher.

After the unsuccessful presidency of Andrew Johnson, the Radical Republicans were anxious for a successful candidate. They nominated Grant, who easily defeated his Democratic opponent, Horatio Seymour, to become the eighteenth president. Grant nominated his friends, many of them opportunists, to office; and as a result his administration suffered from incompetence and corruption. He had no economic experience and no way of determining who was qualified to oversee the economy. In 1873 there was a major depression.

Grant's major policy initiative was his "peace policy" with the Indians in the West. He encouraged Quakers to apply for positions as Indian agents. These agents tended to be less corrupt than the men they replaced but naïve when it came to dealing with the Plains Indians. The army refrained from any major campaigns on the Great Plains from the end of Sheridan's winter campaign in April 1869 until the Red River War in June 1874. This war effectively ended the peace policy. Grant's final year in office witnessed Custer's defeat at the Little Bighorn and the dispatch of the army in large numbers to deal with the hostile Lakota and Cheyenne.

Grant's term also spanned the reconstruction period in the South. Grant used the military to suppress terrorist organizations like the Ku Klux Klan in the South and to promote equality for blacks. This resulted in a record number of blacks in office in the South. But the South resented having Northern policies forced upon them. This, combined with the bitterness of the Civil War, resulted in the South becoming a virtual Democratic kingdom. Grant wanted to run for a third term, but the Republican Party decided that he had been in office long enough and did not want to overturn the tradition of limiting the president to two terms.[17]

Rutherford B. Hayes was a successful criminal lawyer before the Civil War. He married into a liberal, politically active family and became a believer in abolition and women's rights. At age thirty-nine, with no military background, he volunteered for a position in the Union Army at the beginning of the Civil War. He was commissioned a major and through bravery and hard work rose to the rank of major general by war's end. He was chief of staff to General Rosecrans and had served in General George Crook's corps. Then he took up the seat in the House from Ohio that he had been elected to during the war. He served for three years in Washington in the House before being elected governor of Ohio. After two terms as governor, he was nominated for president at the Republican convention for his reputation for honesty and bravery. In November 1876 in the dirtiest presidential campaign in American history, he ran against Samuel Tilden of New York. The election was so ridden with fraud that a special congressional electoral commission was set up to examine the voting and award electoral votes. Hayes won narrowly, with a minority of the popular vote, earning him the title of "Rutherfraud" B. Hayes and "His Fraudulency."

Hayes moved to reassure the electorate by announcing plans for electoral reform, announcing that he would limit himself to one term; and after a month in office, he pulled federal troops out of the South thereby ending reconstruction and black rights for ninety years. Some saw in this a payment on a deal reached during the election. But Hayes claimed that the troops were merely creating bitterness and preventing reconciliation between the North and the South.[18]

James Garfield was probably the poorest man ever elected president of the United States. Raised on a farm on the outskirts of Cleveland, Garfield became a carpenter and janitor in order to work his way through college. After graduating from college he studied law on his own and passed the Ohio bar exam in 1860. Even before becoming a lawyer he was elected to the state senate in 1859 as a Republican. After the fall of Fort Sumter, Garfield formed the Forty-Second Ohio Infantry Regiment and quickly rose from lieutenant colonel to full colonel in the early months of the war. At the time in 1863, he was the youngest officer promoted to major general; this was after his brigade performed very well in battle in January 1862, and he was cited for a daring raid under fire at the Battle of Chickamauga in September 1863.

Garfield was elected to the House from Ohio without campaigning and resigned his commission in December 1863 to take up his seat. He served for seventeen years in the House, serving on several important economic and budgetary committees, including the Banking and Currency Committee, the Appropriations Committee, and the Ways and Means Committee. He developed a reputation both as a financial expert and a moderate; he voted for impeachment of President Johnson, supported Grant for two terms, and then backed Hayes. He was elected to the U.S. Senate in 1880.

In 1880 the Republican convention looked set for a fight between Ulysses Grant and James Blaine. But Garfield emerged as a dark-horse candidate during the course of balloting and ended up walking away with the nomination. His opponent in the general election was Democrat and former General Winfield Scott Hancock, a hero of Gettysburg. This was the only election between two Civil War heroes and the third between two former generals, the last having been in 1852. There were few differences on the issues between the two candidates, except over the tariff—which Hancock labeled a "local question." It was the closest election on record between 1876 and 2000: although Garfield won with 214 electoral votes to 155 for Hancock, he had a plurality of less than seventy-five hundred popular votes, or about one-tenth of 1 percent of the vote. Both candidates won nineteen states apiece, with Garfield taking the Northern and Midwestern states and Hancock the Southern and border states. Had only two very close states, New York and Indiana, gone Democratic, Hancock would have won in the electoral college. Hancock was the first Northern candidate to carry the South. In order to prevent the loss of New York, Garfield struck a deal with New York political boss Senator Roscoe Conkling, promising to consult him on political appointments. Conkling's protégé, Chester Arthur, had already been nominated as Garfield's vice-presidential running mate.

As president, Garfield appointed James Blaine as secretary of state and favored his faction of the Republican Party over that of Senator Conkling of New York. Four months into Garfield's term an emotionally disturbed disappointed office seeker, Charles J. Guiteau, assassinated him. His vice president, Charles Arthur, from whom he had already become estranged, succeeded him.[19]

Garfield's election opponent, Winfield S. Hancock, was the last Mexican fighter prominent in American politics. He graduated from West Point in 1844 and served in Mexico where he won brevet rank for bravery. Hancock began the Civil War as a brigade commander and served with distinction in the early fighting. He was promoted to division commander, major general, and served in that capacity with distinction in the Peninsular Campaign in June 1862 and then at the Battles of Antietam (September 1862), Fredericksburg (February 1863), and Chancellorsville (May 1863). He was appointed to corps commander in time for Gettysburg in July and made the crucial decision to stand and fight there. He was a hero of the battle and was severely wounded. He then served under Grant in the 1864–65 campaign. In 1867 Hancock was George Custer's superior in his first Indian campaign in Kansas, but Hancock did not take the field. He was an army district commander in charge of Texas and Louisiana during Reconstruction. There he clashed with Radical Republicans for not promoting carpetbaggers and blacks over local whites. After losing the presidency he returned to the army as a department commander.[20]

Benjamin Harrison, grandson of William H. "Old Tippecanoe" Harrison, graduated from Miami University at the top of his class and then apprenticed with a top law firm in Cincinnati. In 1852 he became the city attorney of Cincinnati, a position he retained for eight years before becoming the reporter of the Indiana supreme court in 1860. In 1862 he resigned and volunteered for the army joining the Seventieth Indiana Volunteers. This renewed his family's acquaintance with Indiana. He served for three years, reaching the rank of brigadier general before he finished his service. When Hays gave up the governor's office to run for president, Harrison received the Republican nomination to succeed him but lost the election. He became an influential king-maker in the Ohio Republican Party, supporting both Hayes and Garfield for the presidency. In 1880 the Ohio legislature nominated him to the Senate. In 1887 the Democrats took control of the legislature and Harrison was not returned to the Senate.

Harrison then ran as a "rejuvenated Republican" for president in 1888 against incumbent Grover Cleveland. The race was polite and centered on economic issues. Cleveland won the popular vote, but Harrison won the electoral vote and so became the twenty-third president. He supported business interests as president by supporting a high tariff and the use of silver in coinage. Harrison supported the preservation of forest reserves. In foreign policy he supported expansion of American presence in the Pacific through the building of a world class navy, at a time when the U.S. Navy lagged far behind several South American powers. He also supported the building of a transoceanic canal in Central America. He negotiated a protectorate over the Samoan Islands. Harrison nearly took the United States to war over an assault on American sailors in Chile. But he proved to be a one-term president, losing to Former President Cleveland in 1892—the only instance of a president having terms that were not consecutive. Harrison was a cold and aloof figure who ended up alienating many of his own key supporters.[21]

Three of the Civil-War-veteran presidents—those after Grant—plus Chester Arthur make up the group that historians refer to as "the four lost presidents," because their terms were relatively uneventful and they have been forgotten by history. This was a period of legislative supremacy, like the period before the Civil War. The one president—Garfield—who was equipped by experience and intellect to deal with the issues of the day was tragically murdered before he had a chance. Garfield was also the last of the so-called "log-cabin presidents"—those presidents who were born in log cabins. Indian-fighter Andrew Jackson had been the first log-cabin president.

Grover Cleveland's second term began the "gay nineties," so-called because they were a period of economic contentment.

The conquest of the North American continent between the two oceans and north of the Rio Grande in fulfillment of the doctrine of Manifest Destiny helped to bring on the Civil War. The Civil War ended the last leftover unsettled issue from the American Revolution. The frontier was officially ruled to be closed in 1890, meaning that within the continental United States there was no clear boundary of settlement from wild unsettled areas. The last major Indian trouble took place on the Sioux Reservation at Wounded Knee and Standing Rock in South Dakota in December 1890–January 1891. It resulted from the "Ghost Dance" religion that was sweeping Indian tribes in the West as an escapist refuge from their then state of abject poverty and servitude. An attempt to pacify the reservation led to the death of Sitting Bull in a fight with reservation police. A full revolt broke out, with the army called in. The army put down the revolt with severe loss of life after an outbreak of shooting led troops to open fire on fleeing Indians with a rapid-fire Hotchkiss cannon. When the firing ended more than 150 Lakota lay dead, including forty-four women and sixteen children, with fifty wounded; and twenty-five troops were dead and thirty-nine wounded. It was neither a battle nor a massacre but something in between; but it was definitely a tragedy.[22] Miles put an end to the revolt and then pulled the army back from the reservation.

In the twentieth century only two presidents who were major war heroes were elected. Theodore Roosevelt led the Rough Riders, a volunteer cavalry unit that fought on foot, up San Juan Hill (it was actually the neighboring hill) in July 1898, helping to win the Spanish-American War. A successful New York City police commissioner and assistant secretary of the navy before the war, Roosevelt was nominated as the vice-presidential running mate with McKinley. After President McKinley was assassinated in office, Roosevelt became the president in 1901. He was elected in his own right in 1904. After allowing his own vice president, William Howard Taft, to serve a term as president, Roosevelt felt betrayed by Taft and challenged him as a third-party candidate, throwing the race to Democrat Woodrow Wilson in 1912. General of the Army Dwight Eisenhower was elected president in 1952. He served two terms and could most likely have easily won a third term in 1960, but Republicans had passed an amendment limiting presidents to two terms.

NOTES

1. Sibley then served on army expeditions against the Sioux in the Dakota Territory in 1863 and 1864. See "Sibley, Henry Hastings," *Webster's World Encyclopedia 2000*.

2. Marjory Stoneman Douglas, *The Everglades: River of Glass* (Sarasota, FL: Pineapple Press, 1988), p. 266.

3. William E. Lass, *Minnesota: A Bicentennial History* (New York: W. W. Norton, 1976), pp. 104–110.

4. Kenneth S. Davis, *Kansas: A Bicentennial History* (New York City: W. W. Norton, 1976), pp. 101–105.

5. Michael D. Pierce, *The Most Promising Young Officer* (Norman, OK: University of Oklahoma Press, 1993), pp. 3–5; Charles M. Robinson III, *Bad Hand* (Austin, TX: State House Press, 1993), p. viii. This was based on Mackenzie's ability to deliver the surprise attack on Indian villages.

6. Robert M. Utley, *Frontier Regulars: The United States Army and the Indian, 1866–91* (New York: Macmillan, 1973), pp. 54–55, 179, 220; on Custer's place see Utley, *Cavalier in Buckskin* (Norman, OK: University of Oklahoma Press, 1988), pp. 206–207. Greene is a specialist on the Great Sioux War of 1876–77 and the author of several books on it and on the Nez Perce war.

7. On Crook's military background see Peter Aleshire, *The Fox and the Whirlwind* (New York: John Wiley & Sons, 2000), pp. 41–60, 77–100, 111–38, 187–226; on the Geronimo campaign specifically see Aleshire, pp. 239–58, 279–90; and Utley, *Frontier Regulars*, op. cit., pp. 369–96.

8. See Robert Wooster, *Nelson A. Miles & The Twilight of the Frontier Army* (Lincoln, NB: University of Nebraska Press, 1993), pp. 1–95; and Robert M. Utley, *Frontier Regulars: The United States Army and the Indian, 1866–1890* (New York: Macmillan, 1973), pp. 269–70, 272–81, 286–90.

9. Wooster, pp. 96–110; Utley, *Frontier Regulars*, pp. 310–19, quote is on p. 317.

10. Pierce, op. cit., pp. 28–52, 57, 66, 146–53, 186–91.

11. Pierce, op. cit., p. 52 for quote from Grant; Wooster, op. cit., pp. 67, 71, 74, 115; Utley, *Cavalier*, pp. 27–28; Utley, *Frontier Regulars*, pp. 277–78.

12. Pierce, op. cit., pp. 181–83, 192, 194, 196, 205, 208, 210, 212, 217, 221–23, 224–25, 229.

13. Utley, *Cavalier*, op. cit., pp. 13–35.

14. See Stan Hoig, *The Battle of the Washita* (New York: Doubleday, 1976), pp. 126–44, for a description of the battle and Appendix C, pp. 200–201 for estimates of Indian casualties. The band only played a few notes before the instruments froze up, but enough to make it the regimental tune of the Seventh Cavalry.

15. Utley, *Cavalier*, pp. 118–21 on the Yellowstone expedition and pp. 165–93 on the Battle of the Little Bighorn.

16. On Red Cloud, see Utley, *Frontier Regulars*, pp. 134–36, 237, 239, 282–83.

17. "Ulysses S. Grant: The Troubled President," *The American President* at www.americanpresident.org accessed in October 2002.

18. "Rutherford B. Hayes, The Healer President," *The American President* at www.americanpresident.org accessed October 2002.

19. "James Garfield: The Martyred President," *The American President* at www.americanpresident.org accessed October 2002; "Garfield, James," *Grollier's Multimedia Encyclopedia 1995*.

20. "Hancock, Winfield Scott," *Grollier's Multimedia Encyclopedia 1995*.

21. "Benjamin Harrison: The Iceberg President," *The American President* at www.americanpresident.org accessed in October 2002.

22. Utley, op. cit., pp. 406–407; Wooster, op. cit., p. 186.

Appendix: The Indian Fighter and the Arab Fighter

INTRODUCTION: THE NATIVE FIGHTER

In 1968 Israeli radical journalist and future peace activist Uri Avnery coined the term *Arab fighter* to describe Moshe Dayan. He used it as a parallel to the term *Indian fighter*, which was in common usage in nineteenth-century America to describe military leaders and politicians who based their careers on fighting Indians. Avnery never developed the concept, but he did claim that native fighters were common in the second generation of settler societies.[1] This author decided to investigate Avnery's claim. After investigating the history of many democratic settler colonies (Australia, Canada, New Zealand, Northern Ireland, Rhodesia, and South Africa), I could find evidence for only three societies that had classes of *native-fighter* politicians: the United States, whose history I have covered in the preceding chapters; Israel; and the South African Republic (Transvaal), which existed between the Vaal and Limpopo Rivers and between British Bechuanaland (Botswana) and Swaziland and Mozambique from 1859 to 1900. As the Afrikaners were always a minority within this territory and never reached a large number during the nineteenth century, they are much less relevant to compare with either Israel or the United States. They are more comparable to the Texas Republic of 1836–45, and I do not cover them in this appendix. I define *native-fighter politician* as one whose political career is at least assisted, if not based upon, his status fighting the native population of his country.

If one examines the histories of Latin America it may be possible to find Indian fighters who became *caudillos*—that is, dictators or strongmen in a nondemocratic context. But among the Western democracies of Europe, even if one expands the definition to include the native population of important colonies, one finds only individuals, such as Arthur Wellesley—the Duke of Wellington—who gained fame fighting in India before going on to fight in the Peninsular War. Only in Spain does one find a class of native-fighter politicians, from Spanish Morocco, and they came to power through a coup ending the democracy that had briefly existed. The only member of the Spanish Cortes who was a prominent Morocco veteran was Ramon Franco, Francisco's brother, who was elected more for his fame as an aviation pioneer in breaking records than as a combat pilot.[2]

THE ARAB-FIGHTER POLITICIANS OF ISRAEL

One historian of Texas compared the Texas settlers on the frontier and their problems with the Comanche with the Israelis and their conflict with the Palestinian.[3] Actually, initially the Texas republic had more parallels with the South African Republic. But after statehood, Texas became more like the Orange Free State with its mixture of an educated professional class and Indian fighters as politicians. But, demographically, Texas was like Israel—an immigrant society that was expanding exponentially in population.

Israel's Arab-fighter politicians have much more in common with American-Indian- and Mexican-fighter politicians than they do with the Afrikaner African fighters. Because the Palestinians and Israel's neighbors are all Arabs, those who fought the Palestinians from 1938 to 1948 and after 1987 and those whose experience was primarily in wars with Israel's neighbors from 1948 to 1982 are both Arab fighters. Thus they combine the categories of Indian fighter and Mexican fighter by analogy. Initially the Israeli experience was similar to the American experience. Only a few generals who were war heroes—such as Yigal Allon, Moshe Carmel, Israel Galili, Moshe Dayan, and Ezer Weizman—were elected to parliament. But this changed starting in the Labor Party in the late 1960s and early 1970s and then proceeding to the Likud and smaller parties. Today entrance into the Knesset (parliament) is nearly automatic for former chiefs of staff. In the first two decades of Israeli independence it was quite rare.

Unlike the United States, which had only three major wars in the first eighty to eighty-five years after the Revolution, Israel has had six major wars in half that period: the 1948 War of Independence, the 1956 Sinai War, the 1967 Six-Day War, the 1969–70 War of Attrition, the 1973 Yom Kippur War, and the 1982 Lebanon War. Since then it has had two "internal" rebellions in the occupied territories: the 1987–93 Intifada and the 2000–2002 Al-Aksa Intifada. These are comparable to the 1936–39 Arab Revolt and the opening stages of the 1948 war. So it is quite common to have Israeli generals who have had experience in three or four wars by the time they make chief of staff. In the United States a few figures at best had experience in two major wars: the Revolution and the War of 1812, the War of 1812 and the Mexican War, or the Mexican War and the Civil War (this latter combination being fairly common). In South Africa the era of the Boer War generals ended because they had died out. The same is true in the United States with the Civil War generals—they became too old to have political careers. But Israel is continuously producing new Arab fighters.

Israel is today in a period comparable to the early 1850s in American terms: three Arab-fighter generals have served as prime minister, and there were direct competitions between two Arab-fighter generals in 2001, comparable to the 1848 and 1852 elections in the United States.

Most Israeli Arab fighters follow a different career path than the Indian-fighter politicians. The Indian fighters had simultaneous military and political careers that overlapped. This was only true of a few early Arab-fighter politicians who were politicians in the prestate era of the 1940s and then served in the 1948 or 1956 war. Ariel Sharon began his political career in 1973, just as his military career was ending with his return to active duty in the Yom Kippur War. Yigal Allon and Israel Galili were actively involved in politics as disciples of socialist leader Yitzhak Tabenkin. Moshe Dayan was a protégé of David Ben-Gurion and attended a Zionist Congress in Switzerland in 1946. But since this first generation there has been a radical separation and sequencing of the two career phases. After Ezer Weizman "parachuted" directly into the cabinet for the Herut Party in 1969, a mandatory "cooling-off" period of six months was instituted between ending military service and election to the Knesset or service in the cabinet.

Most Indian-fighter politicians were also lawyers or entrepreneurs. That is not the case with Arab fighters. Sharon, who has a law degree but has never practiced law, is a notable exception. Most Arab fighters are wanted solely for their electoral appeal and security expertise. If they have a civilian occupation besides politician, it is farmer as many come from collective settlements, kibbutzim and moshavim. In fact, the career path for many Arab fighters is to join the government as the minister of either labor or agriculture and then work their way up. Dayan and Sharon both started as agricultural ministers, whereas Allon and Rabin started as labor ministers. Weizman was minister of transport—this was unique to his background as an air force general, as El Al is the main responsibility of the minister of transport.

Israel is lacking any second tier—state or provincial government—and has only local government and national government. Thus, cities—the three largest cities are Haifa, Jerusalem, and Tel Aviv—and political parties must serve the equivalent function as states in launching Arab fighters on their careers or serving as the basis for the second tier of Arab-fighter politicians. The equivalent of politicians like John Sevier, Isaac Shelby, William Carroll, Sam Houston, and so on is to be found among the smaller parties of the Israeli system: *Tsomet* (crossroads), *Tehiya* (renaissance), and *Moledet* (homeland), which collectively formed the settler parties supported by

West Bank and Gaza settlers; the Center Party; and the Democratic Movement for Change. Arab fighters go into these smaller parties for three reasons or at two different points in their career: first, when they are transitioning from one major party to another as when Ezer Weizman was going from the Likud to Labor via his *Yahad* (together) party or when Sharon was going from the Liberal Party to Herut via *Shlomzion* ("peace of Zion"); second, at the beginning or end of their political careers as when Moshe Dayan formed his Telem party in 1981 to run for the Knesset after having quit the Likud government; or third, because they want to be big fish in a small pond rather than small fish in a big pond. This gives more scope for their egos and the possibility of ideological purity. The generals' lists did not really become important until the appearance of both the Democratic Movement for Change and Shlomzion in 1976. They then multiplied in the 1980s.[4]

In 1977 General Mattityahu Peled became one of the founder members of *Shelli* (an acronym for both peace for Israel and equality for Israel) along with Meir Pa'il, and both were elected to the Knesset. Peled had been an arch-nationalist like Weizman up to June 1967 and then underwent a dramatic conversion to the Left after the war when he did a doctorate in Arabic literature. He joined with Yoav Eliav, former secretary-general of the Labor Party, and Shulamit Aloni in a temporary alliance in the early 1970s. Then Peled, Eliav, and Pa'il joined together with other figures on the Left to form *Shelli*. But *Shelli* does not fit the profile of the typical general's list: it was a far-Left party, similar to the old Mapam with a focus on social issues and peace with the Palestinians through a two-state solution and negotiations with the PLO. Peled, head of the quartermaster corps of the IDF, was not a major Arab fighter. Pa'il was director of the education branch of the IDF and a military historian by vocation. *Shelli* collapsed during 1981 due to a dispute over its internal rotation agreement, which specified that the two MKs were to give up their seats to the next two people on the list halfway through their term. At least one failed to deliver on the agreement, costing the party the support of the Sephardic or Oriental community during the 1981 election. There were also problems with the party's stance during the Lebanon War.[5]

America only had a multiparty system from 1848 to 1860 and then only with three or four major parties. Most of the Indian fighters stayed in the major parties (the Democrats, the Republicans, the Whigs) during this period. So there is no real equivalent to the smaller Israeli parties in the American party system for the Indian fighters.

The era of the Arab-fighter politicians really began in 1954–55 with the creation of the *Ahdut Ha'Avoda* (Unity of Labor) paramilitary party and the election of Yigal Allon and Moshe Carmel to the Knesset in 1955. I define "paramilitary party" as a party that is either the political wing of an existing paramilitary group or the continuation of a former paramilitary group in political form. In Israel paramilitary parties were of the latter type, which is in contrast to Ireland and Northern Ireland, the only other Western democracies with paramilitary parties, where they are primarily of the former type. Ahdut Ha'Avoda was the continuation of the Palmach, the standing army portion of the Hagana, the mainstream militia organization. There were two underground paramilitaries in the prestate period: the *Irgun Zvai Leumi* (National Military Organization) or Etzel and the *Lohemei Herut Israel* (Fighters for the Freedom of Israel) or Lehi. Both had paramilitary parties to the 1949 Knesset elections, but Lehi's party, which won only one seat, soon disappeared. Etzel's party was Herut, which merged with the Liberal Party and two smaller parties in 1973 to form the Likud (union). It remained a paramilitary party into the early 1980s and retained a paramilitary leader, Yitzhak Shamir, until 1992. Ahdut Ha'Avoda had in its Knesset caucus the 1948 commanders of the northern (Carmel) and the central and southern (Allon) commands and the head of the Hagana staff (Galili). Carmel served as minister of transport in Israeli governments in the mid-1950s and again in the mid-1960s. In 1965 Ahdut Ha'Avoda formed the first *ma'arakh* or alignment with the ruling Mapai party. In 1968 these two parties were joined by the Rafi party to form the Israeli Labor Party. Initially the component parties retained their identities as separate factions within the Labor Party, but the Labor Party soon split into two camps: the Allon camp and the Dayan camp. Eventually these would become the Rabin camp and the Peres camp.[6]

In 1959 Moshe Dayan, the chief of staff during and architect of the Sinai War, joined the Labor Party and Knesset as minister of agriculture. He remained in the government until 1964. In 1961 Allon became minister of labor. The Arab fighters were in third-tier positions—minor cabinet posts. In June 1967 they moved up to the second-tier level when Dayan became defense minister, Allon became deputy prime minister, and Galili became minister without portfolio. In 1969 when Prime Minister Levi Eshkol died and was replaced by Golda Meir—as a compromise figure between Allon and Dayan—and all three Arab fighters became members of the "kitchen cabinet" that made security decisions, the Arab fighters demonstrated their power within the system. This was the first wave of Arab fighter—equivalent to the Revolutionary war veterans like Sevier, Shelby, Sullivan, and Washington. They were all senior officers during the War of Independence.[7]

The second wave arrived beginning in 1969 and continued through 1976. In the following, the date in parentheses is the year the general entered politics. The second wave consisted of: Weizman (1969), Haim Bar-Lev (1972), Aharon Yariv (1972), Sharon (1973), Yitzhak Rabin (1973), Yigael Yadin (1976), and Meir Amit (1976). Rabin grabbed the prize that had eluded both Allon and Dayan in 1974 after a short apprenticeship as minister of labor. The Arab fighters had finally reached the first tier. But Rabin was forced to yield this in 1977 and descend first to the opposition and then to the second tier as defense minister from 1984 to 1990. The second wave consisted mostly of senior officers from the Sinai War and the Six Day War, except for Yadin who had a second career as an archaelogist and academic. Rabin was also a senior officer in 1948, Allon's deputy on the central and southern fronts. Yadin created his own list, the Democratic Movement for Change or *Dash* (from its Hebrew acronym), which included Amit. The others joined the two main parties.[8]

A third wave followed in the early 1980s. It consisted of: Raphael "Raful" Eitan (1983), Benyamin "Fuad" Ben-Eliezer (1984), and Rehavam "Gandhi" Ze'evi (1988). Ben-Eliezer hooked up with Weizman, after he had briefly entered the ethnic religious party *Tami*, and followed him into the Labor Party. Eitan and Ze'evi both founded their own parties, *Tehiya* (renaissance) and *Moledet* (homeland). They all served in minor government positions except for Ben-Eliezer who became Sharon's defense minister in 2001.[9]

A fourth wave followed in the early 1990s. It included: Avigdor Kahalani (1992), Dan Shomron (1992), Amram Mitzna (1994), Ehud Barak (1995), Amnon Lipkin-Shahak (1999), and Yitzhak Mordechai (1996). These were figures that were generals in the 1980s and 1990s. Kahalani, a hero of the Yom Kippur War and the Lebanon War, joined the Labor Party in 1992. He formed his own list, The Third Way, in 1996 to pressure for retention of the Golan Heights in any future deal. Kahalani was joined by Dan Shomron, a hero of the Entebee Rescue of 1976, who also joined the Third Way. The party ended up with three seats in the 1996 election, and Kahalani became minister of internal security in the Netanyahu government. He failed to win a single seat in 1999, and the party dissolved.[10]

Barak and Lipkin-Shahak were both chiefs of staff during the second Rabin government of 1992–95. Barak was Israel's most decorated soldier, a hero of commando operations in the early 1970s. Barak joined Labor in 1995 and became a minister of the interior under Rabin before becoming minister of foreign affairs under Peres. Barak was elected prime minister in the second direct election, against Benyamin Netanyahu, in 1999. He defeated Netanyahu in a major upset and was himself destroyed by Sharon in a landslide in 2001 as a result of the failure of the peace process and the Al-Aksa Intifada. Lipkin-Shahak, who left the IDF in 1998, joined with a couple of Likud defectors, Dan Meridor and Roni Milo, to form the Center Party. Lipkin-Shahak was initially the leader of the new Center Party, but Netanyahu's defense minister Mordechai quit the government in late 1998 and joined the new party. Polls showed that Mordechai was more popular than Lipkin-Shahak, so he became the new leader. He was convicted of sexual assault in 2001, from when he was a senior general, and so his political career came to an abrupt end. At the end of February 2001 the Center Party dissolved itself, with Dahlia Rabin-Pelossof, Lipkin-Shahak, and Savir forming a new faction called "The New Way." Meridor and Milo were looking to return to the Likud.[11]

Israel is now in its fifth wave of Arab fighters. These are Arab fighters who were generals in the late 1990s and in the early twenty-first century.

The first two are Matan Vilnai in the Labor Party and Effi Eitam in the National Religious Party. Eitam's best role model would probably be Paul Kruger, the conservative Christian nationalist Kaffir fighter.

Starting with Barak it has almost become automatic for a chief of staff to join the government or at least become elected to the Knesset upon retiring from the IDF. Initially only lieutenant generals (chiefs of staff) and major generals (regional or branch commanders) could aspire to becoming ministers. Now, Ben-Eliezer has lowered the bar to brigadier general. The last brigadier general who served in the government was Yigal Allon, and under the rank system instituted after he left the army he would have been a major general.[12] There have been so many waves of Arab fighters that Israelis should develop a Hebrew term (possibly *yeridot*) to refer to them equivalent to the waves of immigration, or *aliyot*, that have been used by Israeli historians.

One way in which the Arab fighters seem to represent a corporate interest of the military is their success in capturing the defense ministry. Since 1967 only three defense ministers have not been former generals: Shimon Peres (1974–77), Menahem Begin (1980–81) and Moshe Arens (1982–84, 1990–91). Peres was offered the same rank as Dayan and Rabin during the War of Independence but turned it down because he thought that it would limit his authority. He was a former deputy director general and director general of the defense ministry, and so in American and British usage it would have been permissible to address him as "General." Peres by American or European standards would have been considered very qualified to be defense minister. Yet Rabin was able to convince the Israeli public a decade later that Peres was unsuited for the job. Arens, a former professional aircraft designer for the Israeli Aircraft Industry, was also well qualified for the position. But Arab fighters have—starting with Dayan and continuing to this day—turned the position into a sort of super chief of staff who is there to second-guess the chief of staff and supervise the conduct of military operations rather than administer the running of the IDF. In this conception the IDF is a sort of mufti priesthood or rabbinate with the defense minister as pope or chief rabbi. Only Begin was unqualified by Western standards to be defense minister, and he basically let the IDF run its own show while he was in charge.

Because all Israelis serve as conscripts and reservists in the IDF, we cannot refer to every war veteran who is a politician as an Arab-fighter politician. But there is a category of civilian politicians who are equivalent to the Davy Crocketts of American history. In addition to the victorious generals and colonels of the early wars, there was also the category of *frontiersman* that included Daniel Boone, David Crockett, and Kit Carson. The Israeli equivalent would be the *commando*. This is a soldier who specializes in cross-border reprisal raids and antiterrorist operations. Sharon and Barak both started out in this category until they became generals. Bibi Netanyahu also falls into this category because he was a captain under Barak in the

Seyeret Matkal (Headquarters Reconnaissance Unit) and took part in the Sabena airliner rescue of 1972 at Ben-Gurion airport. He ran in 1996 on the basis of his expertise as an antiterrorist expert. Thus, he falls somewhere in between the typical Arab fighter and a normal civilian politician.

ARAB FIGHTERS IN POWER

Arab fighters have been involved in negotiations with Israel's Arab neighbors and the Palestinians since the armistice negotiations of 1949. Two Arab fighters, Yitzhak Rabin and Moshe Dayan, were involved in the armistice negotiations. Rabin played a minor role; Dayan played a fairly substantial role as Jerusalem front commander. Dayan was also the Israeli military representative to all four of the Mixed Armistice Commissions that dealt with any border disputes between Israel and its neighbors in the period immediately following the armistice agreements.

Dayan as defense minister had an opportunity to engage in discussions with quite a few Palestinian notables in the territories—particularly those loyal to Jordan—in his six years as defense minister, particularly in the first two years. It was Dayan who decided upon the "open bridges" policy of keeping the borders open between the occupied territories and the Arab countries. This policy continued until the Intifada, when it was modified due to security considerations.

Dayan advocated negotiating a separation-of-forces agreement with Egypt along the Suez Canal in 1971, but Golda Meir was opposed and President Anwar Sadat's starting price for any agreement was too high. Dayan finally got his chance to negotiate this agreement through Aharon Yariv, who was acting as the Israeli military representative at the Kilomoter 101 talks, in January 1974. Kissinger basically ratified what the Israelis and Egyptians had already agreed to. In addition to Dayan, Arab fighters Yigal Allon and Yitzhak Rabin were involved in the Kissinger shuttle negotiations of 1974–75. These resulted in separation-of-forces agreements with Egypt and Syria and the Sinai II interim agreement with Egypt in September 1975. The Arab fighters saw these agreements in strategic terms: neutralizing the most powerful opponent so that they could deal with lesser, more radical enemies like Syria and the Palestine Liberation Organization (PLO). Dayan, Rabin, and Allon all met with King Hussein of Jordan in numerous secret meetings between 1967 and 1977, but Hussein was too weak in stature to be able to make any concessions in his territorial demands from Israel so no agreement was reached.

Dayan and Weizman were involved in the Camp David negotiations for a peace treaty with Egypt that lasted from December 1977 to March 1979. Rabin and Barak were involved with peace negotiations with Syria; Rabin was involved in negotiations with both the PLO and Jordan; and Barak was involved in negotiations at Camp David with the PLO and—through intermediaries—at Taba.

From all these negotiations the following conclusions can be drawn about Arab fighters in general. First, Arab fighters are at least as flexible, creative, and moderate in peace negotiations as their civilian counterparts from the same party if not more so. Dayan was more flexible and creative in dealing with Egypt and Jordan than Meir was. Dayan and Weizman were much more interested in making peace with Egypt than were the Herutniks in Likud. Rabin was slightly less flexible in dealing with the PLO than Peres was, but Peres was unusual among Israeli politicians in the degree of his commitment to peace. Barak was more moderate and forthcoming than any previous leader when he negotiated with the PLO.

Second, Arab fighters have the personal and professional credibility—that civilians lack—to sell agreements involving major Israeli concessions. *Los Angeles Times* reporter and biographer Robert Slater dubbed both Dayan and Rabin "Mr. Security." Dayan was a source of comfort to the Israeli public during both the Six Day War and the War of Attrition. He could have sold a separation-of-forces agreement with Egypt to the public in 1971 or 1972. He lost this status in October 1973 and was forced to resign with Meir in June 1974. The presence of four former generals in Begin's cabinet in 1977 helped to induce Begin to negotiate with Sadat and vice versa. Peres was able to conclude the Oslo agreements with the PLO and sell them to the public only because Rabin was prime minister. Barak was able to make major concessions in Jerusalem, "Israel's eternal and undivided capital," because of his heroic past. Average Israelis treat the Arab fighters as "personal security advisors"—treating them the way Americans and Europeans treat financial advisors.

Third, Arab fighters—especially those newly released from the IDF—tend to monopolize decision-making control over security matters and surround themselves with aides who were former high-ranking officers, usually those who were their friends in the army. Rabin in his second government and Barak were both their own defense ministers. Rabin would have liked to have been his own defense minister in 1974, but he needed to give Peres a powerful position in the government because of the latter's status as the number two man in the party. Rabin also limited Peres to dealing with Europe and the Third World and with multilateral peace negotiations while he personally handled relations with the United States and bilateral negotiations. An organizational chart of the second Rabin government would show many lines of control running straight from Rabin to subordinates and not running through other ministers. Sharon has not become his own defense minister primarily because he is in a government of national unity with Labor and has needed to offer the ministry to Labor. Sharon has taken personal control of all relations that he considers important. He has repeatedly bypassed Foreign Minister Peres in dealing with the United States through his own aides, and he often contradicts Peres when it comes to policy toward the Palestinians. This pattern seems to indicate that the Arab fighters distrust civilian politicians as either disloyal, incompetent, or both. Barak was notorious for not consulting other cabinet members when he made decisions. It is as if the Arab fighters imagine themselves to be in a presidential system rather than in a coalition parliamentary system.

THE FUTURE OF THE ARAB-FIGHTER POLITICIAN

Israel looks set to experience another generation of Arab-fighter politicians. Sharon, the last of the second generation, is busy attempting to defeat the Palestinians by military means. This could result in another generation without peace between Israel and the Palestinians. Yasir Arafat seems too discredited among the Israeli public to allow any Israeli politician to make peace with him. This means that Israel—and the Palestinians—will have to wait for his successor. If Arafat is killed by Israeli military action or forced into exile abroad, his successor could be another hard-liner. There is still a group of third- and fourth-generation Arab fighters who became war heroes in 1973 and 1982 and who served as chiefs of staff or senior commanders in the 1990s. This generation includes Barak, Amnon Lipkin-Shahak, and others. Lipkin-Shahak still has yet to make his mark as a politician now that Yitzhak Mordechai has retired from the Center Party and politics. Barak could make a comeback, just as Netanyahu is doing today. Amram Mitzna, busy as mayor of Haifa until now, won the leadership of the Labor Party in November 2002. He was greeted by the centrist electorate as the next Yadin or Lipkin-Shahak but lost badly to Sharon in elections at the end of January 2003 due to his dovish positions on peace with the Palestinians. He resigned as head of the Labor Party a few months later.

If Israel's northern border heats up due to Hizbullah rocket attacks on Israeli settlements, Israel could be involved in another war with Syria. This would produce a similar set of Arab fighters. The reign of the Indian-fighter politicians partly came to an end because the Indian wars in the East came to an end. When the Indian wars resumed in the West, they were too remote from the East Coast to be of electoral significance and they were quickly forgotten once they ended, thereby releasing their heroes for politics. The United States had two major wars and two minor wars that produced Indian-fighter politicians.

Israel has had five major wars and three minor wars to produce its Arab fighters. We have only seen the politicians that resulted from the major wars and not from the Intifada and the Al-Aksa Intifada.

Unlike the U.S. Army in the Indian wars in the West, the IDF is a conscript army led by a professional officer corp. The Intifadas have taken place close to Israel's main population centers and not at a great distance as in the case of the Indian wars. In America the Indian fighters were replaced by the Mexican fighters and then by the Civil War veterans. In Israel, those who have fought the Palestinians, the Egyptians, the Syrians, the Jordanians, and so on are all different brands of Arab fighters. Thus they are equivalent to both the Indian fighters and the Mexican fighters. Military figures remained important in American politics as long as the United States was fighting its wars in North America. When the theater of warfare moved to Europe and the Pacific, the victors became less important. After Theodore Roosevelt was elected president following the Spanish-American War, the only major war-hero president was Dwight Eisenhower who was elected in 1952. Starting with John Kennedy and ending with George Bush (senior) all presidents were veterans of World War II, with the exception of Lyndon Johnson.[13] But this was simply because they were of the age group when all able-bodied men, except farmers and those with critical occupations, were in the military. Kennedy was president at a very young age (forty-three) and Bush was president at an advanced age (sixty-nine).

PERSONAL AND PARTY COMPARISONS BETWEEN AMERICA AND ISRAEL

While writing this book the author kept in mind similarities between particular American Indian fighters and Israeli Arab fighters. The clearest parallel is between Andrew Jackson and Ariel Sharon. Jackson and Sharon have similar personalities—always imagining that someone is challenging their integrity. If dueling were still in fashion in Israel in the twentieth century, it would not be hard to imagine Sharon dueling with opponents over insults, real or imagined. He probably would have fought duels with Eitan, Weizman, and possibly even Begin. Jackson and Sharon are also similar in imagining that they had a monopoly on the definition of national security and were legally empowered to protect it by any means they sought fit, whether through a secret invasion of Florida or one of Lebanon. They are also similar in their level of military skill and determination to win. Jackson imposed a military solution to the Indian problem, and Sharon appears to be attempting to impose a military solution to the Palestinian problem.

The next parallel is between William H. Harrison and Moshe Dayan or Ezer Weizman. All three of these individuals belonged to powerful families that could be considered part of the social aristocracy of their countries. Just as Harrison played a role in the Battle of Fallen Timbers, Dayan and Weizman played significant roles in the War of Independence. Both Dayan and Harrison benefited from political patronage. But Harrison was an obscure figure for a longer time before reaching the political summit; Dayan, in contrast, was only in the wilderness for three years and he never reached the very top. Likewise Weizman was in the wilderness for about a decade and he never reached the top politically. If Dayan is the Israeli Harrison and Sharon is the Israeli Jackson, then Allon must be the Israeli John Sevier. But in his importance to the War of Independence, Allon is more like Anthony Wayne who never had a successful political career. Allon was a much more important military and political figure than Sevier ever was.

The final parallel is between Yitzhak Rabin and Richard M. Johnson. On April 1, 1948, while Rabin was in command of the Harel Brigade, Abdul Kader al-Husseini, the leader of the Palestinian irregulars attached to the Mufti of Jerusalem—Haj Amin al-Husseini, was killed in the battle at Kastel, outside Jerusalem, with Rabin's forces. Rabin never made any personal claim to having killed the guerrilla leader as he was probably elsewhere at the time, but it distinguished him from Dayan and others of his rank during the war. Abdul Kader al-Husseini was the most important Arab leader to be killed in combat with the Israelis and the closest thing to a Palestinian Tecumseh. After his death the Palestinian resistance began to deteriorate significantly.[14]

But there is a greater correlation between political parties. The Labor Party with its hawkish and dovish wings is comparable to the Whig Party. For decades it could not really be considered an anti-occupation party, but the most influential anti-occupation politicians were in the Labor Party. Peace with the Palestinians and the occupation are the Israeli equivalents of slavery and territorial expansion in the mid-nineteenth century. The Conscience Whigs are comparable to the politicians who left the Alignment in 1984 (Mapam, Yossi Sarid) to later form Meretz. Making Shamir prime minister was for them the equivalent of making Taylor president—it would have been complicity in the promotion of an individual who was antithetical to their principles. But it is unlikely that Meretz will ever turn into an Israeli Republican Party. Also Sarid lacks the social stature or ancestry of Charles Adams; Adams's Israeli equivalent would be Yael Dayan or Dahlia Rabin-Pelosoff.[15] Meretz is the equivalent today of the Free Soil Party, attempting to become another Republican Party. If Yossi Beilin were to carry through with his threat to leave Labor and form a new party merging Laborites with Meretz, it would be the equivalent of the creation of the Republican Party in the United States. And of course, Likud is comparable to the Democratic Party. Possibly the Center Party was the Israeli equivalent of the Know-Nothings with its opportunistic empty platform that appeared and disappeared almost overnight. It would be worthwhile for Meretz leaders to study in greater depth the story of how the second-party system came to an end in the United States and was replaced by the present party system.

POLITICAL MYTHOLOGY

Richard Slotkin, an American professor of English at Wesleyan University, argues that "the Myth of the Frontier" is the central American political myth. This myth that began in the legends of Daniel Boone and the novels of James Fennimore Cooper ended in the myth of Custer's last stand at the Little Bighorn and the mythology of the gunfighters. In the nineteenth century it helped pave the way for the log-cabin presidents, from Jackson to Garfield, which coincided with the era of the Indian-fighter politicians. It concerned the ideal of the self-made man, remaking oneself in a new place, and ideas of racial supremacy and Manifest Destiny.

Likewise, the Israeli Arab fighters are connected to the Israeli "Myth of the Sabra." This myth is an Israeli version of the Communist idea of the "new Soviet man." The sabra myth is the idea of a new Jew who is both a warrior and a farmer. The Arab fighters, most of whom come from a collective settlement background, were the embodiment of this myth; and Moshe Dayan was the icon. Dayan first became a celebrity when he was featured in *Life* magazine in 1949 as the symbol of the new Israel. For twenty years, from the time when he became chief of staff until the Yom Kippur War, Dayan was the human face of the sabra myth. Dayan's own biography fit the needs of this myth to a tee. He was the first child of the first kibbutz and was then raised on the first moshav. He was, along with Yigal Allon, one of the first two company commanders chosen for the Palmach. A dashing commando officer during the War of Independence, he was promoted over other officers by Ben-Gurion starting in late 1949 so that he could purge the IDF of officers loyal to rival socialist parties. Dayan benefited from a form of political affirmative action but was up to the positions he was given. His reputation as a womanizer only served to further endear him to the macho Israeli public.[16]

Dayan suffered in that he and Allon canceled each other out. Neither could be given the top office without tearing the party apart. So it was given to a gray grandmother figure, Golda Meir, who soon became a national Jewish mother. Dayan, who benefited from unearned praise for his figurehead role as defense minister in June 1967, suffered from it six years later. The new icon was the man Dayan partly eclipsed in 1967, Yitzhak Rabin.[17]

Rabin also suffered from having a rival. Shimon Peres could not prevent Rabin from becoming premier, but he did help to make Rabin's first term as prime minister less successful than it could have been.[18] Through cooperation Rabin and Peres were able to temporarily establish a peace with the Palestinians. By his martyrdom in 1995 Rabin was able to establish the sort of mythical stature that Custer and Kennedy had established in the United States. Rabin was not only the great Arab fighter but the peacemaker as well. This was a role pioneered for him by Dayan and Weizman. Dayan never achieved this mythical status as the peacemaker because he was a political maverick who was isolated at the time of his death in 1981. Although still recognized as a national hero, Dayan was too much of a traitor to be embraced by the Left or Center and not from the right background to be accepted by the Right. Weizman suffered from the same problem in reverse—he became a traitor to the Right and was too much of a rival to Rabin to be embraced by the Left after 1995.

The sabra myth was expanded in the 1970s as the Likud gained political respectability to include members of the Revisionist undergrounds. the

Irgun Zvai Leumi or Etzel and the *Lohemei Herut Israel* or Lehi. The Right had always had its own political mythology based on the underground struggle against the British—the Revolt—from 1942 to 1948 with its own martyrs and heroes. In the seventies these entered the national mythology and joined with the Arab fighters from the socialist parties.[19] This facilitated the migration of figures like Sharon and Ze'evi from the Left to the Right starting in 1973. This then allowed the various governments of national unity between the two main secular parties, Labor and the Likud, to take place. The first government of national unity ended because there was too much ideological separation between the two main components, Labor and Gahal, and Begin was experiencing problems of control within his own Herut Party. But after this union of mythologies occurred in the seventies, the second national unity government was much more stable. At this point neither of the two main parties wanted a peace agreement with the Palestinians through the PLO.

Today national mythology in Israel is starting to unravel. The Left sees Rabin, a man dismissed by most of the Left during most of his political career as being too hard-line, as a martyr, figuratively—if not literally—assassinated by a Rightist conspiracy that included all those opposed to the Oslo Agreements. Today the Right feels comfortable in creating a countermyth of Oslo as national treachery. Rabin is not attacked directly by mainstream Likud politicians but rather by inference through Peres and Barak. Some have suggested an investigation into Oslo and Palestinian interference in Israeli elections in 1996 and 1999. Thus we have the ideological instability characteristic of the United States from 1845 to 1860 displaying itself in Israel.[20]

COMMON FEATURES

The three societies that had native-fighter politicians had a long history of military involvement and have several things in common. First, they are all *independent settler colonies,* that is, immigrant countries where the settlers replaced the native population and gained independence. Second, they all had people's armies based on conscription and universal participation rather than a military caste system. Third, the countries are/were all democracies at least for the settler population; but there are or were several significant limitations on that democracy. In South Africa the whites were always a minority within the territory. In the United States blacks could not vote until after the Civil War and slavery existed on the basis of race. In Israel Arabs did not have civil rights other than the right to vote until late 1966. Even today they are legally second-class citizens with a distinctly different legal status from Jews. Fourth, these societies were all what Conor Cruise O'Brien has termed "siege societies" as they have a sense of being surrounded by a numerically significant if not superior native population.[21]

It is the combination of these four characteristics that has produced the native-fighter phenomenon. The elimination of any of these features is enough to eliminate the native fighter as a political class. Thus, in *dependent settler colonies* controlled by a colonial metropole throughout the process of colonization and expansion such as Australia, Canada, New Zealand, and South Africa, no native-fighter class developed. The same is true of Northern Ireland, whose settler population provided the stock for many of the Indian-fighter politicians in America and for the British general staff during the two world wars. Had Northern Ireland declared independence during The Troubles, as advocated by some loyalist elements like the Ulster Defense Association, it would have produced its own military or official paramilitary forces. These in turn would have produced Fenian-fighter politicians. As it was, The Troubles produced only one Fenian-fighter politician—Ken Maginnis of the Ulster Unionist Party. He is much more in the local American tradition of Tennessee or Texas than in the Israeli mold.[22]

Once conscription was replaced by a professional standing army following the Civil War in the United States, the Indian-fighter politician disappeared even though the Indian wars continued. Once the bulk of the population no longer felt threatened by the native population or by foreign allies of that population, the conquest of the native population became less a reason for honor and political reward. Thus, Crook and Miles had no chance of being president. And obviously, if the country is not a democracy or at least a settler democracy, we cannot really talk about politicians using their military backgrounds to electoral advantage. This means that Latin Indian fighters are not a source of historical relevance for Israel.

As long as all of these conditions apply to a particular society, it will continue to produce native-fighter politicians. When the state of siege is lifted, the threat disappears, and conscription ends, the generals will remain confined to their offices and farms after a lag of a decade or two. We can only look forward to that day arriving in Israel. The first sign of this will probably be the reconquest of the defense ministry by civilians; the second sign will be the end of the generals' lists as a phenomenon; and last will come the disappearance of the generals from the lists of the two main parties.

NOTES

1. Uri Avnery, *Israel Without Zionism* (New York: Macmillan, 1968), p. 153.
2. Ramon was at this stage a liberal whose politics were very different from his brother's. But he died in the Spanish Civil War fighting on the nationalist side as a bomber pilot.
3. T. R. Fehrenbach, *Lone Star: A History of Texas and the Texans* (New York: Macmillan, 1968), pp. 445–47.
4. Susan Hattis Rolef, *Political Dictionary of the State of Israel* (New York: Macmillan, 1987), pp. 20–21, 76, 224, 235, 250, 328.
5. The person that should have gotten the seat was Sa'adia Marciano, a member of the Israeli Black Panthers civil rights group. See Rolef, op. cit., pp. 224, 235, 250.
6. See Rolef, op. cit., pp. 14, 15, 18–19, 121; resumes of Galili and Carmel provided by Yad Tabenkin, an institute to commemorate Yitzhak Tabenkin.

7. Ibid.; Ezer Weizman, *On Eagles' Wings* (New York: Macmillan, 1976), p. 216.

8. Ned Temko, *To Win or To Die* (New York: William Morrow and Co., 1987), p. 175; Howard M. Sachar, *A History of Israel from the Rise of Zionism to Our Time* (New York: Alfred Knopf, 1996), pp. 746, 1013; Rolef, op. cit., pp. 20–21, 76, 328.

9. Rolef, p. 90; Ehud Sprinzak, *The Ascendance of Israel's Radical Right* (New York: Oxford University Press, 1991), pp. 169, 174; Hanan Sher, "A Hard-Liner and a Gentleman," *The Jerusalem Report,* Nov. 5, 2001; Leslie Susser, "The Man in the Hot Seat," *The Jerusalem Report,* Sept. 10, 2001, p. 18.

10. "Ehud Barak," at www.abcnews.go.com/reference/bios; and "Ehud Barak" at *Jewish Virtual Library* at www.us-israel.org/jsource/biography; Yitzhak Mordechai," *Jerusalem Post Elections Primer '99,* at www.info.jpost.com/1999/Supplements/Elections99/candidates; "Yitzhak Mordechai," *Jewish Virtual Library* at www.us-israel.org/jsource/biography; "Center Party Dissolves," *Jewish Virtual Library* at www.us-israel.org/jsource/biography. The source on Mitzna is Leslie Susser, "The Haifa Comet," *Jerusalem Report,* Sept. 9, 2002. All websites in this footnote were accessed in April 2002. Meridor returned to the Likud in late 2002 but did not compete to run for the Knesset.

11. "Yitzhak Mordechai," *Jerusalem Post Elections Primer '99,* at www.info.jpost.com/1999/Supplements/Elections99/candidates; "Yitzhak Mordechai," *Jewish Virtual Library* at www.us-israel.org/jsource/biography; "Center Party Dissolves," *Jewish Virtual Library* at www.us-israel.org/jsource/biography.

12. Two new officer ranks were added in the early 1950s: colonel and lieutenant general.

13. Johnson was in the Pacific for a special mission following Pearl Harbor and had a book written about his mission by aviation writer Robert Caiden, which made him out to be a war hero.

14. Howard M. Sachar, *A History of Israel from the Rise of Zionism to Our Time* (New York: Alfred Knopf, 1996), pp. 300, 307; Robert Slater, *Rabin of Israel* (New York: St Martin's Press, 1993), p. 65; Yitzhak Rabin, *The Rabin Memoirs* (Los Angeles, UC Press, 1996), p. 42.

15. Dayan joined Meretz along with Yossi Beilin in December 2002 after they were not allocated realistic positions on the Labor list.

16. Robert Slater, *Warrior, Statesman: The Life of Moshe Dayan* (New York: St. Martin's Press, 1991), pp. 7, 11, 58, 126, 130.

17. Ibid., pp. 310; Robert Slater, *Rabin of Israel* (New York: St. Martin's Press, 1993), pp. 149–50, 207–210.

18. See Slater, *Rabin,* pp. 305–312.

19. The first step in this process was the reburial of Vladimir "Ze'ev" Jabotinsky in Israel on Mt. Zion in 1965; it continued with the issuance of stamps commemorating underground heroes in the 1970s and the renaming of streets to commemorate Jabotinsky, Etzel, and Lehi in Jerusalem and Tel Aviv.

20. See Amiel Ungar, "Now Its Time to Investigate Oslo," *Jerusalem Report,* October 21, 2002.

21. Thomas G. Mitchell, *Native vs. Settler: Ethnic Conflicts in Israel/Palestine, Northern Ireland and South Africa* (Westport, CT: Greenwood, 2000).

22. Maginnis retired from provincial level politics in 2001.

Bibliography

Adams, James T. *The Adams Family* (New York: Literary Guild, 1930).
Alden, John R. *George Washington* (Baton Rouge: Louisiana State University Press, 1984).
Aleshire, Peter. *The Fox and the Whirlwind* (New York: John Wiley & Sons, 2000).
Bauer, K. Jack. *Zachary Taylor: Soldier, Planter, Statesman of the Old Southwest* (Batan Rouge: Louisiana State University Press, 1985).
Beck, Roger B. *The History of South Africa* (Westport, CT: Greenwood, 2000).
Biographies of the Presidents of the United States: 10th to 18th Presidents (Phoenix Multimedia [Video], 1985).
Boorstin, Daniel J. *The Americans: The Colonial Experience* (New York: Random House, 1958).
Brauer, Kinley J. *Cotton versus Conscience* (Lexington: University of Kentucky Press, 1967).
Brown, Fern G. *Franklin Pierce: 14th President of the United States* (Ada, OK: Garret Educational Corp., 1989).
Callaway, Colin G. *The American Revolution in Indian Country* (New York: Cambridge University Press, 1995).
Catton, William and Bruce. *Two Roads to Sumter* (New York: McGraw-Hill, 1963).
Channing, Steven A. *Kentucky: A History* (New York: W. W. Norton, 1977).
Collins, David R. *Zachary Taylor: 12th President of the United States* (Ada, OK: Garret Educational Corp., 1989).
Davenport, T. R. H. *South Africa: A Modern History, Third Edition* (Toronto: University of Toronto Press, 1987).
Davis, Kenneth S. *Kansas: A Bicentennial History* (New York: W. W. Norton, 1976).
Davis, William C. *Three Roads to the Alamo* (New York: Harper Collins, 1998).

De Villiers, Marq. *White Tribe Dreaming* (New York: Viking, 1988).
Derr, Mark. *The Frontiersman* (New York: William Morrow, 1993).
Douglas, Marjory S. *The Everglades: River of Grass* (Sarasota, FL: Pineapple Press, 1988).
Drake, Richard B. *A History of Appalachia* (Lexington: University Press of Kentucky, 2001).
Driver, Carl. *John Sevier: Pioneer of the Old South West* (Chapel Hill, NC: University of North Carolina Press, 1932).
Egan, Ferol. *Fremont: Explorer for a Restless Nation* (Garden City, NY: Doubleday, 1977).
Eisenhower, John S. D. *Agent of Destiny* (New York: Free Press, 1977).
Eisenstadt, Abraham S. *American History: Recent Interpretations Book 1: To 1877* (New York: Thomas Crowell, 1969).
Elazar, Daniel J., and Shmuel Sandlar, eds. *Who's the Boss in Israel* (Detroit: Wayne State University Press, 1992).
Elting, John R. *Amateurs, To Arms!: A Military History of the War of 1812* (New York: Da Capo Press, 1995).
Farragher, John Mack. *Daniel Boone* (New York: Henry Holt, 1992).
Fehrenbuch, T. R. *Lone Star: A History of Texas and the Texans* (New York: Macmillan, 1968).
Finger, John R. *Tennessee Frontiers* (Bloomington: Indiana University Press, 2001).
———. *The Eastern Band of Cherokees* (Knoxville: University of Tennessee Press, 1984).
Folmsbee, Stanley et al. *Tennessee: A Short History* (Knoxville: University of Tennessee Press, 1969).
Fritz, Jean. *Make Way for Sam Houston* (New York: G. P. Putnam's Sons, 1986).
Gurko, Miriam. *Indian America: The Black Hawk War* (New York: Thomas Crowell, 1970).
Harrison, David. *The White Tribe of Africa* (Berkeley: University of California Press, 1981).
Havighurst, Walter. *Ohio: A Bicentennial History* (New York: W. W. Norton, 1976).
Hoig, Stan. *The Battle of the Washita* (New York: Doubleday, 1976).
Holt, Michael F. *The Rise and Fall of the American Whig Party* (New York: Oxford University Press, 1999).
Howard, Robert P. *Illinois* (Grand Rapids, MI: William Eerdmans, 1972).
Klein, Philip S. *President James Buchanan* (University Park, PA: Pennsylvania State University Press, 1962).
Lass, William E. *Minnesota: A Bicentennial History* (New York: W. W. Norton, 1976).
Mahon, John K. *History of the Militia and the National Guard* (New York: Macmillan, 1983).
Mayer, Henry. *All on Fire: William Lloyd Garrison and the Abolition of Slavery* (New York: St. Martin's Press, 1988).
Nagel, Paul C. *Descent from Glory* (Oxford: Oxford University Press, 1983).
Nevin, David. *The Texans: The Wild West Series* (New York: Time-Life Books, 1975).
Oates, Stephen B. *With Malice toward None: The Life of Abraham Lincoln* (New York: Harper Row, 1977).
Pakenham, Thomas. *The Boer War* (New York: Random House, 1979).

Patrick, Rembert W. *Jefferson Davis and His Cabinet* (Baton Rouge, Louisiana State University Press, 1944).
Perlmutter, Amos. *The Life and Times of Menachem Begin* (Garden City, NY: Doubleday, 1987).
Peterson, Merrill D. *The Great Triumvirate* (New York: Oxford University Press, 1987).
Peterson, Norma L. *The Presidencies of William Henry Harrison & John Tyler* (Lawrence, KS: University Press of Kansas, 1989).
Pierce, Michael D. *The Most Promising Young Officer* (Norman, OK: University of Oklahoma Press, 1993).
Remini, Robert V. *Martin Van Buren and the Making of the Democratic Party* (New York: Columbia University Press, 1959).
———. *The Life of Andrew Jackson* (New York: Harper & Row, 1988).
———. *Henry Clay: Statesman for the Union* (New York: W. W. Norton, 1991).
———. *Daniel Webster: The Man and His Time* (New York: W. W. Norton, 1997).
———. *Andrew Jackson and His Indian Wars* (New York: Viking, 2001).
———. *John Quincy Adams* (New York: Times Books, 2002).
Robinson, Charles M. III. *The Men Who Wear the Star: The Story of the Texas Rangers* (New York: Random House, 2000).
Russell, Francis. *Adams: An American Dynasty* (New York: American Heritage Publishing, 1976).
Sachar, Howard M. *A History of Israel from the Rise of Zionism to Our Time* (New York: Alfred Knopf, 1996).
Seitz, Don C. *The Also Rans* (Freeport, NY: Books for Libraries Press, 1968).
Slater, Robert. *Warrior, Statesman: The Life of Moshe Dayan* (New York: St. Martin's Press, 1991).
———. *Rabin of Israel* (New York: St. Martin's Press, 1993).
Slotkin, Richard. *Fatal Environment* (New York: Harper Perennial, 1994).
———. *Regeneration Through Violence* (New York: Harper Perennial, 1996).
Steloff, Rebecca. *William Henry Harrison: 9th President of the United States* (Ada, OK: Garret Educational Corp., 1990).
Strode, Hudson. *Jefferson Davis: American Patriot Volume 1: 1808–1861* (New York: Harcourt Brace & Co., 1955).
Sugden, John. *Tecumseh* (New York: Henry Holt, 1998).
Taylor, Alan. *American Colonies* (New York: Viking, 2001).
Temko, Ned. *To Win or To Die: A Personal Portrait of Menachem Begin* (New York: William Morrow, 1987).
Utley, Robert M. *Frontier Regulars: The United States Army and the Indian, 1866–1890* (New York: Macmillan, 1973).
———. *Cavalier in Buckskin* (Norman, OK: University of Oklahoma Press, 1988).
Webb, Walter Prescott. *The Texas Rangers: A Century of Frontier Defense* (New York: Houghton Mifflin, 1935).
Wilson, Major L. *The Presidency of Martin Van Buren* (Lawrence, KS: University of Kansas Press, 1984).
Wilson, Monica, and Leonard Thompson, *The Oxford History of South Africa, Vol. 2* (New York: Oxford University Press, 1971).
Wooster, Robert. *Nelson A. Miles & The Twilight of the Frontier Army* (Lincoln, NE: University of Nebraska Press, 1993).

Index

Adams, Charles Francis, 75, 89, 97–99
Adams, John, 13, 30, 74
Adams, John Quincy, 69–72
   in Congress, 74–75, 88
   1824 election, 69–71
   1828 election, 71–72
   presidency, 74
Afrikaners, 17, 215, 216, 221
Allon, Yigal, 216–19 passim, 225, 227
Antimasons, 72–73, 75
Apache, 152, 175, 181, 190, 200–202
Arapaho, 177, 180–81

Barak, Ehud, 220–24 passim
Baylor, George, 189–90
Baylor, John, 189–90
Bell, John, 95
Bell, Peter, 186
Ben-Eliezer, Benyamin, 220
Benjamin, Judah, 144–45
Black Hawk, 54, 91, 137
Black Hawk War, 20, 91, 137
Blue Jacket, 35, 48
Boers, 215
Boone, Daniel, 13, 31–37

Bowlegs, 198
Brant, Joseph, 31, 47
Breckenridge, John C., 141, 143
Buchanan, James, 96, 117–19
Burleson, Edward, 182–83
Butler, William O., 96, 103

Caddo Indians, 175
Calhoun, John C., 43, 63, 69–70, 88, 133
California, 115–17
   Californios, 116
   statehood of, 117
California Battalion, 116
Carmel, Moshe, 216, 218–19
Carrol, William, 163
Cass, Lewis, 55, 57, 96–97
Catawba, 27
Cherokee, 27–28, 38–40, 47, 58, 65–66, 134–37, 157–59
Cheyenne, 51
Chickamauga, 47
Chickasaw, 65–66
Choctaw, 65, 135
Clark, George Rogers, 32, 35–36, 153

Clay, Cassius M., 155
Clay, Green, 154–55
Clay, Henry, 80–81, 103
　as candidate, 69–72, 73, 80, 83–85, 95–96
　and 1850 Compromise, 139
　and John Tyler, 82–83
　as War Hawk, 46, 165
　and Whig Party, 73
　and Zachary Taylor, 99–100, 140
Cleveland, Grover, 211
Comanche, 180–82, 185–88, 189–91
Conscience Whigs, 75, 89–91, 97–99
Cotton Whigs, 75, 88–90, 91
Crawford, William, 65–66, 69–70
Creek, 46, 59–60
Creek Rebellion (1836), 101
Creek War (1813), 59–61, 163–64
Crittenden, John J., 56–57
Crockett, David, 76–78, 164–67
　in Congress, 76–77, 164–67
　as Indian fighter, 76, 165
　as presidential potential, 77
Crook, George, 193, 198, 200–202
Custer, George A., 200, 205–6

Davis, Jefferson, 87, 107–9, 151–56
　as Indian fighter, 107
　as Mexican fighter, 108
　political career, 107–9
　as president, 87, 151–56, 157
Dayan, Moshe, 215–19 passim, 221–23, 225–27
Democratic Party
　origin of, 71
　and secession, 119–21, 123
　in Tennessee, 160–67 passim, 168–69
　in Texas, 185, 191
Douglas, Stephen, 105, 120–23, 149

Elections
　1824, 69–71
　1828, 71–72
　1832, 72–73
　1836, 79
　1840, 80–81
　1844, 84–85

　1848, 95–97
　1852, 103–4
　1856, 118–19
　1860, 121–23
Etowah, 40

Fallen Timbers, Battle of, 48
Filibustering, 110–11
Fillmore, Millard, 96, 97, 100, 103–4, 118
Ford, John S., 185–86
Fountain, Albert, 190–91
Free Soil Party, 97–99
Fremont, John C., 114–19
　after 1856, 119
　as explorer, 115, 117
　as Mexican fighter, 115–16
　presidential campaign, 117–19

Garfield, James, 209–11
Grant, Ulysses S., 208–10

Hamilton, Alexander, 128–29
Hardin, John, 129
Harmer, Josiah, 129
Harrison, Benjamin, 211
Harrison, William H., 47–49, 50–56, 79–82
　as Indian fighter, 52–56
　as politician, 79–81
　as president, 81–82
　Thames, 54–56
　Tippecanoe, 52–53
Hayes, Rutherford, 209
Hays, Jack, 172, 187
Herut Party, 219
Houston, Sam, 60, 163–64, 171, 182–84 passim
Huston, Felix, 171

Israel, 215–29

Jackson, Andrew, 41, 45, 57–73, 76–78, 80, 84, 152, 161–63, 164–68 passim
　early life, 57–58
　1824, 1828 elections, 69–72
　as Indian fighter, 58–61
　as president, 132–37

Johnson, Richard M., 55–56, 155–56
Jones, John B., 191–92

Kansas, 199
Karankawa Indians, 175
Kaufman, Daniel, 187–88
Kentucky, 132–36, 152–56
King Philip's War, 6–8
Kiowa, Kiowa-Apache, 175–77, 179–81
Know-Nothing Party, 106, 117–19, 226

Labor Party, 216, 218, 223, 224, 226
Lane, James, 94, 111–14
   in Civil War, 113–14
   Kansas, 112–13
   as Mexican fighter, 94, 111
Lane, Joseph, 114
Lawson White, Hugh, 79
Liberty Party, 85, 99
Likud Party, 218–19, 226, 228
Lincoln, Abraham, 80, 95, 99, 120–23
   in 1840 election, 80
   in 1848 election, 95, 99
   in 1860 election, 122–23
Lipkin-Shahak, Amnon, 220
Little Turtle, 46–48
Lubbock, Francis, 187

Mackenzie, Ranald, 193, 198, 200–205
McCulloch, Ben, 186–87
McLean, John, 95
Miami Indians, 46–49
Miles, Nelson, 193, 198, 200–205, 207

Netanyahu, Benjamin, 221–22
Northern Ireland, 229

Ohio, 47–49, 152, 154, 156–57
Osceola, 137

Pierce, Franklin, 101–3, 105–7
"Prophet, The," 50–53
Prophetstown, 51–53

Quitman, John, 109–10

Rabin, Yitzhak, 217–28 passim
Red River War, 103–4, 152, 181

Republican Party, 117–19, 120–22, 191
Robertson, Jerome, 188–89
Ross, Lawrence "Sul," 177–78, 189
Rusk, Thomas, 184–85

Scott, Winfield, 18–19, 53, 61, 62, 73, 92, 93, 100–101
   1840 election, 80, 93
   1848 election, 90, 95–96
   1852 election, 94, 102–4, 168
   as Mexican fighter, 93–94, 101
Seddon, James, 143
Seminole
   First Seminole War, 63
   Second Seminole War, 21, 91–92, 137–38
   Third Seminole War, 138, 198
Sevier, John, 38–41, 158–62
   in Congress, 162
   early career, 38, 168
   feud with Jackson, 41, 161–62
   as governor, 41, 161–62
   as Indian fighter, 38–40, 158–59, 170
Seward, William, 117, 120–22
Sharon, Ariel "Arik," 217–19, 223, 225, 228
Sheridan, Philip, 179, 180, 203
Sherman, John, 157, 204
Sherman, William T., 157, 180, 203
Smith, James, 194
South African Republic, 215

Taylor, Zachary, 53–54, 88, 91–100, 138–41
   as candidate, 94–97
   early life and career, 53
   as Indian fighter, 53–54, 91–92
   as Mexican fighter, 92–94
   as president, 99–100, 138–41
Tecumseh, 46–56 passim
   death of, 56
   early life, 46–50, 51
   in War of 1812, 52, 54–55
Tennessee, 39–41, 158–69
   politics of, 160–69
   settlement of, 39–41, 158–60
   Whig Party in, 167–69
Tenskwautawa (The Prophet), 50–53

Texas, 152, 169–93
  Indian warfare in, 170–72, 175–82
  politics in, 173–75, 177–79, 182–92
  Republic of, 173–74
  Revolution, 169–70
Texas Rangers, 169–72, 177–79, 180
  captains of, 172, 177, 185,
  Frontier Battalion, 180–81
  origins, 169–70
Thames, Battle of, 54–56
Tyler, John, 73, 80–83, 84–85

United States
  American Revolution, 11–16, 26–28, 30–35, 37–39
  Civil War, 123, 141–46, 169, 179, 185, 188–90, 192, 204, 205, 208–12 passim
  growth of, 4–5, 32–33, 151–54, 156–57, 158–60, 169, 174–75, 197–201
  war with Britain (1812), 18–20, 45–46, 53–62
  war with Mexico, 92–94, 102, 108, 116

Van Buren, Martin, 71–72, 77, 79, 81, 84, 98–99

Walker, William, 106, 110–11, 190
Washington, George, 4, 5, 9, 28–30, 48, 127–32, 147
  as Indian fighter, 28–29
  as president, 48, 127–32, 147
  in the Revolution, 29–30
Webster, Daniel, 20, 73, 79–83 passim, 85, 88, 90–91, 95–97, 99–100, 103–4, 139
Weizman, Ezer, 216, 218–19, 222, 225
Whig Party, 73–85 passim, 87–106 passim
  collapse of, 104–6
  1836 election, 79
  1840 election, 80–81
  1844 election, 83–85
  1848 election, 87, 90–91, 93, 94–97
  1852 election, 102–4
  1856 election, 118
  origin of, 72–74
Wood, George, 184

Yadin, Yigael, 219–20

Ze'evi, Rehavam, 220, 228

About the Author

THOMAS G. MITCHELL is the author of *Indispensable Traitors* (Greenwood, 2002) and *Native vs. Settler* (Greenwood, 2000). His research concentration has been on ethnic conflicts in settler societies. He has also served with the army in Bosnia and Kosovo.